The Calling of History

The Calling of History

Sir Jadunath Sarkar and His Empire of Truth

DIPESH CHAKRABARTY

The University of Chicago Press
Chicago and London

Dipesh Chakrabarty is the Lawrence A. Kimpton Distinguished Service Professor of History and South Asian Languages and Civilizations at the University of Chicago. He is the author of several books, including *Habitations of Modernity: Essays in the Wake of Subaltern Studies*, also published by the University of Chicago Press.

The University of Chicago Press, Chicago 60637
The University of Chicago Press, Ltd., London

Printed in the United States of America

24 23 22 21 20 19 18 17 16 15 1 2 3 4 5

ISBN-13: 978-0-226-10044-9 (cloth)
ISBN-13: 978-0-226-10045-6 (paper)
ISBN-13: 978-0-226-24024-4 (e-book)
DOI: 10.7208/chicago/9780226240244.001.0001

Illustration on page ii: Jadunath Sarkar (ca. 1926). Photographer unknown. Courtesy of the Archives, Centre for Studies in Social Sciences, Calcutta. Used with permission.

Chakrabarty, Dipesh, author.
The calling of history : Sir Jadunath Sarkar and his empire of truth / Dipesh Chakrabarty.
pages cm
Includes index.
ISBN 978-0-226-10044-9 (cloth : alk. paper)—ISBN 978-0-226-10045-6 (pbk. : alk. paper)—ISBN 978-0-226-24024-4 (e-book) 1. Sarkar, Jadunath, Sir, 1870–1958. 2. Historians—India—Biography. 3. India—Historiography. 4. Historiography. I. Title.
DS435.7.S26C53 2015
907.2′02—dc23
[B]
2014041928

♾ This paper meets the requirements of ANSI/NISO Z39.48-1992 (Permanence of Paper).

To those who showed me the way:

the late Barun De and Asok Sen in Calcutta;
Anthony Low and Ranajit Guha in Canberra;
the late Greg Dening in Melbourne

And to Rochona, who shares the journey every day.

Contents

Abbreviations

DCL, Deccan College Library

GOI, Government of India

IHRC PROCEEDINGS, *Indian Historical Records Commission, Proceedings of the Meetings*

IHRC RETROSPECT, *Indian Historical Records Commission: A Retrospect, 1919–1948*

IRD, Imperial Record Department

JSP, Jadunath Sarkar Papers

NAI, National Archives of India, Delhi

NL, National Library, Calcutta

SP, Sardesai Papers (Kamshet), digital copies in the author's personal collection

Introduction

> Rhetoric is the dialectic of the public square, the *agora,* in contrast to the dialectic of the lyceum or the academy.
>
> CARL SCHMITT, *The Nomos of the Earth*

The book in your hands, dear reader, comes out of a chance encounter in the library. I would not be the first person to report an experience of stumbling upon material that gave rise to a research project. A gifted New Historicist might even make something theoretical of what may be called "librarial" luck. But let me be more modest and just recall, in a gesture of gratitude to the very existence of physical libraries in this digital age, how one day sometime in the mid-1990s and as someone new to the riches of the Regenstein Library at the University of Chicago, I came across a book with an appendix excerpting about 250 letters exchanged between two Indian historians, Sir Jadunath Sarkar (1870–1958) and Rao Bahadur Govindrao Sakharam Sardesai (1865–1959). The letters covered the years from 1907 to 1952. The book was a collection of essays edited by Dr. Hari Ram Gupta and published from Punjab in 1958 as a tribute to Sir Jadunath in the final year of his life.[1] As a physical object, the book was not particularly attractive. The font seemed too large for serious prose, the paper coarse, the general appearance ordinary, and the printing uneven. But Jadunath Sarkar was once a name every educated Indian knew. A Bengali by birth, he was easily the most highly regarded Indian historian, and he had a very strong public presence in late-colonial India. Sardesai, his correspondent, was similarly a well-known and respected historian, from what is now the state of Maharashtra in India. Browsing these excerpted letters in the library, I vaguely sensed their importance. Here were two of India's pioneering historians writing to each other for decades about issues crucial to historical research, and yet I had not seen any significant discussion of

1. Hari Ram Gupta, ed., *Life and Letters of Sir Jadunath Sarkar* (Hoshiarpur: Panjab University, 1958). Gupta's preface is dated 10 May 1957 (p. ix). Sarkar died on 19 May 1958.

these letters by scholars of South Asia. I felt fortunate in having stumbled upon them. It is only now, after I have finished writing this book, that I have some sense of exactly how fortunate I was. I now know that the publication of Hari Ram Gupta's book was dogged by financial uncertainty. And I would not even know this factoid except through a second stroke of luck in October 2012, when some colleagues and I discovered, in a heap of waste paper in the locked-up residence of Sardesai in Kamshet (near Poona), some letters from another historian, Dr. Raghubir Singh, a princely historian from what used to be the native state of Malwa and a student of Sarkar's. In a couple of these letters, Dr. Singh spoke of the financial uncertainty that once threatened the publication of these excerpts.[2] Dr. Gupta did not know until near the very end, it now seems, that there would be money available to pay the expenses of including a large appendix containing these extracts. Finding Sardesai's house was an adventure in itself, which I briefly describe in chapter 2.

There was, however, nothing particularly serendipitous or surprising about why I found the excerpted letters arresting. Barring the prominent exceptions of Damodar Dharmanand Kosambi (1907–1966) and Ranajit Guha (1923–) in the twentieth century, there are not many known instances of Indian historians discussing, in a truly sustained and original manner, methodological issues involved in the production of historical knowledge. History has been an important subject in India from the colonial times and is among the most successful—along with economics and anthropology (often folded into sociology in India)—of the social sciences that have flourished in the country since the attainment of political independence in 1947. India has been blessed with many gifted historians. Yet on questions pertaining to methods or epistemology fundamental to the discipline—and I should make it clear that I am not speaking of historiography here—even the best Indian historians have usually been content to let Western savants make pronouncements

2. SP, letter from Raghubir Singh to Sardesai, dated Sitamau, 25 January 1956, mentions Singh's receiving a letter from Dr. Hari Ram Gupta "where-in he had informed about your [Sardesai's] wishes that the entire correspondence between you and Sir Jadunath be sent down to him so that after he has taken down necessary excerpts the same may be sent away to the Poona University." However, a second letter, dated 4 February 1956, states: "I do not know if Dr. Hari Ram Gupta's efforts will bear any fruit. His original idea was to give a selection of some extracts from this correspondence. But the final decision can only be taken when it is known as to what funds could be available and how many pages would be spared for this particular section." Ultimately, the excerpts made up the major part of the book, and the correspondence went to the National Library in Calcutta and not to the University of Poona, as originally intended. I have camera copies of these letters in my possession. The originals are probably still rotting away in Sardesai's house at Kamshet.

from time to time on what history was, while they, the Indian scholars, busied themselves with producing learned and good histories that, though attentive no doubt to global methodological debates, did not aim to contribute in any fundamental way to the issues being debated.

It was therefore intriguing to come across letters between two prominent Indian historians—one of them recognized generally as one of the greatest modern historians that India has produced—discussing in private, and with passion and fury sustained over a period spanning the entire first half of the twentieth century, questions of critical importance to the very procedures that make history an academic discipline: What did it mean to do "research" in history? How would one weigh historical evidence? What would be a defining distinction between "facts" and the "raw" materials of history? How might one go about collecting sources for writing history in a context where no effective public archives were available? How would one explain the historical absence of public archives in India and make a case for building them? And other related questions. The letters did not produce any new philosophical or methodological insights as such, but the unflagging energy, intensity, and interest with which Sarkar and Sardesai pursued these questions was impressive. They were, moreover, not asking the questions in an abstract vein; it was clear that the questions were integral to their own research and to the debates they were actually engaged in with their contemporaries in India. Given the absence of any vigorous discussions of these issues in the scholarly world of Indian history today, I felt curious to understand why they seemed so urgent to these Indian historians in the first half of the twentieth century, what provisional answers the two fashioned for themselves, and why. The larger narrative of this book addresses that initial and immediate curiosity that Gupta's book sparked in me as I stood riveted to those epistolary excerpts in the immense and overwhelming presence of books in the famed Regenstein Library.

But my interest in these letters had other origins as well, which have become clearer to me in the course of working on this book. First, the concern that was displayed in these letters with the idea of "historical truth" immediately contrasted with the idea of history I was brought up on. I had known—both from E. H. Carr and from the general state of South Asian history—that history was, ultimately, about the clash of perspectives. Carr had already taught us—in India, through the cheap Penguin version of his Trevelyan lectures titled *What Is History?* that our professors recommended and that we could afford to buy—that only the nineteenth century made a "fetish" of "facts" and "documents," that we now knew, following the classicist A. E. Housman, that "accuracy was a duty, not a virtue" and that the "modern" historian was engaged in a "continuous process of moulding his facts to his interpretation and his interpretation to his facts."[3] Carr's subtle recommendation for striking a balance or "equality" between facts and interpretation was soon lost in the din of the battle cries that rent the airs of the scholarly world of Indian history in the decades that followed the achievement of political independence. The most celebrated debates in modern Indian history from the 1960s on were about the beneficial or deleterious impact of colonial rule on Indian society. It was generally understood that whatever evidence scholars marshaled in these debates, the lines of division very much reflected contradictory points of view, mainly between "nationalist" and "imperialist" camps. The well-known *Subaltern Studies* project, in which I participated almost from its inception, positioned itself on the battlefield of a perspectival war between three historiographical approaches to the study of modern South Asia: the "Cambridge-imperialist" one, the "nationalist-Marxist" versions of history, and the strand to which we belonged, "we" being the scholars associated with *Subaltern Studies*.

Sarkar's letters spoke of another age, when accuracy was indeed considered a "virtue," when the idea of historical truth made sense to historians, who presumably, on their part, combated their own biases and perspectives to get to the "truth." I was interested to find out more about why the idea of historical truth could seem so plausible to a past generation of scholars and about the architecture of ideas that may have subtended the conception of such truth. I did not want to consign the nineteenth and the early twentieth centuries to a land of "errors," from which the progression of knowledge and ideas had simply rescued us. But I did not want to go back to the nineteenth century, either. I wanted to understand what made "facts" once so valuable and "historical truth" a matter of virtue for these historians in colonial India.

Browsing the letters, I also realized that Sarkar, aided manfully by Sardesai, had struggled all his life to give history a "proper" academic form in India. But neither Sarkar nor Sardesai was, in today's terms, a "professional" historian; they were what we would, without intending any insult, call "amateurs." But this is what lent their struggle a certain historical peculiarity: it took place not within the institution we call the university but in the public domain, through intense and sometimes vituperative argumentation with other "amateur" historians writing for the general readership in an age when feelings of regional, caste, and religious identities, as well as those of anti-imperial nationalism, were on the rise. The excerpted letters were their private testimony, as it were, to how much these debates mattered to them. And it was

3. E. H. Carr, *What Is History?* (1961; Harmondsworth: Penguin, 1970), pp. 8, 10, 16, 29.

through such debates, as I shall endeavor to show in this book, that the discipline of history began to take an academic shape in colonial India.

These considerations made me reflect on my own involvement in the intellectual skirmishes over skepticism and historical knowledge that generally followed the publication of Hayden White's *Metahistory* (1973) and that were rekindled in the 1980s and the 1990s when issues having to do with memory and with postmodern, poststructural, or postcolonial critiques of historicism (itself an imprecise term open to multiple interpretations) exploded across the scene of the humanities that I inhabited. It is not so much the details of these debates that I want to discuss here, for they would not be relevant to what I have to say.[4] My point is that the Sarkar-Sardesai correspondence reminded me, by way of contrast, how so many of those academic debates of the 1980s and the 1990s were about history-in-general or historical knowledge in the abstract. Think, for instance, of some of the key books published in those years: Eric Hobsbawm's *On History*, Richard Evans's *In Defense of History*, Jacques Le Goff's *History and Memory*, Paul Ricoeur's *Memory and History*, Carlo Ginzburg's *History, Rhetoric, Proof*, and, on the other side of the "history wars," Hayden White's various texts, Keith Jenkins's *The Post-Modern History Reader*, Ashis Nandy's incendiary essay "History's Forgotten Doubles," and even books judiciously straddling the divide, such as Alan Megill's *Historical Knowledge and Skepticism* and Constantin Fasolt's *Limits of History*. The list could easily be expanded.[5] All these texts treat history as an abstract and general form of knowledge whose academic protocols are determined by certain rules and procedures. There is, of course, a long and venerable tradition of treating history thus—going back at least to the beginnings of the nineteenth century, and perhaps even earlier if one remembers

4. I pursue some of these thoughts in a book provisionally titled *History and the Time of the Present* (Durham, NC: Duke University Press, forthcoming).

5. E. J. Hobsbawm, *On History* (New York: New Press, 1997); Richard J. Evans, *In Defense of History* (New York: Norton, 1999); Jacques Le Goff, *History and Memory*, trans. Stephen Rendall and Elizabeth Claman (New York: Columbia University Press, 1992); Paul Ricoeur, *Memory, History, Forgetting*, trans. Kathleen Blamey and David Pellaeur (Chicago: University of Chicago Press, 2006); Carlo Ginzburg, *History, Rhetoric, and Proof* (Hanover, NH: University Press of New England, 1999); Hayden White, *Metahistory: The Historical Imagination in Nineteenth-Century Europe* (Baltimore: Johns Hopkins University Press, 1973); Hayden White, *The Content of the Form: Narrative Discourse and Historical Representation* (Baltimore: Johns Hopkins University Press, 1987); Keith Jenkins, ed., *The Post-Modern History Reader* (London: Routledge, 1997); Ashis Nandy, "History's Forgotten Doubles," *History and Theory* 34, no. 2 (May 1995), pp. 44–66; Alan Megill, *Historical Knowledge, Historical Error: A Contemporary Guide to Practice* (Chicago: University of Chicago Press, 2007); Constantin Fasolt, *Limits of History* (Chicago: University of Chicago Press, 2004).

Koselleck's remark that it was only toward the end of the eighteenth century that it began to make sense in Europe to speak of history in general, to say that one was interested in "history" as such and not simply in the history of a very particular this or that.[6] For it was within this tradition that Benedetto Croce, R. G. Collingwood, Fernand Braudel, E. H. Carr, and others spoke of history. They spoke of it as an abstraction, a universal form of knowledge, something that indeed made E. H. Carr's question "What Is History?" legitimate not only to scholars who saw themselves as defending this form of knowledge against the attacks of skeptics but also to those who critiqued and questioned it. This is the tradition of academic historians speaking to one another with a shared sense of the academic discipline of history.

The Cloistered and Public Lives of History

We could see this way of speaking of history—of history-in-general—as a sign of what I have elsewhere called the "cloistered" life of the discipline, in order to distinguish it from its opposite, something Bain Attwood, Claudio Lomnitz, and I christened "the public life of history" in 2008 in a special issue of the journal *Public Culture* dedicated to the latter theme. History is more prone than many other disciplines to having such a public life. I should clarify that the distinction between the "public" and "cloistered" lives of history is not the same as the otherwise useful distinction between "professional" and "lay" history that Peter Burke recently made, following the language of the title of Hugh Trevor-Roper's 1957 inaugural lecture, *History: Professional and Lay*. Burke's category "lay" history includes not only histories written by "amateurs" and novelists but also pasts performed on the stage and through audiovisual materials.[7] By the "public" life of a discipline, I mean the way that "lay" history or discussions in the public domain actually come to shape the fundamental categories and practices of the discipline's "cloistered" or academic life. "Public" and "cloistered" lives are interactive categories, and the discipline of history is molded by the pressures of both

6. See the discussion in Reinhart Koselleck, *Futures Past: On the Semantics of Historical Time*, trans. Keith Tribe (Cambridge, MA: MIT Press, 1985; first published in German, 1979), pp. 27–35.

7. Bain Attwood, Dipesh Chakrabarty, and Claudio Lomnitz, eds., "The Public Life of History," special issue, *Public Culture* 20, no. 1 (2008); Hugh Trevor-Roper, *History: Professional and Lay* (Oxford: Clarendon Press, 1957); Peter Burke, "Lay History: Official and Unofficial Representations, 1800–1914," in *The Oxford History of Historical Writing, 1800–1945*, ed. Stuart Macintyre, Juan Maiguascha, and Attila Pók (Oxford: Oxford University Press, 2011), pp. 115–132.

sides; Burke's distinction, as I understand it, is mainly inert and classificatory in function.

All disciplines, needless to say, have a cloistered life. This is the life that a discipline lives through journals, reviews, specialized conferences, university departments, professional associations, and so on. It is a life fostered by and confined to academic institutions. It is what gives a discipline its social and institutional authority, making people look upon the practitioners of the discipline as experts. Disciplines have their thresholds, which act as barriers to entry: one must have a minimum degree of specialized training to enter conversations or controversies internal to a discipline. History usually does not have many such barriers, not strong ones, anyway, except in certain specialized subfields such as economic history or the history of science and technology, and some other areas (e.g., parts of environmental history) where technical training may indeed be necessary. But generally speaking, history is probably the least technical of all social science disciplines. Almost any person, academically trained or not, can presume to write and debate history (and sometimes people do so, alas, even in areas that actually require special training, say, in old or medieval languages). This creates, potentially, a field of tension between the two lives of the discipline, the cloistered one and the public one. Sometimes a middle ground is occupied creatively, as in the case of academically trained historians who write successful trade books or popular blogs and magazine columns; sometimes, the relationship is awkward or tense, particularly when trained historians find historical claims made in public life by particular groups—who may even have claims to historians' political sympathies—difficult to justify in terms of their professional knowledge. Being the kind of discipline that it is, history remains perennially open to the pressures emanating from its public life. The difference between the "cloistered" life of history and its "public" life is similar to the distinction that Carl Schmitt once made between the agora and the academy. In the academy, one seeks to instill a version of knowledge for which the protocols of the knowledge are designed to ensure veracity in the judgment of the practitioners of the discipline. In the agora of public life, the function of rhetoric is different. As Schmitt puts it, "What one person says to another is debatable, plausible, or convincing only in a given context and a given place."[8] What I do in this book is to study the interaction between these two domains to see how that dynamic shaped the academic discipline of history in a particular con-

8. Carl Schmitt, *The "Nomos" of the Earth in the International Law of "Jus Publicum Europaeum,"* trans. G. L. Ulmen (New York: Telos, 2006), p. 50n1.

text, that is, late-colonial India, even as "academic" history emerged through debates that were often conducted outside of academe.

The cloistered life of history—that is to say, its academic disciplinary life the world over—may look the same everywhere, with minor variations. We may even be able to provide this cloistered life of the discipline with more-or-less global histories, such as in books on the general history of historiography, that helpfully educate and inform us from time to time.[9] These are necessarily histories of different traditions of historical writing. I do not dispute the plausibility or the utility of such histories. My point is different. It is that historical writings end up being embedded in different public contexts in very different ways. Monika Baár has recently argued that historical knowledge is peculiarly vulnerable to the context in which it is generated. Her work demonstrates how the "nature" of historical writing is always "influenced not only by temporal but also by local circumstances."[10] I am pushing the argument a little further by saying that it is not only the "nature of historical writing" that is influenced by the places in which such writing is produced; the valence of even the basic categories of the discipline—such as "research," "facts," "truth," "evidence," "archives"—can be molded by the interaction between history's cloistered and public lives.

Now, answers to the question of how much pressure the discipline's public life exerts on its cloistered existence will understandably vary from one context to another. In places where the university has come to be valued as an institution of "experts," historians are less exposed to the pressures of the pasts that are invented, claimed, and contested in the popular domain. I imagine nineteenth-century German historians to have enjoyed this kind of authority at a time when they also played a world-historical role in establishing the discipline itself.[11] In the contemporary United States, academic historians are somewhat distanced from the strife and intellectual clamor of the public sphere by the strength of their numbers and by the strength of their professional associations and related activities. Often—though not always—one finds a clear distinction drawn in the United States between those who write only trade books for the public and those historians who write mainly

9. There are some excellent and useful books of this genre. See, for example, John Burrow, *A History of Histories* (New York: Vintage, 2007); and, on a more ambitious global scale, Daniel Woolf, *A Global History of History* (Cambridge: Cambridge University Press, 2011).

10. Monika Baár, "East-Central European Historical Writing," in Macintyre, Maiguascha, and Pók, *Oxford History*, p. 326. See also Monika Baár, *Historians and Nationalism: East-Central Europe in the Nineteenth Century* (Oxford: Oxford University Press, 2010).

11. See William Clark, *Academic Charisma and the Origins of the Research University* (2006; Chicago: University of Chicago Press, 2007).

for other historians in universities and other research institutions.[12] Historians in Australia, however, inhabit a different situation on the whole. The emergence of Australian Aboriginal history in the 1980s, for example, was a much-debated phenomenon, both among academics qua academics and in the larger public context. Debates about the claims of memory, oral history, and experience over those backed by archival documents (mostly of settler-European origin) raged as much in the halls of academe as in discussions in the media, in courtrooms, and sometimes on the streets as well (as fracas and also as questions of historical reenactments and public history, as during the celebrations of the Australian bicentennial in 1988).[13] The same would be true of contestations between Maori and Pakeha histories in New Zealand or between native and European histories in many regions of Africa.[14] In India, again, history has acquired a strong but different public life. Universities in general do not carry much social authority there, and members of the "public" outside do not much depend on what history professors say to make up their own minds about what "really" happened in the past. Such popular

12. Peter Novick's *That Noble Dream: The "Objectivity" Question and the American Historical Profession* (1988; Cambridge: Cambridge University Press, 1993) is an excellent account of the historical strength the profession of history in the United States possessed to marginalize, in effect, the concerns of "popular" histories. His comments (p. 522) on how the university defeated the resistance of the countercultural movements of the 1960s is telling in this regard. He also shows how the profession absorbed the pressures coming out of black, feminist, and other "sectional" histories in the 1970s and the 1980s.

13. Some of these developments are summarized in Stuart Macintyre and Anna Clark, *The History Wars* (Carlton, Victoria: Melbourne University Press, 2003).

14. The literature here is immense. For a sample biased by the accidents and preferences of my own reading, see Bain Attwood, ed., *The Age of Mabo: History, Aborigines and Australia* (St. Leonards, NSW: Allen and Unwin, 1996); Bain Attwood, *Telling the Truth about Aboriginal History* (Crows Nest, NSW: Allen and Unwin, 2005); Andrew Sharp and Paul McHugh, eds., *History: Power and Loss: Uses of the Past—A New Zealand Commentary* (Wellington, NZ: Bridget William Books, 2001), in particular J. G. A. Pocock's essay, "The Treaty between Histories," pp. 75–96; Deborah Bird Rose, *Hidden Histories: Black Stories from Victoria River Downs, Humbert River, and Wave Hill Station* (Canberra: Aboriginal Studies Press, 1991); Judith Binney, *Redemption Song: A Life of Te Kooti Arikorangi Te Turuki* (Auckland, NZ: Auckland University Press, 1995); Minoro Hokaru, *Gurundji Journey: A Japanese Historian in the Outback* (Sydney: University of New South Wales Press, 2011); Deborah Posel and Graeme Simpson, eds., *Commissioning the Past: Understanding South Africa's Truth and Reconciliation Commission* (Johannesburg: Witwatersrand University Press, 2002). See also the essays by Bain Attwood, Miranda Johnson, and Deborah Posel in the 2008 issue of *Public Culture* devoted to the theme of "The Public Life of History"; and Miranda Johnson's doctoral dissertation, "Struggling over the Past: Decolonization and the Problem of History in Settler Societies" (PhD diss., University of Chicago, 2008).

reconstructions of history—often tied to identity politics associated with regions, religions, caste, or sects—end up fueling activism on the streets, a form of politics that, for good and bad, has become an integral part of Indian democracy.[15]

It may thus be argued that the outcomes of particular debates in history in the 1980s and the 1990s—the value of "memory," for instance, or that of "myth" over that of history—were decided, in many national or regional contexts, not by what historians said in specialist books and in learned and specialized conferences but by the pressure that the realm of public disputations about the past brought to bear on the discipline of history and vice versa. Thus, debates about whether or not Aboriginal myths, songs, poetry, and dance forms constituted history could not be decided in the Australia I lived in by the strictures of the discipline alone. Instead, the discipline was under pressure to find room to accommodate forms of the past that it tended usually to rule out as invalid. New Zealand scholars have had to experiment with telling the same historical story twice, once in the White or Pakeha way, and again in the Maori way.[16] Or consider the importance of undocumented "historical" characters like Jhalkari Bai and of myth-history in Dalit struggles for recognition in Uttar Pradesh, as demonstrated in the work of Badri Narayan, Ramnarayan Rawat, and others.[17] Myth-history has loomed large in Dalit politics of the past in the Indian state of Uttar Pradesh.

Reading the letters between Jadunath Sarkar and Govindrao Sakharam Sardesai made me realize what was missing from the purely academic debates around history in the 1980s and the 1990s. These debates about history-in-general were conducted with very little attention to the transactions between the two lives of the discipline inside and outside academia. (Joyce Appleby, Lynn Hunt, and Margaret Jacob's *Telling the Truth about History* remained an exception in acknowledging the role of identity politics in the United States

15. On history as parleyed in the popular domain, see Badri Narayan, *Women Heroes and Dalit Assertion in North India Culture, Identity and Politics* (New Delhi: Sage, 2006), in particular chaps. 3–6. Ramnarayan S. Rawat, *Reconsidering Untouchability: Chamars and Dalit Histories in North India* (Bloomington: Indiana University Press, 2011); chap. 4 of Rawat's book provides a good discussion of the kind of histories leaders of the Chamar caste in UP (present-day Uttar Pradesh; the United Provinces in the colonial period) wrote for themselves in the early twentieth century. I discuss some of the issues in involved here in my "History and the Politics of Recognition," in *Manifestos for History*, ed. Keith Jenkins, Sue Morgan, and Alan Munslow (New York: Routledge, 2007), pp. 77–86. Also, Neeladri Bhattacharya, "Predicaments of Secular Histories," *Public Culture* 20, no. 1 (Winter 2008), pp. 57–73; and "Teaching History in Schools: The Politics of Textbooks in India," *History Workshop Journal* 67 (Spring 2009), pp. 99–110.

16. See the references cited in note 14 above.

17. See Narayan, *Women Heroes*; Rawat, *Reconsidering Untouchability*.

in stoking debates within academe.) In other words, what was often missing from books defending or critiquing history-in-general during the clamorous decades of the 1980s and the 1990s was any sense of the diverse and changing relationship between the cloistered and public lives of the discipline of history in different contexts, for the tension between the two is probably what gives historians' debates in many places a flavor and a taste missing from academic disciplines that are more "protected" from the public. This is probably why, when a distinguished Indian historian turned his attention to debates in the West that followed the publication of Hayden White's essay "The Burden of History" in the journal *History and Theory* in 1966, he could not quite see what the fuss was all about. To him, the talk of "crisis in history" appeared to be "a problem affecting the historical sciences in the West rather than in the Afro-Asian countries." For in these latter countries, history was so tied up with nationalism that there was little chance of history getting "displaced from its pre-eminent position," as he thought had happened in the West. Satish Chandra, the historian just quoted, actually went on to make the self-regarding observation that in countries such as India, historians that he called "national" "command a measure of public esteem which is becoming rare elsewhere."[18] Chandra wrote this in 1972, too early for anyone to foresee that this "public esteem" of "national" historians in India did not translate into anything like the authority assigned to experts; it was not able to stop sections of the "Hindu" public in India in December 1992 from destroying a sixteenth-century mosque in Awadh on the flimsy and intolerant ground that it had been built on a demolished Hindu temple—which they did in a frenzy of political vandalism, throwing all historians' and archaeologists' advice to the winds.[19]

But Chandra had a point. He was drawing the attention of his European colleagues to a particular feature of public life in "Afro-Asian countries" where multifarious conflicts involved claims made about the past by groups with different and often mutually opposed interests. This is what made many aspects of the past into matters of lively political interest in the present; but

18. Joyce Appleby, Lynn Hunt, and Margaret Jacob, *Telling the Truth about History* (New York: Norton, 1994); Satish Chandra, "Decentring of History," in his *Essays on Medieval Indian History* (New Delhi: Oxford University Press, 2003), p. 505. The essay was first published in *Diogenes* (Paris) 72 (1972), pp. 92–109.

19. A melancholy witness to the ineffectiveness of professional historians' attempt to prevent this mass-political act of vandalizing a historical site is Sarvepalli Gopal, ed., *Anatomy of a Confrontation: Ayodhya and the Rise of Communal Politics in India* (London: Zed, 1993). The book was published originally in Delhi in 1991 as an intervention in the debate about the targeted historic mosque in Ayodhya. It was a well-intentioned intervention but did not have much impact on the events as they unfolded—as acknowledged in Gopal's preface to the 1993 edition.

it also left historians in places like India exposed to the vagaries of the public life of the discipline. Sarkar and Sardesai were no exception to this observation. I want to show, through the example of these two, that it was actually the tension generated by this exposure that shaped the career of the discipline in the subcontinent, for Sarkar and Sardesai did most of their research and writing *before* historical research was introduced as a subject in Indian universities. Their struggle to put history on a "proper" footing in the early part of the twentieth century demonstrates, in this sense, the popular origins of academic history in India. Their debates, even quarrels, with their contemporaries, as well as their own disagreements, serve as a reminder that the fundamental concepts, institutions, and practices that define history as a discipline—facts, truth, evidence, bias and objectivity, research, the weighing of evidence, public archives—were actually hammered out in India through lively contestations and exchanges across the public domain and the institutional space of the university. It needs to be borne in mind, in addition, that universities in India before independence were few in number, only seventeen in 1947, whereas more than six hundred exist today. The educated were a small minority. At the same time, the growth of mass politics, entailing the creation of modern identities at various levels—that of the nation as well as those of region, religion, and caste—created popular demands for multiple stories about the past. These multiple stories clashed just as often as did different imaginations of regions, communities, and the nation in colonial India. The Indian university as an institution often did not provide a venue for debates that would subject issues of public life to rigorous and academic examination. The struggle to give history a "proper" academic form was part of public life well into the 1930s and the 1940s.[20]

Sarkar was a child of the empire, embraced its highest abstract ideals, and struggled all his life—with loyal, fraught, but constant support from his friend Sardesai—to give Indian history a "scientific" and academic status, to free it

20. Religious studies would be an even more powerful example of this phenomenon. Perhaps because of their concern to avoid interfering in Indian religions, the British built universities in India in which one of the most important aspects of Indian life in the nineteenth century, religion, was never made a subject of academic study. The questions that the young Narendranath Datta (Swami Vivekananda), for example, put once to the scholar Pramadadas Mitra of Benares about "Hindu" scriptures while traveling in north India in the 1880s, were clearly questions worthy of discussion in a university; but religious studies has never been made into an academic subject in India, while debates unrestrained by any academic rigor rage in Indian public life. See *The Complete Works of Vivekananda*, Mayavati memorial ed. (Calcutta: Advaita Ashram, 1995), pp. 201–224.

of what he saw as the shortcomings of histories popular in the public domain. But all of this embroiled him in lifelong controversies with other historians, both amateur and professional, and their conflicts sometimes took even ugly or unpleasant turns. Sarkar's attempt to sever the connection between populist histories and their academic counterparts failed. This book tries to show how enmeshed the academic and the popular domains were in colonial India in the period 1900–1950, in terms of history as a knowledge form. This in turn has indeed had long-term effects on debates within and about the discipline in independent India.

What made Sarkar's work particularly contentious to many were the two figures much of his research focused on: the last great Mughal emperor Aurangzeb (1618–1707; r. 1658–1707), who was an orthodox Sunni Muslim, and the Maratha ruler Shivaji (1627/30–1680; r. 1674–1680), who remained, for much of his later life, a rebel in Aurangzeb's empire and eventually (1674) declared himself an independent Hindu king. Aurangzeb was a debated figure in his own time and attracted loyalties in the twentieth century that were often divided along religious-political lines. Hindus considered him an "intolerant" Muslim ruler in a predominantly Hindu land, while many if not most Muslims respected his strict observance of Islamic tenets both in personal life and in his policies, especially in the latter half of his rule. Shivaji, on the other hand, emerged by the early twentieth century as a symbol of Maratha and Hindu pride at a time when nationalist politics in India began to be fractured along the lines of cleavage that religion, language, and caste provided. So just as most Hindus came to look upon Akbar (1542–1605; r. 1556–1605) as the ideal Mughal ruler, Shivaji became both a hero of the non-Brahman movement in the twentieth century (in addition to being a hero to Hindus in general) and anathema to many Muslim nationalists.

As we will see, Sarkar found himself often at the center of many of these debates. Many Maratha historians and admirers of Shivaji felt unhappy at Sarkar's criticisms of their hero. They blamed this on Sarkar's dependence on Mughal sources and his pro-Mughal sympathies. Many Muslim intellectuals, on the other hand, were unhappy with Sarkar's praise of Shivaji and with his criticisms of Aurangzeb's religious orthodoxy. Through all the disputes and argumentation recounted in this book, it is clear that the historical debates that have informed and constituted modern South Asia have mostly concerned personalities from the early-modern period, mainly the Mughal times, and in particular from the seventeenth and eighteenth centuries. Sarkar was the preeminent historian of two such debated—and celebrated—personalities: Shivaji and Aurangzeb.

Introducing the Two Historians

I should at this point briefly introduce the main protagonist of my story, Sir Jadunath Sarkar, and his lifelong friend and collaborator from 1904 on, Rao Bahadur Govindrao Sakharam Sardesai (fig. 1). Born in Rajshahi in present-day Bangladesh, Sarkar was described on his death by A. L. Basham as "probably the greatest Indian historian of his generation."[21] Throughout most of his working life, his official duties were to teach literature and sometimes history at undergraduate institutions such as Ripon College, Calcutta; Ravenshaw College in Cuttack, Orissa; Patna College in Bihar; and Banaras Hindu University. He retired in 1926, when he was appointed the vice chancellor of the University of Calcutta for two years. From 1929 on, he continued his work as an independent scholar.

A self-taught historian, Sarkar was a prolific writer. The most exhaustive bibliography of his works that I have seen lists 4 books and 158 essays and addresses in his native Bengali and about 17 books—some of them with multiple volumes—and 260 essays in English, plus some 110 essays and addresses he published in newspapers and magazines. These are in addition to the many Persian and French documents he translated and published, the volumes of documents he edited on his own or in collaboration with others, and the numerous books in a variety of languages for which he wrote forewords.[22] Basham's obituary spoke for many when it said of Sir Jadunath: "The greatness and importance of his work was largely due to the thousands of unpublished documents of the Mughal period which he was able to bring to light and utilize, bringing to bear upon them a sound historical judgment, unprejudiced by communal, religious, or national sentiments."[23] Sarkar's detractors would have disagreed with the last part of the statement, but it described well Sarkar's ideals, whatever his failures in achieving them. Sarkar was knighted in 1929 and was the first Indian historian ever to have been elected—as he was in 1952—an Honorary Foreign Member of the American Historical Association.[24] He was also elected an honorary member of the Royal Asiatic

21. A. L. Basham, "Sir Jadunath Sarkar, C. I. E.," *Journal of Royal Asiatic Society* 90 (1958), p. 222.

22. These numbers are taken from the detailed lists provided in Anirudhha Ray, *Jadunath Sarkar* (Kolkata: Poshimbanga bangla akademi, 1999), pp. 70–118.

23. Basham, "Sir Jadunath Sarkar," p. 223. An excellent account of Sir Jadunath's career and achievements until 1926—probably furnished by Sarkar himself—was published under the title "Sir Jadunath Sarkar" in the *Modern Review* (September 1926), pp. 347–348.

24. NL, JSP, letter no. 102, Sardesai to Sarkar, Bombay, 15 June 1929, congratulates Sarkar "upon [his] being a recipient of the high honour of knighthood."

FIGURE 1. G. S. Sardesai, 9 February 1957. A photograph found framed at Sardesai's bedside. Photograph by Ranu Roychoudhuri. Private collection of the author.

Society of Great Britain and Ireland in 1923 and an honorary corresponding member of the Royal Historical Society of England in 1935.

We will not be concerned here with the entire oeuvre of Sarkar. Apart from the letters exchanged between him and Sardesai, our focus will be limited mainly to Sarkar's five-volume history of the last great Mughal, Aurangzeb, published between 1912 and 1924, and the four volumes of *Fall of the Mughal Empire*, published between 1932 and 1950. The other two books of Sarkar that will concern us in some detail are those on the seventeenth-century Maratha hero and king Shivaji (1630–1680): *Shivaji and His Times* (1919) and *The House of Shivaji* (1948).

Sardesai's role in my narrative is mainly as Sarkar's friend, collaborator, interlocutor, and correspondent. A self-taught but celebrated historian of the Marathas, who was employed by the maharaja of Baroda (from 1889 on), he took voluntary retirement in 1925 to devote his time entirely to his historical scholarship. The maharaja did not take kindly to this decision and slashed Sardesai's pension by more than half, which forced him to live in a village called Kamshet near Poona, where his brother had a house.[25] He also was the author of many books and articles, most famously his eight-volume single-authored series in Marathi on Maratha history, known as *Marathi Riyasat* and published between 1898 and 1939 (making him known as the *Riyasatkar*), and his three volumes in English, *New History of the Marathas*. On the recommendation of Jadunath Sarkar, Sardesai was allowed access to the collection in the Alienation Office in Poona of the records of the eighteenth-century peshwas, rulers of the Marathas, in order to bring out edited collections of these documents. Some forty-five volumes of *Selections from the Peshwa Daftar* were published under Sardesai's editorship. He collaborated with Sarkar in editing and publishing the records of the Poona Residency, the office of the East India Company official who acted as the resident at the Peshwa Court in Poona.

Sarkar and Sardesai came into contact in 1904. They were interested in using complementary historical sources. Sarkar wanted to use Marathi documents for his work on Aurangzeb; Sardesai needed to know about Persian sources for Maratha history. Sarkar knew Persian, French, and Portuguese in addition to English, Bengali, Sanskrit, Hindi, and later Marathi. Sardesai could read early-modern Marathi script. And thus flourished a friendship that only the emergence of a modern, academic discipline of history could make possible and that lasted until Sarkar's death in 1958. Sardesai died the next year.[26]

Their long-term conflicts with other historians over access to sources and over judgments having to do with evidence and history were also something that brought Sarkar and Sardesai together emotionally. Their opponents were

25. His pension was restored in 1939 to its full amount, Rs 237 and 8 annas per month. In 1926 it had been slashed to Rs. 93 and 8 annas per month. But some twenty thousand rupees due to him, he said, were never paid. "All the same," commented Sardesai, "I need not hereafter feel a pinch in life." NL, JSP, letter no. 564, Sardesai to Sarkar, Kamshet, 24 April 1939.

26. Vasant V. Rao, "Govind Sakharam Sardesai," in *Historians and Historiography in Modern India*, ed. S. P. Sen (Calcutta: Institute of Historical Studies, 1973), pp. 222–234. I have included here only such information as I thought necessary for a minimal introduction. Much of the necessary biographical information about both is spread throughout this book, with the relevant sources mentioned.

mainly the independent scholars associated with the Bharat Itihas Samshodhak Mandal (Association of Researchers in Indian History), set up in Poona in 1910. Much of my narrative here brings in the sense of rivalry and occasional hostility between Sarkar and Sardesai on one hand and the Poona historians—joined by Surendra Nath Sen from Calcutta and Sir Shafaat Ahmad Khan from Allahabad—on the other. This hostility, at once intellectual and personal, finds a place in my narrative because it became an important factor in shaping both historical research and the nature of Indian institutions that were meant to foster and promote such research in the country.

The Fall from Grace of Sir Jadunath

Sarkar's reputation as a historian survived the debates of his lifetime. Immediately after Sarkar's death, the eminent Bengali historian, Professor N. K. Sinha, prophesied: "It is not likely that Sir Jadunath Sarkar will ever be displaced. His wonderful accuracy will secure to him immunity from the common lot of historical workers. So far as we can visualize, in the near future, in his chosen field, there will be only scanty gleaners after his copious harvest." So probably it seemed in Calcutta in 1958. But even as Professor Sinha was writing these lines, a group of younger scholars at Allahabad, Aligarh, and Oxford were conducting research that would ensure that by the time someone like me came into the world of South Asian history as a young novice in Calcutta in the early 1970s, Jadunath Sarkar's name would be all but forgotten among the prominent historians of India. Everybody, of course, knew his name and knew that he was without doubt once the greatest authority on Mughal India—particularly for the seventeenth and eighteenth centuries—but his academic status suffered a steep decline in the late 1950s and the early 1960s. We dutifully bought copies of his five-volume history of Aurangzeb, his four volumes of the *Fall of the Mughal Empire*, and some of his other works when the Indian publisher Orient Longman reprinted them in the 1970s. But we did this with the knowledge that Sarkar's approach to history had been discredited. Our teachers did not do emperors, battles, and the character of kings anymore. Unlike Sir Jadunath Sarkar and other historians of his time, they did not believe in the role of heroes in history. Heroes had been replaced by "causes." As Satish Chandra said, "[Sir Jadunath] . . . projected Aurangzeb's struggle to conquer the south as a Greek tragedy . . . [but] the search for causal relationships cannot be given up by historians."[27]

27. N. K. Sinha, "Sir Jadunath Sarkar: An Obituary Notice and Appraisal" (1958) reprinted in his *The Historian as an Archivist*, ed. Pradip Sinha (Midnapur: Vidyasagar University, 1999),

"Cause" was a code word for institutional analysis. Into the list of "causes" fell economy, institutions, parties and politics at the Mughal court, money, wages, exploitation, histories of the state and of revenue crisis, peasant revolts, provincial autonomy, and so on. Chandra's generation studied the Mughals with an eye on the question of India's transition to capitalism. Could India have become a capitalist economy on her own, without the mediation of British colonial rule? Were underdevelopment and "distortions" of Indian institutions results of colonial rule? Those were their (and our) questions. We were decidedly anti-empire in our attitude. We knew that Sir Jadunath was not. This transition in historiography is captured well in something Satish Chandra wrote in 1989, discussing "Mythifying History" in the Indian journal *Seminar*. For Jadunath Sarkar, "the personal qualities of Aurangzeb . . . became a negative point," wrote Chandra; current research, he contended, showed Aurangzeb to be "neither a hero nor a villain," but someone representing an old order that could not "recognize . . . the stirrings and incipient growth of a new socio-economic system."[28]

Chandra's criticisms were backed up by the work of his student M. Athar Ali, whose pathbreaking study *The Mughal Nobility under Aurangzeb*, a revised version of a PhD thesis submitted to the Aligarh Muslim University in 1961, was published in 1966. Ali emphasized the need to study in detail "all the elements of the *structure* of the Mughal Empire" before its decline could be attributed to what he called "text-book formulae" such as "personal degeneracy of the kings, luxurious life at the court, inefficiency of administration," all reminiscent, as we shall see, of Sarkar's analyses in his multivolume *Fall of the Mughal Empire*. The historiography of Mughal India underwent further

p. 26; Chandra, "The Deccan Policy of the Mughals (I)—Up to Shah Jahan," in his *Essays*, p. 447. This essay was first published in *Indian Historical Review* 4, no. 2 (January 1978), pp. 326–335.

28. Satish Chandra, "Reassessing Aurangzeb," *Seminar* (Delhi), special issue, "Mythifying History," 364 (December 1989), p. 35. Indeed, this criticism has been repeated many times over the past five decades. For some late instances, see Robert C. Hallisey, *The Rajput Rebellion against Aurangzeb: A Study of the Mughal Empire in Seventeenth-Century India* (Columbia: University of Missouri Press, 1977), pp. x, 85; and Andrea Hintze, *The Mughal Empire and Its Decline: An Interpretation of the Sources of Social Power* (Aldershot, Hampshire: Ashgate, 1997); Hintze sees Sarkar's emphasis on "character" as a "monocausal" approach to history. The Bangladeshi scholar Mohammad Shah squarely places Sarkar among "pro-imperialist, colonial and communal historians of the colonial era" in his article "Jadunath Sarkar's Interpretation of Aurangzeb's Reign," *Journal of the Asiatic Society of Bangladesh (Humanities)* 28, no. 2 (December 1983), pp. 133–141. Douglas E. Streusand, in *The Formation of the Mughal Empire* (Delhi: Oxford University Press, 1989), p. 2, sees Sarkar as both anachronistic and partisan to Hindus: "Sarkar represents one of the three present-minded approaches to Mughal history: the Hindu communalist approach."

significant changes with the publication of Muzaffar Alam's *The Crisis of Empire in Mughal North India* in 1986, based on research conducted under the supervision of Satish Chandra and S. Nurul Hasan, both trained at the University of Allahabad and later professors at the Aligarh Muslim University. As a matter of fact, much of the ire and sarcasm of Athar Ali's introduction to the second edition of his *Mughal Nobility* was directed at Alam (and the perceived congruence of Alam's propositions with those made by Christopher A. Bayly of Cambridge). Yet, it is interesting to see how, in spite of all the vitriol that Ali reserved for Alam and Bayly, Alam's own position on Sarkar remained consistent with the criticisms that Sarkar's work had already received from the generation that taught Alam, in which Ali was included. Alam described Sarkar's attribution (and that of Sarkar's mentor William Irvine, an Indian Civil Service officer) of "the decline of Mughal power" to "a deterioration in the characters of the emperors and their nobles" as failing to "lead us beyond the perspective of the seventeenth and eighteenth centuries' Persian chroniclers, with the difference that Sarkar also read evidence of a 'Hindu reaction' in the Rathor, Bundela, Maratha and Sikh wars against the Mughal[s]." "Sarkar's views," Alam concluded, "are to be set against the ambience of the times that lent legitimacy to communal interpretation of Indian history in the late-nineteenth and twentieth centuries."[29]

However, a silent but perhaps the most magisterial dismissal of Sarkar came in the form of Irfan Habib's 1958 doctoral thesis from Oxford, eventually published in 1963 as the awesome *The Agrarian System of Mughal India*, a classic in its own right, which played a key role in displacing Sarkar from the canon. Habib wrote about the "agrarian crisis" that plagued the Mughal Empire and contributed to its "destruction," but he did so without any reference to Sarkar's propositions in the latter's *Fall*, as if the volumes did not exist for Habib.[30] Sarkar features rarely in Habib's book. No mention of him is to be found in the original preface, dated Aligarh, August 1962, and the few

29. M. Athar Ali, *The Mughal Nobility under Aurangzeb*, rev. ed. (New Delhi: Oxford University Press, 1997), p. 1; the first edition was published by Aligarh Muslim University in 1966. The text of the 1966 edition was not changed much in the revised edition of 1997; see "Preface to the New Edition," p. ix. Muzaffar Alam, *The Crisis of Empire in Mughal North India: Awadh and the Punjab, 1707–48* (Delhi: Oxford University Press, 1986), pp. 2–3.

30. Irfan Habib, *The Agrarian System of Mughal India (1556–1707)* (London: Asia Publishing House for Department of History, Aligarh Muslim University, 1963), chap. 9, the last paragraph of which begins, referencing Mao Zedong: "Thus was the Mughal Empire destroyed." Habib's bibliography mentions Sarkar's (somewhat ephemeral) *Mughal Administration* (1920) and his 1906 translation of Aurangzeb's *farman* to Rasikdas.

references in footnotes are mostly confined to Sarkar's *The India of Aurangzib* (1901) and his errors of translation or his mistakes in dating events.[31] The one time Sarkar figures directly in the text is in an appendix on revenue statistics, where Sarkar is acknowledged as one of the pioneers, after Edward Thomas's *The Revenue Resources of the Mughal Empire in India* (1871), who "attempted a study of . . . [Mughal] statistics." The reference, again, is to *The India of Aurangzib*.[32]

The India of Aurangzib was a work of Sarkar's youth, published in 1901 when he would have been about thirty-one. The book was a product of the thesis that won him the prestigious Premchand Roychand Scholarship at the University of Calcutta, a fellowship named after a Gujarati merchant who "suddenly amassed a large fortune during the cotton boom of 1866 [precipitated by the American civil war] and spent much of it in various useful charities."[33] Sarkar obtained this prize scholarship in 1898, and the book version was published in 1901. The book contained partial translations of two relevant seventeenth-century Persian manuscripts Sarkar could locate in India, which supplied some key statistics of the late Mughal period: *Khulasatu-t-tawarikh* by Sujan Rai, who composed it between 1695 and 1699, and *Chahar Gulshan* (c. 1759–60), by Rai Chatar Man (or Chaturman) Kayath.[34]

Sarkar actually explained in the book how he had to translate "this work [*Chahar Gulshan*] without any critical apparatus of the text." The "only copy" he could lay his hands on in India had "numerous" mistakes; some "proper nouns" were missing and the text was in "corrupt condition." Sarkar was apologetic about his work even though it had involved an enormous amount of labor on his part. He pointed out in his preface that the title of the book did not "fully express its content," and its size gave "an inadequate idea of the labour it ha[d] involved, especially in making out proper names and abbreviated Arabic word-figures (*raqam*) from badly-transcribed Persian." "If the net results of the researches embodied in this work be imperfect and wanting in finality," he pleaded, "I hope the difficult nature of the subject and our want of the requisite materials will be taken into account before sentence is pronounced

31. Habib, *Agrarian System*, pp. 3n4, 15n44, 22n75, 343n24.

32. Ibid., p. 395.

33. Rao Bahadur Dr. G. S. Sardesai, "Jadunath Sarkar as I Know Him," in Gupta, *Life and Letters*, p. 26.

34. Both of these authors and their respective texts receive extended discussion in Muzaffar Alam and Sanjay Subrahmanyam, *Writing the Mughal World: Studies on Culture and Politics* (New York: Columbia University Press, 2012), chap. 9. The name of Sujan Rai's text is given by Alam and Subrahmanyam as *Khulasat al-Tawarikh*, which I take to be the more correct transliteration.

upon it." His very first chapter began with a formal "apology." "Nobody can be more sensible of the imperfections of this book than the author," reads the very first line of the book. Yet it was his hope that "nobody who knows what it is to translate a Persian work bristling with obscure geographical names from a single and incorrectly transcribed manuscript, will be hard upon" the author for "these imperfections." The manuscripts available to him were unpublished and unedited, he often had "no second manuscript to collate [with] the one lying in front of him," and the "Pandits and Maulvis" who helped him were "ignorant of historical criticism." "The historical student in India," observed Sarkar, "is thrown almost entirely on his own resources. He may, therefore, claim a partial, if not a plenary, pardon for his sins."[35]

Meant probably more for his contemporaries than for researchers after his time, these words of "apology" did not win Sarkar much reprieve from the criticisms, if not the condescension, of posterity. Habib, then probably about the same age as Sarkar was when the latter published his *The India of Aurangzib*, rubbed the point in while rejecting Sarkar's translation: "The *Chahar Gulshan* has not been printed, but the geographical and statistical portion was translated by Sarkar in his *India of Aurangzeb* [*sic*]. Bodl[eian] Elliot 366 is not only the earliest among catalogued MSS . . . but is also probably the most authoritative, being a copy of the original work and not of its later recension. Its reading has generally been preferred here to that of Sarkar's *India of Aurangzeb*, which on the admission of the translator, was based on a carelessly transcribed manuscript and contains many errors in the statistical portions."[36]

But more than his rejection of specific sources used by Sarkar, it was the themes that Habib worked on that signaled the remarkable shift in historiography I have already mentioned. Habib was avowedly Marxist—his very last footnote in the book is a reference to the *Selected Works* of Mao Zedong. He was "secular" (in the Indian sense of the word) and did not shy away from decrying "Muslim communalism"; and he sought the causes of Mughal decline in a revenue crisis of the empire and the attendant rebellions in the countryside. Habib was, however, not the first person to signal the shift. Anecdotal evidence suggests that the story of Sarkar's fall from grace with younger generations of Indian historians had its origins in the decade before Indian independence in 1947. The Department of History at the University of Allahabad, where later historians like Satish Chandra and Nurul Hasan were trained, had

35. Jadunath Sarkar, *The India of Aurangzib (Topography, Statistics and Roads) Compared with the India of Akbar: With extracts from the "Khulasatu-t-tawarikh" and the "Chahar Gukshan" translated and annotated* (Calcutta: Bose, 1901), pp. xxi–xxii; preface, p. i; chap. 1, p. ix.

36. Habib, *Agrarian System*, p. 3n4.

a critical role in disseminating critiques of Sarkar's approach to history. Chandra and Hasan both migrated later as teachers to the Aligarh Muslim University, where Muhammad Habib, father of Irfan Habib, began a "secular" and left-leaning tradition of historical research in the 1920s.[37] "When I entered the portals of the Allahabad University in 1940 as an undergraduate," recalls Satish Chandra, "the University had established its reputation as a centre . . . which attracted in large numbers those who aspired to enter the sanctum of the civil services." The Department of History, "considered one of the leading centres of historical research in the country," had Sir Shafaat Ahmad Khan at its head. Khan, who became India's high commissioner in South Africa in 1940, was one of the main adversaries of Sir Jadunath Sarkar through the 1920s and the 1930s. After Khan's departure from the scene, the intellectual leadership of the Allahabad school of historians passed on to Professor R. P. Tripathi, who, having trained with Harold Laski in London, was extremely critical of Sarkar's focus on rulers and their ideas and characters.[38] Apart from Sarkar's personal dislike of Shafaat Ahmad Khan, what fueled this criticism was also the publication of the third volume of Sarkar's *History of Aurangzib* in 1916, which had a heavy emphasis on Aurangzeb's orthodox Islamic policies. Many read the book as a straightforward indictment of Islam.[39] "Appar-

37. The rise of Marxist approaches in the historiography of Muslim and particularly Mughal India deserves a separate study. For an elucidation of such an early framework blending Islamic exposition with some broadly Marxist-cum-socialist principles of historiography, see Mohammad Habib's introduction and Khaliq Ahmed Nizami's preface to a reprinted version of *Elliot and Dowson's History of India as Told by Its Own Historians*, vol. 2 (Aligarh: Cosmopolitan, 1952).

38. It appears that Tripathi did not publish any books in the 1930s, but the preface to his 1959 book *Some Aspects of Mughal Administration* (Allahabad: Central, 1959), p. iv, published while Tripathi was the vice chancellor of Saugor University, clearly states that it was based on his 1926 University of London D.Sc. dissertation, written under the supervision of Harold Laski, Denison Ross, and Henry Dodwell. This edition describes itself as "second, revised edition" but gives no detail about the publication of the first edition. Tripathi's influence on his students seems to have come about mainly through his lectures. In his memoirs of Nurul Hasan, the historian Barun De mentions the "great admiration" that Hasan felt, while a student at Allahabad, for Tripathi, a "systematic thinker" on Muslim administration in India. See Barun De, "Prof. S. Nurul Hasan: A Memoir," Occasional Paper no. 1, 2006, Raj Bhavan (Governor's House), Calcutta, pp. 2–14.

39. Aurangzeb has always been, indeed from his own lifetime on, a disputed character. The discussion in the two books so far published on Sarkar, both based on PhD dissertations—S. K. Srivastava, *Sir Jadunath Sarkar: The Historian at Work* (Delhi: Anamika Prakashan, 1989), pp. 77–99; and Kiran Pawar, *Sir Jadunath Sarkar: A Profile in Historiography* (New Delhi: Books and Books, 1985), pp. 43–74—offer contradictory points of view. Srivastava, having trained with Sumit Sarkar (see his preface), is critical of Jadunath Sarkar's views of Aurangzeb and predictably finds Pawar's study, critical of the critics of Sarkar (Pawar, p. 65), lacking in "critical insight and analysis" (p. xviii). Pawar (p. 80) points out that in the first decade of the twentieth century, Mus-

ently," writes Chandra, "R. P. Tripathi wanted . . . a critical study of the *causes* of the fall of the Mughal Empire" that would put Sarkar's exclusive focus on Aurangzeb's "religious policy" in "proper perspective." For "it was well known that the Allahabad school of history"—and this must have included its founding leader, Sir Shafaat Ahmad Khan—"was bitterly opposed to Sir Jadunath Sarkar's representation of Aurangzeb as a religious fanatic and his view that in a truly Islamic state religious toleration was an impossibility." They never put their criticisms into print, but, as Chandra remembered it, "he was not spared in the lectures." Sarkar returned the compliment later when Chandra, as a research student, went to work in Sarkar's library. Sarkar, while generous in giving Chandra unfettered access to his library, also said to him: "The students of the history department at Allahabad are good and hard-working . . . but your teachers are lazy." Chandra thought this a "gibe at R. P. Tripathi's easy lifestyle," but, as will become clear to the reader of this book, it could have been aimed at Shafaat Ahmad Khan as well. It is entirely possible that Tripathi owed some of his criticisms of Sarkar to discussions with his close colleague Khan.[40]

---

lim intellectuals like Maulana Shibli Nomani (1857–1914) wrote several articles in Urdu defending Aurangzeb's religious policies against criticisms by colonial historians. Some of these have been published in English in Maulana Shibli Nomani, *Alamgir*, trans. Syed Sahabuddin Abdur Rahman (Delhi: Idarah-i-Adabiyat-i Delli, 1981). One of the best-known protests against the third volume of Sarkar's *Aurangzeb* was the lawyer Zahiruddin Faruki's book *Aurangzeb and His Times* (1935; Delhi: Idarah-i-Adabiyat-i Delli, 1972), where he pronounced: "Sarkar's attempt to prejudice Aurangzeb's case by denouncing Islam itself is altogether futile" (p. 92n1). See also the discussion in Alam and Subrahmanyam, *Writing the Mughal World*, pp. 6–8, where the authors write that "for the most part," Shibli's "realm was not properly Indian history."

40. Chandra, introduction to *Essays*, p. 3. Sarkar served on a selection committee of the University of Allahabad in the 1940s for the position of professor of history. Dr. Ram Prasad Tripathi and Dr. Ishwari Prasad were the "internal" candidates for this position. Sarkar's opinions on the Allahabad history department were quite damning: "After its first start with a fanfare of trumpets under Prof. Rushbrook Williams 28 years ago, it has done nothing to leave a mark." On Dr. Tripathi, his comments were acerbic:

> The writing of 'best seller' cribs for I.A. or even for B.A. standards, is not regarded as *original* research by the learned world. It is not a valid title to this post to have taken a doctorate by a really creditable thesis twenty years ago and to have gone to sleep ever after. . . . Dr. R. P. Tripathi is definitely inferior to Dr. Ishwari Prasad; his intellectual attainments are of a lower type than Dr I. Prasad's and his thesis nowhere touches the level of first-rate research; moreover, ever since his appointment, he has been an increasingly habitual absentee from the schoolroom of research worker.

NL, JSP, from file titled "Jadunath Sarkar: Misc. Papers," undated "Confidential Note on a Selection Committee of the Department of History, Allahabad University."

In the past few decades, however, beginning perhaps with the late J. F. Richards's *Mughal Administration in Golconda* (1975), the tide has slowly turned for Sir Jadunath. Richards began his acknowledgments in the book with a glowing tribute to Jadunath Sarkar: "I have relied again and again on the writings of that master historian, Jadunath Sarkar. Today, in 1974, his narrative approach and his intellectual concerns appear a bit old-fashioned. Only a historian who has tried to develop an accurate narrative of political and public events, using fragmented sources typical of this period, can appreciate the magnitude of Sarkar's contribution. He set the narrative frame for the late Mughal period virtually single-handed. Because I have been trying to fill in a peculiar regional gap in his narrative, I am most aware of his skills." Similarly, Irfan Habib's preface to a "second, revised" edition of his *Agrarian System* mentions Sarkar directly in the text as one of the pioneers to whom Habib *now* feels indebted: "In the preface to the first edition, I especially acknowledged my debt to W. H. Moreland and P. Saran. . . . My consciousness of the debt to them and to others like H. M. Elliot, S. H. Hodivala, Jadunath Sarkar and Ibn Hasan, has only grown with time." Muzaffar Alam's new introduction to a forthcoming edition of his *The Crisis of Empire* carries a detailed analysis of precisely the very sources that he once thought exposed the likes of Sarkar to the danger of simply reproducing the "biases" of the eighteenth-century chroniclers who wrote out their own experiences of the decline of the Mughals.[41]

But these changes have been slow to come. The consensus about Sarkar that one comes across in histories written in India even today reflects the dominance of the historiography established by the Aligarh and Allahabad schools. From questions related to the "character" of the emperor to "causes" and "structures" of the Mughal decline, the main direction of the historiographic movement away from Sarkar was clear. It is also entirely understandable that in postwar decades, when academic history was emerging globally as a branch of the social sciences and favored sociological explanations over literary ones, historians working on the decline of the Mughal empire should find accounts that assigned a determining role to the character of emperors limiting and restrictive. Indeed, the new consensus against Sarkar found a nice summary in S. K. Srivastava's 1989 book on Sir Jadunath, which was based on his thesis submitted to the University of Delhi: "Jadunath in his

41. J. F. Richards, *Mughal Administration in Golconda* (Oxford: Clarendon, 1975), p. vii; Irfan Habib, *The Agrarian System of Mughal India, 1556–1707*, 2nd, rev. ed. (New Delhi: Oxford University Press, 2000), p. xiii. I am grateful to Muzaffar Alam for letting me see his penultimate draft for his new introduction.

efforts to highlight the religious orthodoxy in Islam as a factor for Aurangzeb's failure, has totally overlooked some of the important aspects [sic]—the inherent contradictions of the Jagirdari and Zamindari systems, the tensions and contradictions within the nobility, and the social tensions which existed in the agrarian community."[42]

If Srivastava's position may be regarded as reporting what stood as the left consensus in India on Sir Jadunath in the 1970s and the 1980s, Peter Hardy, an English historian of Muslim India, who wrote a foreword for Srivastava's book, provides an interesting case showing how long the postindependence consensus against Sarkar held. Writing as early as the 1950s under the intellectual influence—a little too heavy an influence, one might say—of Collingwood's *The Idea of History* (1938), Hardy once accused the likes of "Doctors Lane-Poole and Vincent Smith, Sir Wolseley Haig [all colonial amateur historians] and Sir Jadunath Sarkar" of depicting "the history of medieval times as a succession of battles, rebellions and of depositions of one Muslim soldier of fortune by another." These were, in Hardy's eyes, antiquated approaches: "The working hypotheses of most modern historians—that a society must be studied in its own terms and that all aspects of the life of a people, a society or civilization are to be assumed to be interconnected and interdependent—seem not have greatly influenced . . . [their studies] of medieval Indian history."[43] Hardy's position appears to have solidified further in the late 1980s, when he wrote a foreword to Srivastava's book. Sarkar now looked to him like the epitome of a colonized intellectual—a middle-class person, "Indian in colour and blood, but English in taste, in opinions, in morals and *in intellect*"—a realization of Macaulay's imperial dream. Not only was Sarkar someone who simply recycled British, colonial propositions about "medieval" Indian history—propositions that made the British feel good about themselves as rulers of India—he was anachronistic as well. He assumed "human nature" to be the same "in the present and the past"—that humans were "motivated by much the same passions and inclinations and prejudices"—and was therefore always engaged in "hurrying on his historical personages past their own contexts into his." Hardy was convinced that C. A. Bayly's *Rulers, Townsmen, and Bazaars: North Indian Society in the Age of British Expansion, 1770–1870* had "shown Sarkar's representations of the eighteenth century to be more rhetorical than historical." While Sarkar's work, Hardy thought, was still "essential

42. Srivastava, *Sir Jadunath*, p. 108. Srivastava's references here are to the work of Irfan Habib and Satish Chandra.

43. Peter Hardy, *Historians of Medieval India: Studies in Indo-Muslim Historical Writing* (London: Luzac, 1960), p. 3.

reading for the tiros," it was "vital" that he should be shown to have ("as have the rest of us," Hardy qualified) "feet of clay," so that "subsequent historical investigation" was not "trampled into the earth."[44]

The Forgotten Question about Jadunath Sarkar

Historiography is not my main concern in this book. What interests me here is a certain intellectual and historical amnesia implicit in the historiographical turn discussed above, a forgetting that today seems as surprising as it seems also interesting. Historians who criticized Sarkar's emphasis on "character" as "monocausal," or as seeming like "text-book formulae," missing out on the "structural" aspects of Mughal rule, never stopped to ask why someone of Sarkar's erudition, intelligence, and sense of engagement with the politics of his time would be so obsessed with the role of character in political history. Did Sarkar mix up the past with the present in an anachronistic way, write about heroes and fallen heroes, of the character of individuals as determining their destiny, simply because he was gullible and colonized enough to adopt as his own the propositions that British colonial historians had developed about Mughal India out of self-serving motives? This book is a long answer to that question. It is an attempt to bring into view a larger architecture of ideas regarding empire and nation, from which the analytical categories of "character" and "the hero" once derived their legitimacy and intelligibility. It is to draw our attention to forms of relations between imperial and patriotic thought that coexisted with, gave competition to, and later lost ground to virulently anti-imperialist and triumphalist forms of nationalism in colonial India. I do this to understand two fundamental methodological obsessions of Sarkar: his near-fanatic zeal for a positivist idea of "fact" and his spiritual pursuit of a metaphysical idea of "truth" in history. Very few, if any, historians today would share Sarkar's passion on these questions. So my exercise is also an attempt to relativize E. H. Carr's question, What is history? by asking, after Anthony Grafton: What *was* history?[45] For a patriot like Sarkar, who, growing up within the intellectual horizons of the British Empire, sought to ground the discipline in certain positivist and metaphysical conceptions, respectively, of fact and truth, what indeed was history?

44. Peter Hardy, foreword to Srivastava, *Sir Jadunath*, pp. vi–xi, Hardy's emphasis; C. A. Bayly, *Rulers, Townsmen, and Bazaars: North Indian Society in the Age of British Expansion, 1770–1870* (Cambridge: Cambridge University Press, 1983).

45. Anthony Grafton, *What Was History? The Art of History in the Early Modern World* (Cambridge: Cambridge University Press, 2007).

Sir Jadunath and the Question of Character

Sarkar was remembered as much for his contribution to historiography as for his personal discipline, reflected even in something as small as his steady and clear handwriting, which others often remarked on. I knew all this before proceeding to read the correspondence between Sarkar and Sardesai in the original in the Rare Books Section of the National Library in Calcutta. I also knew, from reading about him, that Sarkar had been seriously influenced by his father, who combined a love of Vaishnava devotional literature with a deep respect for nineteenth-century Brahmo reformers of Hinduism and kept in touch with their leaders, Devendranath Tagore and Keshab Chandra Sen.[46] I had read the historian Niharranjan Ray's description of Sir Jadunath as someone of "nineteenth-century Victorian, puritanical habits" whose ideals had been shaped by "the classical and historical outlook and prose of Gibbon, Mommsen, Macaulay, and Trevelyan, and by the encyclopedic ideals of liberal humanism." But I was not prepared for the archival presence he came to have for me. I had read in Hari Ram Gupta's tribute to Sarkar that "Jadunath's handwriting does not vary at all, indicating no hurry. It is [a] beautiful, steady and regular hand. Not a word is illegible, and . . . mistakes and corrections are very few." The letters themselves were very impressive in what they said not only about Sarkar's scholarship—that was legendary—but also about his spectacular memory. I was impressed with the ease with which sentences such as the following would flow out of his pen in letters to Nana, as Sardesai was called by those close to him: "The verse about the contrast between a child's birth and an old man's death scene was written by Hafiz [1320/25–1388/89], from whom both Tulsidas [1532–1623] and your Tukaram [1577–1650] stole it."[47] Copying some twelve hundred letters day after day by hand—for the rules of the National Library would not allow me to copy them in any other way—I could not help being affected by the difference between Sarkar's and my handwriting.[48] His was a clear and steady hand, unhurried, as Gupta put it; mine was rushed and illegible. After a while it was impossible not to feel the presence of a person who paid attention to every detail of the task in front

46. Moni Bagchi, *Acharya Jadunath: Jibon o sadhana* (Calcutta: Jijnasa, 1975), pp. 1–2; Anil Chandra Banerjee, *Jadunath Sarkar* (New Delhi: Sahitya Akademi, 1989), pp. 2–3.

47. Niharranjan Ray, preface to Moni Bagchi, *Acharya Jadunath*, p. 11; Gupta, *Life and Letters*, p. 17; NL, JSP, letter no. 870, Sarkar to Sardesai, Calcutta, 22 February 1946.

48. It is not clear how many letters from their correspondence were actually preserved. Gupta, *Life and Letters*, p. 13, mentions that the letters written by Sarkar before 1907 and those from Sardesai predating 1914 could not be found anymore. According to him, a total of 1,320 letters were still available. The National Library collection that I consulted actually had about 1,200.

of him, from copying historical documents to writing letters. Sheer historical reasoning—that his handwriting may have owed its clarity to colonial education that encouraged scribal skills—was of little help to me in warding off this presence, for Sardesai's handwriting, from the same historical period, was just as bad as mine. One could not avoid being reminded of Sarkar's forbiddingly methodical and disciplined personality. It was as if Sir Jadunath reprimanded me from behind every sentence of his that I copied, for there was so much difference between his writing and mine. "What's the big rush, my friend?" I could hear him say to me silently. "Do you work even harder than I did?" It was perhaps under the pressure of that silent rebuke that I could not shake off that I found myself buying a new pen one day, one with a rough point, so that I wouldn't "slur" my pen across several letters at once as was my wont!

It was difficult not to be moved by what I discovered in the archives about Sarkar's relationship to the Indian civil servant William Irvine (1840–1911), whose unfinished book *Later Mughals* Sarkar completed and published after Irvine's death. In 1915 Sarkar entered into a contract with Margaret Seymour, Irvine's daughter, whereby he agreed to publish the book at his own expense. To Mrs. Seymour were owed fifteen copies of the book and a part of the profits.[49] Sarkar worked hard to add 109 pages and many new notes to the book. This was purely a labor of love, as Sarkar considered Irvine to be a sort of mentor to himself. *Later Mughals* came out in two volumes in 1922. It was twelve years before Sarkar's expenses were recovered, and he then started sending regular checks to Mrs. Seymour every year from 1934 on. Margaret Seymour died on 17 June 1954, when Sarkar was about eighty-four, three years away from his death.[50] On the death of Mrs. Seymour, Sarkar must have learned the whereabouts of Irvine's son, H. W. K. Irvine, who, it turned out, lived in extreme poverty in Cuba. The files in the National Library contain only one letter from this man, dated 1955, in which he wrote: "I am very old, 83, and sick for many years and very poor indeed, but in the last two years in . . . very, very bad conditions. Scarcely walk and cannot write myself. My wife does all the writing for me." A few months later Irvine's wife, Eloina, wrote to Sarkar to say: "I am very sorry to have to tell you that my husband, H. W. K. Irvine died in 7 January after a long illness."[51] Sarkar then started sending the royalty checks to Eloina.

49. NL, JSP, Irvine File, letter from Margaret Seymour to Sarkar, London, 9 December 1915.

50. NL, JSP, Irvine File, letter from the manager of Midland Bank to Sarkar, London, 9 December 1955.

51. NL, JSP, Irvine File, letter to Sarkar from H. W. K. Irvine, 23 September 1955; NL, JSP, Irvine File, letter to Sarkar from Eloina Irvine, Calcutta, 10 May 1956.

That someone like Sarkar would be dutiful until his very last day is not surprising. But his dutifulness to William Irvine's daughter and son takes on a poignant color when we remember that these were perhaps the worst years of his own life, the last ten or twelve years. Between 1942 and 1957, as Sarkar's biographer Moni Bagchi writes, Sarkar had to cope with six deaths in his immediate family: "the death of his third son-in-law; the deaths, within four months of each other, of his eldest son and the eldest son-in-law; the death of his daughter in England in 1949; his youngest son's in 1955, and that of his second eldest grand-son (from a daughter), Captain Amit Kumar, in 1957."[52] In addition, his mother died in 1939 and a brother in 1951.[53]

The few personal letters preserved in the National Library—all his diaries appear to have been destroyed, except for few torn pages from the 1890s—portray an old man buffeted by many unfortunate blows in life, including his unceremonious removal from the organization he helped to build, the Indian Historical Records Commission (I detail this in chapter 7).[54] With the onset of the Second World War, he was worried about his son-in-law Major Sushil Ghosh, who was married to his second daughter, Sudha. Major Ghosh was missing in action around Singapore for five long years. The letters reveal a deeply caring side of Sir Jadunath, when the "rationalist" in him yielded to practices that he would have otherwise dismissed as "superstitious"—consulting astrologers, clairvoyants, performing religious vows (*brata*)—all in the aid of locating Major Ghosh.[55] Not given to expressing to others his private feelings, Sarkar wrote just a line through all this time to Nana, saying, "My anxiety about my son-in-law . . . is growing more agonising, and has

52. Bagchi, *Acharya Jadunath*, p. 223.

53. NL, JSP, letters from Sarkar to Sardesai—no. 589, Calcutta, 18 September 1939; no. 1064, Calcutta, 21 March 1951; no. 914, Calcutta, 23 January 1947. In the last-mentioned letter, Sarkar describes the death of his eldest son-in-law as an "unlooked for calamity."

54. Sarkar wrote to Sardesai as late as 1951 to say, "All my diaries since my college days (1889 onwards) have been preserved, except for the one for 1926 which was lost in changing houses." But these, sadly, were not handed over the National Library; nor do they seem easily accessible to researchers. The "face" of the family or lineage (*parivar*, *vamsa*) being considered very important in India, Indian families are usually extremely wary about handing over to outsiders such documents. NL, JSP, letter no. 1063, Sarkar to Sardesai, Calcutta, 14 March 1951. The few personal letters available at the National Library were found among discarded rubbish by the authorities of the Centre for Studies in Social Sciences when they took possession of Sarkar's residence at 10 Lake Terrace, Calcutta 700029 in the early 1970s. See the introductory note by Barun De to the file named "Miscellaneous" among the Sarkar papers in the library.

55. NL, JSP, Miscellaneous File, Sarkar's letters to his daughters Sudha and Roma, Calcutta, 30 December 1945, 25 May 1946. See also his letters to Sudha, Calcutta, 16 December 1941, 14 December 1943, 15 January 1944.

prevented me from doing my work."[56] It was not until the night of 11 October 1946 that the family was informed that Major Ghosh had died in action on 13 February 1942.[57]

This was not the end of Sarkar's troubles. In 1945 his second son, Satyen, returned from England because of illness. That Sarkar was morally strict with his children can be easily seen from letters he wrote to Satyendranath when the latter was young.[58] But Satyendranath's death on 8 September 1955 broke his heart. "Last Thursday night," he wrote to Nana, "Satyen's sufferings came to an end, and I now stand entirely son-less [his other son, Abani, had been stabbed to death during the Hindu-Muslim riots of 1947 in Calcutta by an unknown assailant] like you; only you are free from my anxieties about orphan young grandsons coming from sons and daughters."[59]

The other personal problems, about which Sarkar remained entirely private in these years, were his wife's chronic ill health and her manic obsession with washing herself repeatedly, indicative of a pathological concern with "purity" and "pollution" that was common among middle-class Bengali women of a certain period. There is only a cryptic reference to all this in a letter to Sardesai, written in 1950, where Sarkar mentioned in passing the "many domestic quarrels and illness of which I cannot speak."[60] But he was understandably more forthcoming in letters to his daughters.[61] Two letters of 1944–45, only five months apart, suggest that sometimes he would go through a prolonged period of depression and unrest in his mind. In a letter of 1945 to Sardesai, he made an unusually emotional reference to his own life: "Were it not for my wife's sake, I could have gone to some obscure village like Kamshet [where Sardesai lived] and buried myself there for three months, severing my connections with the outer world." Five months before that, in December 1944, he had expressed himself in Bengali and without reserve to his daughter Sudha: "I am old now, and my capacity for toleration is exhausted. I want to

56. NL, JSP, letter no. 745, Sarkar to Sardesai, Calcutta, 16 November 1942.

57. NL, JSP, Miscellaneous File, Sarkar to son Satyen, 11 October 1946.

58. See NL, JSP, Miscellaneous File, Sarkar's letters to Satyendranath, Darjeeling, 23 March 1933. There is also some family correspondence (mainly letters written by Abani to his younger brother Satyen while the latter was in England) preserved in the archives of the Centre for Studies in Social Sciences, Calcutta, that supports this point.

59. NL, JSP, letter no. 1189, Sarkar to Sardesai, Calcutta, 10 September 1955. On the death of Abani, see Srivastava, *Sir Jadunath*, p. 13.

60. NL, JSP, letter no. 1051, Sarkar to Sardesai, Calcutta, 19 October 1950.

61. NL, JSP, Miscellaneous File, Sarkar's letters to Sudha, Calcutta, 18 December 1944, 26 April 1945, 14 May 1945, 17 February 1946.

make financial provisions [for your mother], leave this place, and spend a year with you or in Kamshet sometime in the future."[62]

All of Sarkar's references to his personal life in his letters to Nana from the 1950s on are heavy with depression. In 1954, informing Sardesai of Satyen's incurable illness, Sarkar wrote: "I keep good health . . . though my writing has necessarily stopped."[63] In 1954, his wife slipped in the bathroom and was bedridden for a long time, confirming some of Sarkar's worst fears.[64] The octogenarian still kept himself busy with his writing, especially on military history. But the letters to Nana in these years reveal a profound sense of being tired: "A certain languor seizes me after any work and old things have begun to escape my memory." Later in the same year: "I see only darkness before me. This distracting thought is sapping my vitality and has put an end to my literary activity."[65]

The point of this long excursus into Sarkar's private sufferings in the last decade of his life is not to psychoanalyze or psychologize him: I am not competent for that task, and this book is not a biography. But reading these letters and those between Sarkar and the children of Irvine together made me realize that even his darkest years of experiencing the most profound sense of exhaustion could not stop Sarkar from carrying out what he thought was his duty—to keep paying Irvine's children the royalties due to them. I have no idea how much of an effort it was, but Sarkar clearly overcame his "languor and darkness" enough to go to the post office to send the money, never an easy task in the Indian system. The last letter we have from Irvine's daughter-in-law Eloina from Cuba is dated 16 July 1956, nearly two years before Sir Jadunath died. Eloina thanked Sarkar for the fifty pounds he had mailed and sent him in return her "liveliest gratitude" along with her thanks to God. The letter ends by saying: "Please excuse my bad English but perhaps you can't read Español, my idiom."[66]

Let me briefly explain why this encounter in the archives with the "character" of Sir Jadunath was of more than passing interest. Most people who came into academic contact with Sarkar remembered him for his work habits, a

62. NL, JSP, letter no. 843, Sarkar to Sardesai, Calcutta, 18 June 1945; NL, JSP, Miscellaneous File, Sarkar's letter to Sudha, Calcutta, 18 December 1944.

63. NL, JSP, letter no. 1173, Sarkar to Sardesai, Calcutta, 15 December 1954.

64. NL, JSP, letter no. 1182, Sarkar to Sardesai, Calcutta, 15 April 1954; Miscellaneous File, Sarkar's letter to his wife, Dehradun, 25 June (1945?).

65. NL, JSP, letter no. 1175, Sarkar to Sardesai, Calcutta, 1 February 1955; letter no. 1194, 7 December 1955.

66. NL, JSP, Irvine File, letter from Eloina, 16 July 1956.

heightened sense of time, his unusual reserve, his strictly disciplinarian personality, and his attention to details even when it came to issuing ordinary instructions—in short, as a character. The reminiscences in the book edited by Gupta are full of telling anecdotes, some impressive, some amusing, but all pointing to his rigorous, almost manic, insistence on discipline and rectitude: Sarkar's angry refusal of personal gifts from students; his "regularity and punctuality"; his moral revulsion toward the theater in his student days; his "honesty of conduct and complete obedience to the law"; his meticulous habit of keeping accounts of everyday expenses; the perception of him by others as "a misanthrope . . . who preferred books to men"; his generosity to trusted research students in accommodating several of them, sometimes simultaneously, in his own house and at his own expense; his parsimoniousness with time—seeing students (and guests) with an eye on his pocket watch so that he did not lose any time in small talk, and yet his dedication to them as a teacher, and so on.[67] The eminent historian Jagadish Narayan Sarkar, who was once Sir Jadunath's student, recalls: "When in 1939 I approached him for carrying on research [on the Mughal noble] 'Mir Jumla,' the first question he put to me was whether I knew Persian. When I replied in the negative he went away without any further useless talk." Not until two years later, when Jagadish Narayan Sarkar had learned enough Persian, did Sir Jadunath happily relent; then he "placed the entire resources of his library" at his student's disposal.[68] One could go on adding to such stories, all indicative of a man given to appreciating disciplined "character" in men both living and dead.

Some of this may have merely pointed to quirks of personality. If so, I am in no position to discuss or analyze them. What cannot be missed, though, is the connection that existed between Sir Jadunath's insistence on cultivation of a certain truthfulness on the part of the historian—the demand that the historian make a sincere attempt to rise above his or her own times and interests—and his ideas about historical truth. For facts and truths had to be faced up to even if they were unpleasant and did not confirm the historian's

67. Gupta, *Life and Letters*, pp. 5, 6, 41, 44, 46, 51, 75, 79, 85, 91, 92. For more on Sir Jadunath's closeness to and affection for students while teaching at Patna, Benares, and other places, see Pawar, *Sir Jadunath Sarkar*, pp. 6–8. N. M. P. Srivastava, *Rise of Militant Nationalism in Bihar: Sir Jadunath Sarkar with Bihar Revolutionaries* (Patna: NMPS, 2004), chaps. 2–4, documents in detail how Sarkar had to pay, professionally, for the official suspicion that he was in league with anticolonial, revolutionary students in Patna. For Sarkar's own ideas about teaching, see his "The Higher Teaching of History in Our Colleges" and "Confessions of a History Teacher," both in *Modern Review* (July 1915), pp. 25–27; (December 1915), pp. 662–667.

68. Jagadish Narayan Sarkar, "Thoughts on Acharya Jadunath Sarkar," *Indo-Iranica* 24, nos. 1–2 (March–June 1971), p. 7.

biases (unlike today, when we proudly wear our biases, Marxist or otherwise, on our sleeves). A certain cultivation of self-denying ethics in the personhood of the historian, a practice of ascesis, was therefore essential, for without that, the historian could not receive the truth the facts told. This demand will sound strange to historians today, when we have moved away from all metaphysical ideas of historical truth to a more procedural idea of historical objectivity, the execution of which depends not on the ethics of the historian's personal life but on procedures having to do with journals, presses, and peer reviews, both formal and informal. What history was for the likes of Sir Jadunath was indeed something different. Historical research and writing was a way of preparing oneself for a truth that was beyond partisan interests.[69] The claim was not that the historian was disinterested to begin with but that he (or, later, she) tried to be so, and precisely because one could never be fully successful in such an effort, the struggle to be truthful was ceaseless. In other words, it was not a mere accident that students and colleagues remembering Sir Jadunath would remember the self-denying quality of the discipline he willingly imposed on himself. It was part of his historical method; the man *was* the method. Or that is how he staged himself to himself and to his contemporaries in the scholarly persona he made his own.[70] Sarkar's "personality" interests me only to the extent that it was an integral part of the methods of research he advocated. This is why, even though this is not biographer's account of the historian Sir Jadunath Sarkar, and is definitely not a book about historiography, Sarkar is central to my enterprise. The book is certainly written *around* him.

The Public and Cloistered Lives of Academic History in India

In the history of erudition, Jadunath Sarkar was by no means unique in insisting on a certain severity of self-discipline and an austere devotion to

69. The historian of Japan Tessa Morris-Suzuki discusses this shift in terms of a distinction between truth and truthfulness. See her *The Past within Us: Media, Memory, History* (London: Verso, 2005), pp. 27–30.

70. I say this because one must not confuse a "character"—a textual construct, after all—with the all the messiness, inconsistencies, and unaccountable contradictions of a flesh-and-blood human being. See the discussion in Martin Price, "People of the Book: Character in Forster's 'A Passage to India,'" *Critical Inquiry* 1, no. 3 (March 1975), pp. 605–622; and Rawdon Wilson, "On Character: A Reply to Martin Price," *Critical Inquiry* 2, no. 1 (Autumn 1975), pp. 191–198. Sarkar comes across as a somewhat different person in the Bengali letters he wrote to his daughter (available in his papers at the National Library) and in the fragments of the correspondence of his family now held in the archives of the Centre for Studies in Social Sciences, Calcutta.

"disinterested pursuit of knowledge" as absolutely necessary to the life of the scholar. One could study him in a comparative framework from diverse points of view. His attitude to archives and sources bear some resemblance, for example, to that of the "doyen" of twentieth-century Egyptian historiography, Muhammad Shafiq Ghurbal (1894–1961). And given the close connection between modern historiography and nationalism in many parts of the colonized or European-dominated regions of the world, it would not be hard to find broad similarities with scholars in other geographical contexts.[71] Another possible path of comparative inquiry could be defined around the question of life-forms: is a certain kind of asceticism a universal demand of scholarly life? A detailed and comparative discussion of K. M. Elisabeth Murray's biography of her great lexicographer grandfather, James A. H. Murray (1837–1915), the editor of the *Oxford English Dictionary* from the 1870s to his death, or A. D. Nuttall's study of the study by Mark Pattison (1813–1884) of Isaac Casaubon (1559–1614), or Tom Stoppard's portrayal of A. E. Housman (1859–1936) in his play *The Invention of Love*, would no doubt help us to see Sarkar not simply as the solitary and defeated figure that he became in his own context in the 1950s; it would enable us to place him in a global history of scholarship as a modern form of life.[72] Additionally, such a comparative exercise would let us appreciate the difficult and specific problems that dogged the pursuit of scholarly life in late colonial India, where political passions came to acquire an all-consuming force and where academic institutions were too weak to resist them.

Such comparative exercise, however, is not my aim. My aim is to tell the story—partial and incomplete, no doubt—of the academic formation of the discipline in India, through its involvement in what I have called its "public life." I have thus taken some of the ideas, institutions, and practices central to the very definition of academic or professional history—such the ideas

71. See the extremely informative discussion in Yoav Di-Capua, "The Thought and Practice of Modern Egyptian Historiography, 1890–1970" (PhD diss., Princeton University, 2004), vol. 2, chap. 5. George Iggers and G. Edward Wang (with contributions from Supriya Mukherjee), *A Global History of Modern Historiography* (Harlow, UK: Pearson Longman, 2008), chap. 5; and Woolf, *Global History of History*, chap. 8, discuss other comparable characters in their accounts of historiographies in non-Western nations.

72. See K. M. Elisabeth Murray, *Caught in the Web of Words: James A. H. Murray and the Oxford English Dictionary* (New Haven, CT: Yale University Press, 1977); A. D. Nuttall, *Dead from the Waist Down: Scholars and Scholarship in Literature and the Popular Imagination* (New Haven, CT: Yale University Press, 2003); Tom Stoppard, *The Invention of Love* (London: Faber and Faber, 1997). I am grateful to Anthony Grafton for suggesting to me this fruitful line of inquiry, which I hope to be able to pursue in the future.

of facts and historical truth, the practice of research, and the institution of the archive—and written the history of their coming into their own in the Indian context by looking at the role that Sarkar and his colleague Sardesai and their hostile and friendly interlocutors played in this process as they all pursued whatever they fancied as "scientific" history. I thus begin with a chapter discussing the absence of the university at a moment when the idea of "scientific" history seized the imagination of several amateur scholars in late-nineteenth- and early-twentieth-century colonial India. Chapters on research, sources, facts, imperial imagination and the nation, character as method, and archiving and the archives follow. I have used the story of Sarkar, I might say, to speak of the "birth" of academic historical writing in colonial India. I borrow this word *birth* from the Nietzsche-Foucault lexicon to indicate that I do not see Jadunath Sarkar as a single point of origin for the history of academic history in India. I see him as a part of what Foucault called "genealogy," an idea that in its in very conception was opposed to the idea of origins. The story could be told around other scholars and in other ways. The story remains necessarily partial and incomplete. The very fact that I tell the story on the basis of Sarkar's and Sardesai's letters to each other means that in spite of my best efforts, I have inevitably missed out on other possible perspectives that might have enriched and complicated our understanding of the issues I discuss.

I have been recently, and somewhat hastily, accused of "remaining rather faithful to the position of Jadunath Sarkar" in what I have written about him up to now.[73] I have to clarify again that this is not an intervention in historiographical debates about Mughal India. That task would be beyond my competence: I would need to have a command of his "sources" and linguistic competencies that I simply do not have.[74] So the question of being faithful to Sarkar's historiographical positions does not arise. And besides, as the book should make clear, Sarkar is not my hero, though I cannot but respect and admire him deeply—but not uncritically, I hope. I personally do not share either the premises or the world of his thought.[75] Sometimes he comes across as

73. Alam and Subrahmanyam, *Writing the Mughal World*, p. 27n49.

74. For an account of historiographical debates in India, see Vinay Lal, *The History of History: Politics and Scholarship in Modern India* (Delhi: Oxford University Press, 2003).

75. In his old age, Sarkar made certain remarks about East Pakistan and about Hindu refugees from East Pakistan that many today, including myself, would find abhorrent and absurd. They were the only statements where I found him completely out of sympathy with Bengali Muslims, then citizens of the newly formed state of East Pakistan. Jadunath Sarkar, "Brothers from Over the River: The Refugee Problem of India," *Modern Review* (August 1948), pp. 236–237. In May 1947, he joined a number of Hindu-Bengali intellectuals—including Meghnad Saha

simply prejudiced, and I have not discussed prejudices that I could not make intellectually interesting for myself.[76] Nor do I share his style. He would not have liked the personal form of address to the reader that I began this introduction with. His approach would have been stern and formal. I do not share his view of historical knowledge, either. He thought of historical knowledge as endlessly perfectible. While I grant him that proposition in some limited areas, I think of historical knowledge as conversational, as a series of statements that relate sequentially to one another without any overall movement toward an imagined goal of finality. But for close to two decades now, I have lived, off and on and often intimately, with the minor tragedy of Sarkar's academic life. Separated by generations, ideas, debates, and a world he could not have foreseen, I have felt it impossible, while involved in this project, not to engage him in conversations in my head, if only to understand and confront our differences. In the 1970s I worked for two years as a fellow in history of

---

and Sunitikumar Chatterjee—in asking for a permanent partition of the province of Bengal along broadly Hindu-Muslim lines. See Bidyut Chakrabarty, "The 1947 United Bengal Movement: A Thesis without a Synthesis," *Indian Economic and Social History Review* 30, no. 4 (1993), p. 477 (I am grateful to Partha Chatterjee for drawing my attention to this reference). This was, of course, only a few weeks after his eldest son, Abani, had been stabbed to death "at the junction of Dharamtolla and [the] Esplanade" toward the end of April 1947 by a Muslim assassin as part of the communal madness that gripped Calcutta in those years. Nerode Baran Roy reported to Sardesai that Sir Jadunath was "outwardly calm and resigned" but "I have seen him sitting alone looking out vacantly into the open." NL, JSP, Miscellaneous Papers, letter from N. B. Roy to Sardesai, Calcutta, 29 April 1947. This personal bereavement does not absolve Sarkar of the responsibility for the statements he made. I have not discussed these statements (mostly made around the insane years of 1947–48), for they are not relevant to the topic of this book. Besides, one has to read these unacceptable statements of Sir Jadunath alongside the many lines he wrote throughout his life in appreciation of Islam's contribution to Indian history and culture. In his book *Mughal Administration* (1935; reprint, New Delhi: Orient Longman, 1972), p. 164, he mentioned the significant fact that a "huge mass of Sufi literature in the Persian language was produced by the Hindus." One of my personal favorites is an observation he made in a Bengali essay in 1923: "The soul of India took refuge in the religion of the Sufis in the seventeenth and eighteenth centuries." Sarkar, "Nutaner modhye puratoner prokash" [The expression of the old in the new], *Prabhati* 1 (Summer 1923 [Bengali year 1327]), reprinted in *Jadunath Sarkar rachana sambhar*, ed. Nikhilesh Guha and Rajnarayan Pal (Calcutta: M. C. Sarkar, 2011), p. 159.

76. Some of Sarkar's ideas on degeneracy, for instance, carry the stamp of eugenic stereotypes. For instance, he summarily described "the Muhammendans of India, particularly those of Turkish and Afghan breeds" once as "a military race, but not eminently intellectual nor industrial." Hence they "declined" when the "utmost possible limits of their conquest was reached." Of their womenfolk, he was even more damning. Women in the harem suffered "degradation" because the mixing of local and foreign women tended "to degrade their children." Sarkar, *Mughal Administration*, p. 171. Thankfully, this is not a dominant motif in Sarkar's writings analyzed here.

the Centre for Studies in Social Sciences, housed in what used to be the residence of Sir Jadunath Sarkar, at 10 Lake Terrace, Calcutta 29. My first teacher of history, the recently deceased historian Barun De, a close colleague of the Aligarh scholars who were critical of Sarkar, was the founding director of this Centre. The house, built in 1940, was more than thirty years old but still had a homely and lived-in feeling about it. Almost every day of those two years, I would spend time in what used to be Sir Jadunath's study—then converted into the office of the registrar of the Centre, my good friend Susanta Ghosh—indulging in what Sarkar despised, the Bengali habit of "idle chat," daily palavers, idealized and treasured within Bengali tradition as a cultural practice called "adda."[77] The seventies historiography that was dismissive of Sarkar perhaps protected us from any malevolence the venerable historian's outraged spirit may have wished on us, seeing the abuse of this "sanctum" he once zealously guarded for the use of only those he considered "genuine researchers." I end the book with a snippet of an impossible and perhaps implausible conversation, for that is what this project has been—a long conversation with Sir Jadunath Sarkar, in an effort to understand what possibilities were once open to the discipline of history in a place called India, possibilities that we cannot, and some might argue need not, ever open up again. But they at least help us present-day historians to develop a perspective on our own times and thus to historicize our own concerns and practices.

The larger point of such an exercise would be to return us to the proposition with which I began. It makes sense in the context of the university to discuss and debate the knowledge protocols of history in the abstract, for one could legitimately imagine in that context a form of knowledge that was something like history-in-general. But more often than not, as history as an academic discipline has spread its wings away from the centers in Europe where it was born, its actual practice in particular national or regional contexts has been shaped by the interaction between its two lives, the lives that I have described here as "cloistered" and "public." This book is an attempt to show how history's cloistered or academic life began in colonial India in disputations that took place in what I have called its "public life," and this decades before the discipline found a home in the research programs of Indian universities. That fact, I try to show in this book, had a profoundly determining influence in shaping some of the basic institutions, practices, and categories that have come to constitute the discipline of history in postcolonial India.

77. See the chapter on this practice of "adda" in my book *Provincializing Europe: Postcolonial Thought and Historical Difference* (2000; Princeton, NJ: Princeton University Press, 2008).

1

The Popular Origins of Academic History

History was not a university subject in India at the postgraduate level until after the First World War. The first postgraduate department for the study of modern and medieval history was created by the University of Calcutta in 1919, and most graduate-level history departments in other universities began in the 1920s and 1930s. The precarious nature of the profession in its early days may be seen in that the sole journal representing the discipline in India, the *Journal of Indian History*, brought out initially in 1921–22 from the University of Allahabad, ran into financial trouble in the third year of its existence because of the "lack of support" from the authorities. It survived by being relocated to Madras, where it was edited and rescued by the archaeologist S. Krishnaswamy Aiyangar of the University of Madras.[1]

The historian Sabyasachi Bhattacharya is probably right to observe that "the [original] site of modern Indian socio-economic and political thinking and contestation was not the university" but public life. The colonial university, he further argues, was an institution created primarily to "attribute cognitive authority to western civilization exclusively" and to transmit, passively, knowledge produced in the West. Indian thought on society and the social sciences, he concludes with reason, was molded in the informality of public life.[2] While this statement is broadly true, it can also be seen with

1. "Ourselves," *Journal of Indian History* 4, nos. 1–3 (1926), 1.

2. Sabyasachi Bhattacharya, "Introduction: New Approaches to Indian Thought in Relation to the Social Sciences in Modern India," in *Development of Modern Indian Thought and the Social Sciences*, ed. Bhattacharya (Delhi: Oxford University Press for Centre for Studies in Civilizations, 2007), pp. xxvii–xxviii. This work is vol. 10, part 5, of *History of Science, Philosophy and Culture in Indian Civilization*, general editor D. P. Chattopadhyyaya (Delhi: Oxford University Press for Centre for Studies in Civilizations, 2007).

little reflection that no academic subject worth its name could emerge in the modern world without the blessings of the institution called the university and without the creation of professional associations and other related institutions. These latter institutions developed late in India. Self-taught researchers debated issues fundamental to the discipline of history—such as historical facts and truth, evidence, sources, archives, research—for a long time before Indian universities began to teach history for research degrees. As a result, the relationship between academic and popular histories in India has been marked by a certain kind of closeness and tension that we will encounter as we study the debates and activities that engaged the energies of Sir Jadunath Sarkar.

Popular "Scientific" Histories

The cult of "scientific history" began in India in the 1880s and more seriously in the early years of the 1900s—particularly in Bengal and Maharashtra, the two regions I will mostly concentrate on in this book—amid what could only be described as enormous public "enthusiasm for history." The expression "enthusiasm for history" is not mine. The poet Rabindranath Tagore used it in an essay he wrote in 1899 in the Bengali literary magazine *Bharati*, welcoming the decision of Akshaykumar Maitreya (a pioneering amateur historian) to bring out a journal called *Oitihashik chitra* (Historical vignettes) from Rajshashi in northern Bengal (now in Bangladesh). Tagore wrote: "The enthusiasm for history that has arisen recently in Bengali literature bodes well for everybody. . . . This hunger for history is only a natural consequence of the way the vital forces of education[al] . . . movements are working their way through Bharatbarsha [India]."[3] Tagore was correctly describing his own times. A host of young Bengali scholars had begun to take an interest in the past and in debating ways of gaining access to it: Rajendralal Mitra (1822–1891), Akshaykumar Maitreya (1861–1930), Dineshchandra Sen (1866–1939), Rakhaldas Bandyopadhayay (1885–1930), the young Jadunath Sarkar (1870–1958), and others come to mind. There were, similarly, a bunch of "amateur" scholars taking an active interest in regional history in western India: V. K. Rajwade (1864–1926), D. B. Parasnis (1870–1926), V. V. Khare (1858–1924), K. N. Sane (1851–1927), R. G. Bhandarkar (1837–1925), G. S. Sardesai (1865–1959), and others. They worked on and from a variety of sources ranging from old literature to family genealogies, sculptures, and coins; they debated

3. Tagore cited in Prabodhchandra Sen, *Bangalir itihash shadhona* [The Bengali pursuit of history] (Calcutta: General Printers, 1953–54), p. 36.

among themselves "scientific" ways of studying the past; but they were all votaries of the new science of history.[4]

The English word *research* was actually translated into Bengali and Marathi in the first decade of the twentieth century and incorporated into names of organizations such as the Varendra Anusandhan Samiti (Varendra Research Society), established in Rajshahi in 1910, and the Bharat Itihas Samshodhak Mandal (Association of Researchers in Indian History), founded in Poona the same year. The Bengali word *anusandhan* was a neologism translating literally the English word *research*, while *shodhak* in Marathi literally meant "the searcher," and hence *samshodhak* "the researcher."[5] The Kamarupa Anusandhan Samiti was set up in Assam in 1912.[6] K. P. Jayasawal and others set up the Bihar and Orissa Research Society—later Bihar Research Society—in 1914.[7] Speaking before an assembly of Indian historians and officials in 1943, the director-general of archaeology of India, Rao Bahadur K. N. Dikshit, who presided over the Indian History Congress meeting in Aligarh that year, commented on the growth of societies and departments devoted to historical research in many parts of India: the government of Bombay had established the Department of Kannada Research in 1939; a "new Journal of Andhra History and Culture" had been "recently started at Guntur," where Andhra University was located; the Andhra Historical Research Society already existed in the

4. See Tapati Guha-Thakurta, *Monuments, Objects, Histories: Institutions of Art in Colonial and Postcolonial India* (New York: Columbia University Press, 2004), chaps. 4 and 5; and Prachi Deshpande, *Creative Pasts: Historical Memory and Identity in Western India, 1700–1960* (New York: Columbia University Press, 2007). See also Shyamali Sur, *Itihash chintar shuchona o jatiyotabader unmesh: Bangla 1870–1912* [The beginning of historical thought and the emergence of nationalism: Bengal 1870–1912] (Calcutta: Progressive, 2002); Gautam Bhadra, *Jal rajar golpo* [The story of the fake king] (Calcutta: Ananda, 2002); Kumkum Chatterjee, "The King of Controversy: History and Nation-Making in Late Colonial India," *American Historical Review* 110, no. 5 (December 2005), pp. 1454–1475; Sumit Guha, "Speaking Historically: The Changing Voices of Historical Narration in Western India, 1400–1900," *American Historical Review* 109, no. 4 (2004), 1084–1103.

5. On the history of these two organizations, see Nirmalchandra Choudhuri, *Akshaykumar Maitreya: Jibon o shadhona* [Akshaykumar Maitreya: Life and endeavors] (Darjeeling: North Bengal University, [1984?]), the chapter on the Varendra Research Society. For the Poona Mandal, see the brief remarks of Jadunath Sarkar in his *Maratha Jaitya Bikash* [The development of the Maratha nation] (Calcutta: Ranjan, 1936–37), p. 44; and Deshpande, *Creative Pasts*, pp. 117–119.

6. For an extended discussion, see Arupjoyti Saikia, "History, *Buranjis* and Nation: Suryya Kumar Bhuyan's Histories in Twentieth-Century Assam," *Indian Economic and Social History Review* 45, no. 4 (December 2008), pp. 473–507.

7. B. P. Sinha, "Kashi Prasad Jayasawal," in *Historians and Historiography in Modern India*, ed. S. P. Sen (Calcutta: Institute of Historical Studies, 1973), p. 83.

Nizam's dominions; and the Gujarat Research Society had been established "recently."[8]

Jadunath Sarkar was a lifelong member of the Bangiya Sahitya Parishad (Bengal Literary Academy) and the Bharat Itihas Samsodhak Mandal in Poona. He was also associated with the Bihar Research Society and with the nationalist student conference in Bihar that was started by Rajendra Prasad, who went on to become the first president of independent India. Sarkar even presided over some of the sessions of this conference.[9] But more than the research associations and academic institutions in Bengal, it is really the historians of Poona, both Sarkar's collaborator Govindrao Sardesai and other members of the Bharat Itihas Samshodhak Mandal, who loom large in our story. Sarkar's interest in the history of the Marathas, both at the time of their ruler Shivaji (1630–1680) and when the peshwas ruled (1713–1818), led to many clashes of opinions and conflicts of perceived interests between Sarkar and Sardesai on the one hand and some Poona scholars on the other. Those conflicts underpin much of the story told in the following chapters. But Sarkar's engagement with the Poona circle of historians is seen not only in his friendship with Sardesai but also in the fact that he actually wrote, for the journal *Modern Review*, detailed obituaries of four of these of Marathi stalwarts when they died around 1926–27, bringing to a close the early history of modern historical research in Maharashtra. However, Sarkar's clashes with some of the surviving historians of Poona, such as Datto Vaman Potdar (1890–1979) and scholars such as Surendra Nath Sen (1890–1962) and Shafaat Ahmad Khan, from Calcutta and Allahabad, respectively, but both associated with Potdar, continued for almost another two decades.

At the heart of these conflicts were clashing conceptions of nationalism. Indian interest in historical knowledge and research, from the 1870s onward, clearly had something to do with the rise of cultural nationalism in various forms in the different parts of the country. There was an emerging consensus that dissemination of historical and other forms of knowledge in public life was a crucial ingredient for building a nation. Tagore expressed the sentiment well while addressing a gathering of students organized by the Bangiya Sahitya Parishad during the years of the Swadeshi movement (1905–07). He said:

8. Rao Bahadur K. N. Dikshit, "Presidential Address," in *Proceedings of the Indian History Congress*, sixth session, 26, 27, and 28 December, Aligarh Muslim University (Allahabad: General Secretary, Indian History Congress, 1944), pp. 14–15, 18–19.

9. Moni Bagchi, *Acharya Jadunath: Jibon o sadhana* [Jadunath, the teacher: Life and endeavors] (Calcutta: Jijnasha, 1975), pp. 52–53.

> Bengal is the country nearest to us. The Bengali Literary Academy has made the language, literature, history, sociology, etc., of this land into subjects for their own discussions. My appeal to the Academy is that they invite students to be part of these discussions. . . . If students, led by the Academy, can collect details about religious sects among the lower orders of their own country, then they will both learn to observe people with attention and do some service to the nation at the same time.

For Tagore, the criterion for judging knowledge to be "true" was that it aided public life. Simply reading "ethnology"—Tagore used the word in English—was not enough, for instance. If such reading did not generate "the least bit of curiosity for a full acquaintance with the Haris, the Bagdis, and the Doms [all "untouchable/low-caste" groups] who live around our homes," said Tagore, "it immediately makes us realize what a big superstition books have become for us."[10] The new knowledge was thus welcome because it could aid the formation of the nation by acting as a bridge between the educated minority and the nonliterate masses.

In Bengal, the likes of Akshaykumar Maitreya and Jadunath Sarkar shared Tagore's sentiments. They thought of the historian as a custodian of the nation's or the people's memories. Presiding over a conference of the North Bengal Literary Association at Rangpur (now in Bangladesh) in 1908, Akshaykumar announced a three-step program with respect to "scientific" history: "(a) knowledge had to be acquired, (b) discoveries had to be made, and (c) they had to be publicized among ordinary people in accordance with scientific methods." Otherwise, he feared, the scientific pursuit of history would be reduced to "mere argumentation among the learned."[11] Addressing, in 1915, the History Branch of the eighth convention of the Bengal Literary Association held in Bardhaman, Sarkar similarly echoed Maitreya's and Tagore's sentiments about the need to make connections between education

10. Rabindranath Thakur [Tagore], "Chhatroder proti shombhashon" [Address to students], in *Rabindrarachanabali* [Collected works of Rabindranath], centenary ed. (Calcutta: Government of West Bengal, 1961–62), 12:728–729.

11. Maitreya cited in Choudhuri, *Akshaykumar Maitreya*, pp. 94–95. Maitreya's interventions in debates on literary and visual representations of the past gave rise to many lively debates involving many literary luminaries. For more on that, see Ratna Ghosh and Pranab Barman, eds., *Bangalir itihashchinta* [Bengali historical thought] [in Bengali] (Danton, Midnapur: Ashadeep for Department of History, Bhattar College, 2012); and Samir Patra and Arindam Chakrabarty, eds., *Itihash o sahitya: Prasanga Rabindranth o Akshaykumar* [in Bengali] [History and literature: On Rabindranath and Akshaykumar] (Calcutta: Ashadeep for Tamluk Itihashcharcha Kendra, 2012). The subject of the portrayal of history in nineteenth-century Bengali poetry has received extended and stimulating discussion in Rosinka Chaudhuri's *The Literary Thing: History, Poetry, and the Making of a Modern Literary Culture* (Delhi: Oxford University Press, 2013).

of the masses and historical research: "Some people say with regret that historical essays have banished the short story from the pages of the Bengali monthly magazine. If this piece of good news . . . is indeed true, then literary leaders and the learned academies are faced with a crucial duty with regard to the development of the nation's mind. . . . Our duty is to help tie together this newly-awakened endeavor to serve history, to contain and direct this initiative through advice so that the Bengali brain[-power] is not mis-spent."[12] Such direction could come about only through the popularization of "scientific" history. It is perhaps with such popularization in view that Sarkar wrote for nonspecialist readers all his life in magazines and newspapers such as the *Modern Review*, *Prabasi*, and the *Hindusthan Standard*.

"The best way of cultivating history is the scientific way," Sarkar emphasized. The scientific way of writing history was "the first step in national development. The more we discover the real truth about the past, the more the minds of our people will proceed along the right lines. . . . True history teaches people the causes of the rise and fall of nations, their health and illness, their death and regeneration." Having said this, Sarkar proceeded to notch up the rhetoric. He likened "scientific" history to the old medical and religious scriptures of the Hindus: "Without this *mahashivatantra* [lit., a Tantric text on the Great Shiva], this national *ayurvedashastra* [lit., Vedic science of life], this dedication to truth, and without an irrepressible urge for continuous improvement, there is no gain."[13]

Brave and optimistic words, but the reality was stark. Making "scientific" history a popular preoccupation was not easy. Historians such as Sarkar and others would find themselves pitted in a struggle with many forces at once. First of all, while there was a broad agreement that "scientific history" began with the collection of original contemporary sources, there was no agreement on what else being "scientific" entailed. Of particular contention was the question of how sources, once collected, would be examined and evaluated. Would a poetic text be amenable to the methods of the historian? Would historical facts always end up supporting nationalist sentiment? In what ways could the methods of history help the nationalist movement along? Indian researchers differed vehemently among themselves in answering these questions, not because some were nationalists and others not, but because they subscribed to different imaginations of the nation. But there were some other problems

12. Jadunath Sarkar, "Presidential Address to the History Branch," Eighth Bengal Literary Convention (Bardhaman), Proceedings of the History Branch, p. 1. My copy of this report, lent kindly by Gautam Bhadra, does not have a printer's line.

13. Ibid., pp. 1, 8–9.

as well, and some of these were quite beyond their immediate control. Access to original "official" sources was often made very difficult throughout India by some very restrictive policies of the colonial government. And most crucially, the academic neglect in Europe of "modern" Indian history (though not of ancient India or Indology) meant that this historiography was cut off from contemporaneous debates in European universities about historiography in general. Indian researchers knew about Ranke, though not in much detail. The likes of Sarkar, as we will see, read Macaulay and the *Edinburgh Review* and Gibbon and some Mommsen, and they read the English historian Gooch about historiographical developments in Germany.[14] But the kind of rebellion against the Rankean tradition that marked the German academic scene in the late nineteenth century—for example, the one that we associate Jacob Burckhardt with—completely passed them by. Instead, when not too swayed by aggressively nationalist sentiments, they found their actual mentors in colonial administrator-scholars, some of whom, after retirement in India, took up academic positions in institutions such as the School of Asian and African Studies in London and wrote positive and encouraging reviews of Indian scholarship in journals like that published by the Royal Asiatic Society of Britain.

The Colonial State and the Problem of Sources

There is a long history, in British India, of the government's dragging its feet on the question of—as contemporary officials put it—"removing obstacles to historical research" in the country. Soon after they assumed the formal charge of India in 1858, the British formed a state that required documentation for its daily operations. "As early as 1861," says an official history of the Indian Historical Records Commission, "the Government of India appointed a Committee to report on their archives."[15] J. Talboys Wheeler, who served the committee as its secretary, eventually published, on his "own account," a compilation titled *Early Records of British India* that the government allowed on consideration that this was a "literary venture."[16] The question of throwing open the records of the central and provincial governments in British India was raised anew in 1914, on the publication of the Report of the Royal Com-

14. G. P. Gooch, *History and Historians in the Nineteenth Century* (London: Longman and Green, 1913).

15. *IHRC Retrospect* (Delhi: Manager of Publications, GOI, 1948), p. 1.

16. Syamalendu Sengupta, *Experiencing History through Archives: Restoration of Memory and Repair of Records* (Delhi: Munshiram Monaharlal, 2004), p. 75.

mission on Public Records. The India Office now wanted the Government of India to take responsibility for the use by researchers of their own records.[17] The response of the officials of the Government of India to this issue leaves us in no doubt that, from the very beginning, historical knowledge was a matter that touched some raw political nerves of the colonial administration.

Correspondence that passed between the marquess of Crewe, the secretary of state for India at the India Office, London, and the governor of Madras in 1913 clearly showed that the very idea of letting researchers into colonial record rooms had something unnerving about it for the administration. Crewe felt the need to reassure the nervous Madras government, whose officials were "under a misapprehension" that the India Office was proposing to "allow private persons unrestricted access to . . . unpublished [public] records." He enclosed with his letter a copy of rules "regarding applications to search the India Office records," showing that no one was allowed such unrestricted access even in London. Every request, he said, was "carefully considered"; the applicant was "required to state the object he [had] in view" and, if necessary, to "submit notes or extracts he may have made" and was not "allowed to make use of any to which objection is raised."[18]

Crewe wrote again the following year, in February 1914, this time to the governor general of India, pointing out that the records in London were "largely duplicates of those in India" and that "it [was] obviously undesirable that there should be any difference . . . between the practice adopted by . . . [the India] Office and that obtaining in India" with regard to researchers in history.[19] A. F. Scholfield, the officer in charge of records in the Imperial Record Department in Calcutta, disagreed strongly and in terms that revealed the political fear that guided the government in India in these matters. In a note dated 28 April 1914 and addressed to his colleagues and superiors, Scholfield countered Crewe's letter by saying that "the argument from the Records in the India Office is specious. If the Records in London are the same as those in Calcutta, the 'public' is different." Elaborating, he added that there had never been "any wide-felt want, any loud or insistent demand for the throwing open of the Records." For Indian scholars, in his opinion, had "no knowledge of what is evidence and how to use it." "There is in India," he said, in words that must have guided him in 1919 when he was appointed, ex-officio, the

17. *IHRC Retrospect*, p. 2.

18. NAI, IRD, April 1914, Proceeding (hereafter Proc.) no. 53, letter dated 5 December 1913 from the India Office to His Excellency the Right Honourable the Governor in Council, Fort St. George [Madras].

19. NAI, IRD, April 1914, Proc. no. 53, letter dated 27 February 1914 from the India Office to His Excellency the Right Honourable the Governor General of India in Council.

first secretary to the newly formed Indian Historical Records Commission, "no Aristocracy of erudition, no school of history; historical research, scientific use of evidence[,] critical scholarship are rarely understood and seldom achieved."[20] He would rather prevent any "abuse of records" by (a) "admitting only persons who have given proof that they are serious researchers" and (b) "publishing press-lists and calendars of all of our Records, forestalling those who for whatever ends would distort or suppress evidence, by placing the whole in the hands of the public."[21]

When contacted on this matter, the provincial governments of Madras and Bombay expressed similarly conservative opinions. The government of Madras was "willing to allow free access" for the period before "the permanent settlement of British rule in the greater part of Southern India," that is, before the nineteenth century. "The records from the year 1801 . . . possess . . . [a] peculiar importance in regard to the origin of the present system of revenue administration and they may furnish material for litigation against Government." The Madras government therefore was of the opinion that even the India Office should adopt the same precaution.[22] The government in Bombay preferred an even more restrictive system. It was "opposed to the giving of general permission to search and examine" government records because "there is no guarantee that even records bearing a comparatively remote date do not contain documents or information the disclosure of which to the public would be prejudicial to the interests of the State." Records could be opened to only "the acknowledged historical student and, then too, subject to restrictions which would ensure the undoubted loyalty and honesty of the recipient."[23] Emboldened by the expression of such concerns on the part of provincial officials about historical research, the officers in Calcutta only felt reinforced in the opinions they had already given to London. Scholfield wrote in an internal note that even putting a time limit on the documents that

20. NAI, IRD, April 1914, Proc. no. 53, note by A. F. Schofield dated 28 April 1914. Alwyn Faber Scholfield succeeded Edward Denison Ross (later director, School of Oriental and African Studies, University of London) in the position of the officer in charge of records of the Imperial Record Department in 1914 and retired soon after the first session of the Indian Historical Records Commission (1919), having been its first ex-officio secretary. See *IHRC Retrospect*, pp. 48–52.

21. NAI, IRD, April 1914, Proc. no. 53, note by Scholfield, dated 28 April 1914.

22. NAI, IRD, December 1914, Proc. no. 224, letter no. 1392, A. Butterworth, I.C.S., acting chief secretary to the Government of Madras, Public Department, to the secretary to the Government of India, Education Department, dated Fort St. George, 30 October 1914.

23. NAI, IRD, December 1914, Proc. no. 224, letter no. 7460, from J. L. Rieu, I.C.S., secretary to the government of Bombay, General Department, to the secretary, Government of India, Education Department, General Branch, dated Bombay Castle, 21 September 1914.

could be made public was "not an adequate safeguard, [but] a *subject*-limit might be, if such a thing were possible."[24] His superior, L. Porter, was not even prepared to go that far. He dismissed the relative liberality of the government of Madras with the remark, "If the proposal is mischievous in Calcutta and Bombay it is equally so in Madras."[25] An official letter dated 4 February 1915 addressed to Lord Crewe and signed by the governor-general and several provincial governors summed up the position of the Government of India. There was no question of "placing the whole [archives] in the hands of the public," as historical research was "still in its infancy in India." In such a situation, the "encouragement and opportunities which the opening of records would afford to irresponsible writers . . . might be a source of inconvenience to the Government."[26]

The Government of India's hands were eventually forced, it seems, when the home government in England adopted some of the recommendations of the Royal Commission on the question of allowing private scholars access to government records in the interest of promoting historical research. In itself, this development is perhaps testimony to the growing importance at this time, globally, of the idea of "historical research." On 21 March 1919 the Government of India published an official resolution announcing its intention to make official records in India "more accessible than at present to students of history and of removing, so far as possible, any existing obstacles to *research*." The government acknowledged that it had been influenced by "the recommendations of the Royal Commission on the Public Records of England and Wales."[27] Perhaps also at issue was another factor, as suggested in a long, liberal-minded but unpublished note by R. H. Blaker, the keeper of records in the late 1910s and the 1920s. This was the changing legal status of the records of the India Office in England. So long as the India Office was itself maintained "out of Indian revenue," there was some doubt as to "whether its records could be looked upon as coming within the scope of the [English] Public Records Acts." "But the same hesitation," noted Blaker, "no longer seems to exist in England for the India Office records have lately come

24. NAI, IRD, December 1914, Proc. no. 224, Scholfield's note I.R.D.U.O.R, no. 679, dated 23 November 1914.

25. NAI, IRD, December 1914, Proc. no. 224, note by L. Porter dated 21 November 1914.

26. NAI, IRD, June 1915, Proc. no. 94; and IRD, April 1918, Proc. No 47, appendix.

27. NAI, IRD, April 1919, Proc. no. 60, Department of Education (General Branch), Resolution no. 77, dated 21 March 1919, emphasis added. See also NAI, IRD, April 1919, Proc. no. 60, HGB's note dated 14 April 1919, referring to particular sections of the report of the Royal Commission: "Please see the references in 'Records: public access to' at p. 207 of vol. I, pt III and p. 113 of Vol. II, pt III of the first and second reports."

within the purview of the Royal Commission on Public Records in England." In theory, then, the master of the rolls in England could legally compel the India Office "to deposit its records down to the year 1837 in the Public Record Office."[28] This looming change in the legal situation must have also weighed on the minds of the otherwise conservative colonial administrators in India.

Feeling the need "to have at their disposal a permanent body of expert advisers whose opinions would carry weight with the Record officers and the public," the Government of India decided to constitute not anything like the Public Record Office in England—a national archive, that is—but the Indian Historical Records Commissions (IHRC), consisting of both government officials, the keeper of records of the Indian government being ex-officio the secretary of the commission, and four historians (for a term of three to five years) nominated to be "Ordinary Members" by the Government of India.[29] The idea seems to have been first broached by an Indian official, J. M. Mitra, an assistant secretary in the Department of Education. In a note dated 17 November 1917, Mitra noted the importance the Royal Commission on Public Records gave to the "needs of historians." He agreed with others who said, "Historical research is still in its infancy in this country," but he made that the basis for the argument, "We should do our best to encourage scholars to make use of our records and not sit with folded hands in the vain hope that scholars will come to us without any active encouragement on our part." He therefore recommended the appointment of an "Advisory Committee on the lines of the English Advisory Committee in connection with all the important record offices." Its main purpose would be to "advise the Record Office how . . . earlier historical documents should be dealt with." He further recommended that men of "undoubted abilities in matters of historical research, such as Archdeacon [W. K.] Firminger and Professor Jadunath Sarkar" be inducted into such a commission.[30]

28. NAI, IRD, April 1920, Proc. 41, K.W. [Keep With], R. H. Blaker's note on "Questions of making the official records in India more accessible to students of history and the public," dated 27 November 1919.

29. Government of India, Department of Education, Resolution no. 77 (General), dated 21 March 1919, reproduced as Appendix A to *IHRC Proceedings*, vol. 1, *First meeting, Held in Simla, [19–20] June 1919* (Calcutta: Superintendent of Government Printing, 1920).

30. J. M. Mitra's note dated 17 November 1917, in NAI, IRD, December 1917, Proc. no. 18 and K.W. Mitra's note has an interesting citation from an article in the *Quarterly Review* that remarked on the different traditions of the French and the British with regard to the role historians played in the governance of their official archives on foreign relations. "In England the question of the fitness of the applicant [for access to government records] . . . is settled entirely by the officials of the department. In France there is a system which is much more satisfactory to historians. There an application is judged by the Comité des Archives Diplomatiques, a body

The argument received broad endorsement from the historian-cum-politician Ramsay Muir, whose opinions the Government of India appears to have solicited in 1917. Muir agreed with others that the number of historical researchers in India did not justify opening up the records in the way they had been in England. But he emphasized the pedagogical role that a "permanent Historical Materials Commission" could play in the development of history as an academic subject in India. Muir's thoughts were expressed in language redolent of some of the oldest European charges against "the Indian mind." One of "the gravest defects of the Indian mind," said Muir "is its lack of the historical sense. We will never remedy this by compelling Indian students to learn by heart any number of half-crown text books; we can only do it by introducing the method and spirit of historical enquiry and criticism, and that must be done, in the first instance, among the teachers." Muir underlined the importance of this point by enunciating a principle of what may be called an "imperial liberalism": "The remedying of this defect seems to me to be of primary importance, not merely from an intellectual but a political point of view; if educated India is to attain full political sanity, it must be by training in criticism and in the evaluation of evidence." It was with such educational aims in mind that Professor Muir suggested that the proposed commission should be headed by a "trained historian brought out from Europe—"a man stronger . . . on the historical than on the archival side." It would then be his responsibility to train Indian history teachers and graduates by involving them—under his "supervision and guidance"—in the work of editing and translating into English selections from regional records in British India and the native states that existed in different Indian languages such as Persian, Marathi, Gurumukhi, and so forth.[31]

There remained a gap between the principles of "imperial liberalism" that Ramsay Muir spelled out in his letter and the sentiments of the officials involved in the running of the commission that was finally set up in 1919. The official resolution that led to the establishment of the Indian Historical Records Commission made "the training of Indian students . . . in methods of historical research and the selection of competent editors" the very last of the "duties" of the commission, the highest being that of advising the gov-

---

consisting partly of historians, partly of officials so that the candidate can be sure that his qualifications are judged by persons conversant with his studies." This particular file has also been indexed under NAI, Education Department–General, A Proceedings, April 1918, Nos. 1–17. I owe this last reference to Ms. Parnisha Sarkar.

31. NAI, IRD, December 1917, Procs. no. 18 and K.W., demi-official letter dated 7 December 1917 from Professor Ramsay Muir to Sir Edward D. Maclagan, secretary, Education Department, Government of India.

ernment on "the treatment of archives for the purposes of historical study," for example, "the cataloguing, calendaring and reprinting of documents" and "the extent and the manner in which documents should be open to inspection by the public."[32] The latter is what the government meant by the phrase "removal of obstacles to historical research." A foreword written by A. F. M. Abdul Latif (Ali), the then keeper of records, to an official 1925 guide to the records of the department explain the book itself as something intended to "obviate difficult[ies]" faced by "a research scholar."[33]

Comments by Scholfield, the first secretary of the commission, scribbled on an official note by one "H.G.B." and dated 14 April 1919—some two months before the IHRC had its first meeting at Simla—reveal some deep currents of resistance to the government's stated aim of "removing obstacles" to research. When H.G.B. asked if "the handlist of the gazettes, which [was] in ms." should be included in the category of documents to be printed for a public readership, Scholfield firmly commented on the margin, "Certainly not." H.G.B.'s remark that "there need not be any hurry" in the matter of printing ten volumes of lists of records "in the custody of this office," as the business would have to wait until "the arrangement of all the related records, which was in hand, was complete," received a hearty marginal tick of approval from "A.F.S." To H.G.B.'s suggestion that "there should be *no shifting of records or splitting up* of lists consequent upon the transfer of heads of work from one department to another," A.F.S. responded with an enthusiastic "I agree." On the question of whether or not the Imperial Record Department should expedite the listing of the old Thugee and Dacoity records—which, though not in the custody of the Imperial Record Department, possessed "considerable historical interest"—Scholfield's instruction was clear: "I don't think we need yet at any rate." His response was similarly firm on the question of "sale to the public . . . [of] our lists of records." "Of course not," he wrote. "They are merely for office purposes and could be of no interest to any one." When H.G.B. suggested that a "large portion of the duty of training students in methods of historical research will perhaps devolve upon the K[eeper] [of] R[ecord] and this office," Scholfield demurred on the margin of the page with a wry "I think not."[34]

32. Government of India, Department of Education, Resolution no. 77 (General), dated 21 March 1919, reproduced as Appendix A to *IHRC Proceedings*, vol. 1.

33. *A Hand-Book to the Records of the Government of India in the Imperial Record Department, 1748 to 1859* (Calcutta: GOI, Central Publication Branch, 1925), foreword by A. F. M. Abdul Latif.

34. NAI, IRD, April 1919, Proc. no. 60, H.G.B.'s note dated 14 April 1919 and A.F.S.'s marginal comments.

Scholfield's generation of officials, on the whole, deemed it enough service done to research if—in addition to weeding, repairing, and maintaining records—they would bring out hand lists, calendars, index volumes, and some selections of government records from time to time. Throughout the 1920s, the bureaucracy saw the IHRC as an advisory body for this purpose.[35] They would use the commission's, and in particular Professor Jadunath Sarkar's, expertise, for example, to determine whether a manuscript by James Tod (of the East India Company) entitled "Origin, Progress, and the Present State of the Pindaries," written around 1811 and found among the Central Provinces secretariat records, was worthy of publication.[36] The commission, similarly, would play a role in dissuading the provincial government of Bombay in 1920 from financing the publication of English translations of old Marathi texts published by the "amateur" Marathi historian Rao Bahadur D. B. Parasnis in his magazine *Itihasa Samgraha*. "The Commission . . . were of opinion," reported R. H. Blaker in this case, that the documents in question were "not of sufficient historical or economic importance to merit translation."[37] And so the situation continued for decades. While the government in Delhi did relent a little around 1940 over the question of allowing Indian researchers to consult documents in its custody, the Imperial Record Department created in the 1890s was made into the National Archives of India *only* after independence in 1947. In chapter 7 of this book, we will continue the story of how Indian scholars serving on the commission struggled in the 1920s and 1930s to have the records opened up to researchers in India.

The Academic Neglect of Indian History

"Modern," meaning roughly sixteenth- to early-nineteenth-century, Indian history became an academic subject in India first in the 1920s and primarily in the 1930s, when Indian universities began to produce some PhDs on the subject. And no established university even in Britain, the country that

35. See, for instance, the correspondence between the Bengal government and the Imperial Record Department in June–July 1920 that provides explanations for such terms as press-list, hand-list, calendar, etc. NAI, IRD, July 1920, Proc. no. 27.

36. NAI, IRD, March 1920, Proc. no. 40. Also see Jadunath Sarkar's report dated 31 December 1919 on "the Tod Manuscripts relating to the Pindaries and Rajputana," in *IHRC Proceedings*, vol. 2, *Second Meeting, Held at Lahore,* [8–9] *January 1920* (Calcutta: Superintendent of Government Printing, 1920), Appendix C, p. xiii.

37. NAI, IRD, March 1920, Proc. no. 44, Blaker's letter to the chief secretary, government of Bombay, dated Calcutta, 22 January 1920. One hears in the commission's remarks the voice of Jadunath Sarkar, always critical of amateur historians such as Parasnis.

ruled India, considered the topic worthy of study before the Second World War. It attained a certain degree of respectability with the publication of five volumes—the projected second volume was never published—of the *Cambridge History of India* between 1922 and 1938.[38] But mostly old India hands produced these—British administrators who had served in India and who pursued scholarship either on the side or in retirement. The first volume, on ancient history, was not very historical in approach. E. J. Rapson, who edited it, was a professor of Sanskrit at the University of Cambridge, and much in the volume was concerned mainly with questions of philology. Lt.-Col. Sir Wolseley Haig, who planned the fourth volume but died before it could be sent to press and who edited and wrote seventeen of the twenty-three chapters in volume 3, *Turks and Afghans*, was a retired army officer who later worked as lecturer in Persian at the School of Oriental Studies of the University of London. Professor Henry Dodwell, the editor of volumes 5 and 6, had worked in the Indian Education Service and was appointed, on retirement, the first professor of the history and culture of the British dominions in Asia at the School of Oriental Studies. The only two historians to contribute from India were Sir Jadunath Sarkar in volume 4 and S. Krishnaswamy Aiyangar, professor of Indian history and archaeology and fellow of the University of Madras, who wrote a chapter for volume 3.[39]

The autobiography and other writings of Sir Cyril Philips, a pioneer among twentieth-century British academic historians of India who rose to be the vice chancellor of the University of London after the Second World War, clearly convey a sense of how marginal Indian history was in Britain between the two world wars and how it was structured like an academic ghetto where retired colonial scholars and their Indian, and later African, students would congregate. "In England Chairs of Arabic had existed at Oxford and Cambridge since the seventeenth century," recounts Philips in his short history of

38. There was an attempt by A. L. Basham in 1950 to edit, revise, and publish the manuscript prepared earlier, ostensibly under the editorship of E. J. Rapson. The proposed volume included contributions from U. N. Ghoshal and D. R. Bhandarkar. Clearly, there were differences between the points of view of Rapson and Bhandarkar over a chapter they authored together. Ghoshal's nationalist phrases—with respect to Assamese kings—such as "characteristic of the lofty sense of dignity of both rulers" were edited by Rapson to read: "in which both rulers asserted their claims to precedence." Eventually, it seems, the essays proved too difficult to update and the volume was never published. See British Library, Mss. Eur. D 863/27, 863/19, and 863/20A.

39. *The Cambridge History of India* (Cambridge: Cambridge University Press, 1922–38), vols. 1, 3–6. Sarkar contributed two chapters on Aurangzeb, one on the later Mughals, and one on the Hyderabad State. *The Cambridge History of India*, planned by Lt.-Col. Sir Wolseley Haig and edited by Sir Richard Burn (Cambridge: Cambridge University Press, 1937).

the School of Oriental and African Studies at the University of London. Sanskrit and Chinese began to be taught in the middle of the nineteenth century. Chinese and Hindusthani (the original form of Hindi and Urdu) were taught at the University College, London, from the time when it was founded in 1826. Later King's College and the University College joined hands "in forming a 'School of Modern Oriental Languages,' which was formally inaugurated by Professor Max Müller in 1890," but the effort to combine the resources of the two institutions was not very successful.[40]

Indian history was not taught at a British university until the formation of the School of Oriental Studies in 1917 (from 1938 it was Oriental and African Studies), with Dr. Denison Ross, himself an old India hand "who had served with distinction in the Indian Education Service," as its first director.[41] The first professor of Indian history there—and, it would seem, in Britain itself—was Henry H. Dodwell, who, again, had served in India as the curator of the Madras Records Office and who had written a book on Dupleix and Clive and had brought out selections of documents.

Oxford had a readership in Indian history from at least the early part of the twentieth century.[42] But the position and the subject were both marginal to the mainstream. Besides, Indian history produced in Britain did not yet mean the history of the Indian people. It was mostly about the British and their doings in India. William Holden Hutton held this position, for instance, between 1913 and 1920. Hutton's only original contribution to the subject, it would seem, was a volume on Marquess Wellesley in the Rulers of India series, apart from a couple of chapters on the late eighteenth century that he contributed to *Cambridge History*. He moved on to become a lecturer in ecclesiastical history at Trinity College in Cambridge and published numerous volumes on subjects unrelated to India.[43]

C. H. Philips's reminiscences provide additional evidence of this rather bleak picture. Philips himself may have been the first British student in the School of Oriental and African Studies (SOAS) to be involved in postgraduate research in Indian history.[44] But even he had to be careful in selecting his research topic, as there were no designated lectureships, outside of SOAS, for

40. C. H. Philips, *The School of Oriental and African Studies, University of London, 1917–1967: An Introduction* (London: Design for Print, n.d.), p. 10.

41. Ibid., p. 14.

42. Tapan Raychaudhuri tells me that this was a position in Indian studies in the nineteenth century before it was converted into a position in history.

43. See the obituary notice in the *American Historical Review* 6, no. 2 (January 1931), p. 460.

44. C. H. Philips, *Beyond the Ivory Tower: The Autobiography of Sir Cyril Philips* (London: Radcliffe Press, 1995), pp. 40, 41.

the teaching of the history of India. "In choosing a field of research," he writes, "I had to bear in mind that there were still no departments or posts in British universities offering a career specifically in Indian history. . . . Moreover, the entrée scholars like Henry Dodwell and Ralph Turner, for example, had enjoyed through an early career in the Indian education service was no longer open to British candidates." He therefore had to make sure that his topic of research also spoke to imperial and European history and thus chose to work on the politics of the East India Company in the eighteenth century. Even so, when it came the question of publishing his thesis, a person no less than Sir Lewis Namier, who acted as an examiner of the thesis, advised him to give the prospective book "a popular title like *The East India Company* to underplay its 'precise subject' which was 'Indian politics in London.'"[45]

It was not until after the Second World War, when Philips became the head of the history department at SOAS, that he could find "a rich crop of young scholars with first-class degrees and wartime personal experience of India," such as Kenneth Ballhatchet, John Harrison, and Peter Hardy, all contributors to the volume that Philips later edited on the historiography of the subcontinent. Most of the research students in the 1920s and 1930s working at the School of Oriental Studies in London, he says, were Indians who were "more often than not treated by the staff as second-class citizens."[46] Philips offers a telling anecdote about the difficulties he faced when he once attempted to "mainstream" (in today's jargon) the subjects of Asian and African histories by merging the seminars held at SOAS with the series hosted by Professor Vivian Hunter Galbraith, director of the London Institute of Historical Research (later Regius Professor of History at Oxford University), who, according to Philips, was "one of its most influential figures." Confronted against his wishes with Philips's proposal, the professor is said to have asked, "How many students would you be bringing?" "About 60," answered Philips. And this is how the rest of the conversation went: "'Where from?' 'Mainly Asia and Africa,' [Philips] said, upon which, with his face flaring red, he [Hunter] jumped to his feet shouting, 'You would drown us, and anyway I don't want any bloody niggers here!'" Philips left, "accepting regretfully" that, "unlike every other major field of history in London, seminars on Asia and Africa for the time being at any rate would have to remain within the confines of [his] own college."[47]

Later, in fact as late as 1950, Philips mobilized his "young colleagues at . . .

45. Ibid., pp. 47–48, 51.

46. Ibid., pp. 157, 45.

47. Ibid., p. 163.

[SOAS] to join [him] in preparing a *Companion to Oriental History*," with a view to getting it published in the series of handbooks published by the prestigious Royal Historical Society—in order precisely to "place Asian history firmly within the tradition of the British framework of historical study." His efforts "came to nothing." He wrote in the preface to the volume: "As the interdependence of the countries of the world increases, the realization grows that the histories of all peoples form a common heritage. European political activities and the spread of western ideas and technology in the Orient have long since convinced the peoples of Asia of this fact; and daily the nations of the West are becoming more aware of the significance for them of the study of and understanding of the languages and cultures of the East." The handbook was meant to guide the reader "through the more important difficulties." Yet, as Philips acknowledged in his autobiography, the volume had "minimal" impact on the society's "lecture and publications programme."[48]

This depiction of the 1950s is also confirmed by the noted Indian historian Tapan Raychaudhuri's reminiscences of the years when he went to Oxford for a second doctoral degree. "The University," writes Raychaudhuri, "made no other formal provision for the instruction of graduate students working on Indian history beyond appointing a supervisor."[49] That supervisor was "Dr C.C. Davis, once a Major in the Indian army, [who] supervised all students working for research degrees on Indian history, irrespective of subject or period." Thus, Raychaudhuri continues, "Irfan Habib who worked on the agrarian history of the Mughal period, Dr. Puri whose thesis concerned the rule of the Kushanas, I who worked on the Dutch Company's trade were all his supervisees." Davis's own work was on the northwest frontier and Warren Hastings, and his lectures on Warren Hastings constituted "the only course on Indian history included in the history syllabus."[50] Davis's election to the readership was determined, it seems, on the basis of considerations that were at least as political as they were academic. He told Raychaudhuri that his "competitor for the post was [Edward] Thompson, but the latter's attitude to the Indian national movement was too sympathetic to allow his election." Nor did the university treat Davis particularly well. In Raychaudhuri's words, "no one told him what was wrong with him but he was never elected a Fellow of any college, but only given dining rights at Balliol." His readership in modern

48. C. H. Philips, ed., *Handbook of Oriental History* (London: Offices of the Royal Historical Society, 1951), p. vii; Philips, *Autobiography*, pp. 163–164.

49. Tapan Raychaudhuri, *The World in Our Time: A Memoir* (New Delhi: Harper Collins, 2011), p. 218.

50. Ibid., p. 124.

Indian history was not even a permanent position until toward the very end of his career. He was elected to the position for five-year terms. Raychaudhuri describes him as "an old fashioned political historian who had certainly achieved a level of excellence within those limits," but he "was not an intellectual familiar with modern approaches to historical interpretation or with the social sciences."[51] Whatever his personal shortcomings and strengths as a scholar, Davis's situation no doubt reflected in part the marginal status of the subject he taught: Indian history.

Colonial Scholars as Mentors

Denied access to official sources and relegated to a low status in the Western academic world, Indian enthusiasts of "scientific" history at the beginning of the twentieth century turned, understandably, to colonial administrator-scholars in search of mentors, interlocutors, or just people to argue against. The relationship between the Indian researchers and these officials-scholars was always close and cordial, though always somewhat fissured by the ideological differences of nationalism and, for want of a better word, imperialism. Yet the relationship was important. The Bengali antiquarian Rajendralal Mitra remained in conversation with colonial administrator-scholars throughout his career. Sita Ram Kohli of Punjab owed his inspiration to a visit to Lahore by the prominent British historian Ramsay Muir in 1913–14.[52] The administrator-scholar Edward Gait's 1906 publication *History of Assam* had a tremendous influence on the scholarship and imagination of young Assamese historians and led to the formation of the Kamrupa Anusandhan Samiti, which nurtured future historians like Suryya Kumar Bhuyan.[53] Sir Edward also played a prominent role in the founding, in 1915, of the Bihar and Orissa Research Society.[54]

51. Ibid., p. 215.

52. Fauja Singh, 'Sita Ram Kohli,' in Sen, *Historians*, pp. 250–264. On Rajendralal Mitra, see Kalyan Kumar Dasgupta, *Indian Historiography and Rajendralal Mitra* (Calcutta: Satchidananda Prakashani, 1976), chap. 2 in particular.

53. See Arupjyoti Saikia's essays, "History, *Buranjis*, and Nation," 473–507; and "Gait's Way: Writing History in Early-Twentieth-Century Assam," 142–171, in *History in the Vernacular*, ed. Raziuddin Aquil and Partha Chatterjee (New Delhi: Permanent Black, 2008).

54. See the discussion in Aryendra Chakravartty, "Territorial Self-Fashioning: Place-Making in Late 19th Century and Early 20th Century Colonial India" (PhD diss., Pennsylvania State University, 2013), chap. 4. I am grateful to Dr. Chakravartty for letting me consult a copy of his unpublished dissertation.

This relationship played a large part in promoting a love of European books and scholarship—particularly in history—in Bengali educated and well-to-do households. Sir Jadunath himself relates in an essay on his personal library how his father "as a zamindar [landlord] in Rajshahi [North Bengal] used to buy books of the retiring Magistrates and Judges of that district." Books in his father's libraries sparked Sarkar's initial interest in history. He also mentions that this practice of colonial officials selling their libraries to Indians on retirement was an old one: "In the days before the Suez Canal, the British officers who came to serve in India, often passed fifteen or even twenty years here before taking furlough Home. Most of them, therefore, brought with themselves a collection of good books. . . . Wellington, when he came to India as a Colonel [1798] brought a fairly large library in his ship. So also did Elphinstone and others. At the time of their retirement, they used to sell their furniture and libraries . . . [to] Indian grandees."[55]

As time wore on, and especially in the twentieth century, nationalism divided British and Indian historians along predictable lines. Even the best among the nineteenth-century British administrator-scholars in India, Eric Stokes once wrote, had two aims: first, "to discredit the Whig interpretation of Indian history which had taught that the founders of British rule were stained by greed, fraud, and innocent blood"; and second, to "demonstrate that [British dominion] was the result of long-working forces and was an inseparable part of the history of Europe and of Britain." This "continued to be the mainspring of later administrator historians, of Vincent Smith and the archivists, Foster, Forrest, Hill, or of Lovett and his colleagues in the *Cambridge History of India*" in the twentieth century. Thus Henry Dodwell's preface to the fourth volume of the *Cambridge History of India*, published in the 1930s, could see the Great Rebellion of 1857—one that Indians had already come to see as their "First War of Independence"—only as India's "first [ungrateful] answer" to the "benevolent changes" brought about by British rule. "In the ultimate analysis that movement was a Brahminical reaction against influences which, given free play, would revolutionize the mental, moral, and social conditions of the country." Similarly, Sir Verney Lovett's popular book *A History of the Indian Nationalist Movement* (1920) dismissed Gandhi's noncooperation movement with the comment: "It is directed by men who thoroughly understand how to play on the pathetic gullibility of the masses and the uncritical, easily aroused ardour of the youth of the educated classes. . . . Their object is

55. Jadunath Sarkar, "A Chapter of My Life: How My Library Grew Up," *Modern Review* (January 1958), p. 21.

to subvert the central and provincial British-cum-Indian Governments and Councils recently established by law."[56]

Eric Stokes described this division around nationalism as somewhat inevitable: "When the whole case against their [the British historians'] obvious bias and national prepossession has been made, it has yet to be shown that there is any adequate alternative to national pride and prejudice for keeping alive an active interest in Indian history in this country." T. G. P. Spear and A. L. Basham have made similar remarks on modern histories of India.[57] Basham cites the case of Vincent Smith, who had worked in the Indian Civil Service from 1869 to 1900 and whose books *Early History of India* (1904, with second and third editions in 1908 and 1914 and a fourth edition after his death, in 1924), *History of Fine Art in India and Ceylon* (1911), and *Oxford History of India* (1919) were popular texts in India. Smith admired objectivity as a value but remained "a lamentable failure" at practicing it, as he had an undying faith that India's inherent tendency toward chaos could be kept in check only by a despotic force such as the imperial British.[58] By the same token, Basham also mentions, as examples of partisan histories, nationalist arguments claiming for India an ancient capacity for democratic self-rule, made in texts such as K. P. Jayasawal's hugely successful *Hindu Polity* (1918) and *History of India, 150 to A.D. 350* (1933); or in R. K. Mukerjee's *Indian Shipping and Maritime Activity* (1912), *Fundamental Unity of India* (1914), and *Local Government in Ancient India* (1919); and R. D. Banerji's *Age of the Imperial Guptas* (1933).[59] Partisanship also often marked the varieties of caste, regional, or Hindu or Muslim histories that proliferated in the 1930s and 1940s.[60]

In this context, the great Maratha *itihasachayra* (teacher of history) Viswanath Kashinath Rajwade and the "doyen of Indian history" Sir Jadunath Sarkar represented mutually opposed tendencies. Even though Rajwade was influenced by such European figures as Ranke and Comte and has even been called

56. E. T. Stokes, "The Administrators and Historical Writing in India," in *Historians of India, Pakistan and Ceylon*, ed. C. H. Philips (London: Oxford University Press, 1961), 403; *Cambridge History of India*, vol. 6, *The Indian Empire, 1858–1918*, ed. H. H. Dodwell (1932; Delhi, 1964), pp. v–vi; Sir Verney Lovett, *A History of the Indian Nationalist Movement*, 3rd ed. (1920; London: John Murray, 1921), preface, no pagination. This work was reprinted in 1968.

57. Stokes, "Administrators and Historical Writing," p. 403; A. L. Basham, "Modern Historians of Ancient India," pp. 260–293; and T. G. P. Spear, "British Historical Writing in the Era of the Nationalist Movement," pp. 404–415, both in Philips, *Historians*.

58. Basham, "Modern Historians," pp. 268, 271. See R. C. Majumdar's essay "Nationalist Historians," also in Philips, *Historians*, p. 418, for a nationalist critique of Smith.

59. Basham, "Modern Historians," pp. 283–284.

60. See, for instance, Peter Hardy, "Modern Muslim Historical Writing on Medieval Muslim India," in Philips, *Historians*, pp. 295–309.

"the Ranke of Maharashtra," and even though he translated many European texts in his journal *Bhashantar*, he took a vow, quite early on his career it appears, not to write a "single line in any language other than Marathi." It has been observed of him that so strong were his "pure nationalistic tendencies" that he "was of the firm belief that if anybody were to take any help from the foreign government, he would be unable to make a proper search for truth even in non-political and cultural fields." Jadunath Sarkar tells of Rajwade's aversion to those who wrote in English: "When I first met Rajwade, in 1908," writes Sarkar, "he urged me to write in my mother-tongue (Bengali) and not in English."[61] A pro-Rajwade and anti-Sarkar version of the same incident published in the journal the *Mahratta*, by a Mr. B.M.B. from Dhulia (where Rajwade lived after separating from the Mandal in Poona), runs somewhat differently:

> The late Mr. Rajwade told me the incident in connection with the first interview that Yadunath Sarkar had with him. The late Hari Narayan Apte and Yadunath had attended one of the meetings of the Bharat Itihasa Samshodhak Mandal at Poona. At that time Mr. Apte happened to introduce Yadunath to Rajwade. After introduction Mr. Rajwade asked Prof. Yadunath as to why he wrote his books in English instead of writing them in Bengali, his mother tongue; was it because he wanted praise from European scholars? Mr. Rajwade told him at the same time that he would be serving his countrymen better and the Bengali language better if he would write them in his own language.[62]

Sarkar's version does not have these details. He simply says: "A mutual friend, himself a Deccani Brahman, asked Rajwade, 'If Sarkar had written in Bengali could you have read his histories, or even heard his name?' There was no answer."[63] The account in the *Mahratta* had a significantly different conclusion: "The interview ended with the remark that he [Rajwade] had nothing but contempt for such people [those who wrote in English]. Rajwade did not have the soft and polished manners and the suave mode of speech of the courtiers of the Mogul Emperor Aurangzeb with whose court-life Sarkar had . . . become familiar. Sarkar was naturally shocked by what Rajwade spoke to him and thereafter contracted a strong dislike for him and thenceforward he did not spare Mr. Rajwade but tried to slur him whenever he could."[64]

61. G. H. Khare, "Vishwanath Kashinath Rajwade," in *Historians and Historiography in Modern India*, ed. S. P. Sen (Calcutta: Institute of Historical Studies, 1973), p. 205; Jadunath Sarkar, "The Historian Rajwade," in his *House of Shivaji* (Calcutta: S. C. Sarkar, 1948), p. 268.

62. B.M.B, "The Late Mr. V. K. Rajwade and Prof. Yadunath Sarkar," in *Mahratta* (27 March 1927), pp. 166–168.

63. Sarkar, *House*, p. 268.

64. B.M.B., "The Late Mr. Rajwade," p. 168.

Whatever the truth of this particular incident, it is clear that Sarkar and Rajwade belonged to opposite ends of the spectrum of where a nationalist seeker of "scientific history" stood with regard to historical researchers among the British colonial officials in India. In his public statement on Rajwade, Sarkar described the former's "hatred of modern Europe" as "insane."[65] Privately, he described Rajwade as simply "mad." Once, in 1947, disagreeing strongly with Sardesai's handling of a particular document while the latter was engaged in writing the third volume of his *New History of Marathas*, Sarkar wrote: "What pained me most was your attitude to historical evidence and certain political theories. Old Vishubhai [Rajwade] was *known* to be mad, therefore what he wrote did not matter much; nobody read his *udgar* [in Marathi: ejaculation, exclamation, interjection] running into four times the length of his documents. But why should the passages noted by me in your vol. III go out to the public and cause you to be ranked with Rajwade?"[66]

Sarkar never explicitly mentioned any particular administrator-scholar as his ideal and would rather refer to Macaulay or some other European historians as worth learning from. He admired Sir William Foster (1863–1951), the formidable archivist at the India Office. When Foster edited the memoirs (1735) of Clement Downing, an English sailor who served the East India Company between 1715 and 1721, worked for a Mughal army in 1723, and eventually died at sea, Sarkar's praise for the editor was quite effusive, betraying many of his own ideals. Downing "had suppressed or garbled many facts . . . in order to leave a falsely glorifying account of his own doings." "But," wrote Sarkar, "he counted without Sir William Foster who, with his unrivalled knowledge of the India Office Manuscripts records, had tracked his lies to their lair, confronted them with . . . facts, and at last left Downing a poor jackdaw shorn of all his glittering plumage."[67] It pleased Sarkar immensely when the administrator-scholar of Mughal history Henry Beveridge compared his writing to that of a Mughal miniature artist. Years later he recalled the incident in a letter to "Nana," unconsciously displacing the figure of the colonial official to that of the more general "European critic." "Many years ago a European critic called me 'a master of the miniature' style of history writing—i.e. of the art of putting many things into a small readable compass, where nothing of use is omitted," he wrote to Sardesai, with some pride.[68]

65. Sarkar, *House*, p. 275.

66. NL, JSP, letter no. 938, Sarkar to Sardesai, Calcutta, 19 August 1947.

67. See Sarkar's review of *A History of the Indian Wars*, by Clement Downing, ed. W[illia]m. Foster (Oxford University Press, 1924), in *Modern Review* (February 1926), p. 183.

68. NL, JSP, letter no. 389, Sarkar to Sardesai, Calcutta, 30 December 1935.

Clearly, by the beginning of the twentieth century, ideas, manuscripts, journals, documents, books, and articles went back and forth between Indian and colonial-European scholars. When S. M. Edwardes, a retired member of the Indian Civil Service (ICS), took it in hand to revise the well-known *The Early History of India*, by the venerable Vincent A. Smith, for a fourth edition to be published in 1924 after the author's death, his preface gave readers a glimpse of a scholarly world in which (ex-)colonial officials with educational interests and Indian historians and archaeologists frequently exchanged ideas, hypotheses, and discoveries. Edwardes thanked "Indian scholars like Messrs. R. D. Banerji, K. P. Jayasawal, D. R. Bhandarkar" for their excavations and the archaeologist S. Krishnaswamy Aiyangar for an important article that the latter had "kindly sent to [him]." When D. B. Parasnis tried unsuccessfully to open up the Holkar records in Indore, "the usual obscurantist and obstructionist policy of Native State officials," writes Sarkar, " had perversely baffled him." The person who came to Parasnis's rescue was "a very influential political agent in his retirement in England," who wrote strongly to the Government of India on Parasnis's behalf. Sarkar writes: "The Darbar gave to fear that permission which it had refused to scholarship."[69] The lines of cooperation between individual administrator-scholars and their Indian counterparts thus ran both ways.

The connections often ran deeper than what mere sharing of information would suggest. It was from the administrator-scholar that Indian historians learned to write historical narratives. Vincent Smith's invocation of Goethe on the duty of the historian—"to separate the true from the false . . . [to] look upon himself as one who is summoned to serve on a jury"—is not only reminiscent of how Sardesai began the second volume of his *Marathi Riyasat* with a citation from Goethe, but the voice itself could have been that of Sir Jadunath Sarkar. Or think of the affect that Sarkar would sometimes strike in his prose by frequently referencing the imperial theme of heroism in the canonical English literature in which he had been formally trained. Even that belonged to a tradition of writing particularly colonial in its provenance. For instance, reading Sidney Owen—a professor of history in Bombay's Elphinstone College and a one-time reader in Indian law and history at Oxford, whom we will have occasion to refer to again—one comes across instances of the use of literature in ways that are strongly reminiscent of Sarkar's prose. Owen thus used the Scottish poet Thomas Campbell in describing the Indian

69. Vincent A. Smith, *The Early History of India, from 600 B.C. to the Muhammadan Conquest Including the Invasion of Alexander the Great*, 4th ed., rev. by S. M. Edwardes (Oxford: Clarendon Press, 1924), p. vi; Jadunath Sarkar, "D. B. Parasnis," *Modern Review* (June 1926), p. 653.

ruler Akbar in a series of lectures he delivered in Oxford on the history of India from 1627 to 1761: "This truly heroic king's heart was in the beneficent works of peace; and he might without hypocrisy have made the profession: 'Ye are brothers! Ye are men!/And we conquer but to save!'"[70] Just two lines. No reference to the context in which these lines were written or to their author. There is the only the assumption that the reader would also be familiar with the poetic refrain. But in one fell swoop, as it were, the quotation blended the heroism of Akbar and that of the British in a general gesture of glorifying the possible nobility of all empires and thus confirming the reader's prejudices in favor of imperial themes. As we shall see in chapter 5, Sarkar's own prose adopted these very rhetorical strategies, but in the service of his own patriotic and imperial-liberal imagination of a self-governing India.

The one colonial administrative-scholar whom Sarkar felt undoubtedly close to was the ICS officer William Irvine (1840–1911), whose unfinished tome *Later Mughals* Sarkar both completed and published at his own expense (see the introduction to the present volume). And with respect to Sarkar, Irvine played the role of the older scholar, happy to lend a helping hand to the younger. When Sarkar produced his first book on Mughal history, *India of Aurangzib* (1901), Irwin reviewed it the following year for the *Journal of the Royal Asiatic Society* of London. "It . . . is the first attempt," said Irwin in praising the book," by an English-educated Indian to deal with the modern history of his own country in the critical and scientific spirit. . . . Mr. Jadunath Sarkar has gone . . . to the original sources, qualifying himself for dealing with them by first acquiring a knowledge of Persian." The review ended with words that were indeed mentorial in tone: "Mr. Sarkar's work is of a very meritorious nature, but if it is to be perfected he must keep it constantly by him, amending and altering it as his researches extend. . . . We shall look for and welcome the other works announced as in preparation. But we beseech him on the next occasion not to forget an index, without which any work of this kind is nearly useless."[71]

Irvine and Sarkar exchanged several manuscripts over the years. Sarkar wrote, in a Bengali essay on Irvine, "Whenever I found out about any rare

70. Smith, *Early History*, p. 3; Govind Sakharam Sardesai, *Marathi Riyasat*, 4th ed. (Mumbai: Popular Prakashan, 1988), 4:3; Sidney Owen, *India on the Eve of the British Conquest: An Analytical History of India, 1627–1761* (Calcutta: Susil Gupta [India], 1954), p. 5. This work was first published in London in 1872.

71. W[illia]m Irvine, review of *The India of Aurangzib*, by Sarkar, *Journal of the Royal Asiatic Society* 34 (1902), pp. 687–692.

manuscripts related to Indian history, he got me to make copies for him."[72] And Irvine, in turn, would help Sarkar with materials from his own collection. Sarkar wrote: "The most charming feature of Mr. Irvine's character was the spirit in which he gave unfailing and eager help and appreciation to younger men engaged in researches connected with his own subject. . . . I am one of the many students of Indian history who were indebted to him for help, guidance and light on obscure points." Irvine "freely lent" manuscripts from his own collection; and without "his assistance in securing . . . loans or transcripts of rare Persian MSS. from England, France, and Germany," Sarkar wrote, his own *History of Aurangzib* "could hardly have come into being." "Mr. Irvine also criticized and emended the first five chapters of my *History* as freely and carefully as if it were his own work."[73] Those who know anything of the fierce and intense pride that Sarkar took in his own scholarship and in his skills as a historian will know that he could have written this only of someone he placed in the position of a teacher.

In this informal world of scholarship, whatever the political differences dividing various groups of scholars, everybody was agreed on one assumption: that Indian history was at a stage where the most urgent task of the serious scholar was to collect sources and to create repositories and archives that would make them accessible to present and future researchers. Rajwade, it is said, "wanted to write a comprehensive and authentic history of Maharashtra, [but] . . . had to abandon that idea and concentrate on the fulfillment of the triple conditions of discovery, collection and publication of historical sources as the pre-condition to scientific history-writing." Irvine expressed very similar sentiments in *Later Mughals*: "If this book cannot claim in the highest sense of the word the name of History, it is at least the result of some research and labour, things sadly required in Indian history as a preparatory clearing of the ground for more ambitious work. . . . At some future day the genius may arise who shall make these dead bones live; and when in a footnote this 'Gibbon of the future' flings me a word of acknowledgement, I shall be satisfied." Sarkar said pretty much the same in defending Irvine against those who were "inclined to deny him the title of the Gibbon of India on the ground that he wrote a mere narrative of events, without giving those reflec-

72. Sarkar, "William Irvine, I.C.S" [in Bengali], in *Jadunath Sarkar rachana sambhar* [A collection of Jadunath Sarkar's writings], ed. Nikhilesh Guha and Rajnarayan Pal (Calcutta: M. C. Sarkar, 2011), p. 113.

73. Jadunath Sarkar, "William Irvine: A Biography," in *Later Mughals*, by William Irvine, ed. and augmented with *The History of Nadir Shah's Invasion*, by Jadunath Sarkar (New Delhi: Munshiram Manoharlal, 1996), 1:xxii–xxiii.

tions and generalizations that raise the *Decline and Fall* to the rank of a philosophical treatise and a classic in literature." "They forget," said Sarkar, "that Indian historical studies are at present at a much more primitive stage. . . . We have yet to collect and edit our materials, and to construct . . . the bed-rock of ascertainable and unassailable *facts* . . . on which alone the superstructure of history could be raised by our happier successors."[74]

Ironically, this understanding that Indian history was in a "primitive" stage precluding the possibility of the emergence of a truly great historian came to haunt Sarkar's students when they sat down to evaluate their teacher's success at the historian's craft. "Old Beveridge," wrote the historian and Sarkar's student Kalika Ranjan Qanungo, referring to Henry Beveridge of the Indian Civil Service, "once hailed Jadunath as [a] 'Bengali Gibbon.'" "But a review compliment," he continued, "however sincere and just, cannot make a Gibbon of him in the estimate of the world at large." Qanungo acknowledged Sarkar's "vast learning," "the excellence of his English," "his power at drawing a magnificent background for [the]tragic canvass of the *Fall of [the] Mughal Empire*." These qualities may have elicited "this high compliment" from "the greatest modern British authority on Muslim India." But there still remained vast gaps between the respective stages of development that European and Indian histories found themselves in:

> If Jadunath like Gibbon had written this epic of history in his own language, if he could have had the advantage of Gibbon in having the raw materials dug out by generations of scholars before him, if decaying Delhi had been smouldering Rome, and above all if the historical knowledge of the present generation had been on a par with that of Roman history of Gibbon's contemporary Europe, only then could Jadunath have had the scope to rise to the stature of a Gibbon. Jadunath could not afford to be picturesque without being suspected and challenged at every step. He was under the necessity of letting chronicles and news-letters speak. . . . This means interference with the even flow of narrative.[75]

Qanungo's passage points to problems much larger than the simple question of assessing Sarkar's skills as a historian. Without being aware of it, Qa-

74. Raja Dixit, "Historical Writing and Research," in *A History of Modern Marathi Literature*, ed. Rajendra Banhatti and G. N. Jogalekar (Pune: Maharashtra Sahitya Parishad, 2004), 2:252; Irvine, "Author's Foreword," in *Later Mughals*, 1:xxxii; Sarkar, "William Irvine," in Irvine, *Later Mughals*, 1: xxiv. See also Sarkar's Bengali essay "William Irvine, I.C.S.: Sangkhipta jibani" [William Irvine, I.C.S.: A brief biography], in Guha and Pal, *Jadunath Sarkar*, pp. 111–122.

75. K. R. Qanungo, "Jadunath Sarkar as a Historian," in *Life and Letters of Sir Jadunath Sarkar*, ed. Hari Ram Gupta (Hoshiarpur: Panjab University, 1958), p. 71.

nungo probably spoke for generations of Indian historians (including mine) who have had to write academic history in a language of which they were not "native speakers." An idealization of European historiography is also evident in the shared understanding that as a modern form of knowledge, Indian history was in a "primitive" state of development. It needed to "catch up" with European historiography. These were inescapable problems, stemming from how Indians understood and negotiated the meanings of being modern while living under the compulsions of alien rule. We will encounter these themes again as our narrative unfolds (see chapter 5 in particular). But for now, let us focus on what researchers in Indian history did when they were faced with the new tasks of finding "sources" and defining to their own satisfaction what it could mean to be a researcher of the past. Those are the themes we take up in the next two chapters.

2

Debating Research

I present here a mostly ethnographic, as distinct from an intellectual, history of the birth of the practices that came to be known as historical research in colonial India. So, for example, I do not ask who first mooted the idea of "research" among historians in India and how the idea was disseminated. I am interested in that question, but the questions of more immediate interest here are Geertzian in spirit, with maybe a few sociological twists added to them: How would one write the history of the activity called historical research in the Indian context? What kinds of activity would be designated historical research, and by whom? What would make such activity socially meaningful to those engaged in it? In what way would such social meaning differ from whatever meaning the act of writing history assumed in the past, when writing history was not necessarily the same as researching it? In other words, how would those who initiated research in Indian history distinguish themselves as doing something new and thus set themselves apart from those they perceived as *not* doing research proper? What would give research its prestige and thus constitute it as some form of distinction (in Pierre Bourdieu's sense of the word), that is, as some kind of cultural capital? These are some of the questions that motivate this chapter. What makes these questions interesting in the Indian context is a fact that I have already described as being at the heart of this book: that debates about the idea of historical research among Indian scholars began long before Indian history became a researchable subject in Indian universities, not to mention the emergence of Indian history as an area of specialization in the universities of the West, including Britain. The latter, we have seen, is a much more recent story (see chapter 1).

But even as the word *research* began to become popular in the years following 1910, there was no universal agreement on what deserved the nomenclature of *research*. The idea of research came to be clarified through discussions and disagreement among scholars participating in the emerging public life of the discipline. The Sarkar-Sardesai correspondence is fascinating in this regard: it was, directly or indirectly, all about research. The two scholars saw themselves as engaged in "true" research, while they often criticized others for failing to understand what research was. Even their correspondence, Sardesai thought, was worth preserving mainly as a guide for future scholars looking for models of research in history. He wrote to Sarkar on 4 May 1943: "Your own letters to me, all of which I have carefully preserved, are valuable insofar as they record a complete account of historical research in Maharashtra during the last 30 years; and as you have doubtless preserved my letters, the two collections together will form a guide to future workers if a selection could be published, when easy times come dealing with the various problems of research."[1] Indeed, when such a selection of the Sarkar-Sardesai correspondence was published as an appendix to the volume edited by Hari Ram Gupta, Sarkar wrote a foreword summing up his life as that of a researcher emphasizing—as the letters in the selection do as well—the idea of the "genuine researcher." He wrote: "When I first set my hand to the plough in 1891, research (except in Sanskrit) meant only the pirating or translation of modern English or French books. . . . But today no *genuine* worker on Indian history is content unless he has mastered the language of the *original* authorities and can utilise the original records, despatches, state papers and inscriptions, which are the primary responsible sources."[2]

What Was Research?

Like many other terms fundamental to the academic discipline of history, the word *research* was born in India as a contested category. There were "true" researchers—at least in Sarkar's eyes—and researchers who did not deserve that name. What then was research? By way of approaching this question, we will distill some answers from what Sarkar and Sardesai professed, both to each other and in public, and then proceed to see, in this and the following chapters, what was at stake in the answers they provided.

Sarkar's understanding of historical research echoed, though not without some Indian modifications, Ranke's emphasis on "original narratives of eye-

1. NL, JSP, letter no. 762, Sardesai to Sarkar, Kamshet, 4 May 1943 (the letter is in nephew Arvind's handwriting).

2. Sarkar's "message" dated 20 April 1957, in *Life and Letters of Sir Jadunath Sarkar*, ed. Hari Ram Gupta (Hoshiarpur: Panjab University, 1958), emphasis on "genuine" added.

witnesses" and the "strict presentation of facts, no matter how conditional and unattractive they might be." As Sarkar understood the word, research was, first and foremost, an attempt to reconstruct history by getting as close as possible to eyewitness accounts of the past. Presiding over the meeting of the History Branch of the Eighth Bengali Literature Conference, held in April 1915, Sarkar underlined—following in the footsteps of Ranke—the importance of original, primary sources, the significance of which, Sarkar complained, Indian historians tended to overlook: "Consider how in writing histories of the Pathan period we depend blindly on Ferishtah and Al Badayuni and on Khafi Khan for the histories of seventeenth-century Mughal emperors, but all three of them were born long after the events and were mere collectors of contemporary descriptions."[3] This practice had to be abandoned.

The second task for a researcher in history was to "verify . . . references" (Sarkar used these English words). He likened the process by which historians should interrogate evidence to the interrogation of witnesses in the court of law under criminal jurisprudence in India—a ready reference to the everyday practice of criminal cases in colonial (and present-day) India, beginning with the lodgment of a First Information Report, or FIR: "(a) Who made the first report? Has any copy of the *first information* [in English] [report] been collected? How do we get copies of confidential police diaries? Did this particular witness have the opportunity to find out about the event? (b) Did he witness with his own eyes or is he repeating what he has heard from others? (c) Are his interests tied up with those of any of the parties in dispute?"[4]

Collecting and verifying evidence, however, was merely "hard work," wrote Sarkar. It did not require the application of any special merit, though the ideal of "hard work," as we shall soon see, was critical to this new idea of research. The next step was for the historian to avoid "personal mistakes" by looking at a character or an event in the round, from many directions at the same time—hence the need for the historian to adjudicate between different kinds of sources with different perspectives: "The modern historian cannot remain satisfied with later compilations and secondary sources; he must go to the very fountainhead of information, to the written words of the men who made history or their contemporary recorder. He also tries, as far as is

3. See Leopold von Ranke, "Preface to the First Edition of *Histories of the Latin and Germanic Peoples* (1824)," in his *The Theory and Practice of History*, ed. Georg Iggers, trans. Wilma A. Iggers (London: Routledge, 2011), p. 86; Jadunath Sarkar, "Presidential Address," *Proceedings of the Eighth Bengal Literary Conference*, Burdwan, Chaitra, 1321 [April 1915], p. 3. My copy—lent to me by Gautam Bhadra—does not have a printer's line.

4. Sarkar, "Presidential Address," p. 3.

humanly possible, to concentrate on each event from every side, instead of accepting the testimony of one party only."[5]

Finally came the question of the narrative, or what Sarkar would call the historian's "philosophy of history."[6] But the biggest item in Sarkar's reformist agenda was the question of truth. The search for original and contemporary sources was ultimately in aid of realizing "the whole and undistorted truth about the past." History must stand, as he put it, "on the solid rock of truth."[7]

Each of the terms in Sarkar's schema marked a break with what we might call the Indian tradition of writing history under the Mughals and before. Because India did not have any identifiable archives that survived into the British times—the mature Sarkar spent much time explaining and pondering why this was so—the insistence on finding and using original and contemporary sources made for an entirely new activity, which produced much rivalry among generations of historians over the question of who got to particular sources first (more on this in the next chapter). I cannot imagine historians in pre-British India seeking credit or feeling jealous of each other for being the first to spot an original source. Indeed, as Sarkar himself says, many of the older historical accounts repeated other accounts already available to them.

But, most importantly, by this call for "hard work" and "abandoning laziness," Sarkar signaled that research by its very nature was an activity primarily of the young, a value that most historians of the older times did not have (and I shall soon explain why). One of the most remarkable aspects of the Sarkar-Sardesai correspondence is a particular strand of their lament over old age that had not so much to do with the disabilities of old age as such—Sarkar sometimes wrote, as on 12 February 1947, "My health is my only solace but my age is my despair"—as with the fact that getting old actually prevented them from stomping around the countryside looking for original historical sources.[8] Thus, Sarkar wrote to Sardesai in 1940: "You probably realize that in view of our advanced age this is likely to be the last historical excursion we shall undertake together."[9] Nearly a year later, in 1941: "We are both of us turned 70, and you had recently a severe attack. And we have therefore sadly to discontinue our old pleasant practice of roving from place to place—which are romantic in name only but yield absolutely no historical material at present. No

5. Sir Jadunath Sarkar, introduction to *Selections from the Peshwa Daftar* (Bombay: Government Central Press, 1933), p. 1.

6. Sarkar, "Presidential Address," pp. 6–7.

7. Ibid., p. 2.

8. NL, JSP, Sarkar to Sardesai, letter no. 915, Calcutta, 12 February 1947.

9. NL, JSP, letter no. 647, Sarkar to Sardesai, Calcutta, 21 October 1940.

more for us Kanakgiri and Tanjore and similar delusive attractions!"[10] Sardesai reciprocated these sentiments in some of his letters. The "monotony of [his] existence in Kamshet," he remarked in a letter of 1943, made him remember wistfully their research trips in 1925 when they "stayed together" at the Servants of India Society. "I am languishing here in my loneliness and yearn for some stimulation from you," he wrote with even more pathos in 1950.[11] I don't think this particular way of experiencing old age would have been available to historians of Mughal or late-Mughal India, and not just because their average lifespan would have been shorter. Even if we could describe some of the preparatory work they did for writing historical accounts as "research," it would not have been for them such a necessarily youthful activity.[12]

When Writing History Entailed No "Research"

While histories in the Mughal or in the late-Mughal period were written for a variety of reasons, some instrumental, some theological, some motivated by other reasons, the work was seldom undertaken as idealistic, youthful activity. Most historians were not "young" by the reckoning of their own ages. Peter Hardy points out in his *Historians of Medieval India* that Zia al-din Barani, arguably "the most important historian" of the sultanate period, was "at least seventy-four lunar years old" when he completed his *Tarikh-i-Firuz-Shahi* in 1357.[13] There is some disagreement between Hardy and K. A. Nizami as to whether or not Barani used eye-witness accounts, but there is broad agreement that he wrote both this book and *Fatawa-i-Janhandari* out of concern for "his own rise and fall" and "during his last years of exile from court" as a means of influencing the sultan of Delhi with a view to his eventual rehabilitation.[14] The seventeenth-century Hindu historian Ishwardas Nagar's *Futuhat-i-Alamgiri*, dealing with the period 1657–1700, was written when the author

10. NL, JSP, letter no. 690, Sarkar to Sardesai, Calcutta, 17 September 1941.

11. NL, JSP, Sardesai to Sarkar, letter no. 753, 9 January 1943; no. 1050, 14 October 1950.

12. Cf. what Ranke said about archives and old age in his sixties: "I still study the archives with the greatest imaginable pleasure. There is some gleam of youth or rather of youthfulness in these studies, where one always learns something new and important, with the idea of communicating it to the world—a sentiment which makes one forget a little that one is getting old." Ranke to Clara Ranke, June 1862, in *Briefwerk*, p. 441, cited in Leonard Krieger, *Ranke: The Meaning of History* (Chicago: University of Chicago Press, 1977), p. 105.

13. Peter Hardy, *Historians of Medieval India: Studies in Indo-Muslim Historical Writing* (London: Luzac, 1960), p. 20.

14. Ibid., p. 24. K. A. Nizami, "Zia-ud-din-Barani," in *Historians of Medieval India*, ed. Mohibul Hasan (Meerut: Meenakshi Prakashan, 1968), pp. 38, 43.

was forty-seven years old (1699–1700). It was written as an act of secular piety: "After going through it, the educated may derive intellectual benefits, the illiterate knowledge, . . . the brave inspiration, . . . [and] the cowards may . . . long to undertake valorous deeds."[15] Written histories were often used to secure favors. Sarkar himself translated, among other things, three eighteenth-century Persian histories of Bengal nawabs. Of these, Azad-al-Husaini's *Nau-bahar-i Murshid Quli Khan* was clearly used by the author as part of an application for a literary pension, while Yusuf Ali's *Ahwal-i-Mahabat Jang* was written as a distraction—"to compose his mind" when the author was going through a difficult time brought about by illness, unemployment, his father's death, and the danger of "imprisonment and confiscation of . . . property."[16]

It was, in fact, this very different cultural location of history that allowed European administrators and soldiers to collect historical manuscripts in India in the late eighteenth and early nineteenth centuries. Histories were often written and given as gifts to secure favors with officials. Think of the famous Henry Miers Elliott (1808–1853) and John Dowson's (1820–1881) nine-volume collection of Muslim histories. Elliott, who was the foreign secretary of Lord Dalhousie, was interested in the history of old Indian families. Gifts of Persian manuscripts pleased him. So, as Sarkar explained in a Bengali essay, "presenting him with very rare or hitherto unknown historical manuscripts smoothed the passage to his *durbar*; it could even make it possible to save a small kingdom or increase the pension of a *nawab*. Thus the hapless descendants of the imperial or old courtly families gave Elliott gifts of highly valuable and beautifully written Persian manuscripts preserved in the imperial palace of Delhi. Among them were some of which there were no other copies in the world." Earlier, in the eighteenth century, between 1765 and 1775, when the English became the main power in northeast India, Europeans began to acquire illustrated Persian manuscripts in Lucknow and elsewhere through the force of money and power. Again, Sarkar's description is full of insight:

> Supplicants who knew Persian wrote up histories in that language (or collected what they had at home) to give as gifts [to Europeans] in order to please the Europeans and thus smooth their passage to employment. Especially, the stories to do with the occupation of Delhi by Ghulam Kadir towards the end of 1788, the extraction of Shah Alam's eyes, looting of the royal family, and

15. Tasneem Ahmad, trans. and ed., *Ishwardas Nagar's Futuhat-i-Alamgiri* (Delhi: Tadarah-i-Adabiyatri-i-Dilli, 1978), pp. xvii, 2.

16. *Bengal Nawabs Containing Azad-al-Husaini's "Naubahar-i-Murshid Quli Khan," Karim Ali's "Muzaffarnamah," and Yusuf Ali's "Ahwal-i-Mahabat-Jang,"* trans. Jadunath Sarkar (1952; Calcutta: Asiatic Society, 1985), pp. 1, 79.

> the insults suffered by them created great excitement and curiosity among Europeans inside and outside India. Then the very next year saw the beginning of the French Revolution. There also the royal family was humiliated and harassed, the nobility killed or incarcerated and tortured. For this reason, many of the English in India asked their *munshis* to write the history of the last phase of the Mughal emperors.

Sarkar includes Gholam Hussein Tabatabai's famous *Seir-ul Mutaqherin* in his list of such European-induced Persian histories.[17]

There is an incident in John Malcolm's biography that also gives us some insight into the social place historical manuscripts may have held in rules of etiquette and social transaction in late-Mughal or early-British India. Malcolm describes with mixed emotions his meeting, during a visit to Nizam's Hyderabad in July 1817, with an old acquaintance—an ex–dancing girl named Chandah—who, by the time Malcolm saw her that July, had moved up in the world: "She has high titles, . . . [and] has the distinctions of a noubut, or kettle-drum, rides on an elephant, and keeps up a good deal of state." Malcolm's responses to the lady were mixed. Even though she "chanted her Hindostanee and Persian odes" on seeing Malcolm again, they did not quite "charm" Malcolm "as they were wont." "After all," remarks Malcolm, "eighteen years do make some difference in the appearance and feelings both of man and woman." Following a dinner at the minister Chandu Lal's place, the lady sent Malcolm a copy of "her history of the Nizam and his ancestors, to which she ha[d] added a general essay on universal history." Malcolm writes:

> Though I knew this compilation had been made for her, I could not refuse her vanity, . . . the tribute of a compliment. "You are certainly," I said to her, "one of the cleverest women of the age." "That observation," the old lady replied, quite gravely, "is one of the truest you ever made." Her dress this evening was very splendid, but she looked haggard and old. Her eyes were painted overmuch, and their blackness, joined to a look of intoxication, which I fear was not feigned, made this celebrated woman an object of disgust more than of admiration.[18]

17. Jadunath Sarkar, "Mughal jug-e bharotiyo oitihashikgon" [Indian historians during Mughal rule], *Sahitya Parishad Patrika* 45, no. 1 (1345 [1938–39]), p. 62; 46, no. 2 (1346 [1939–40]), pp. 75–76. The fascinating story of the social transaction through which "Nota-Manus" came into possession of some broken leaves of the manuscript of *Seir* in the Murshidabad Nawab household is told in Seid Gholam Hossein Khan, *Seir Mutaqherin*, trans. Nota Manus (1789) (Lahore: Sheikh Mubarak Ali, 1975), vol. 1, *Proposal*, p. 5.

18. John William Kaye, *The Life and Correspondence of Major-General Sir John Malcolm, G.C. B., Late Envoy to Persia, and Governor of Bombay; from Unpublished Letters and Journals* (London: Smith, Elder, 1856), 2:164–165.

Malcolm obviously found the lady's pretensions pathetic, but it is significant that the gift from the lady should be a history of the ruling family coupled with a history of the world.

Research and the Relocation of History

What changed, then, by Sarkar's time with the advent of "scientific" and academic visions of history were not only the methods of the discipline and ideas about authorship—one could not simply attach one's name to a compilation put together by others—but the social and cultural location of history as well. Thus what was new about the idea of historical research that Sarkar promoted was its absolutely noninstrumental, disinterested character, a kind of truth-for-truth's-sake attitude. The joy of research partook of this pure, that is, disinterested, character of the truth being sought, as expressed, for example in a letter written in 1933 when Sarkar was able to locate the village of Palkhed on the map: "Eureka! I have found *Palkhed* on the map." The discovery depended on "correct dates to make estimates for duration of journey, direction, etc."[19] Similarly, a letter of 1936 described how reading Sardesai's translation of "Bussy's march on Poona" led Sarkar "to a restudy of the Maratha accounts of it," and he found "*Purandaré Daftar* of such absorbing interest" that he "stole a day and a half from work on [his] third volume [of *Fall of the Mughal Empire*] and translated the whole of the account of this expedition given in *Purandaré* and identified *all* the places." "There is an unspeakable joy," added a jubilant Sarkar, "when one succeeds in tracing every minute movement of a campaign on large maps like those I possess. I had done the same thing with regard to the Palkhed campaign three years ago."[20]

Sarkar's presidential speech to the Bengal Provincial Literature Conference of 1915 articulated this idealism in very a clear form. And there was a distinctly nineteenth-century German ring to what he said. "The best method of researching history," he pointed out, "is the scientific method. This method does not vary with time and place because it is equally effective in all departments of knowledge and is inherent in all that is truthful." "Nationalist pride" should not lead Indians to dismiss it simply because "modern Europeans" had adopted it; for then the "histories we write will be imperfect because they will be unscientific." By pointing to "nationalist pride" as an obstacle to research, Sarkar was obviously also making the point that the question of methods in

19. NL, JSP, letter no. 278, Sarkar to Sardesai, Darjiling, 20 September 1933.

20. NL, JSP, letter no. 427, Sarkar to Sardesai, Darjiling, 20 August 1936.

"scientific history" could not be separated from the cultivation of a certain kind of disposition or "character" on the part of the historian:

> What is the method for ascertaining the [historical] truth? Firstly, one has to prepare one's mind for this task. Casting aside the greed for fame, wealth or power, suppressing one's own feelings of attachment or anger, abandoning all previous prejudices, one has to firmly resolve:
>
> To Truth this day we will dedicate our minds,
> It is only the Truth that we shall endeavor to understand and worship
> The treasure of Truth is what we will seek.

(The three lines of verse are a quotation from a song composed by Rabindranath Tagore in 1901). Sarkar then went on to underline what such commitment to truth might entail emotionally for a historian:

> We will not worry about whether or not the truth [we seek] is pleasant or unpleasant, or if it accords with or differs from received public opinion. Whether it pleases or hurts our sense of patriotism will not be our concern. If telling the truth invites taunts and complaints from our friends or societies, we will put up with that, for it is the vow of the historian to seek, understand, and accept the truth. We will have to [for instance] uproot the idea from our minds that treating the ancient stories of India—say, the *Ramayana* or the *Mahabharata*—as fictional will stain the glorious image of India. We have to resolve that we will believe nothing without proof.[21]

What Meinecke wrote about Ranke—"Ranke was always anxious to show 'what things really had been like.' . . . [A] serious and priestly approach lay concealed in this desire, and Ranke was indeed filled with something of the priest's exaltation"—finds an echo in what Sarkar said throughout his life on the question of historical truth.[22] There was a difference, though, as will become clear as our narrative progresses. If Ranke's idea of scholarship as vocation was "a secular version of the Protestant clerical calling, serving God's social order and yet with an independent mission transcending it," the place of God, in Sarkar's case, was taken by the idea of the nation. It was the ideal of serving a certain vision of the nation that necessitated the elevation of research to the status of an idealistic activity.[23]

21. Sarkar, "Presidential Address," p. 2. For the song quotation, see Prabhatkumar Mukhopadhyay, *Gitabitan: Kalanukromik shuchi* [A chronological index to Tagore's book of songs, *Gitabitan*] (Calcutta: Tagore Research Institute, 1994), p. 142.

22. Friedrich Meinecke, *Historism: The Rise of a New Historical Outlook*, trans. J. E. Anderson (London: Routledge and Kegan Paul, 1972), p. 498.

23. Krieger, *Ranke*, p. 45.

Many of Sarkar's biographers have noted that he looked upon history as some kind of a calling, a call to truth, its objective method something to be practiced as a matter of personal virtue. The historical truth he looked for was indeed the "universal truth" that many European savants spoke of even in the early part of the twentieth century. "Our history of India," he said in 1937, "in order to find acceptance in the wide world of scholarship, must appeal to universal reason by transcending the narrow limits of national prejudices and beliefs[;] it must be scientific in its method, and science knows no barriers of country or race and owes no homage except to truth." In speaking of himself in a radio broadcast in 1948, he spoke of the "eternal vitality" that was always there in honest efforts and true words. He thought it impossible that someone could be a historian without "the right mental attitude." Historical research, he said, called for *sadhana*, a highly spiritualized Sanskrit word denoting a pursuit that had a distinctly ascetic and religious quality about it, perhaps not far from what Meinecke may have meant by the word "priestly" with reference to Ranke.[24]

Marc Bloch's observation about the importance of historians' being able to question and correct their sources is also reminiscent of Sarkar's practices. "Incorrect evidence," wrote Bloch, was not "the only stimulus to the first efforts for a technique of the truth," but "it continues to be the first starting-point from which that technique must necessarily proceed in order to develop its analysis." Sarkar, too, spent many of his working hours in correcting errors in primary sources. A typical letter of his (from 1937) reads: "I spent a couple of days correcting the dates in Dongre's volume and Maheshwar D['s] *Batani Patrén* which also I corrected laboriously."[25] In fact, the different editions of his *Shivaji and His Times* carry a remarkable instance of Sarkar's insistence on

24. Sarkar's speech at the Indian Academy of History, proceedings of the inaugural session at Benares, 30–31 December 1937, pp. 20–23, cited in Raghubir Singh (1993), "Jadunath Sarkar as a Historian of the Marathas," in *History in Practice: Historians and Sources of Medieval Deccan—Marathas*, ed. A. R. Kulkarni (New Delhi: Books and Books, 1993), p. 66; Sarkar's radio talk (12 October 1948) published in *Betar jagat*, October 1948, cited in Moni Bagchi, *Acharya Jadunath: Jibon o sadhana* (Calcutta: Jijnasa, 1975), p. 3. The talk was also reprinted in *Prabashi* and the daily *Jugantar* and has now been reprinted in a volume of Sarkar's Bengali writings. See Jadunath Sarkar, "Amar jiboner tantra" [The principles of my life], in *Jadunath Sarkar rachana sambhar* [in Bengali] [A collection of Jadunath Sarkar's writings], ed. Nikhilesh Guha and Rajnarayan Pal (Calcutta: M. C. Sarkar, 2011), pp. 1–5.

25. Marc Bloch, *The Historian's Craft*, trans. Peter Putnam (Manchester: Manchester University Press, 1983), p. 90; NL, JSP, letter no. 458, Sarkar to Sardesai, Darjiling, 15 April 1937. Correcting dates in Mughal documents was not easy. Sarkar's student Raghubir Singh notes: "In the early years of this [20th] Century, when that great work 'Indian Ephimeries' had not been published, Sir Jadunath Sarkar found great difficulty in converting the dates of one calendar into

the correctness of historical facts. Describing Shivaji's escape from Aurangzeb's prison in 1666, Sarkar had written in 1920 that by the time the emperor found out about it, "Shiva[ji] had had twenty four hours' clear start over his pursuers." He retained that figure in the 1929 edition, but, having consulted other material, changed it in later editions to "fourteen."[26] The change did not affect the narrative much, and most readers would not have noticed the difference. The change was simply a testimony to Sarkar's commitment to facts. Accuracy, pace Carr, was indeed a virtue for him.

Sarkar's sense that there was something spiritually lofty about this commitment to historical truth was, however, no mere copy of Ranke's Protestantism or some other European creed. He had translated the Rankean urge into Hindu-mystic categories and drew on traditions that belonged to the metaphysics of a certain variety of Hindu nationalism that, by his time, had both politicized and spiritualized the word *truth* itself—witness Gandhi's use of the word *satya* (truth) in *satyagraha* and Tagore's glorification of the same word in the lines that Sarkar quoted in his 1915 address cited above. This translational turn was once again clear in Sarkar's use of the Sanskrit word *chittashuddhi*—the act of cleansing (*shuddhi*) one's mind or consciousness (*chit*)—while responding to an occasion in the early 1950s when his admirers organized a formal celebration of his achievements. "If we want to keep alive in our country the [tradition] of original research," he said, "our researchers will need to practise *chittashuddhi*." And this is how he proceeded to explain what *chittashuddhi* meant for a researcher in history:

> The truth-seeking, disinterested person engaged in historical research will need to go beyond the confines of his time, country, and society, and hold in check the desire for cheap appreciation from the people of his own country. The thought that some Hogolkuria University will give me a doctorate degree or that the literary society of Chhoku Khansama Lane will recognize this book with a prize—such desires cannot be the ideal of a true researcher. I cannot afford to be satisfied with the fruits of my labor until the world outside—the society of the learned in what is called *the republic of letters* [in English]—recognizes my research,—such is the difficult vow we have to take in our hearts.[27]

[those] of another." Singh, preface to Jadunath Sarkar, "A Short Chronology of Indian History—XVIIth Cent. (1624–1710 A.D.)," typescript, NL, JSP.

26. Sarkar, *Shivaji and His Times* (Calcutta: S. C. Sarkar, 1920), p. 168; Sarkar, *Shivaji* (Calcutta: M. C. Sarkar, 1929), p. 152; Sarkar, *Shivaji* (1952; Delhi: Orient Longman, 1973), p. 151.

27. "Banglay oitihashik gobeshonar shomoshya" [Problems of conducting historical research in Bengal], in Guha and Pal, *Jadunath Sarkar*, p. 34. There is a Chhoku Khansama Lane in Calcutta but no Hogolkuria University in Bengal; that was just Sarkar's way of referring to imagined insignificant institutions.

Sarkar's immediate reference for the word *chittashuddhi* was to the theology of the sixteenth-century (though some place it in the early seventeenth century) Vaishnava text of a biography of the Bengali saint Chaitanyadeva, Krishnadas Kaviraj's *Chaitanyacharitramrita*, the middle portion of which Sarkar was the first person to translate into English in 1913 (with revised editions published subsequently).[28] But *chittashuddhi* was a much older expression; we can find it in the *Gita*, for instance. Gandhi and other nationalists used the category or something akin to it in their expositions of the *Gita* in the twentieth century.[29]

The Practice Called Research

"Nothing without proof" became Sarkar's battle cry against histories that were produced in India in the first part of the nineteenth century, when European administrator-scholars were more accommodative of "native knowledge." Early East India Company officials who wrote up histories of particular regions of India out of a combination of curiosity and a desire for fair governance often depended on already existing genres of narratives about the past and absorbed these into their own narratives. Consider the case of the eighteenth-century legendary queen of Indore, Ahalya Bai (1735–1795), to whom John Malcolm devoted about thirty-eight pages in the first volume of his *Memoirs of Central India* (1823). Malcolm found that, much like the proverbial peasant in modern historiography, the queen was more remembered than documented.[30] This forced Malcolm to become one of the earliest among colonial-European students of modern Indian history to use as sources what he knew to be "legends" and "anecdotes," the stuff of "oral history" or, even better, "memory."[31] Similarly, James Grant Duff's *History of*

28. See Jadunath Sarkar, *Chaitanya's Life and Teachings from His Contemporary Bengali Biography the Chaitanya-charit-amrita* (1913; Calcutta: M. C. Sarkar, 1922).

29. See the discussion in Dipesh Chakrabarty and Rochona Majumdar, "Gandhi's *Gita* and Politics as Such," in *Political Thought in Action: The Bhagavat Gita and Modern India*, ed. Shruti Kalipa and Faisal Devji (Delhi: Cambridge University Press, 2013), pp. 66–87.

30. I should qualify my statement by saying that even within India, many different traditions of documentation reigned. Muslim rulers, for instance, were frequently well documented. Ahalya Bai was documented too, but Malcolm did not have access to those sources. The Maratha historian D. B. Parasnis, for instance, published "two thick volumes of despatches sent to Poona by the Peshwa's agent at the court of Ahalya Bai Holkar." Jadunath Sarkar, "D. B. Parasnis," *Modern Review* (June 1926), p. 653.

31. Malcolm's history of Ahalya Bai was almost entirely based on stories people told him. This generated a very visible dilemma in his footnotes, as he was a child of the Enlightenment, in fact an avid reader of Hume's *History of England*. Malcolm was therefore always at pains to

the Marathas (1826) was based, in part, on information supplied by one Abdool Hoosain Qazee, "a venerable and sensible old man, the most respectable person now in Beejapore," who, Duff wrote, was "full of legendary information, and on . . . conversing with him, in the midst of lofty domes and falling palaces, one fancies himself in company with the last of the inhabitants of that wonderful place." The same may be said of James Tod, who, in his classic *Annals and Antiquities of Rajasthan*, borrowed equally from his knowledge of European medieval history and from bardic poems and ballads about Rajput clans.[32] On the Indian side, Kaviraj Shyamaldas, the famous author of *Vir Vinod* (1886), a compilation of the history of Mewar in Rajasthan, found his inspirations in Tod's *Annals*. So did his twentieth-century successor-historian, Gaurishanker Hirachand Ojha. Grant Duff remains a point of reference for Maratha historians even today.

It was not as if there was no research involved in the efforts of these early European soldiers, doctors, and administrators to find out about Indian pasts. As is well known, the English word *research*—a word of seventeenth-century vintage—was in common use in India in the eighteenth century, as for instance in the name of that reputed journal *Asiatick Researches*, published by the Asiatic Society of Bengal.[33] But what did *research* mean for eighteenth-century Europeans in India? W. Francklin's history of the reign of Shah Alam, first published in 1798, gives us an example of a conscious use of the word *research* by a European inquirer in eighteenth-century India and therefore makes it easier to see what word meant in practice. Francklin was a captain in the East India Company's service, Bengal establishment, and a member of the Asiatic Society.

---

assure the reader that his anecdotes were reliable. Sometimes he believed a particular Indian man's story because the teller, "Khealee Ram," was "two years ago one of my principal writers." At other times, he simply relied on his own historical experience, as when he heard a story about the queen while himself visiting her palace: "This anecdote was related to me by Baramul Dada ["the venerable manager of Mhysir"], when sitting on the terrace of her [Ahalya Bai's] place at Mhysir [Maheshwar], which overhangs the Nerbudda." Major-General Sir John Malcolm, *A Memoir of Central India Including Malwa, and Adjoining Provinces, with the History and Copious Illustrations of the Past and Present Condition of That Country*, 2 vols., 3rd ed. (1823; London: Parbury, Allen, 1832), 1:183n, 192n, 193.

32. James Grant Duff, *History of the Marathas* (1826; Bombay: Times of India Office, 1878), 1:82–84n; Sukumar Bhattacharya, "James Tod," in *Historians and Historiography in Modern India*, ed. S. P. Sen (Calcutta: Institute of Historical Studies, 1973), pp. 416–423.

33. The online etymological dictionary shows the word to be of sixteenth-century origin and to mean "scientific inquiry" from the 1630s on. Online Etymology Dictionary, www.etymonline.com/index.php?allowed_in_frame=0&search=research&searchmode=term, accessed 1 October 2013.

A footnote in Francklin's book tells us something about contemporary ideas regarding what constituted "research." Writing on the history of the Sikhs, the author informs us that in the years 1793–94, he "was at Paneeput in company with Major Charles Reynolds of the Bombay establishment employed by the British government on a survey through the Do-Ab[,] the results of which, when communicated to the public, will no doubt prove a valuable addition to the geography already acquired." At that time he saw "a body of Sikhs then in the service of the great Sindiah; they were about one thousand in number, under the command of Doolchee Sing, from whose brother most of the information above-mentioned was received." Francklin apologized "for giving a sketch so imperfect, though he is happy to learn that there is another and far better account already before the public from the late Colonel James Browne, of the Bengal establishment, but which account the author has not seen." But he did say that his account given here stood "merely on his own *researches*."[34]

The word *research* here refers primarily to informal inquiries made in the field. For example: "For the following detail of the Malwah province, the author is happy to confess his obligations to Major Charles Reynolds, Surveyor-General on the Bombay establishment, who furnished him with materials collected by himself *on the spot*."[35] Francklin used parliamentary reports and accounts of British officers as well as indigenous accounts, but the idea of verifying one's sources was clearly not important. One "Doolchee Singh's brother's narrative" was accepted without any verification, though Francklin was aware that the sketch was "imperfect." What did make manuscripts seem reliable may be seen from the following statement relating to an account of Rajpootana: "In this description, the author has availed himself of a Persian *MS.* entitled *Hudeeka Al Akaleem*, or a geographical account of several . . . cities and provinces of Hindostaun. It is written by a learned native, and contains much curious and useful information."[36]

It would also be wrong to say that these early European historians had no concern with historical truth. Without that concern, they, like their counterparts in the Mughal world, would not have been historians in any sense. But their ideas about verification of sources were substantially different from those that Sarkar came to apply and advocate. Once, for example, when

34. W. Francklin, *The History of the Reign of Shah-Aulum, the Present Emperor of Hindustaun* (1798; Allahabad: Dr. L. M. Basu, M.B., Panini Office, Bahadurganj, 1934), p. 81, emphasis added.

35. Ibid., p. 123n, emphasis added.

36. Ibid., p. 84n.

Francklin did want to test the veracity of the Delhi legend that, even though Mahadji Sindhia had promised Shah Alam an annual grant of Rs 9 lakhs, no more than Rs 50,000 was ever received in any one year, he checked the story with a Delhi resident, Syud Rezzi Khan, "a nobleman of the court" and "Colonel Palmer's Vakeel" and learned that "this was an actual fact."[37] Or note this following statement of his on the Awadh ruling family: "An historian [Colonel Dow] . . . has informed the world that the reigning family in Oude were obscure in their origin and of low birth; but as that information . . . appears to be incorrect, we have, with the deference to fidelity which the impartiality of history demands, detailed a more authentic account of the rise of that family." But where did Francklin's more "authentic account" come from? He writes: "In this detail, the author has principally followed a small genealogical work, entitled *Owsaf-i-Asuph*, or the Genealogy of Asuf Al Dowla, the present vazir, which was procured by the friendship of Mr. George Johnstone, many years Resident at Lucknow."[38]

Between the second half of the eighteenth century and the first part of the nineteenth, a number of British officials—both civil and military—began to research India's past as amateur antiquarians. The most famous of them include Sir William Jones, Thomas Colebrook, and Captain Colin Mackenzie (1754–1821), who became the first surveyor general of India after the fall of Tipu Sultan and carried out the Mysore survey between 1800 and 1810.[39] There is no question that they saw themselves as doing "research" and that they, taken together, constituted a research community of a sort. A blend of practical concerns and historical curiosity drove their activities. Think of the French officers working in Ranjit Singh's army who collected and forwarded to Calcutta ancient coins they exhumed or discovered in the Punjab.[40] James Prinsep (1799–1840), whose researches on ancient and Mughal coins and whose decipherment in 1827 of the Brahmi script were foundational to Indian numismatics and ancient Indian history, clearly combined research with his practical work in the Benares and Calcutta mints of the East India Company. A tract he published to help the East India Company issue uniform coins

37. Ibid., pp. 191, 192n. Statements of this nature will be found in Malcolm and also in Grant Duff or Tod.

38. Ibid., p. 63.

39. See Rama Mantena, *The Origins of Modern Historiography in India: Antiquarianism and Philology* (New York: Palgrave Macmillan, 2012); Thomas R. Trautmann, *Aryans and British India* (Berkeley: University of California Press, 1997).

40. "Memoir of the Author," by H. T. Prinsep, in *Essays on Indian Antiquities: Historic, Numismatic, and Palaeographic, of the Late James Prinsep, F. R. S.*, ed. Edward Thomas (London: John Murray, 1858; reprint, Delhi: Asian Educational Services, 1995), p. xiii.

throughout their Indian territories, thus ending the monetary chaos that had come to characterize India at the end of Mughal rule—a policy in fact adopted by Lord Bentinck—contained not only a useful history of coinage in India but also references to Mackenzie's collections of Indian documents and ephemera and to Thomas Colebrook's essays in the *Asiatick Researches*.[41] In Prinsep's own understanding of his efforts, he and these other individuals clearly belonged to a community of researchers. In addition, one could think of the enormous collection of information and research that the British produced simply in the course of administering India—the censuses, gazetteers, land settlement reports, and volumes on tribes and castes of particular regions. All of those activities entailed "research" that was eventually incorporated in the work of late-nineteenth-century colonial institutions such as the Archaeological Survey of India and the Anthropological Survey of India. These institutions, through which European ideas about "scientific" research percolated, no doubt trained many future Indian researchers.[42]

The "True" Researcher in History

The call for "scientific history," however, broke the traffic between European and Indian genres of history that marked the antiquarian researches of the first half of the nineteenth century. Scientific history, one may say with Tapati Guha-Thakurta, participated in a certain kind of denigration of "native knowledge."[43] However, more was at stake here than simply European prejudice, as we shall see. Sarkar's moral-idealist position on historical research and objectivity actually entailed a struggle with his own present, with the discipline of history as it was finding a home in Indian "academies" and other educational institutions in the 1920s, 1930s, and later. This was ultimately reflected in what I think of as his *three great rejections*: of the profession of history as it evolved in India—I distinguish here the idea of "profession" from the idea of history as a calling or vocation (in Max Weber's terms, "an intellectual aristocracy"); of the mass politics of nationalism that emerged under the leadership of Gandhi after the Great War; and of the general Indian world of historical scholarship, which he rejected—while making exceptions for

41. James Prinsep, *Useful Tables Forming an Appendix to the Journal of the Asiatic Society: Part the First, Coins, Weights and Measures of British India* (Calcutta: Baptist Missionary Press, 1834), pp. 15, 16, 76, 87.

42. The historian who initiated the study of these "colonial forms of knowledge" in our time was the late Bernard S. Cohn.

43. See Tapati Guha-Thakurta, *Monuments, Objects, Histories: Institutions of Art in Colonial and Postcolonial India* (New York: Columbia University Press, 2004), pp. 168, 219, 108–111.

individuals—in favor of an ideal republic of letters that he often equated with an idealized Europe. But here again, the story is more complicated than it appears at first sight.

Sarkar was not alone in professing the values he did. Many other amateur researchers in the field of history held similar views. A famous example would be Viswanath Kashinath Rajwade, the great Marathi *itihasacharya* (teacher of history) we have already met. In discussing Rajwade's philosophy of history and his methods of research, the Poona scholar M. R. Kantak has demonstrated clearly that Rajwade's values were all Rankean (in a positivist sense) and often bore close resemblance to positions Sarkar would have held. He valued "first hand evidence" if it was "contemporary," if its factual contents could be verified with the help of other sources, if the writer producing the evidence was "honest" and had had proper training in presenting facts, and so on. On this basis, he was happy to pronounce many of the Marathi "*bakhar*s, *kaifiyat*s, family accounts and genealogies"—the staple of Marathi historians before him—"third grade" and "unreliable." But he was erratic in the application of his own principles to the organization of the very large body of documents that he put together in 22 volumes.[44] Of all his contemporaries, Sarkar probably was the one who upheld and applied positivist values most consistently.

The first professional meeting of Indian historians—called at first the All India Modern History Congress and later renamed the Indian History Congress, the name by which it is still known—took place in Poona in 1935 and was the handiwork of three scholars who became the political and institutional leaders of Indian historians in the 1930s and later: Datto Vaman Potdar, from Poona, a leading light of the Bharat Itihas Samshodhak Mandal; Surendra Nath Sen, of the University of Calcutta, later the first director of the Indian National Archives; and Sir Shafaat Ahmad Khan of the Department of History, University of Allahabad. Sarkar did not consider any of them "true" researchers. Sardesai also expressed the same sentiment in a letter of 1937: "As usual the Mandal people [Potdar was the leader of this group] have been assiduous in their attacks upon you and me. I think a time is come when you

44. See the discussion in M. R. Kantak, "Rajwade's Historical Research Methodology," in *Rajwade and His Thoughts*, ed. M. R. Kantak (Pune: Bharat Itihas Samshodhak Mandal, 1990), pp. 33–54; see especially pp. 33, 37–44. For some points in Rajwade's critiques of *bakhar*s and the history (of Marathas) by Grant Duff, see V. K. Rajwade, "Itihas ka arth kya hai?" [What is the meaning of history?] in *Rajwade lekh sangraha* [in Hindi] [Collections of Rajwade's writings], ed. Tarkatirth Lakshman Shastri Joshi, trans. Vasant Dev (Delhi: Sahitya Akademi, 2000), pp. 32–34.

[must] speak out to the whole Indian world how these people lack *the* real historical spirit and the scholarship."[45]

Moni Bagchi reports that young scholars wanting to study under Sarkar's supervision were handed a piece of paper titled "Guidelines for Researchers," which stated five simple principles: "1. Never play hide and seek with any historical truth. 2. Depend on the purest, most immediate documents. 3. Develop a genuine spirit for research. 4. Armchair research is no research at all. One must come into contact with the outside world. 5. You must take research as one takes religion."[46] However, Sarkar's idealistic-moral criticisms of what he saw as Indian scholars' habitual tendency toward "laziness" sometimes went to ridiculous extremes. He would allow young scholars to use his personal library only if he was convinced that they were "genuine" researchers. When Suraj Narain Rao came from the Jind state to work in his library in Calcutta in mid-December 1948, and worked for long hours every day in the library, Sarkar would see him only at 4:00 p.m. with a cup of tea; he would "silently sip" a cup himself and leave after asking Rao for a "list of the material [he] needed the next day." But that is not my example of a "ridiculous extreme." The test that Rao had to pass is indicated in the following sentence in his reminiscence of Sir Jadunath: "It was, perhaps, *on the third day* that one of his [Sarkar's] grandsons came to me and politely pointed out to me the bath-room for use, if and when I needed it"![47]

But this was an extreme example. More often than not, the idealistic figure of the true researcher found its expression in Sarkar's and Sardesai's private criticisms and in a general assumption that the "not-so-true" researcher fundamentally lacked strength of character, showing the extent to which the idea of research was laden, for Sarkar and his friend, with moral significance. For example, one accusation they privately leveled at the younger historians who started the History Congress was that they were all talk and little work. "The show at Allahabad has proved all hollow as expected," wrote Sardesai to Sarkar in 1938, referring to the recently concluded History Congress. "Even the promised report [of] the 1935 Congress has not been published," he added, criticizing Potdar. "Work alone strikes and no amount of talk."[48] Sarkar had

45. On the first history congress, see *Proceedings of the All India Modern History Congress, First Session, Poona, June 1935* (organized in association with the Silver Jubilee of the Bharat Itihas Samshodhak Mandal) (Poona: Prof. Datto Vaman Potdar, 1938); NL, JSP, letter no. 451, Sardesai to Sarkar, Kamshet, 13 February 1937.

46. Bagchi, *Acharya Jadunath*, p. 157.

47. Gupta, *Life and Letters*, p. 83, emphasis added.

48. NL, JSP, letter no. 537, Sardesai to Sarkar, Kamshet, 30 October 1938.

criticized the Congress in a private letter to one of his students, the "princely historian" Kumar Raghubir Singh, by a reference (I think) to the character of the main founder of the Congress, Shafaat Ahmad Khan of Allahabad: "I never attend vulgar *tamashas* [entertainment] like the Modern History Congress or the Oriental Congress. Their standard is very low, and they are often manipulated by low, self[ish] coteries, like the *Bharat Itihas S. Mandal.* Even your 'Doctor Professor' is an awful drunkard; at the Gwalior Session of the I[ndian]. H[istorical]. R[ecords]. Commission, as we were returning from the dinner at Sardar Sitole's place, he began to crow and sing and there was every fear of his soiling my dinner suit in a fit of . . . sickness."[49] He stuck to his view in a letter to Sardesai on 8 September 1939, when the Congress met in Calcutta: "I always avoid the Indian History Congress and shall do so even when I am here during its sitting. It is a vulgar tamasha [entertainment] started by a drunkard."[50] His feelings were strong enough that he expressed them again in a few weeks' time, in a letter dated 29 September of the same year: "I never attend the mushroom Modern Indian History Congress."[51]

The Indian History Congress invited Sardesai to preside over its annual meeting in Jaipur in 1951. Mollified and pleased, he wrote to Sarkar: "I feel circumstances are so shaping themselves that the mistakes of the past are being slowly rectified. Perhaps some of the vaunting upstarts have been exposed in their true colours. We are both nearing our graves and if we could do some service to history, that may prove a turning point. I am, however, altogether unwilling to accept the invitation unless you can be present." He mentioned that Rajendra Prasad, Sarkar's former student from his days in Patna, now (in 1951) serving as the president of the Republic of India, had himself expressed an interest in seeing Sarkar accept an invitation to the Congress. Trying to assure Sarkar, Sardesai continued, "There is no deep [*sic*] laid scheme nor deliberation. The historians of India desire to pay homage to you for the work you have done."[52] Sarkar was hostile to the suggestion, and his letter to Sardesai drips with sarcasm. "Dear Nana," he wrote,

49. Sarkar to Raghubir Singh, dated Darjiling, 3 June 1937, in *Making of a Princely Historian: Letters of Sir J. N. Sarkar to Dr. Raghubir Singh of Sitamau*, ed. S. R. Tikekar (Bombay: Maharashtra Board of Archives and Archaeology, 1975), p. 49, emphasis original. Shafaat Ahmad Khan replaced R. B. Ramsbotham as a member of the IHRC in 1930—see *IHRC Proceedings*, vol. 12, *Twelfth Meeting, Held at Gwalior, December 1929* (Calcutta: Government of India, Central Publications Branch, 1930), p. 2.

50. NL, JSP, letter no. 586, Sarkar to Sardesai, Calcutta, 8 September 1939.

51. NL, JSP, letter no. 590, Sarkar to Sardesai, Calcutta, 29 September 1939.

52. NL, JSP, letter no. 1057, Sardesai to Sarkar, Kamshet, 17 January 1951.

> It is a great honour that the conclave of history professors have "unanimously elected" you to preside over their meeting next December, *after* Potdar, Sen and the Madrasi wind-bags [a reference to S. K. Aiyangar?] have been so honoured. Probably they became aware of the existence of the living encyclopaedia of Maratha history only after reading in the newspapers a report of his death in a Talegaon hospital in 1948, which was later contradicted. "So the old man is not dead, after all." They no doubt want to see if their President-elect, within five months of his 88th birthday, in the intense cold of Jaipur in mid-winter, will have a voice strong enough to keep order among a pack of noisy unmannerly schoolboys holding a debating club.

And then came his unshakable decision:

> I do not share your optimism that the conference will succeed in dragging Jaipur royal archives into the light of the day, or even in actually publishing a scholarly history of India; their past action—or more correctly, inaction—gives no support to such an expectation. I still hold to my decision of not wasting my time by joining in such futilities. . . . I am more usefully employing my time & energy in pushing through two Calcutta presses Poona Residency Correspondence, vols. X and XIV, so as to have them completed and bound by the 31st March next.[53]

Apart from Potdar and Shafaat Ahmad Khan, another of Sarkar's long-term bêtes noire among the organizers of the Indian History Congress was the Bengali historian Surendra Nath Sen, of whom I will have more to say in chapter 7. Sen was a historian of eighteenth-century Maharashtra. Sarkar's dislike of Sen had a long history. He had never admired Sen's scholarship nor liked his association with D. V. Potdar and the Bharat Itihas Samshodhak Mandal of Poona, who, in turn, were opposed to Sardesai and Sarkar. It is possible that Sen and Sarkar were on friendly terms when Sen was a young lecturer at the University of Calcutta in 1919, for the latter's translation of the seventeenth-century biography (*bakhar*) of Shivaji, *Siva Chhatrapati*, acknowledged how "indebted" he was to Sarkar, "who not only revised my manuscript and gave me many valuable suggestions but also placed his whole library at my disposal."[54] But shortly thereafter the relationship soured: we find Sarkar asking Sardesai in 1922 for a copy of "*vividha-dnana-vistar*,"

53. NL, JSP, letter no. 1059, Sarkar to Sardesai, Calcutta, 23 January 1951.

54. Surendra Nath Sen, *Siva Chhatrapati, Being a Translation of Sabhasad bakhar with Extracts from Chitnis and Sivadigvijaya* (Calcutta: University of Calcutta, 1920), preface, p. ix. Kiran Pawar, *Sir Jadunath Sarkar: A Profile in Historiography* (Delhi: Books & Books, 1985), p. 97, uses this statement to argue that Sen was "assisted and encouraged" by Sarkar.

in which Sen's translation of the Sabhashad Bakhar (*Siva Chhatrapati*) had been reviewed by the Marathi historian Sane, who reportedly "pointed out the many places where the translator has failed to understand the sense of the original."[55] Sen's 1923 preface to *Administrative System of the Marathas*, on the other hand, made an approving reference to "Professor Takakhav and Mr. Keluskar's voluminous life of Shivaji Maharaj," a book that was—as we will see in chapter 5—virulently hostile toward Sarkar's work on Shivaji.[56] A few years later, in 1925, we find Sarkar directly asking the Goan historian Pandurang S. S. Pissurlencar, an authority on the Portuguese in India: "Are Dr. Sen's extracts from Portuguese archives published in the *Calcutta Review* exhaustive and correct?"[57] By 1930 the divisions were clear. Sen was now close to Potdar and the Poona Mandal. Not surprisingly, a letter from Sarkar to Sardesai reads: "You may have now seen Dr Surendra Nath Sen in his true colours? With his elementary knowledge of Marathi language and scanty collection of Marathi printed letters, he has presumed to run down your *Main Currents*, and why? Is it to curry favour of [*sic*] the Potdar gang? His ludicrous mistranslations from Marathi and Portuguese, if made known to the general public of Bombay, would add to [the] mirth of the scholarly world."[58]

I should clarify once again that I am not interested in understanding the personal psychology or motivation behind Sarkar's dislike. Nor is it my objective to assess whether or not Sarkar was right in his judgments. I am interested rather in the language through which he expressed his dislike, for that language spoke always of his imagination of the historian as an ideal-romantic figure, a passionate yet disinterested and diligent researcher. I am interested, shall we say, in the social rather than the purely personal meaning of the hostility that developed between Khan or Sen or Potdar on the one side and Sarkar and Sardesai on the other.

55. NL, JSP, letter no. 31, Sarkar to Sardesai, Darjiling, 9 June 1922.

56. Surendra Nath Sen, *Administrative System of the Marathas* (Calcutta: K. P. Bagchi, 1976), "Preface to the First Edition." I discuss the Takakhav-Keluskar book in chapter 5.

57. Sarkar to Pissurlencar, dated Moradpur, 18 November 1925, in *Bibliography of Dr. Pissurlencar Collection*, ed. B. S. Shastry and V. R. Navelkar, part 3 (Bambolim: Goa University, 1989), p. 114. There are other letters of Sarkar's in this collection containing references to Sen that are critical but indirect—he (without being named), it seems, is included in Sarkar's description of scholars who "borrow" Pandurang's materials and by "quickly publishing them in English" earn for themselves "an undeserved credit as the greatest authority on the Portuguese in India or on the Luso-Maratha relations." Sarkar's letter dated 21 November 1931, pp. 144–145. See also the letter dated 17 August 1929, pp. 140–141. I owe this reference to Gautam Bhadra.

58. NL, JSP, letter no. 123, Sarkar to Sardesai, Darjiling, 22 April 1930.

Europe Imagined as the Republic of Letters

Oftentimes, Sarkar would express his intellectual disrespect for conferences and symposia as a forum for dissemination of research, particularly in India. He also showed little confidence in Indian institutions and faculty, while making exceptions for particular individuals. "I do not share your optimism about an impetus being given to the exploration of regional histories," he wrote to Sardesai in 1933. "The failure of the Maharashtra University scheme is quite irrelevant to the issue. Whence will come the professors who will honestly and industriously take up this work of research? They are a lazy lot, as your university authorities are utterly ignorant of the needs of scholarship and indifferent to learning."[59] He declined the honorary membership offered by the Bombay Historical Society in 1952, "as it is neither a real benefit to them nor an honour to me to allow my name to be borne on the rolls of such a mushroom society. For the same reason I now decline the Hony. Doctorships . . . being showered by the Indian universities."[60] Or consider these lines that Sarkar wrote to Sardesai in 1949, when Professor Tarachand from the University of Allahabad approached Sarkar inviting him to edit a multivolume series on Indian history:

> I know that a debating club—esp. one composed of educated Indians—cannot bring any work to completion. In case Allahabad agrees to have me, they must endow me with full powers, exactly as . . . Cambridge University did to Sir W. Haig [for the *Cambridge History of India* volumes on the Muslim period]. . . . If I have to correct and rewrite the rubbish which our Indian professors of history write—as I found to my bitter experience when editing the second volume of Dacca University's *History of Bengal*—I must be paid an extra fee for this *dhobi* [laundry; lit., washerman] work."[61]

The reference to Cambridge University points to a Europe that Sarkar idealized as the home of scholarship. Sarkar had never personally been to Europe. Nor was he much in conversation with European scholars, except for retired colonial administrators from India who were associated, in a scholarly

59. NL, JSP, letter no. 269, Sarkar to Sardesai, Darjiling, 19 July 1933.

60. NL, JSP, letter no. 1116, from Sarkar, Calcutta, 15 November 1952.

61. NL, JSP, letter no. 989, Sarkar to Sardesai, Calcutta, 5 January 1949. The late forties saw some significant demand for histories written by Indians from an "Indian" point of view. K. M. Munshi, who later edited a series of nationalist volumes on Indian history, wrote to Sardesai in November 1943, saying, "I am most anxious that the world is presented with a history of India written by Indians at the end of the war." Munshi's letter attached to NL, JSP, Sardesai to Sarkar, Kamshet, 19 November 1943.

capacity, with the Royal Asiatic Society and other similar institutions in Britain (see chapter 1 above). Sarkar's mentors, as we have seen, were the scholars that the Raj produced from within the ranks of its colonial administrators. Yet an imaginary Europe worked for him as a constant reference to the ultimate and universal measure of scholarly standards. And because he believed reason was by its very nature universal to humans, even if the Europeans had been the first to deploy it in the writing of history, he did not see his own position as a demeaning one. He was a proud and private man. He would not have voiced this respect for Europe in his letters to Sardesai if such opinions had hurt his sense of self-respect. For reasons of space, only a very few examples will have to suffice. For instance, in 1931, when Sarkar drafted a foreword to the *Selections from Peshwa Daftar* that Sardesai had edited, Sardesai did not like the draft: "Your mention of Khare, Parasnis, Gulgule Daftar and . . . your omission of Rajwade . . . will again give rise to dying embers now happily subsiding." He went on to ask, without irony, "Probably you mean this Foreword for European readers outside India."[62] The earnest tone of Sarkar's reply shows how indifferent he perhaps was to regional pride and how seriously he took his assumption about the intellectual superiority of Europe. "Literary grace," he wrote, "is the *sine qua non* for my Foreword, as for an essay in the *Edinburgh Review* . . . . Rajwade's letters may be mentioned with praise in my Foreword by adding a line. . . . But I do not consider any further change desirable to placate the howling mob of Puna. My Foreword is intended for readers in Europe, where they require such a comprehensible readable survey and not an official report."[63]

Or take this instance from 1932. Sardesai suggested to Sarkar that he should apply for the position of editor of the Poona Residency records, even when the commissioner of the Central Division wanted an English person (such as Professor H. G. Rawlinson, the retired principal of Ferguson College in Poona) for the job and was actively contemplating appointing a local English woman simply because the documents were in English. Sarkar did not immediately want to jump into the fray. He was, by then, a well-known scholar who had been the vice chancellor of Calcutta University. He was not a young person, at age fifty-two. And yet he wanted to wait and prove himself to the English, who remained for him, as it were, in the position of teachers. He wrote back to Sardesai defending the commissioner:

> You see he is justified in holding that this . . . cannot done by your staff, as it requires a special and deep knowledge of the English diplomatic history of

62. NL, JSP, letter no. 166, Sardesai to Sarkar, Kamshet, 31 September 1931.

63. NL, JSP, letter no. 168, Sarkar to Sardesai, Darjiling, 14 October 1931.

> the 18th century. . . . If I can after a week's work convince Rawlinson by *actual* demonstration . . . that a scholar of the highest university distinction and experience of history in *European* languages can do the work not a whit worse—probably better (by reason of my historical information, in which the lady lacks)—than any English man or woman, that will be the stage at which I can require the work to be entrusted to me. I don't care to court a rebuff . . . [now].[64]

Paradoxically, Sarkar's desire to prove himself to European scholars or by European standards of scholarship was self-respecting and pathetic at the same time. It spoke of the predicament of the colonial Indian scholar. He hated the idea of being an Indian scholar for whom a European scholar could make excuses by saying, "Oh, how truly Oriental!" In a letter he wrote to Rabindranath Tagore in 1922, declining the latter's invitation to serve on the governing body of Tagore's new university at Shantiniketan in Bengal, Sarkar referred to a character, a European wanderer, in a Kipling story. This man, on coming to India, exclaims at the sight of an *ekka* car (a carriage driven by only one horse), "Oh, how thruly Orienthal!" This was always Sarkar's fear, that his work might not be judged by the standards of "civilized societies of the world" and might be instead measured by some special standard used for evaluating the work of "the black people" (*kala admi*) and thus be pronounced "How thruly Orienthal!"[65]

An idealized Europe was also an imaginary refuge from the conflicts of the present. This shows clearly in what Sarkar wrote to comfort Sardesai when the latter's edition of documents selected from the Peshwa Daftar came in for criticism from Poona scholars, some of it probably prompted by personal rivalries over access to historical sources. "My dear Nana," wrote Sarkar:

> In Europe, your work as editor of the Peshwa's Dafter records would have been promptly recognized by your own university and every university where Maratha history is taught by conferring on you the honorary degree of D. Litt. In England, Mr Loeb, a mere rich man probably innocent of the classics, was created a Doctor by the Cambridge University because he financed the issue of a new edition of the Greek and Latin classics. True scholars are there honored even more surely and quickly. But here, half the Senate (and Board of History) are blissfully ignorant of the present state of research . . . , and the other half are consumed by jealousy of your achievements. This has been my experience [he continued], but I don't care, as I have secured recognition in Europe in no

64. NL, JSP, letter no. 240, Sarkar to Sardesai, Darjiling, 28 November 1932.

65. Sarkar to Rabindranath Tagore, dated Darjiling, 31 May 1922, reproduced in Bikash Chakravarti, *Byahata sakhya: Rabindranath o Jadunath Sarkar* [Friendship interrupted: Rabindranth and Jadunath Sarkar] (Calcutta: Visva-Bharati, 2011), appendix, pp. 11–12.

> small measure. Here, on the other hand, one man takes the opportunity of his visit to any provincial University as an external examiner, to whisper what he represents as mistakes in my work—and his professor audience, ignorant of Portuguese and Marathi sources (at least, of that particular history) swallow his lies without questions. But as you see, I survive these tactics.[66]

In subsequent letters, too, Sarkar kept emphasizing the importance in India of good reviews in English newspapers and magazines: "Take with you the cutting from the *Times Literary Supplement* giving high praise to the *Selections*, which I had sent you in 1931, when you visit Mr. Chandrachud" [the vice chancellor of the University of Bombay]. . . . When these English papers reach India they will produce a good impression."[67] Or the following, a month later: "Our position will be immensely strengthened when appreciative notices of your work appear in England—as in the *Times* in 1931 (you remember). I am expecting these notices to reach India in the middle of July if not earlier. That will put your university to shame."[68]

Sarkar's letters actually suggest that it was the colonial bureaucracy—and not an abstract "universal Europe"—that was the key to his success with the colonial officialdom: "Governments and Vice-Chancellors have sought and accepted my recommendations in selecting men for high History professorships."[69] It was the European administrator-scholars *in India*, such as Henry Beveridge and William Irvine, scholars of Mughal India, who were his real patrons. In an earlier letter, he had in fact advised Sardesai to send a set of the volumes of the Peshwa Daftar to one of these former administrator-scholars, Sir Edward Gait, who had gone back to England on retirement. His advice itself spoke of a peculiar ethnographic sensibility possible only in a colonial relationship, of which Sarkar himself may not have been aware: "Mr. Hudson will soon issue orders for sending out one set of your selections to Sir Edward Gait in London. Please see that only the soon-to-be-issued *bound* volumes are sent and *not loose parts*, as Englishmen (unlike Frenchmen and [the] Portuguese) care to handle only bound books and dislike brochures in paper cover."[70] It was these colonial administrator-scholars who both practiced an exclusivism—after all, they managed the 1920s *Cambridge History of India* project without asking many Indian scholars to contribute—and played mentor to scholars such as Sarkar.

66. NL, JSP, letter no. 306, Sarkar to Sardesai, Darjiling, 1 May 1934.
67. NL, JSP, letter no. 309, Sarkar to Sardesai, Darjiling, 19 May 1934.
68. NL, JSP, letter no. 314, Sarkar to Sardesai, Darjiling, 19 June 1934.
69. NL, JSP, letter no. 306, Sarkar to Sardesai, Darjiling, 1 May 1934.
70. NL, JSP, letter no. 159, Sarkar to Sardesai, Darjiling, 1 July 1931.

The Imagination of Scholarly Europe

The Europe of Sarkar's imagination was also an entity particularly inflected by Germany's reputation in the nineteenth century as the home of modern historical scholarship. Research was seen as something German historians—Sarkar referred to Ranke throughout his life—had invented, though toward the end of his life Sarkar sometimes called German approaches rather "dry," a description he well may have picked up from criticisms of German scholars in the English press.[71] The way he viewed his own library is reminiscent of the private research libraries once valued by German scholars.[72] Many younger scholars working on the Mughal period used his library, and sometimes he would put them up at his own expense.[73] He wrote to Sardesai in 1932: "A library—with works in six or seven languages—like mine is indispensably necessary for the purpose [of constructing chronology] and your whole Bombay Presidency does not contain a single full or even decent library of Indian history like mine."[74] The pleasure he took in caring for his library may be surmised from the meticulousness with which he got manuscripts bound for the library of his student Raghubir Singh: "I have ordered the *duftary* [binder] to use good English leather (Morocco) green or brown (not black), because this leather never emits a bad smell nor cracks under heat (as Indian leather does). The charge will be necessarily 75 per cent higher than if Indian tanned leather had been used, but the volumes will form a line of beauty and joy on the shelf."[75]

Replying to addresses presented to him on his eighty-first birthday, Sarkar once again emphasized the importance of research libraries: "We must build

71. It is possible, of course, that Sarkar's appreciation of the importance of German historical scholarship owed itself to the writings of colonial administrator-scholars. His informal mentor, William Irvine, praised "the Teutonic genius for research" (referring to an eighteenth-century German researcher) in his introduction to his four-volume translation of Manucci's *Storia do Mogor* that was published in the "Indian Texts" series from London around 1906–7. See his "General Introduction" in William Irvine, *Mogul India 1653–1708 or Storia do Mogor by Niccolao Manucci, Venetian*, 4 vols. (reprint, New Delhi: Atlantic, 1989), 1:xlvii. The dates for the original publication are taken from the "Publisher's Note" in the reprint edition.

72. See William Clark's *Academic Charisma and the Origins of the Research University* (Chicago: University of Chicago Press, 2006); and Bonnie G. Smith, *The Gender of History: Men, Women, and Historical Practice* (Cambridge, MA: Harvard University Press, 2000).

73. See, for example, the reminiscences of P. C. Roy Chaudhury and A. L. Srivastava in Gupta, *Life and Letters*, pp. 74–77, 87–93.

74. NL, JSP, letter no. 221, Sarkar to Sardesai, Darjiling, 22 July 1932.

75. Sarkar to Raghubir Singh, Calcutta, 11 February 1937, in Tikekar, *Making of a Princely Historian*, p. 40.

up full and varied research libraries." His example was the University of Syracuse, which had "purchased and brought away from Berlin the entire library of the famous Prussian historian Leopold von Ranke." He also underlined the importance of research languages: "For my history of Shivaji, I had to study the original sources by learning Persian and Marathi and a little Portuguese, besides English, Sanskrit, French and a little of Rajasthani Hindi."[76] When V. Dighe, once Sardesai's research assistant and later a records officer at the Bombay Secretariat, requested a few lines from Sarkar by way of endorsement for Sardesai's *New History of the Marathas*, this is what Sarkar wrote: "In addition to indefatigable industry and intellectual alertness characteristic of German scholarship, he has cultivated the German habit of methodological arrangement, docketing and indexing every scrap of information or thought, and drawing up chronological lists and genealogical tables with meticulous accuracy and detail. . . . But his German thoroughness has not weighed his writings down with German heaviness of style."[77]

Sarkar's Rankeanism, the seeds of which lay in a nineteenth-century understanding of—and a sense of loyalty to—the British Empire, interests me here for its untimeliness in twentieth-century India, when mass nationalism became the mainstay of politics in the subcontinent. In other words, what made it untimely was precisely the rise of anticolonial mass movements. It is well known that, from time to time, many illustrious Indians who grew up in the nineteenth century, from Gandhi to Nirad Chaudhuri, declared themselves proud subjects of the British Empire. As Rome did in the view of Ranke or Neibuhr or Gibbon, the British Empire signaled to them the political possibility of realization of some universal principles, a state that stood above all particular conflicts in society and upheld ideals that were good for all, ideals they thought the future Indian nation should make its own. The great Indologist Sir R. G. Bhandarkar (1837–1925), for example—older than Sarkar by a few decades—pronounced it "an act of Divine Providence that the English alone of all the candidates who appeared about the same time for the empire of India should have succeeded."[78] Like Sarkar, Bhandarkar connected the very issue of "critical methods" in Indology to the question of learning from European scholars. "It is no use ignoring the fact that Europe is far ahead of

76. Jadunath Sarkar, "The Progress of Historical Research in India," *Modern Review* (January 1951), pp. 35–36. For Sarkar's own history of his library—not quite a Benjaminian exercise but telling for what it reveals—see his fascinating essay "A Chapter in My Life: How My Library Grew Up," *Modern Review* (January 1958), pp. 21–23.

77. NL, JSP, from file titled "Jadunath Sarkar: Misc. Papers," letter from V. G. Dighe, record officer, Secretariat, B'Bay, 29 September 1948.

78. A. D. Pusalkar, "R. G. Bhandarkar," in Sen, *Historians*, p. 42.

us in all that constitutes civilization. And knowledge is one of the elements of civilization," he declared in 1888 in a lecture entitled, significantly, "The Critical, Comparative, and Historical Method of Inquiry."[79] Bhandarkar has often been described as an early Rankean in India and compared to Sarkar: "Sir Ramakrishna Bhandarkar was the father of scientific historical scholarship in the ancient period of Indian history as Sir Jadunath Sarkar was in [the] medieval and early British period. . . . He could have easily passed muster as a historian in the view of Ranke."[80]

Much like Sarkar, Bhandarkar did not like the identity politics of nationalism insofar as it impinged on questions of knowledge. And, like Sarkar again, he was a patriot and not an anticolonial nationalist. Bhandarkar held that the "true patriot" considered it his duty to "fearlessly expose" the faults in "the character of his people" and criticized the nationalists of "Bengal and our part of the country" for their "false race-pride."[81] The difference was that Bhandarkar died in 1925, just as nationalism was beginning to assume a mass form. Sarkar, a younger person, lived on until 1958, preaching and practicing his untimely faith in the ideals of the empire when younger historians—and the question of Indian history itself—were caught up in the vortex of anti-imperial nationalism. Sarkar (and, to some degree, his friend Sardesai) never had any sympathy for the street politics of *satyagraha* or for other forms of agitation such as the strike that, in combination with limited franchise, became the language of mass politics in the India of the 1930s and 1940s. As official funds for their project of bringing out selections of *Marathi* documents seemed to run dry around 1930, Sardesai complained to Sarkar about the British commissioner in Poona: "He is altogether pre-occupied with Civil-Disobedience-wallas [lit., peddlers] and has no room in his brain for anything else."[82] Sarkar's reply was clearly sympathetic to the government. Referring to a confidential letter he had received from the land revenue member of the Bombay government, he said: "I cannot blame the government. It has been compelled to make cuts blindly, because our educated and well-to-do

79. R. G. Bhandarkar, "The Critical, Comparative, and Historical Method of Inquiry, as Applied to Sanskrit Scholarship and Philology and Indian Archaeology," in *Collected Works of Sir R. G. Bhandarkar*, ed. Bapuji Utgikar and Vasudev Gopal Paranjpe (Poona: Bhandarkar Oriental Research Institute, 1933), p. 390.

80. Pusalkar, "R. G. Bhandarkar," pp. 44–45; R. N. Dandekar, "Ramkrishna Gopal Bhandarkar and the Academic Renaissance in Maharshtra," in *Writers, Editors, and Reformers: Social and Political Transformations in Maharashtra, 1830–1930*, ed. N. K. Wagle (Delhi: Manohar, 1999), p. 138.

81. Pusalkar, "R. G. Bhandarkar," p. 45.

82. NL, JSP, letter no. 136, Sardesai to Sarkar, Kamshet, 21 September 1930.

countrymen consider it fine sports to encourage reckless and malicious attacks on . . . public servants and the revenue sources, under the holy name of Gandhi. None had the sense or the courage to denounce it." Sarkar also once complained to Nana in 1940, referring to Gandhi in terms that he would never have used in public: "I am sick of this cat and mouse game which the blind Congress is trying to play with Pax Britannica under the 'whip' of a demented Gujarati bania's son, who believes himself *buwa* [original in Nagari] or *avatar* [original in Nagari; incarnation]."[83] "This is the age of democracy and demagogy," Sardesai said in 1934, expressing feelings of frustration and resignation, having failed to move the vice chancellor of the University of Bombay into taking an active interest in his selection of peshwa documents.[84]

The First and Last Research Seminar

Whatever the age was, and however Sarkar and Sardesai understood it—of "democracy and demagogy" or something else—there was no question that they found themselves on the wrong side of it. I want to close this chapter by describing the defeat of the idea of a German-type research seminar that the duo wanted to foster and patronize in a direct spirit of challenge to the Indian History Congress, which, as Sardesai and Sarkar saw it, was all talk and no work. This was the first and the last such "research seminar" in history to be held in India before independence (and perhaps even after). One could say that it died very soon after it was born.

The idea arose in May 1929, when Sardesai was busy preparing his selections from the Peshwa Daftar, a good six years before the first History Congress, led by D. V. Potdar and Shafaat Ahmad Khan, met in Poona. The government of Bombay had approved a budget of Rs. 11,000 for Sardesai's researches in the peshwa papers. Sardesai felt the need "to train a few youngsters on this side [western India] in the work of Maratha history." "The Poona workers," he wrote to Sarkar that month, referring to scholars associated with the Poona Mandal, "have vitiated the whole atmosphere so terribly that the results are all froth, sentiment and words. So I have a mind with your help to institute at Kamshet a sort of two-three weeks' holiday course of lessons—say in October next."[85] Sarkar obviously approved of the idea, for we find Sardesai writing on 12 June to say that he was "happy" that Sarkar agreed "with my idea of a summer class." Sardesai was perhaps galvanized in part by the hos-

83. NL, JSP, letter no. 657, Sarkar to Sardesai, Calcutta, 16 November 1940.

84. NL, JSP, letter no. 315, Sardesai to Sarkar, Bombay, 14 August 1934.

85. NL, JSP, letter no. 100, Sardesai to Sarkar, Kamshet, 11 May 1929.

tile reception to his researches among the scholars of the Bharat Itihas Samshodhak Mandal, for he added again that he was "anxious to set an example to these Poona talkers, what work means and how it can be done." He would finalize a program and send "a few typed copies" to various colleges of Bombay and Poona "to secure proper students," and he added: "I have written to Pissurlencar to attend and I am sure Father Heras and Rawlinson and others will visit our place."[86] Sarkar appears to have been slow to respond. Sardesai wrote again on 12 July 1929, pressing Sarkar for his reactions to the proposed syllabus for the Kamshet school.[87] But Sarkar had just been nominated to the Bengal Legislative Council and pleaded his inability to join Sardesai that year: "This will keep me in Calcutta for a part of August and a good deal of November–December and February–March next. . . . It will now be inconvenient for me to spend three weeks at Kamshet in October next, as I shall have to clear a lot of arrears of work here, especially the rewriting of the 4th volume of Aurangzib. . . . I am grieved to disappoint you."[88]

Nothing came of the idea over the next few years. We find Sardesai returning to it in July 1933 after a conference convened by the government of Bombay to establish a "Maharashtra University" "proved abortive." But "the immediate result" of this move, Sardesai thought, would be "an advance in regional histories, Marathi, Gujarati and Canarese." In that context, he reported that "some leading scholars" had suggested to him that "a practical step might be taken" by him and Sarkar "by showing the way in historical research in a scientific spirit." He had had consultations at Satara and Poona on the subject and "the outcome of it [was] a proposal for starting a vacation course of lectures in historical research, preferably at Satara—during the Puja or Christmas vacation." "You may remember," he reminded Sarkar, "that I made such a proposal to you four years ago for a vacation course of a week or two in intensive study at Kamshet."[89] Sarkar replied that he could come to Poona in December. He said, "I am prepared to spend a week or ten days at Satara, helping you to hold a vacation class, if you can get a number of really competent and earnest students." But nothing happened this time either, for we read of a proposed "vacation course in historical research at Satara" in winter that year falling through, perhaps because of Sarkar's inability to attend.[90]

It seems highly likely that it was the establishment of the rival Indian His-

86. NL, JSP, letter no. 101, Sardesai to Sarkar, Poona, 12 June 1929.

87. NL, JSP, letter no. 103, Sardesai to Sarkar, Poona, 12 July 1929.

88. NL, JSP, letter no. 104, Sarkar to Sardesai, Darjiling 19 July 1929.

89. NL, JSP, letter no. 267, Sardesai to Sarkar, Kamshet, 12 July 1933.

90. NL, JSP, letters nos. 282 and 285, Sardesai to Sarkar, Kamshet, 23 October; and Sarkar to Sardesai, Darjiling, 3 November 1933.

tory Congress in 1935—something Sarkar saw as a wrong-headed effort in organizing historical research in India—that made him and Sardesai come back to the idea of holding a model research seminar in order to guide and train young scholars in "real" research. By April 1938, Sarkar had drawn up a plan for a proposed autumn school in Kamshet. He wrote to Sardesai: "I feel that much is to be gained by sending a *detailed* programme like the one enclosed for printing—though the Allahabad group [a reference to Shafaat Ahmad Khan, who presided over the first History Congress, and his colleagues] will probably steal its best items after reading it. . . . The thing we have undertaken is so novel and so unlike what History Congress, Orientalist Conferences and the like have meant hitherto to the public, that I have been at pains to amplify my sketch."[91] The sense of rivalry is very clearly suggested by a letter to Sarkar from S. R. Tikekar, a young scholar who assisted Sardesai and Sarkar, written in May 1938: "Prof D V Potdar has made a vague announcement re. Allahabad History Congress. . . . He says it will be held sometime about Dussera—at the same time as ours. I had therefore to steal a march over him and through the press agencies, I have announced the date of the conference." Tikekar strongly felt that the "detailed programme [would] . . . have to be issued to the press" to forestall Potdar and company.[92]

Sarkar prepared the draft for a press release that he mailed to Sardesai on 25 May 1938. Young researchers in history were invited to meet for a week at Kamshet, "a Railway station and Post Office, only ten miles east of Lonavla and 29 miles west of Poona." The proposed dates for the meeting were 2–8 October 1938. Board and lodging would be free. "The week will be spent in conversations, lectures, and informal discussions . . . [and] the last three days will be given to a special study of Maratha historiography, the course of its recent advances, its present problems and the location of materials for its further advancement, &c." "Ways and means" would be explored for the purpose of "creating a permanent school of Maratha history at the Deccan College, Poona, which the Government of Bombay [had] recently decided to develop into a research institute."[93]

But there was a problem from the very beginning. The rival Indian History Congress in the meanwhile had already announced the dates of their next meeting to be held in Allahabad: 6–8 October 1938. There was thus a clash of

91. NL, JSP, letter no. 529, Sarkar to Sardesai, Darjiling, 7 April 1938. Sardesai shared Sarkar's fears: "I share your fears that the . . . workers of the Allahabad show will steal our items. However, I strictly believe it is *men* that execute a programme." Letter no. 531, from Sardesai, Kamshet, 13 August 1938.

92. NL, JSP, "Miscellaneous File," NLC, S. R. Tikekar to Sarkar, Bombay, 27 May 1938.

93. NL, JSP, "Miscellaneous File," NLC, draft by Sarkar, dated Darjiling, 25 May 1938.

schedules, for some of the potential attendees at the Kamshet seminar wanted to attend the Allahabad Congress as well. Not good news, from Sarkar's point of view. He wrote to Sardesai, suggesting some flexibility: "Shafaat Ahmad's show will run from the 6th to the 8th October next, so that the few guests at Kamshet who wish to join both the functions can stay on to the afternoon of the 4th or even the 5th of that month."[94] Sardesai's response was colored by a combination of resignation and bravura. Acknowledging, "Several gentlemen have signified their intention to spending a few days here and [then] proceed to Allahabad," he nevertheless claimed to be "happy" about this development, "so people will easily realize what is solid and what is hollow trash." For, as he put it, "Our object is essentially different from that of Allahabad. Paper reading, speech-making and other advertising items are their mainstay, while we here will have quiet heart-to-heart talks, consultations and deliberations, throughout night and day, as we sit together and devote practically all our time to the subject. We will handle a few subjects, not ambitious spectacular plans for the world at large but practical items for those who wish to sit down and *start work at once*."[95]

But Tikekar soon began to negotiate with Shafaat Ahmad Khan to ensure that there would not be an absolute clash of dates between the two meetings. Sardesai was clearly aware of this, for it was he who reported this fact to Sarkar.[96] A compromise was worked out in order to allow scholars to attend both the Kamshet meet and the Congress; the Congress changed its schedule and eventually met over 8–10 October 1938, and the Kamshet program was curtailed to end on the sixth.[97] An angry and somewhat defeated Sarkar wrote to Sardesai on 6 August: "I have just wired to Tikekar to close the Kamshet lectures on sixth October. This will allow the bigwigs to go away by the afternoon of that day. But let there be no false hope on the part of Allahabad people that as a price for their concession I shall attend their function. I will *not*, and as I see from your letter of the 3rd, you will also stay at Kamshet to reorganise the more important work with local scholars. My lantern lectures (in Marathi, with your previous corrections) will fall on the 6th—8th."[98]

Thirty-two scholars from different parts of India met in Kamshet on 2–6 October 1938 for this first (and, alas, the last as well) "research seminar" in history. A report of the meeting was published with a list of the names of the

94. NL, JSP, letter no. 524, Sarkar to Sardesai, Darjiling, 12 July 1938.

95. NL, JSP, letter no. 526, Sardesai to Sarkar, Kamshet, 31 July 1938.

96. NL, JSP, letter no. 527, Sardesai to Sarkar, Kamshet, 3 August 1938.

97. See *Proceedings of the Indian History Congress, Second Session, Allahabad, October 8, 9, 10* (Allahabad: Indian History Congress, n.d.).

98. NL, JSP, letter no. 528, Sarkar to Sardesai, Darjiling, 6 August 1938.

individuals who attended. The report carries the name of S. R. Tikekar (and mentions his association with the Prarthana Samaj) on its cover, but it was Sarkar who drafted the report and got it printed from Calcutta.[99] The report begins by distinguishing this meeting from "Conferences and Congresses on History" that were "too formal" and that "devote[d] too much of their time to delivery of conventional addresses and the reading of long papers which are most likely to be effective if read at leisure than when heard from a platform." This was a meeting where the "visiting scholars lived together as one family without any formality or stiffness." "Sir Jadunath Sarkar who occupied the *guddee* (—no chair being allowed), started every meeting with a sketch of the work of the day and the[n] guided discussions throughout by constantly keeping the points at issue before the members."[100]

The subjects discussed at the Kamshet meeting included "the existing materials bearing upon Indian history in different languages, their classes and relative value and their location both in Europe and India, the means of obtaining transcripts from different European libraries, the range and special character of the more important libraries in India (especially private collections) and the degree of facility that each of them offered to students," and so on. Attendees also discussed the "urgent need" to create "a central Bureau or intellectual Exchange-house for the furtherance of Indian historical studies."[101] In addition, expert scholars spoke of sources in different languages—Sarkar on sources in Persian, Raghubir Singh on microfilms and "Persian news letters" ("hitherto . . . collected and used by Sir Jadunath Sarkar only"), Chevalier Pandurang S. Pissurlencar ("Knight of St. Jago, Member of the Academy, Lisbon, and Archivist to the Government of Goa") on sources in Portuguese, Dr. B. A. Saltore on sources in Kanarese, Dr. M. H. Krishna (of "Mysore Museum and University") on the Vijaynagar Empire,

99. S. R. Tikekar, *Report of the Meeting of Workers in Indian History at Kamshet (Poona District), 2nd–6th October 1938* (Bombay: S. R. Tikekar, Prarthana Samaj, n.d. [1939?]). The logo of "Shree Raghubir Library" on the inside cover suggests that Dr. Raghubir Singh, the prince of Malwa and an attendee at Kamshet, may have contributed toward the costs of printing. I owe this source to the generosity of my friend Gautam Bhadra. The final draft of the report was Sir Jadunath's—see NL, JSP, letter no. 536, Sarkar to Sardesai, Calcutta, 24 October 1938: "I shall soon take in hand a regular report of the Kamshet History meet for printing" [based on Tikekar's drafts of daily reports]. Letter no. 652, Sarkar to Sardesai, Calcutta, 4 Nov. 1938: "I have received from Tikekar the draft reports of our Kamshet week in my own hand, and shall revise and rearrange them after four days. Much time will be saved by printing the report in Calcutta. I am the author." NL, JSP, letter no. 547, from Sarkar to Sardesai, Calcutta, 1 December 1938, informs that the report—"completely drafted by me"—was sent to the press on this day.

100. Tikekar, *Report*, pp. 1, 4.

101. Ibid., pp. 4–5.

FIGURE 2. From left, Sarkar, Sardesai, and other scholars at the Kamshet seminar in 1938. Photographer unknown. Courtesy of the Archives, Centre for Studies in Social Sciences, Calcutta. Used with permission.

Rao Bahadur S. G. Sardesai on Marathi sources, Professor Darbar Singh Sodhi (of Khalsa College, Bombay) on Sikh history, and Dr. Moti Chand (curator of the Prince of Wales Museum, Bombay) on "Art and Craft." Sarkar also "explained the supreme importance of large-scale maps to the worker on Indian history."[102]

The enthusiasm so warmly reported by Sarkar in his account of the meeting was, unfortunately, short-lived. But the Indian History Congress thrived and went on to become *the* professional association of academic historians in India. The Kamshet seminar had pledged to subsidize the printing of Ashirbadilal Srivastava's and Hari Ram Gupta's doctoral dissertations. But the funds committed by 30 March 1939 were as follows: "Sarkar [Rupees] 200, Kumar 200, Sardesai 50, Jadhav 25, Dr. Motichand 25, and Tambe Rs 10."[103] Sardesai reported the next month: "Mr. Jadhav informs he cannot pay the amount he so enthusiastically promised. . . . We have no funds."[104] There were not even enough takers for the report that Sarkar had prepared under Tikekar's name. We find Sardesai asking him in 1940: "Kindly let me know what may be done

102. Ibid., pp. 5–17.

103. NL, JSP, letter no. 563, Sarkar to Sardesai, Calcutta, 30 March 1939.

104. NL, JSP, letter no. 564, Sardesai to Sarkar, Kamshet 24 April 1939.

FIGURE 3. Sarkar (center, writing) Sardesai (to Sarkar's left), and other scholars at the Kamshet seminar, 1938. Photographer unknown. Courtesy of the Archives, Centre for Studies in Social Sciences, Calcutta. Used with permission.

with the 300 odd copies of [the] Report of K[a]mshet meet. Can some publisher at Calcutta buy or distribute them gratis?"[105] The last we hear of such meetings is about ten years later, in a letter from Sarkar to Sardesai in 1951: "Profs. Ashirbadilal, N. B. Roy and others here have expressed their willingness to attend your History Meet at Kamshet next May."[106] I strongly suspect that this second meeting never took place.

When Jadunath Sarkar's residential house at 10 Lake Terrace, Calcutta 29, was bought by the Indian Council of Social Science Research in the early 1970s to make it into a home for the Centre for Studies in Social Sciences, Calcutta, the new residents found some old photographs that had been left there in a pile of rubbish by Sarkar's descendants. Among them were a few photographs taken at the 1938 Kamshet meeting—they were reproduced in Tikekar's (Sarkar's) report (see figs. 2–4). I made a trip—in company of Rochona Majumdar and Ranu Roychoudhuri, colleagues from the University of Chicago—to Kamshet on 3 October 2012, in search of the house in which Sardesai lived and where this first experiment in holding a research seminar in Indian history had been conducted. Kamshet has grown from a

105. NL, JSP, letter no. 612, Sardesai to Sarkar, Kamshet, 13 March 1940.

106. NL, JSP, letter no. 1063, Sarkar to Sardesai, Calcutta, 14 March 1951.

FIGURE 4. Scholars at the Kamshet seminar, 1938. Photographer unknown. Courtesy of the Archives, Centre for Studies in Social Sciences, Calcutta. Used with permission.

sleepy village to a bustling Indian town today, though it is still administered through a panchayat, indicating its formally rural status. Ugly, multistoried buildings have appeared on congested roads, integrating Kamshet into the history of contemporary India. There are plans afoot to make Kamshet into a paragliding center for tourists. Most people in the place have forgotten about the Sardesais, who, I am sure, were once a well-known family in the neighborhood. No one we spoke to could remember the *Riyasatkar* who played such a prominent role in Marathi historiography. Through sheer serendipity, however, we were called into the impressive and well-appointed office of a wealthy-looking Parsee gentleman, a Mr. Fali J. Pastakiya, who was clearly one of the powerful and important real-estate developers of the area. He asked us what it was that we were looking for, and, on being told about the purpose of our visit, he said he knew and could show us the house. His driver and caretaker (Mr. Raju Chauhan) led us to the building, still in a lush and green part of the village. The house looked locked-up and abandoned, surrounded by sheets of corrugated aluminum and a garden grown wild (see fig. 5). Mr. Chauhan opened up the building for us. Making our way through dirt and cobwebs, we found an old photograph of Sarkar's best friend, Nana (see fig. 1, p. 15), by the side of what used to be the latter's bed, and some old correspondence and documents mixed up with some decaying pages of books that no

FIGURE 5. Kamshet House, 2012. Photograph by Ranu Roychoudhuri. Private collection of the author.

longer existed as wholes. We walked on the verandah where the participants in the 1938 seminar met and took photos of the house. For us, as historians, this was like a pilgrimage. Mr. Chauhan found it very puzzling that we should be poring over the very old and dusty papers with such intensity, but he kept saying, with some measure of wistfulness, that he was sure that what we were doing was *nek kaam* (lit., virtuous work). Sardesai and Sarkar would perhaps have agreed with him.

3

Hunters and Gatherers of Historical Documents

The very friendship between Jadunath Sarkar and Govindrao Sardesai stands witness to the growing importance of "sources" among those who thought of themselves as researchers in Indian history at the beginning of the twentieth century. What brought Sarkar and Sardesai together was their respective searches for complementary historical sources—in Marathi and Persian. "Sometime in the year 1904," writes Sardesai,

> a letter in an unknown handwriting indicating vigour and precision with contents severely formal and businesslike, took me by surprise at Baroda. The name of the writer did not solve the mystery as I had not till then heard of him. . . . However, this letter came like a divine windfall. . . . [He] required my help in supplementing with Marathi sources his vast source of Persian materials regarding . . . Aurangzib. And I myself in my scheme of the *Marathi Riyasat* was just then sorely feeling the need of utilizing Persian sources. . . . In short, this letter became the pledge of future co-operation between the Mughal and the Maratha.[1]

In itself, this was a modern development demonstrating how profoundly the practices of an emergent discipline could affect relations between individual scholars. At this time, we do not know of any precolonial historians of, say, Muslim India coming together to be such close and lifelong friends on the basis that, as historians, they had complementary interests in "sources."

That the idea of "scientific" history made "original" documents increasingly valuable to historians of early-twentieth-century India can be seen from small developments. As Rama Mantena and others have shown, the practice

1. G. S. Sardesai, "Jadunath Sarkar as I Know Him," in *Sir Jadunath Sarkar Commemoration Volume*, ed. H. R. Gupta (Hoshiarpur: Department of History, Punjab University, 1958), 1:18.

of collecting documents and inscriptions—and thus the development of an interest in the sheer "facts" of Indian history—go back to early decades of the nineteenth century, when antiquarians like Colin Mackenzie (1754–1821), the first surveyor general of India, collected large amounts of artefacts and paintings relating to India's past.[2] Toward the end of the nineteenth century, Indian scholars themselves got involved in the practice of such collections as the craze for "scientific history" spread among them, emphasizing the importance of "original" sources in reconstructions of the past. The "history enthusiasts" we met in chapter 2 were the pioneers of this movement. Among them, the pride of place must go to Viswanath Kashinath Rajwade, whose unparalleled twenty-two volumes of sources on Maratha history still awaits comprehensive analysis by a modern scholar.

By the time we come to the Great War and the years immediately after, the importance of "original sources" seems clearly established in Indian historical circles. Thus, a 1915 advertisement for the first two volumes of Sarkar's *History of Aurangzib* said: "Based entirely on Original Persian Sources—MSS. & Works which were altogether unknown to previous writers. . . . [They] represent the first attempt to write a critical and Scientific History of India during Aurangzeb's long reign." And publicity for his *Anecdotes of Aurangzeb* stated that these anecdotes had been "translated from Persian MSS. of a work not yet used by any historian."[3] Ishwari Prasad's D.Litt. dissertation from the University of Allahabad, for example, was published in 1936 with the expression "original sources" emphasized both in the preface—"I have primarily relied upon original sources"—and in the title itself: *A History of the Qaraunah Turks in India (Based on Original Sources)*.[4] When Shafaat Ahmad Khan succeeded Rushbrook Williams as the professor and head of the newly formed Department of Modern History at the University of Allahabad in 1920, after having obtained a D.Litt. from the University of Dublin, he established the first research journal devoted to Indian history, *Journal of Indian History*, which made its debut in 1921. All his life Khan understood the "essential task" of the "scientific" historian to be the "collection of material and [its] vigorous examination."[5]

2. Rama Mantena, *The Origins of Modern Historiography in India: Antiquarianism and Philology* (New York: Palgrave Macmillan, 2012).

3. Advertisement in *Modern Review*, January 1915.

4. Ishwari Prasad, *A History of the Qaraunah Turks in India (Based on Original Sources)* (Allahabad: Indian Press, 1936), pp. v–vi. Prasad also thanked *Cambridge History* authors—Dennison Ross, Wolseley Haig, and Rushbrook Williams.

5. Shafaat Ahmad Khan cited in M. M. Rahman, *Encyclopedia of Historiography* (Delhi: Anmol Publications, 2004), 315–316. The biographical details about Khan are also taken from this book.

The first few issues of the journal contained regular reports on searches for historical manuscripts carried out by Khan himself and by some of his colleagues, such as Pandit Ram Prasad Tripathi, Professor Beni Prasad, and Gurti Venkat Rao. In introducing these reports, Khan commented on the plight of the researcher in India: "His main difficulties are not lessened by the confused and disorganised condition in which many of the most precious of our national collections are kept. . . . He must wend his way circumspectly, if he is not to rouse the suspicions of the moody custodians, and indifferent owners, of historical documents." He returned to the same theme in his presidential address at the first meeting of the Indian History Congress—then called the Modern History Congress—in Poona in 1935, and again in the Srimant Sayaji Rao Lectures he delivered in Baroda in 1938.[6]

Historical Papers in the Public Sphere

But where would historians in colonial India, amateur or professional, go in search of sources? Implied in this historical question is a larger one about the relationship between society and the production of academic history: In what sense would history come to occupy a place in the "public sphere" that European rule created in India? Jürgen Habermas wisely characterized the "public sphere" as a "category" of bourgeois society.[7] It was a "category" of thought, an ideational entity, not to be found anywhere on the ground in a full-fledged form, though it could it be approximated by certain institutions. Not every modern nation in the history of the past two hundred and fifty or so years has felt obliged to mint replicas of the so-called European bourgeoisie, but none, one could argue, has been quite able to escape the reach of the categories and themes of public life forged in bourgeois Europe. The ghost of the "public sphere" haunts us all in many different forms. One such form, globally speaking, is the discipline of history. Born in nineteenth-century Europe as a form of knowledge nestled in and nourished by the university—though, of course, with complex and entangled roots reaching back to distant and diverse pasts—the discipline of history had the utopian ideal of the public sphere

6. Shafaat Ahmad Khan, "Search for Historical Manuscripts in Indian Libraries," *Journal of Indian History* 1, no. 2, serial no. 2 (1922), 345–370; Shafaat Ahmad Khan, "Presidential Address," *Proceedings of the All India Modern History Congress, First Session, Poona* (Poona: Datto Vaman Potdar, 1938), pp. 1–63. See also Sir Shafaat Ahmad Khan, *The History and Historiography of British India* (Allahabad: Kitabistan, 1939), where this speech was more or less reproduced.

7. Jürgen Habermas, *The Structural Transformation of the Public Sphere: An Inquiry into a Category of Bourgeois Society*, trans. Thomas Burger with assistance from Frederick Lawrence (Cambridge, MA: MIT Press, 1989).

written all over it. Take, for example, one of the most elementary rules of evidence in academic history writing: that the documents a historian uses as her or his sources must be verifiable by others. The rule derives from a fundamental principle of debate in the construction of modern "public life" (or, after Habermas, the public sphere): that such debates should be based on equal access to information. Equal access to information is what a modern archive represents to researchers in history. Writing history, ideally speaking, is thus very much the act of the "public man" (I don't gloss "man," for obvious reasons). The discipline of history has the story and the telos of the public sphere built into it. These were indeed the issues that animated the frenetic search for sources that Indian scholars carried out between, say, 1890 and 1940. Sarkar almost put these thoughts into the mouth of the Marathi scholar—and an inveterate collector of sources—D. B. Parasnis when he wrote an obituary for the latter in 1926: "But how to make his rich store of original sources accessible to the public? How to preserve them from the vicissitudes of a family's private property and give them to the nation? How to house them in a building worthy of their importance and proof against destruction by fire or flood? These were his anxious thoughts during the last 12 years of his life."[8] These thoughts were Sarkar's as well. And what were they but a demand for a public archive for the nation's past?

The practice of equal access to historical information requires, as a condition of possibility, a process whereby documents held in private possession or available to a restricted group of people turn into public records. For this to happen, however, there must be in place some abstracting mechanisms that actually abstract—that is to say, remove—documents from the particular relations within which they originate and circulate (family, bureaucracy, religious institutions, etc.). Both the state and the market have historically acted as such abstracting forces. The state, for instance, could pass legislation such as public records acts and thus create official or public archives.[9] Archives mark certain old papers as "historical sources" to be made available to bona fide researchers. But the market itself could also be such an abstracting force. Leopold von Ranke, it is known, used to procure some of his key documents

8. Jadunath Sarkar, "D. B. Parasnis," *Modern Review* (June 1926), p. 654.

9. Following in the trails of Sarkar's thoughts and actions, my use of the word *archive* refers in a restricted sense to official or public archives only. Foucault's enlargement of the meaning of *archive* does not concern me here. For an exploration of *archives* in that larger sense in the South Asian context, see Antoinette M. Burton, ed., *Women Writing House, Home, and History in Late Colonial India* (New York: Oxford University Press, 2003).

in the Venetian marketplace for old documents.[10] Without this developed trade in historical records, historians like Ranke would not have been able to build their private research libraries. (The accompanying development of the institution of the university I will keep for now to one side.)

These two processes of abstraction of documents—that of the state acting as a mechanism that abstracts documents from their points of origin and makes them into the signifiers of an abstract entity called "history," and that of the market performing this function of abstraction—can be further described by two different names (though, clearly, their connotations overlap) as the processes of reification and of commodification of documents. The state reifies papers. It declares some papers to be of "permanent" value to the nation's history and hence to be preserved for posterity. It even designates a place for their preservation. As Derrida says, "Archive is not a living memory. It's a location—that's why the political power of the *archons* is so essential to the definition of the archive. So that you need the exteriority of the place in order to get something archived."[11] One could say that in being a particular place, removed from all the diverse places where archived papers actually originated, the archives embody the reified state of these documents.[12] The market, on the other hand, makes ancient documents and books into commodities, available for purchase and sale. We may thus say that modern ideas about history and historical research impart "value" to old documents and that this "value" finds expression through two different logics, both of them, however, being logics of abstraction: I have called them "reification" (archives) and "commodification" (market) of documents.

Yet it is easy to see that these processes of abstraction represent not only the ideal of the public sphere but also some operation of power. For no society—my concrete examples will come from colonial India—is in reality premised on this principle of equal access to information. Information, that

10. Ugo Tucci, "Ranke and the Venetian Document Market," in *Leopold von Ranke and the Shaping of the Historical Discipline*, ed. Georg G. Iggers and James M. Powell (Syracuse, NY: Syracuse University Press, 1990), pp. 99–108. For a longer history of the process, see Filippo De Vito, *Information and Communication in Venice: Rethinking Early Modern Politics* (Oxford: Oxford University Press, 2007).

11. Jacques Derrida, "Archive Fever in South Africa," in *Refiguring the Archive*, ed. Carolyn Hamilton, Verne Harris, Jane Taylor, Michele Pickover, Graeme Reid, and Razia Saleh (Dordrecht, Netherlands: Kluwer, 2002), p. 42.

12. See the engaging discussion of "state secrets" in Ann Laura Stoler, *Along the Archival Grain: Epistemic Anxieties and Colonial Common Sense* (Princeton, NJ: Princeton University Press, 2009), pp. 25–28.

is, knowledge, is always privileged in any society. It belongs and circulates in the numerous and particularistic networks of power, kinship, community, gendered spaces, aging structures, and so on.[13] If that is true, then the archives and the market, insofar as they appear to operate successfully, hide the conflict-ridden history of the public sphere in the same way as the dance of commodities in the marketplace—I am mixing the languages of Marx and Benjamin here—is supposed to hide the inequalities that go into the production of commodities.

Reification and commodification of documents, one could further argue, are never processes that come to a final conclusion. Even in the most effectively functioning of archives or marketplaces, one might need to have recourse to some relations (friendship, family connections, etc.) outside of the logic of bureaucracy or of the marketplace to gain access to certain documents. In other words, the public sphere—a domain where one could discuss and debate matters of public interest on the basis of unfettered access to information—remains a utopia after all; but because it is a utopian ideal, it retains an ideological function as well. The process whereby we create "unfettered" access to historical information can also be seen as the act of prying open the information that was formerly accessible only to a "privileged" community. This is a tension that is central to the very idea of the public sphere: it can act simultaneously both as a utopia of "bourgeois" equality and as an ideology of domination. It can be simultaneously democratic and undemocratic. The agents and advocates of the public sphere are often the bearers of this tension, for we never find a society in which all its members, inspired by the social value of what we call "history," volunteer to convert willingly all "private" documents into "public" records. It is true that the general social acceptance of an academic subject called history imparts value to old documents, and some democratic and historically minded citizens may indeed feel inspired to make "private" papers "public," but a complete correspondence between an individual and the figure of the citizen is exceedingly rare if not altogether nonexistent. The rendering of private papers into public documents must remain, in the end, a question open to the political and institutional features of a country.

The career of the discipline of history in colonial India is interesting precisely because neither of the two processes mentioned—the state reifying or

13. In this and the preceding paragraph, I draw on some thoughts I have lived with for a long time. See my "Trafficking in Theory and History: *Subaltern Studies*," in *Beyond the Disciplines: The New Humanities*, ed. K. K. Ruthven (Canberra: Australian Academy of the Humanities, 1992), p. 106.

the market turning old papers into historically valued commodities and thus into historical records—was in operation on any significant scale. The colonial government, as we have seen, preserved documents but was extremely reluctant to open them up for public examination, even though writing history in a modern form became a popular activity with educated and nationalist Indians from the 1890s on. The work of the Inam Commission set up in the Bombay Presidency in 1852 by the British to inquire into the status of tax-free lands held under previous regimes is an interesting case in point. Owners of such land complained of the way in which the police and government clerks (*karkun*) carried out raids to seize old documents from their houses, sometimes entering by force. It is not at all clear that such seizure of documents was legal—detailed correspondence between the Inam commissioner and the assistant Inam commissioner and a Maratha landholder in one such case shows the government to be extremely reluctant to own up to such raids.[14] However, the point about documents collected or forcibly acquired by the Bombay government was, of course—as Prachi Deshpande has pointed out—that they were not meant to be accessed by any general body of researchers. In fact, as Deshpande puts it, "the Commission [was] reluctant to allow the regular consultation of old revenue records [even] by other institutions of its own government."[15]

Opening up access to government documents was thus a struggle for Indian historians. A recognizable market for antique books in India also did not develop until some time after independence in 1947. Sarkar often had to find ways of procuring his documents from libraries in Europe to which these documents—through European purchase and collection in India—had found their way. He wrote thus in his fascinating history of his own library: "When I undertook original research, . . . I discarded my Calcutta suppliers and began to give large orders, year after year, to the famous second-hand book sellers of England,—Luzac and Trubner, Francis Edwards and Blackwell. George's Sons of Bristol were my first and most copious agent in England (from 1898 onwards)." Parasnis also "bought in England the entire mass of private letters . . . written to Sir Frederick Currie, the British Resident at La-

14. See the correspondence between one Krishnarao Nilkant of Baroda and the Inam Commission reproduced in Appendix C to Robert Knight, *The Inam Commission Unmasked* (London: Effingham Wilson, 1859), pp. 91–111.

15. Prachi Deshpande, "Scripting the Cultural History of Language: Modi in the Colonial Archive," in *New Cultural Histories of India: Materiality and Practices*, ed. Partha Chatterjee, Tapati Guha-Thakurta, and Bodhisattva Kar (New Delhi: Oxford University Press, 2014), pp. 72, 81. I am grateful to Partha Chatterjee for bringing this essay to my attention.

hore, during . . . the Second Sikh War."[16] The historian Ramesh Chandra Majumdar (1888–1980) explains in his autobiography that as a young researcher at the University of Calcutta in the late 1910s, he could bid successfully on British auctions of antique books only because the current vice chancellor of the university, Sir Ashutosh Mukherjee, waived all time-consuming rules and granted him immediate money and authority to do so. When Majumdar moved to the University of Dhaka in 1921, he found it impossible to acquire antique books from abroad, because the process required obtaining clearance not only from the vice chancellor but also from the Finance Committee and the Executive Council of the university, and doing so left him no time in which to bid. The vice chancellor at Dhaka, a European gentleman, actually pleaded his inability to flout rules quite in the way that Sir Ashutosh had done in the interest of research.[17]

Conceptualizing Archives

Jadunath Sarkar was one of the first Indian historians to conceptualize the very problem of archives in India. In the 1920s and 1930s, except for the years 1931 to 1936, when, for financial reasons, the Indian Historical Records Commission was held in "suspended animation," Sarkar was the intellectual center of the commission and a vital force behind its activities and annual meetings.[18] For him, the Indian Historical Records Commission represented an opportunity: it provided a pedagogical and intellectual platform from which to propagate a particular vision of historical research and argue that public ar-

16. Jadunath Sarkar, "A Chapter of My Life: How My Library Grew Up," *Modern Review* (January 1958), p. 22; Sarkar, "D. B. Parasnis," p. 654. For more on how Sarkar procured documents from England, see his letters to Raghubir Singh in *The Making of a Princely Historian: Letters of Sir Jadunath Sarkar to Dr. Raghubir Singh of Sitamau*, ed. S. R. Tikekar, general editor V. G. Khobrekar (Bombay: Maharashtra State Board for Archives and Archaeology, 1975), pp. 10–11.

17. Ramesh Chandra Majumdar, *Jiboner smritideep* [The memory-lamp of life] (Calcutta: General Printers, 1978), pp. 28–29.

18. The expression "suspended animation" was Sarkar's. He used it in welcoming delegates to the 1937 meeting of the commission: "Today, the . . . Commission meets again after seven years of suspended animation due to the financial difficulties of the Government." *IHRC Proceedings*, vol. 14, *Fourteenth Meeting, Held at Lahore, December 1937* (Delhi: Manager of Publications, GOI, 1938), p. 7. See also the discussion in NAI, IRD, January 1937, Proc. no. 18, note by "S.D.U" dated 10 September 1936: "The meetings of the . . . Commission were held in abeyance in 1931 as a measure of retrenchment. It has not yet been possible to revive them though the question is raised by the K[eeper of] R[ecords] from year to year. Last year efforts were made for their revival but they proved unsuccessful. The question will be taken up again shortly in connection with the budget estimates for 1937–38."

chives were indispensable for the writing of history. (As in the case of Ranke, the history Sarkar wrote was mostly political.) Sarkar was acutely aware that it was the absence of proper archives that hindered the progress of modern historiography in India. In a paper presented at the 1925 session of the commission, he focused on the question of archives as the condition of possibility for writing Mughal-Indian history. "The problem of Indian history in the Mughal period," he wrote, "is to find out the most original sources of information."[19] This Rankean enterprise, he explained, was constantly frustrated by the very peculiar nature of how things were done in the Mughal state. "In pre-British days," he explained, "the records of every department of the Mughal Government or a feudatory state were usually kept in the house of the secretary of that department and not in any Government building or archives. . . . Administrative convenience dictated this practice, as, in the absence of a State archivist or general record-keeper, the secretary to a department was the only 'walking index' to the old records of that department." "The result of this old practice," concluded Sarkar, "was disastrous for history. . . . With the decay of the old families . . . much valuable material of first-rate importance has perished. Masses of old paper have rotted in their houses."[20]

Sarkar's 1933 foreword to the *Selections from the Peshwa Daftar* restated the problem. Criticizing Captain James Grant Duff's use of historical sources that were "not always contemporaneous with the events they describe" in writing his "monumental" *History of the Mahrattas* (1826), Sarkar remarked: "Our age recognizes the supreme value of 'unedited documents' of State papers and other contemporary records, as distinct from literature and later compilations." But there was a problem in India:

> As readers of L. von Ranke know, it was the practice in Europe down to the end of the 18th century for official papers relating to a particular document

19. Jadunath Sarkar, "Historical Records relating to Northern India, 1700–1817," in *IHRC Proceedings*, vol. 7, *Seventh Meeting, Held at Poona, January 1925* (Calcutta: GOI, Central Publishing Branch, 1925), p. 28.

20. Ibid., pp. 30–31. Throughout his life, Sarkar returned to this point. He repeated it in his foreword to *Selections from the Peshwa Daftar* (Bombay: Superintendent, Government Printing and Stationery, 1933), pp. 2–3. He later remarked of Sardesai's exploratory research in Hyderabad in the late 1930s that it had "only proved what I had believed, namely, that the Nizam's archives do not contain any state papers of the pre-Panipat period because all the despatches received and copies of despatches sent out were kept in the houses of the secretaries concerned—exactly like the Peshwa's state papers during Nana Fadnis's regime finding their refuge at Manawali, and not in the Peshwa Daftar at Poona. These Moghlai officers lived in Aurangabad and their houses are now in ruins. So farewell to one of your dreams." NL, JSP, letter no. 454, Sarkar to Sardesai, Darjiling, 18 March 1937.

> to go to the private residence of the head of that department, and usually to remain there permanently. As Ranke writes, "A large part of the State papers accumulated during the administration . . . constituted a part of the family endowments (of these officials). Thus, to a certain extent the private collections of Rome (of which Ranke is here speaking) may be regarded as public ones."[21]

But the government in colonial India did not consider papers held by former ruling families as "public" records, though Sarkar thought that they should. He was to make a great deal of this principle in his struggle to gain access to historical documents.

Unsurprisingly, Sarkar returned to this problem on many occasions in his presentations at the meetings of the Indian Historical Records Commission. In a paper on the Jaipur family and the records in their private holdings that he presented at the twelfth meeting of the commission, held in Gwalior in December 1929, he alluded directly once again to Ranke's experience. "In mediaeval conditions of society, State archives often did not exist, and even when they existed and have survived, they are usually surpassed in the extent and importance of their contents by private family records, as von Ranke pointed out long ago." Sarkar then quoted from Ranke's famous introduction to "his monumental *History of the Popes*": "The freedom of access which I could have wished was by no means accorded to me. . . . A large part of the State-papers . . . constituted a part of the family endowments. Thus, to a certain extent the private collections of Rome may be regarded as the public ones." "Even a transcendent historical genius like Ranke," Sarkar went on to say, "failed to give fullness and finality to his *History of the Popes* because he could not open those closed treasuries of information."[22] What hope would Indian history have without a collective effort to imbibe the Rankean love of primary sources? It was clearly this question that engaged Sarkar's passion. As he said in the very first paper he presented to the commission: "I have come across very few historical letters in Persian for these three [second, third, and fourth] decades of Aurangzeb's reign. . . . The missing materials can be discovered only by the combined search of many men at many places."[23]

Sarkar was thus a man with a mission. As the chair of the meeting of the Records Commission in Patna in 1930, he emphasized that the commis-

21. Sarkar, foreword to *Selections from the Peshwa Daftar*, pp. 1–3.

22. Jadunath Sarkar, "The House of Jaipur," in *IHRC Proceedings*, vol. 12, *Twelfth Meeting, Held at Gwalior, December 1929* (Calcutta: GOI, Central Publications Branch, 1930), p. 18.

23. Sarkar, "The Missing Link in the History of Mughal India from 1658 to 1761," in *IHRC Proceedings*, vol. 2, *Second Meeting, Held at Lahore, January 1920* (Calcutta: Superintendent of Government Printing, 1920), pp. 7, 8.

sion needed to interest the research community and the general public in historical documents, for unless the papers in the possession of "historical families" and private persons were "made known and available to scholars it would be as impossible to write a true and full history of India as it would be to write the history of England without using the papers in the possession of the Cecil and Walsingham, Buckingham and Grenville families." The idea therefore was to "interest the outer public" in the work of the commission and "to tempt private records out of their seclusion by . . . [having] a public session." To the public session was also added the attraction of an exhibition of historical artifacts and documents. As Sarkar put it in the same speech: "The exhibition has been our most helpful auxiliary for this purpose."[24]

The Fetish of Documents

In the absence of public archives, both historians and amateur collectors of historical documents turned to the papers in the possession of old historical families in India, including those held by the princely states. The first volume of the *Journal of Indian History*, for instance, had an article reporting on "Dr. Shafaat Ahmad Khan's Tour," "seven weeks in all, of the 'Records Offices of the Indian States.'"[25] Sir Jadunath spent all his life searching for these documents, often arguing that much could be said about the Mughal court if one could gain access to the newsletters (*akhbarat*) sent to these regional magnates by their representatives or ambassadors in the imperial court in Delhi. As he said in his preface to his posthumously published history of the Jaipur state: "Nowhere else in India can we find even a tenth of the mass of *farmans*, *parwanahs*, reports, newsletters and other historical documents exchanged between the Mughal Government of Delhi and the Court of Jaipur, or between the Rajahs and their officers and allies, with the original brocaded covers (*kharitas*) and even the wax seals intact."[26]

Historians associated with the Poona Mandal—Rajwade, Parasnis, Khare, and others—all scoured the countryside in search of family papers. They collected and published them in their journals and in the journal of Bharat Itihas Samshodhak Mandal (BISM) but their editing and arrangements of these documents were often unsatisfactory. While Khare was generally praised for

24. See speech by Jadunath Sarkar in *IHRC Proceedings*, vol. 13, *Thirteenth Meeting, Held at Patna, December 1930* (Calcutta: GOI, Central Publication Branch, 1932), p. 7.

25. *Journal of Indian History* 1, no. 2, serial no. 2 (1922), pp. 371–372.

26. Jadunath Sarkar, *A History of Jaipur, c. 1503–1938*, rev. and ed. Raghubir Singh (1984; Delhi: Orient Longman, 1994), p. ix.

his collections of primary sources, his own book of history, the history of the Ichalkaranji state in Maharashtra, was a text in which he "forgot his rule as a historian and [wrote] like a poet."[27] D. B. Parasnis's journal, *Itihas Sangraha* [lit., history collections], in which he reprinted old historical documents, ran from 1907 to 1916.[28] Viswanath Kashinath Rajwade, who was the most remarkable collector of historical documents in early-twentieth-century India, published twenty-two volumes of Maratha historical records between 1898 and 1921.[29] Yet, as a modern commentator writes, he only sometimes gave the full details of where his sources came from; at other times he maintained "complete silence." "For instance," he wrote "practically not a word by way of introduction to his volumes 9, 12 and 15 to 22."[30] Of his methods of collecting and preserving documents, Jadunath Sarkar wrote in an obituary: "In his passion to save and publish the country's history, he disregarded the laws of ownership. . . . He carried on his own shoulders the bundles of historical papers he could beg, borrow, or steal (or more correctly wheedle out of ignorant villagers),—and deposited them in secret refuges selected by him."[31] But this cult of secrecy was not Rajwade's alone. There was often an intense sense of rivalry between historians over sources available in the collections of historical families in the different native states generally and in the Maharashtra region in particular. S. R. Tikekar reports that the Poona Mandal was so jealous of guarding its historical findings that "when someone read a paper about it [documents in BISM's collection] in the Mandal, the practice [was] to allow no one to use the contents of the paper till the Mandal [had] published it. . . . Students taking notes when papers were being read . . . were stopped from doing so."[32]

It is similarly striking how often in the letters they wrote to each other, Sarkar and Sardesai would emphasize the need for caution and secrecy to keep others off the scent of old documents.[33] Friends for life, the two historians would travel together to different parts of India in search of sources relating to Maratha and Mughal history of the seventeenth and eighteenth centuries, held by descendants of older princely or administrative families of

27. A. M. Vairat, "Vasudeo Vamanshaṣtri Khare," in *Historians and Historiography in Modern India*, ed. S. P. Sen (Calcutta: Institute of Historical Studies, 1973), p. 218.

28. V. G. Khobrekar, "Dattatray Balwant Parasnis," in ibid., p. 209.

29. G. H. Khare, "Vishwanath Kashinath Rajwade," in ibid., p. 201.

30. Khare, "Rajwade," p. 203.

31. Jadunath Sarkar, "The Historian Rajwade," *Modern Review* (February 1927), p. 184.

32. S. R. Tikekar, *On Historiography: A Study of Methods of Historical Research and Narration of J. N. Sarkar, G. S. Sardesai and P. K. Gode* (Bombay: Popular Prakashan, 1964), p. 39.

33. NL, JSP, letter no. 168, Sarkar to Sardesai, Darjiling, 14 August 1931.

the region. Reading their letters, however, makes it manifestly clear that, contrary to their own Rankean beliefs, Sarkar and Sardesai operated in a society where documents seldom had the character of "public" records. Possessed by families and often in a neglectful state, these documents were caught up in invisible but palpable webs of intrigue, rivalry, and regional or family pride, and lay outside the control of the forces of the market or those of the colonial state. Sarkar and Sardesai's competition with other historians over access to these papers reveals another process—distinct from the processes I named reification and commodification of documents in the opening section of this chapter—one that may be likened to the process of fetishization. These early hunters and collectors of historical papers in India often wanted to corner and hoard such documents for their own exclusive use and restrict, at the least for time being, other scholars' access to them. It was as though the "originality" of these documents, irrespective of how useful they were for historical analysis, was in itself a value. The documents thus took on the aura of fetish objects, so that simply being in possession of them lent the researcher some of the glory of the fetish.

It is thus no wonder that Sarkar and Sardesai had to compete with other historians in their search for old documents. Their rivals, on the other hand, as the following remark shows, would go to any length to make access difficult for the duo. "Our Maval tour of 1930 was preceded by a hostile printed handbill signed by Potdar and one of his tools, only because you had beaten the drum in advance in Puna," Sarkar wrote on 14 August 1931, warning Sardesai before undertaking a tour of Tanjore to search for new Marathi sources. "You talk too freely and too unsuspiciously," he added, "while you are surrounded by men who, when not rogues, are fools and proclaim your plans and words to the Poona circle the very next morning, either out of maliciousness or a simple desire to display their own knowledge of your secrets." So his advice was: "Please keep our tour programme next winter strictly secret, or better still, mislead the Poona rascals by carelessly saying that you would accompany me next December on a tour of Panipat, Delhi and Lahore—i.e. exactly the opposite direction. This time never mention Tanjore to anyone there, or if you have done so, say that I am unable to go and you have abandoned the Tanjore project for a new programme of tour in North West India."[34]

The "Poona rascals" of Sarkar's description were the historians and collectors associated with the Bharat Itihas Samshodhak Mandal. The "Potdar" of the passage quoted was Datto Vaman Potdar, who by 1931 was the secretary of the Mandal. The founding scholars of the Mandal—Rajwade, Parasnis,

34. Ibid.

FIGURE 6. Bharat Itihas Samshodhak Mandal (BISM), Pune, exterior, undated. Photograph by Sujit Patwardhan.

Sane, Khare—people Sarkar wrote essays about in the 1920s, as most of them passed away in that decade—had been engaged in collecting historical documents from old Maratha families. A letter from Sardesai dated 14 April 1927 suggests that the process had rather unsavory beginnings: "It is the extremely hostile attitude of these Poona people which has retarded the progress of history in the university and with Government. They are extremely jealous of other workers and would rather damage all other work in the hope of pushing on their own hobbies" (figs. 6–7). "Whatever the Poona apologists of Rajwade might say," he continued, "the whole method of obtaining papers from private houses is nauseating. Of course, we must remember that all sorts of contrivances have to be used in getting hold of papers. There was a scramble between Parasnis, Bhave, Chandorkar, Rajwade, and Mawji[?] and Poona Mandal for a time. But recently the crase [*sic*] has subsided: people have now begun to understand the value of papers and are themselves coming out with them. But the methods about 10 years ago were altogether reproachable."[35]

Unfortunately, the correspondence between Sardesai and Sarkar does not suggest that Sardesai's optimism was warranted. For Sarkar's struggle to gain access to historical documents was not confined simply to the matter of rivalry with the Poona historians. "The old Maratha families," wrote the histo-

35. NL, JSP, letter no. 64, Sardesai to Sarkar, Girgaum, Bombay, 14 April 1927.

FIGURE 7. Bharat Itihas Samshodhak Mandal (BISM), Rajwade Hall, Pune, undated. Photograph by Sujit Patwardhan.

rian Dharma Bhanu in a tribute to Sarkar, “do not allow any one to peep into their family records, much less help a scholar in reading and copying them.” For this reason, Sarkar sometimes had to go about “in the disguise of an orthodox Brahman in *dhoti* and *chadar* and a *tilak* on his forehead, from place to place and copy out relevant portions.”[36] On occasions, Jadunath would have to approach retired civil servants, such as Sir Edward Gait, in England, who would in turn write to “a British Commissioner” in a native state for the ruler of that state to make copies of the relevant records for the commissioner, who would then send them on to Gait in London, and Gait would forward them to Sir Jadunath.[37] M. V. Kibe of Indore, a relative of Sardesai, reminisced about a trip that Sarkar and Sardesai made to Indore to examine the records of a landlord’s family. Knowing the landlord to be an orthodox Hindu, Sarkar “assumed the garb and appearance of an orthodox Brahman by putting . . . sandal-wood paint mixed with saffron on his forehead.” Yet, writes Kibe, the effort was unsuccessful; the two historians were allowed only “a perfunc-

36. Dharma Bhanu, “Our Historian: Sir Jadunath Sarkar,” *Modern Review* (December 1956), p. 456. Dr. Bhanu taught history at Madhava College in Ujjain. Sarkar wrote a foreword for Dharma Bhanu’s book *History and Administration of the North-Western Provinces (Subsequently Called the Agra Province), 1803–1858* (Agra: Shivalal Agarwal, 1957).

37. Bhanu, “Our Historian,” p. 456.

tory approach to records" after trying "for a few days."[38] Sarkar's experience of working in the archives of the Jaipur state in modern-day Rajasthan was not much different. In a letter written in 1935 to his student Raghubir Singh, Sarkar proudly mentioned the *akhbarats* (dispatches) from Aurangzeb's court that he discovered in Jaipur and "brushed them free of centuries of dust with [his] own hands" and put them into a chronological order; but he also mentioned his unwillingness to return to Jaipur "if the officers thwart and insult me (as they did in 1928) by their suspicious attitude."[39]

Evidence of this culture of secrecy around historical documents is not difficult to come by. When Sarkar wrote to Sardesai on 10 August 1935, saying, "When you next visit Poona . . . please quietly pick out all the letters of General Arthur Wellesley (Lord Wellington) . . . and send them to me," Sardesai made a note on the margin of the letter to remind himself: "Keep this a secret from the A[lienation] O[ffice] [the records office] staff and all others."[40] The theme of the need for secrecy in looking for documents is repeated in several of the letters exchanged between Sarkar and Sardesai. Of the two, Sarkar was the scholar more intent on discovering "original" documents, so it should not surprise us that notes for the need for caution and secrecy often came from him. Thus he wrote to Nana on 21 August 1925: "From Gwalior I shall take you privately to Indore, where you must examine the vast State records in Modi in charge of Bhagwat, and also the Wagh Raje daftar. . . . Your presence at Indore can be kept secret, if you desire."[41] Then again on 1 November 1931: "Please see if you can join me in Bombay, but keep our dates and programme strictly secret from the Poona gang."[42] Or this one in 1934: "It would be matter of good policy to keep *strictly silent* there about the mournful fact that the Imperial Record Office, Calcutta, possesses ten times as much records about Maratha affairs after 1785 as the Residency Records of Poona, and that our volumes when issued will be found to be indebted to Calcutta *thrice* as much as to Poona;—and in the case of Mahadji, it is ten to one."[43] He voiced a similar concern as late as October 1940: "Make your confidential arrangements beforehand for securing access to the records in Bangalore."[44]

38. M. V. Kibe, "Reminiscences," in *Life and Letters of Sir Jadunath Sarkar*, ed. Hari Ram Gupta (Hoshiarpur: Panjab University, 1958), p. 81.

39. Sarkar to Raghubir Singh, Darjiling, 26 June 1935, in Tikekar, *Making of a Princely Historian*, pp. 9–10.

40. NL, JSP, letter no. 364, Sarkar to Sardesai, Darjiling, 10 August 1935.

41. NL, JSP, letter no. 42, Sarkar to Sardesai, Moradpur, P.O., 21 August 1925.

42. NL, JSP, letter no. 172, Sarkar to Sardesai, Darjiling, 1 November 1931.

43. NL, JSP, letter no. 328, Sarkar to Sardesai, Calcutta, December 1934.

44. NL, JSP, letter no. 648, Sarkar to Sardesai, Calcutta, 22 October 1940.

The Parasnis Affair

A substantial amount of the correspondence between Sardesai and Sarkar related to what may be called the Parasnis affair. This again gives us some insights into the politics of the process whereby old papers could or could not be converted into "public" documents for use by researchers in history and the ideas that informed this process. While working on the history of the eighteenth-century Maratha ruler Mahadji Sindhia (c. 1730–1794) of the Gwalior state, Sarkar and Sardesai discovered that many of the relevant documents of the Sindhia family—even today an important political family in India—were in the custody of one of the Poona historians, D. B. Parasnis, an inveterate collector of historical documents, which he published in his journal *Itihas Sangraha*.[45] Parasnis collected a vast amount of primary material from the Sindhia family, but he died in 1926 before he could publish it all. Some of these documents formed the collections of a private historical museum he had created, known as the Satara museum, after the town of Satara, where he lived.[46] Parasnis had been granted a lifelong pension of two hundred rupees a month by the government of Bombay for this task. On his death, both the papers and the pension went to his son Amritrao Dattatreya Parasnis, or A. D. Parasnis, who, as far as I can make out, was not a scholar of history but someone who simply held on to these papers without making arrangements to make them available to other historians.

Sarkar and Sardesai tried for many years to get access to these documents. In 1931 Sarkar even suggested to Sardesai an underhanded means of gaining access to some of these documents: "Why not try to get *secretly* one unbound copy of Parasnis's Gwalior Papers vol. I by paying Rs 25 to some compositor or other servant of the Press where the formats of the book are stored? I shall supply the money."[47] They thought long and hard about how they might put pressure on the young Parasnis, forcing him to release the documents for research. Interestingly, a lot of their attempts turned around legal questions, for example, what might have been the nature of the contract between Parasnis and the Sindhias, and who might be the legal owners of these documents. In itself, this was a new way of thinking about historical records. They failed to resolve this question successfully. But the Sarkar-Sardesai correspondence

45. NAI, IRD, March 1920, Proc. no. 44, shows the Bombay government financing in part the publication of Parasnis's *Itihasa Samgraha*, which did not have a wide readership.

46. See Sarkar's question "Will the Satara museum ever be open to the public?" in NL, JSP letter no. 67, from Sarkar, 18 April 1927, Darjiling.

47. NL, JSP, letter no. 168, Sarkar to Sardesai, Darjiling, 14 August 1931.

shows both the utopian and the pragmatic role that the idea of the law played in their arguments. The letters also offer insights into both their use of the category "public records" and their understanding of the nature of young Mr. Parasnis's attachment to these documents.

For a long time, Sarkar and Sardesai were convinced that it was the prospect of making money that made Amritrao hold on to the Gwalior documents, indicating thereby the existence of a historical process whereby these documents were slowly acquiring monetary value. Sarkar writes in March 1931: "Is young Amrit Rao Parasnis trying to play the game of getting more money out of the Gwalior Darbar as the price of yielding these documents . . . ? If so, he deserves no sympathy."[48] Sardesai also was clear from the beginning that what Amritrao Parasnis was after was money. He would part with the documents only if he could make money out of the transaction. In a letter to Sarkar dated 20 January 1927, he wrote that the young Paranis was prepared to sell the unsold but printed volumes of these documents that his father had prepared: "He is in distressing circumstances and would like to secure as much monetary return for these copies as he can." But Sardesai's letter also raised another question, indispensable in discussions of the public life of historical documents: this was the question of the law, especially laws pertaining to the ownership of historical documents. Sardesai was not sure that, legally speaking, Sarkar and Sardesai could simply buy these papers: "We do not know what Parasnis's arrangement with Gwalior was, i.e. whether he has received full payment for all the 15 volumes that he had promised to print for them: and whether the 90 copies now found [to] have been retained by him [were so retained] with the permission of Gwalior." Otherwise, "all the printed works and perhaps even the mss. papers, now in the Satara museum, will form property of Gwalior."[49]

There were two main prongs to what Sarkar and Sardesai developed as their strategy for—as Sarkar phrased it in a letter of 1932—"put[ting] the screw on young Parasnis."[50] One was to bring him under financial pressure by using their contacts in the government to threaten him with a cut in his pension. The other was to persuade the government about its own, that is, the colonial state's, legitimate ownership of these papers that once belonged to a ruling Maratha family. The second entailed the exposition of a certain kind of political theory on the part of Sarkar—but of that, more later.

Parasnis, noted Sardesai in a letter dated 25 June 1932, owed the Rajah of Sangli "over a lac and a half [Rs. 150,000]." "The Raja is quite irritated with

48. NL, JSP, letter no. 150, Sarkar to Sardesai, Calcutta, 1 March 1931.

49. NL, JSP, letter no. 58, Sardesai to Sarkar, Girgaum, Bombay, 20 January 1927.

50. NL, JSP, letter no. 197, Sarkar to Sardesai, Calcutta, 11 March 1932.

young Parasnis and yet he is too shy to take strong action. . . . Barve asks me to make a case against Parasnis. The originals of all papers printed or unprinted by Parasnis must form the property of the museum. . . . If on the day of the opening ceremony Parasnis had not brought all Daftars into the new building, and did not subsequently send them in, it was a fraud and the allowance the family gets can be made liable for it."[51] He later returned to his point about "a kind of fraud played by Parasnis upon Government. . . . We have to move more carefully and threaten him with a cut in his grant."[52] Sarkar concurred in his reply: "I entirely agree . . . that unless he is threatened by Government with a cut in his perpetual pension, he will not disgorge the illegally detained records. Furnish me with full details so that I may approach the Government on the subject. A personal visit from me to the Hon'ble Revenue Member would have been most effective, but it is impossible for me before December next."[53] Writing a few years later on the subject, he repeated, translating into English a Bengali expression about "straightness" that saw "crookedness" as part of the natural order of things:

> This young man can be made to walk straight only by being put in fear of starvation or when he has some additional favour to expect from Government,—and not by appeals to justice or the interests of history. . . . I strongly suspect that ADP, just before his father's death, removed (1) all the pictures, (2) all the Sanskrit illuminated (costly) mss., (3) all the Persian mss., and (4) the letters of Sir F. Currie, Ellenborough, & c.—which I had seen in DBP's house in 1916, as well as the Menavli daftar. . . . These are not in the museum.
>
> I am convinced that valuable Sindhia papers remain unprinted and in ADP's possession. . . . ADP is mainly trying to enhance his importance—and chance of making more money—by pretending he has several rumals [a piece of cloth used to put documents into a bundle] not covered by the material published in *Itihas Sangraha* [in Nagari] and the 5 Gwalior volumes.[54]

As it became clear, however, that "Gwalior Darbar ha[d] no legal claims to Parasnis's Modi daftar," Sarkar also considered the question of a money suit, though "one shadow," he said, "crosses my mind: will not a money suit be barred by time limitations in 1938?" It turned out that Parasnis senior owed some money to the Gwalior family.

> All the letters written by [the late] D.B.P. to the late Maharaja deeply commit him, by stating his remuneration and printing costs per volume. . . . His

51. NL, JSP, letter no. 215, Sardesai to Sarkar, Alienation Office, Poona, 25 June 1932.

52. NL, JSP, letter no. 218, Sardesai to Sarkar, Kamshet, 16 July 1932.

53. NL, JSP, letter no. 221, Sarkar to Sardesai, Darjiling, 22 July 1932.

54. NL, JSP, letter no. 342, Sarkar to Sardesai, Darjiling, 8 April 1935.

> receipts for Rs. 63,150 are there. These will be copied now and sent to V. S. Bakhle [a lawyer] confidentially for his opinion as to . . . whether the sum of Rs 48,150 not cleared by D.B.P. (whose 5 volumes of his own valuation discharge Rs 5 x 3000 = Rs 15,000 only) can be claimed from DBP's remaining assets, viz., his house Happy Vale and his pictures, and his heirs called upon to pay the amount or bring a lawsuit upon their heads. . . . Thereafter Bakhle will formally serve notice of demand on ADP. This, it is hoped, will bring that young man down on [his] knees. If he appeals for mercy to the Gwalior Darbar, Sir Manubhai has agreed to take all the unprinted Modi papers (Mahadji-Nana correspondence) from him and give him a formal quittance.[55]

When these methods failed to produce the desired results, Sarkar and Sardesai experienced much despair about these seemingly unrecoverable sources that they considered indispensable for writing the eighteenth-century history of the Marathas.[56] They made one last desperate attempt to move the colonial government, by exhorting it to take action to recover the documents from the young Parasnis on the ground that these were documents of a precolonial state and hence belonged to the colonial sovereign power, the state that inherited the rulership of Maharashtra from the eighteenth-century peshwas. Sardesai reported on 27 November 1949 that he had had a talk with a Mr. Lad, "who is the present legal Advisor to the Bombay Government" regarding "the question of recovering historical documents" from Amritrao Parasnis "to which he [Parasnis] has no right." Lad proposed to issue a notice to Amritrao "recounting the fraudulent dealings and [threatening that] unless he would deliver all that he has wrongly withheld, the Bombay government would be compelled to suspend his allowances."[57] He urged Sarkar to draft such a note.

It says something about the commitment of these two men to the process of rendering old papers into historical documents that Sarkar actually composed a note for possible use by the government. The note is remarkable for the theory of political sovereignty that informs it. It is also interesting that Sarkar was prepared to do the government's work for this cause. He drafted a quasi-legal letter, for he said in a short prefatory note to the draft: "It will have to be put in a lawyer-like form. . . . remember that a Government Legal Adviser only makes himself ridiculous if he issues an ultimatum which he cannot substantiate in a law-court." Here is the letter that Sarkar drafted for

55. NL, JSP, letter no. 496, Sarkar to Sardesai, Morar, Gwalior, 26 December 1937, c/o Rai Bahadur Bhaduri, labeled "Confidential."

56. NL, JSP, letter no. 792, Sarkar to Sardesai, Calcutta, 4 March 1944.

57. NL, JSP, letter no. 1022, Sardesai to Sarkar, Kamshet, 27 November 1949.

use by the law department of the government of Bombay—I quote it full because the details of this document would repay examination:

> *To A. D. Parasnis,*
> Happy Vale,
> Satara.
>
> In connection with the perpetual pension of Rs 2400 a year granted by the Government of Bombay to the late Rao B[ahadur]. D. B. Parasnis's heirs, I have to draw your attention to the following points.
>
> Throughout his correspondence with the Government of Bombay, the late Rao B[ahadur]. had always given the assurance that all the historical records collected by him would be kept in one place and made available to scholars in an unbroken mass, and for ensuring this object he had solicited government aid. That aid was given conditionally upon this avowed object being fulfilled. . . . That on the above clear understanding Government built the Satara His[torical] Museum, gave your father in his lifetime money aid to the extent of Rs 12,900, and finally sanctioned the perpetual pension to his heir.
>
> But after his death, you as the representative of his heirs withheld from Government a large portion of historical records, without revealing the fact to Government. This was a direct contravention of the contract made by your father, and an act of fraudulent concealment and misappropriation against Government. The grant is therefore liable to cancellation on grounds of fraud.
>
> You should *know that the historical records of a sovereign state belong to the state (and its successors) even though state papers many have been addressed to some minister of the state (like Nana Phadnis) and stored in his private house* (which was the usual practice in pre-British days in India and also in medieval European countries). *The Government's right to these national records cannot be barred by limitation or adverse possession in the hands of others. The Menavli Daftar and other state papers that you hold in your hands are the lawful property of the Bombay Government alone, and you cannot claim them to be the property of Gwalior darbar or any other party.* Your duty is [to submit] these to inspection and recovery by an accredited agent of the Government of Bombay, and you should take notice that by objecting to or delaying such an investigation you are committing a criminal offence.
>
> For your information, I will tell you that Mr. Elphinstone, the first Governor, on taking possession of the peshwa dominions, found many of the state rec-

> ords in the hands of the old hereditary officers of the peshwa, and all these were removed by him to the control of the Government and housed in the Alienation Office. The records that then escaped and reached your father are equally government property.[58]

There was a remarkable assumption underpinning this letter: that the princely states of India were not sovereign entities at all when it came to their pasts, that their historical records could be claimed for the public sphere of British India, and hence the assumption that the government of Bombay could be persuaded to intervene. Both Sarkar and Sardesai actually knew this to be untrue and wished it were otherwise. Sardesai had said as much in a letter to Sarkar in December 1930: "But I am inclined to press the point of last year's beginning at Gwalior [session of the Historical Records Commission], viz., the immediate federation of British India and States for the purpose of history. . . . The records, whether they belong to the British or to the States, form a national property and no one has any individual claims to them. . . . The Jaipur records are no more Jaipur records than the peshwa records are British property."[59]

None of these strategies of Sarkar and Sardesai actually worked. It is possible that the colonial government, now faced with the growing tempo of the nationalist movement and realizing that independence could not be very far off for India, did not want to stir up matters that concerned only Indians. The secretary of the General Department of the government of Bombay informed Sir Jadunath on 30 November 1934: "The Govt. have carefully examined the question of recovering from the de[s]cendants of late Rao Bahadur Parasnis the historical papers forming the bulk of the volumes composed by Rao Bahadur Parasnis for the Gwalior state. They have been advised that they have no legally valid claim to papers relating to the Scindia family referred to by you, as these were among documents housed in the Historical Museum, Satara, in respect of which an agreement was entered into with the heirs of the late Rao Bahadur Parasnis." Sarkar's proposal for intervention by the government was simply "not practicable."[60] Sarkar's letters to Raghubir Singh show that even as late as 1944 Sarkar was trying to get the Gwalior Durbar to negotiate with Amritrao Parasnis—"I should not go beyond Rs. 1,000," Sarkar said in 1941, revising it down to Rs. 500 in 1944—for the release of documents

58. NL, JSP, letter no. 1023, Sarkar to Sardesai, Calcutta, 4 December 1949, emphasis added.

59. NL, JSP, letter no. 144, Sardesai to Sarkar, Kamshet, 15 December 1930.

60. NL, JSP, Jadunath Sarkar Miscellaneous File, letter from Secy., General Department, Govt of Bombay, Bombay Castle, 30 November 1934. This was a reply to Sarkar's letter to the Hon'ble Minister of Education, 10 November 1934.

relating to Sindhia, but to no avail.[61] The issue was dead by the early 1950s as far as either the provincial or the central government was concerned. Sarkar reported to Sardesai in 1951 that the Sindhia papers in possession of the central government were being removed to the newly set up National Archives of India—"no hope of . . . [looking?] into the hands of Amrit D. Parasnis."[62] And in 1955 he reported again that the historian Dr. Saltore had written to him "some weeks ago that the Gwalior Government has entirely forgotten the case of the last Parasnis bundle." "No hope," he added later, "of our doing anything."[63] He also realized, with much sadness, that he was never going to see anything like a public records act in India that would nationalize all historical documents, irrespective of which ruling family had them.[64]

The Archives as a Contradictory Concept

Thus, both in the practical strategies that Sarkar and Sardesai devised to wrest old historical papers out of the hands of the junior Parasnis—by getting the government to reduce his pension and by instituting a money suit—and in their political theory (that one sovereign power simply inherits the documents pertaining to public life created during a previous regime), they were proved wrong. Yet it is noteworthy how central the distinction between the private and the public was to their theoretical and practical thinking. "Parasnis will have to disgorge all he has gulped," said Sardesai in a letter to Sarkar in 1936. Notice the use of the word "public" in the text of this letter: "The main point is [that] . . . it was fraudulent on the part of Parasnis in keeping back these and several other original papers which have been printed by him in his magazines:—that all these should be available to *students of history* as the Parasnis family is granted Rs 200 in perpetuity out of *public* funds."[65] Or his optimism in November 1937 when he felt that an upcoming meeting between Sarkar and the commissioner of the Central Division of the Bombay Presidency could be "utilized for setting right the affairs of the Satara Museum." Sarkar could perhaps explain to the commissioner "how Parasnis defrauded Government and how the originals of the Sindia papers are still possessed by Parasnis . . ." "I feel sure," he added, "they would threaten Parasnis with sus-

61. See, for example, Sarkar's letters dated Kamshet, 1 January 1941, and Calcutta, 28 May 1944, to Raghubir Singh, in Tikekar, *Making of a Princely Historian*, pp. 126–127, 157–161.

62. NL, JSP, letter no. 1084, Sarkar to Sardesai, Calcutta, 6 October 1951.

63. NL, JSP, letter no. 1188, Sarkar to Sardesai, Calcutta, 8 September 1955.

64. NL, JSP, letter no. 144, Sardesai to Sarkar, Kamshet, 15 December 1930.

65. NL, JSP, letter no. 396, Sardesai to Sarkar, Chhindvada, Central Provinces, 21 February 1936.

pension of his allowance if he does not produce Sindia originals, as these are no more *private* property, having been *publicly* given out."[66] The political theory postulated in Sarkar's draft of the semilegal letter reproduced above also turns on this distinction between private and public documents, public documents being seen in his letter as "national" as well: "You should know that the historical records of a sovereign state belong to the state (and its successors) even though state papers many have been addressed to some minister of the state (like Nana Phadnis) and stored in his *private* house . . . . The Government's right to these *national* records cannot be barred by limitation or adverse possession in the hands of others."[67]

What was extraordinary about this application—by the most preeminent Indian historian of British India—of the private-public distinction to pre-British records pertaining to rule in eighteenth-century India was its anachronism. For it did some violence to the very understanding of Indian society through which Sarkar had initially posed the problem of historical sources. Recall Sarkar's own explanation of why it was difficult to find original, eyewitness accounts for the Mughal period: it stemmed from the fact that "in pre-British days . . . the records of every department of the Mughal Government or a feudatory state were usually kept in the house of the secretary of that department," for there were no home-office, and hence private-public, distinctions in that period. Surely, the point made by Sarkar and Sardesai that the documents found in the possession of old Maratha families were "public" documents could not be squared with this observation. Sarkar's and Sardesai's blindness to this problem points to the utopian nature of not only the concepts of "*public* records" and "the archive" that they worked with in thinking politically about historical documents but their instrumental use as well. These bourgeois categories were for them not just visions of the future but also weapons to wield in the present.

Bringing the Story Up to Date

On our 2012 trip to the empty house in Kamshet where Sardesai had lived on retirement from his service with Baroda, my colleagues and I discovered in the accumulated rubbish of the place an entire file containing letters between Sardesai and Sarkar's student Dr. Raghubir Singh of Malwa and some legal documents, dating from 1955–1957 and all relating to the *Gulgule Daftar*, historical papers from the Gulgule family based in Kotah in Rajasthan. Jadu-

66. NL, JSP, letter no. 491, Sardesai to Sarkar, Kamshet, 19 November 1937, emphasis added.

67. NL, JSP, letter no. 1023, Sarkar to Sardesai, Calcutta, 4 December 1949, emphasis added.

nath Sarkar first mentioned these papers in his foreword to *Selections from the Peshwa Daftar*, where he introduced the family in this way: "During the first stages of the Maratha occupation of Malwa under the great Baji Rao I, a Saraswat Brahman named Balaji Yashwant Gulgule of the Ratnagiri district had come as a civil officer [a clerk] in the train of the Maratha invaders in 1733. When the Gwalior territory and the neighbouring parts of Rajputana were assigned to Sindia as his special sphere, Gulgule became his Revenue Collector and Agent (Kamavisdar and Vakil) at Kotah." Balaji Yashwant's son Lalaji Ballal succeeded to his father's office in 1760 and "continued to act for more than forty years afterwards as an important pivot of Maratha affairs in Central India."[68] In a later article he published in 1945 in the *Modern Review*, Sarkar described *Gulgule Daftar* as being of "supreme importance, and in some points our only source, for the history of Mahadji Sindhia from 1792 to 1794 and also for the Sindhia-Holkar relations from the rise of Jaswant Rao Holkar . . . [in] 1799 to the neutralization of Daulat Rao Sindhia by Wellesley in . . . 1804."[69] Some of these records, about five thousand in total, were "carefully preserved and sorted" around 1925 by Pandit Purushottam Rao Gulgule, who also permitted Sardar Anand Raoi Bahu Phalke, "a noble of the Gwalior State," to publish them in two volumes after transcribing them from Modi to Devanagari characters. In 1935, Sarkar hatched an elaborate plan to see if he could use the good offices of Raghubir Singh to obtain the unpublished volumes from an unsuspecting Phalke by promising to him that Singh would publish them at his own expense after Sardesai's clandestine editing but give Phalke's name as the editor. Sarkar feared that Phalke had "taken a jealous alarm at the prospect of Sardesai getting the credit of editing this series" and that Sarkar, being "a lifelong friend and fellow-worker of Sardesai" would be "regarded with the same jealousy." Sarkar and Sardesai were not to be named. But this plan came to nothing, for Phalke would not yield.[70] Later, however, sometime between February 1943 and December 1944, "the present head of the Gulgule family Pandit Chandra Kant" permitted Raghubir Singh—Sarkar's student and "the heir to the Maharajah of Sitamau" in Malwa—to get copies of these unpublished records typed (at Singh's own expense, as we will soon see) for their eventual publication under the editorship of Sarde-

68. Sarkar, foreword to *Selections from the Peshwa Daftar*, p. 4. He had mentioned "Marathi despatches preserved in private possession in Kotah" in an earlier essay—see Jadunath Sarkar, "English Residents with Mahadji Sindhia," *Modern Review* (April 1929), p. 416.

69. Jadunath Sarkar, "A New Source of Maratha History," *Modern Review* (January 1945), p. 14.

70. Sarkar's letters to Singh, dated 6 and 24 November 1935, in Tikekar, *Making of a Princely Historian*, pp. 16–19.

sai, since the two volumes published by Phalke did not contain the letters of Mahadji Sindhia. This arrangement, Sarkar hoped, would "enable the older generation of students of Maratha history like myself to use them before we leave the earthly scene."[71]

Unfortunately, Sir Jadunath ultimately had to leave "the earthly scene" without being able to use these Sindhia-related documents from the *Gulgule Daftar*. But soon after India attained independence in 1947, Sardar Chandrakant Gulgule began to insist on monetary compensation for his family papers. Sarkar wrote to Singh in November 1949 that the Sardar wanted "Rs. 50,000 for his papers—a climb down from three lakhs [300,000]." But Sarkar would not recommend that the Bombay government buy this collection "by paying more than Rs. 12,500 in notes."[72] Nothing came of these negotiations. Sardesai in the meantime was getting anxious to announce through his forthcoming presidential address at the History Congress of 1952 the news of the publication of the *Gulgule Daftar*, "which [was] the sole remaining collection of first class records on Maratha history as yet denied to scholars." Sardar was now asking for Rs. 30,000, but Sarkar doubted that the Bombay government, given its financial concerns, would pay "even Rs. 6,000 for the whole lot."[73] By June 1954, Chandrakant Gulgule wanted back "*all* the transcripts of his ancestral papers typed in Devanagari at [Raghubir Singh's] expense," one set of them having been "sorted, dated, and enriched with notes by Sardesai after months of hard study." Sarkar was afraid that all this "expense and scholarly toil" was "to be lost to Indian history."[74] Sometime around or before 1955, the aforementioned "Pandit Chandra Kant" turned around and brought a case against Raghubir Singh, demanding the immediate return of the papers lent to him and making old Sardesai—who was then ninety-two, infirm and even "unable to walk around the house"—a party to the case.[75] "The anxiety of this lawsuit," wrote the concerned Sarkar to Singh, "will kill him [Sardesai]. Please write directly assuring him of what you plan for your defence at Court,

71. Sarkar, "New Source," pp. 14–15. See also Sarkar's letter, Calcutta, 22 February 1943, to Raghubir Singh, mentioning that Chandrakant P. Gulgule, "fed up with Sardar Phalke," had "decided to hand over" *Gulgule Daftar* in Marathi to Singh for the documents to be edited by Sardesai. Also letter dated Kota, 24 December 1944, from "Chandrakant (Gulgule)" to Sarkar. Tikekar, *Making of a Princely Historian*, pp. 149, 171.

72. Sarkar, letter to Singh from Calcutta dated 16 November 1949, in Tikekar, *Making of a Princely Historian*, p. 233.

73. Sarkar's letter dated Kamshet, 4 June 1951, to Raghubir Singh, in ibid., p. 251.

74. Sarkar to Singh, dated Talegaon, 11 June 1954, in ibid., p. 272.

75. SP, letter from Raghubir Singh to Sardesai, Sitamau, 16 April 1957.

especially if you have engaged a *skillful and noted lawyer* for your defence."[76] The letters in the file we discovered are mostly about this litigation, Singh taking care to spare Nana the trouble of being dragged to the court in connection with a case that they both thought eminently unfair. The case was ultimately settled out of court.

What interested me in this collection of letters and documents was what they indicated about the history of the process by which old papers were still being transformed into historical documents, with different kinds of values, including monetary ones, attached to them. Singh alleges in his deposition, for example, that he had "paid [Rs. 4,000] for the translation of documents from the Gulgule Daftar with [the] understanding that these would be published after editing by Sardesai." Originally, when the discussion of getting to these records began in 1940, Chandrakant, says Singh, was "not himself interested in history but he was legitimately proud of being the possessor of such important historical material." "He had no money motive but he wanted to have the prestige and fame that would accrue to him and the family by the publication of the important records." Phalke was unhelpful and silent when the work of translation was commenced in 1942 and completed in 1945. It was the publication of Sarkar's article in the *Modern Review*, writes Singh, that made Sardar Phalke jealous, and Phalke then "pressed the plaintiff [Chandrakant] to stop supplying copies to the defendant [Singh]," though by then the translation and typing of the documents had been done. However, for three years (1945–48), Phalke, according to Raghubir Singh, made no attempt to publish these documents that Singh then turned over to Sardesai. Sardesai, however, wrote an article about the documents in the *Modern Review* in December 1953. Now, "instigated by Sardar Phalke," or so thought Raghubir Singh, "he [Chandrakant] made a pretext of the article to claim back the transcript copies so that the benefit of the defendant 2's [Sardesai's] editing and scholarship would be available to him without any cost."[77]

Singh's draft deposition makes a fascinating point about the historical situation under which these documents acquired a monetary value—that is, became commodities—and the principles by which their market value could be debated or ascertained (fig. 8). He thought that by the 1950s, when Chandrakant brought the case against him, "money motives" had "probably . . .

76. Sarkar to Singh, Calcutta, 7 March 1956, in Tikekar, *Making of a Princely Historian*, pp. 278–279.

77. SP, "Copy of deposition by Raghubir Singh, Defendant 1, Civil Suit No. 2027 of 1955 in the Court of the Civil Judge, Pune (Draft no. 2)," typescript, p. 8.

become stronger." Even in the 1940s, when Sarkar imagined possible prices that could be paid to Amritrao Parasnis for the purchase of documents in his possession, this is how he reasoned about their monetary value: "So far as I remember, the collection does not contain any first-rate document. It is made up almost entirely of transcripts which means that the originals are to be sought elsewhere. . . . Rs. 500 would not be an unfair price for the whole lot. Rs 1,000 would be too high."[78] A letter from Sarkar to Singh from 1949 thus spells out some of the principles by which the market price of a historical document was to be arrived at: "The value of a MS depends on its penmanship, date of transcription, correctness of the text, and completeness,—also the paper and illuminations if any."[79] Singh's 1953 statement for the court, however, gives us some insight into the recent history of this emerging market for historical documents: "India had won freedom and in the new political set up the *jagirdars* [big landholders] apprehended a deterioration in their condition. In the changed circumstances the plaintiff [Chandrakant] became apprehensive whether he or his family would be able to preserve the valuable records properly. Money motives also entered his mind at this stage and he asked defendant 1 [Singh] what price the records would fetch." Singh gave an estimate of Rs. 10,000. "This being very much below the plaintiff's expectations, he dropped the matter as far as defendant 1 was concerned." Chandrakant claimed in the case he brought against Singh that the documents were so valuable that their "value in money" could not "be computed." Singh, interestingly, contested this claim: "No doubt the Gulgule Daftar and copies thereof contain material of great historical importance. But . . . there are many examples of original historical records being bought and sold. Thus such records have market value which means their value can be computed. The value of the transcript copies is bound to be less than the value of the original; for the original may have some elements of special character such as the handwriting or signature of a great historical personage like Mahadji Sindhia. . . . The plaintiff's original records have been valued at Rs. 10,000 or so." And he defended his right to use the copies for "study and research."[80]

Sardesai pleaded on grounds of his age and infirmity that he be left out of

78. Supplementary note to Sarkar's letter to Singh, dated Calcutta, 28 May 1944, in Tikekar, *Making of a Princely Historian*, p. 160.

79. Sarkar to Singh, dated Calcutta, 16 November 1949, in ibid., p. 233.

80. SP. "Copy of deposition by Raghubir Singh, Defendant 1, Civil Suit no. 2027 of 1955 in the Court of the Civil Judge, Pune. (Draft no. 2)," typescript, 10 pages; and "Draft letter from GSS to the Joint Civil Judge, S.D. Poona 5, Sub. Civil suit no. 2027 of 1956, dated 27.2.1956" (handwritten, 2 pages). This draft names the plaintiff—Sardar Chandrakant Rao Ganpatrai Pandit Gulgule of Kotah.

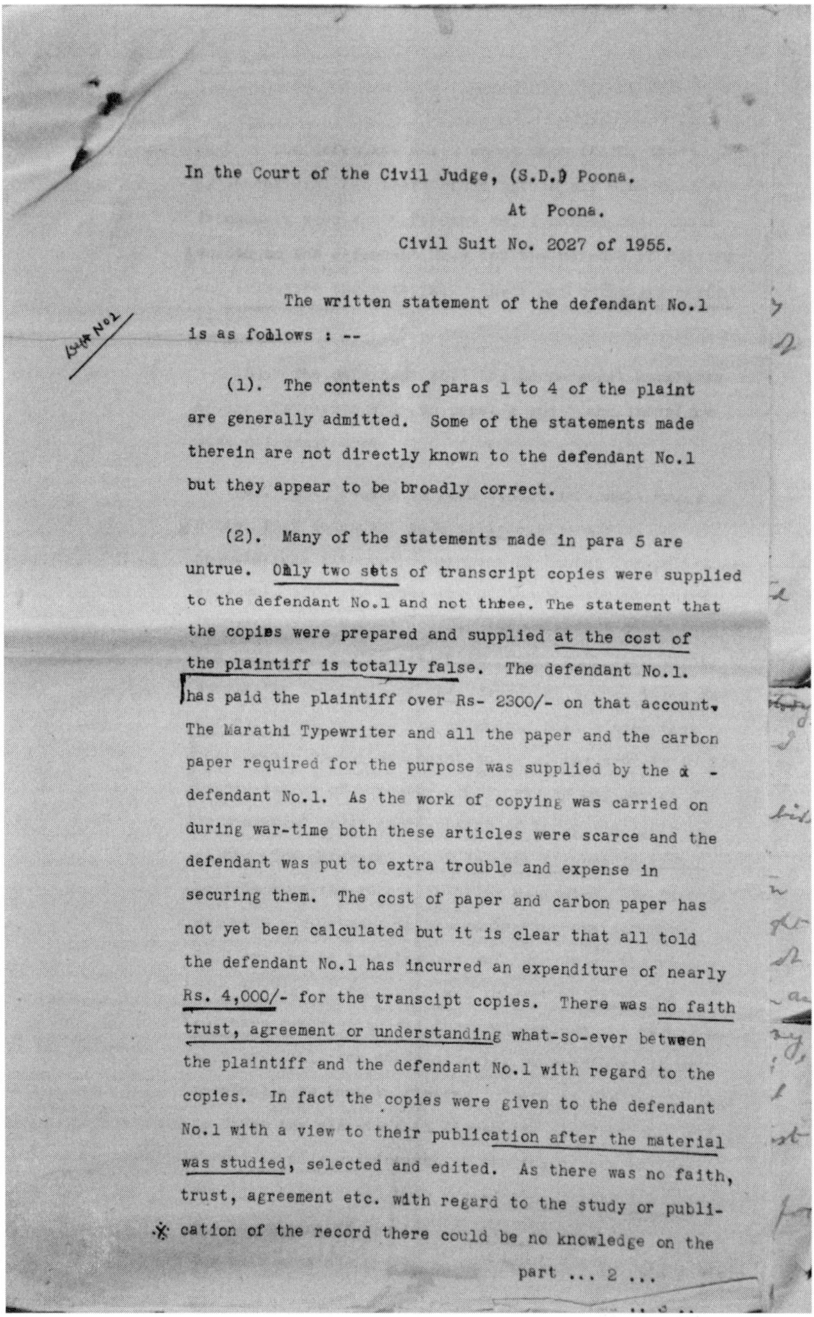
In the Court of the Civil Judge, (S.D.) Poona.

At Poona.

Civil Suit No. 2027 of 1955.

The written statement of the defendant No.1 is as follows : --

(1). The contents of paras 1 to 4 of the plaint are generally admitted. Some of the statements made therein are not directly known to the defendant No.1 but they appear to be broadly correct.

(2). Many of the statements made in para 5 are untrue. Only two sets of transcript copies were supplied to the defendant No.1 and not three. The statement that the copies were prepared and supplied at the cost of the plaintiff is totally false. The defendant No.1. has paid the plaintiff over Rs- 2300/- on that account. The Marathi Typewriter and all the paper and the carbon paper required for the purpose was supplied by the defendant No.1. As the work of copying was carried on during war-time both these articles were scarce and the defendant was put to extra trouble and expense in securing them. The cost of paper and carbon paper has not yet been calculated but it is clear that all told the defendant No.1 has incurred an expenditure of nearly Rs. 4,000/- for the transcipt copies. There was no faith trust, agreement or understanding what-so-ever between the plaintiff and the defendant No.1 with regard to the copies. In fact the copies were given to the defendant No.1 with a view to their publication after the material was studied, selected and edited. As there was no faith, trust, agreement etc. with regard to the study or publication of the record there could be no knowledge on the

part ... 2 ...

FIGURE 8. Excerpt of a 1955 Puna court case document, an excerpt of Raghubir Singh's Draft of Court Deposition, Poona, 1955. Photo by Ranu Roychoudhuri. Private collection of the author.

this legal conflict. Singh was protective of him, and the case was settled out of court. Sardesai never got to edit these documents. But the lone file we found in Kamshet in October 2012 spoke of the long history over which the question of researchers' access to family documents relating to Maratha history—and there is no reason for this to have been any different in other parts of India—was caught up in webs of rivalry, jealousy, litigation, and other forms of fierce competition involving both scholars and historical families. Through this process, however, as Singh's draft deposition suggests, a slow process of commodification emerged, so that questions regarding the monetary value old documents would fetch in the marketplace became legitimate.

The file on the "Gulgule Daftar affairs" in Sardesai's uninhabited house was exciting to discover, but it was also sad to see it in such a neglected condition. I wrote to a couple of esteemed colleagues in higher educational institutions in Poona, requesting that they make efforts to salvage this file and other documents that were simply turning to dust in the old house of the Riyasatkar. My colleagues in Poona were concerned, but their letters also suggested that the process would not be easy. The enthusiasm for old documents that Marathi scholars had once exemplified before the whole nation had indeed seen a decline. It is more than likely that this particular file will never find a place in a properly constituted historical archive, though it deserves better.

4

The Politics of "Unquestionable" Facts

"Please destroy this letter after reading it[;] it is from a sincere friend," wrote Sarkar, concluding a strongly critical letter he had written to his friend Sardesai on reading some draft chapters of the third volume of Sardesai's *New History of the Marathas*. The criticism was indicative of Sarkar's understanding of the relationship that facts bore to interpretation in history: "True, interpretation must differ according to [the] writer's personality; but the basis of the conclusions must be unquestionable facts (as established by latest research) and not mere conjecture. Moreover, the interpretation must be such as to convince an impartial observer."[1] Sarkar's moral insistence that historical narratives, though unavoidably biased, should be based on "unquestionable facts" had a political and polemical point to it. The target of the statement was what

1. NL, JSP, letter no. 882, Sarkar to Sardesai, Dehra Doon, 19 June 1946. Rosinka Chaudhuri has pointed out that Sarkar would sometimes grant great novelists such as Bankimchandra the capacity to speak some "eternal truth" (*chirasatya*). See Rosinka Chaudhuri, "History in Poetry: Nabinchandra Sen's *Palashir Yudhha* (Battle of Plassey) (1875) and the Question of Truth," in *History in the Vernacular*, ed. Raziuddin Aquil and Partha Chatterjee (New Delhi: Permanent Black, 2008), pp. 391–417. But a poetic "eternal truth" was far from what Sarkar himself sought to find in history or through historical research. In fact, in many of the introductory essays he wrote on Bankimchandra's novels, Sarkar went to some trouble to point out many deviations from facts the novels contained while praising the "nectar of high [nationalist] feelings" that issued from Bankimchandra's consciousness. See Sarkar, "Anandamath," "Durgeshnandini," "Debi Chaudhurani," "Rajshingha," and "Sitaram"—these are all his introductions to Bankimchandra's various novels by the respective names—in *Jadunath Sarkar rachana sambhar* [Collection of Jadunath's Writings], ed. Nikhilesh Guha and Rajnarayan Pal (Calcutta: M. C. Sarkar, 2011), pp. 779–837.

Sarkar dubbed "false patriotism," something that remained a target of his intellectual ire throughout his life.

For a complex set of reasons, Indian nationalists in every region felt the need to find "heroes" in their histories, and some of the individuals—such as Rana Pratap (1540–1597) and Shivaji (1630–1680) from precolonial times and the Rani of Jhansi (1828–1858), Swami Vivekananda (1863–1902), and Netaji Shubhas Chandra Bose (1897–1945) from the nineteenth and twentieth centuries—transcended the boundaries of their regions and became heroes for Indians generally, though their appeal was often limited mostly to Hindus. Of them, Shivaji in particular has continued since the early twentieth century to be at the center of many controversies and social conflicts.[2] This search for heroes was influenced also by European romanticism, mediated by the writings of James Tod and Grant Duff, and also, at a more abstract level, the cult of Camillo di Cavour and Giuseppe Mazzini, and by Thomas Carlyle's essays on the hero—particularly the one on "the hero as the king"—that were popular reading for educated Indians.[3]

Sarkar, as we will see, also subscribed to this tendency to view politics in heroic terms, but he wanted all nationalist claims to be based on "unquestionable facts." To this end, he would correct dates given in some of the

2. James Laine's engaging short book *Shivaji: Hindu King in Islamic India* (New York: Oxford University Press, 2003)—as well as the ugly response to it in certain parts of Maharashtra—and Daniel Alan Jasper, "Commemorating Shivaji" (PhD diss., New School University, April 2002) help one to understand the changing fortunes of Shivaji as a modern political icon. See also the essay by Mangesh Kulkarni, "Cultural Memory and the Politics of Intolerance," *Infochange Agenda* 22 (2011), pp. 26–28. Kulkarni explains the many political and contested versions of Shivaji that now circulate in the Maharashtrian public sphere: Bahujan, Nationalist, Hindutva-centric, Communist, and Consensual.

3. For instance, while visiting Stratford-on-Avon sometime in the late 1880s on the occasion of Shakespeare's birthday, the Bengali nationalist poet Dwijendralal Roy described the public adoration of the bard as an act of "hero-worship." "Who says the English or the Europeans do not worship their dead heroes?" he asked. "Carlyle has said, 'hero-worship' [in English] will never disappear from the world." Dwijendralal Roy, "Bilat prabashi" [The England-dwelling Bengali], excerpted in Debkumar Raychaudhuri, *Dwijendralal (jibon)* [Dwijendralal: A life] (reprint, Calcutta: Basudhara, [1964?]), p. 135. The reference to the Carlyle essay "The Hero as King" is clear in Sarkar's statement in the fifth and final edition of his *Shivaji and His Times*, 5th ed. (1952; New Delhi: Orient Longman, 1973), p. 376: "A Government of personal discretion is, by its very nature, uncertain. . . . This has been the bane of all autocratic States in the East and West alike, except where the autocrat has been a 'hero as king' or where a high level of education, civilization and national spirit among the people has prevented the evil." See also Sarkar's foreword (p. v) to V. B. Dighe's *Peshwa Baji Rao I and Maratha Expansion* (Bombay: Karnatak, 1944), where he describes the Peshwa as "truly a Carlylean Hero as King . . . a 'Man of Action.'"

printed versions of eighteenth-century Maratha letters published by Rajwade; uphold, on examination, the dates of some letters published by Rajwade against Kashiraj's 1870 account of the Panipat battle; question, on the basis of contemporary Marathi and Persian documents, some geographical facts relating to this battle given in the *Karnal District Gazetteer*; argue why numbers of soldiers injured and slain at Panipat as stated by Nana Fadnis were more reliable than those given by Kashiraj; question Nana Fadnis's "brag" in his autobiography that "it was only the nightfall [on 7 December 1760] that held the Marathas back" from destroying an Afghan army ("But the truth was otherwise").[4] Or, with reference to the Maratha Malhar Rao Holkar's victory over Jaipur's army at Mangrol in November 1761, Sarkar would write of the English romantic annalist James Tod that he, Tod, had only repeated "the Rajput tradition that this battle . . . was won solely by Zalim Singh and the Kota contingent, while Malhar merely looted the Kachhwa camp!" Sarkar stated, "The detailed and absolutely contemporary Marathi despatches disprove this story." The same, he said, was true of Tod's account of Rajput conflicts with Marathas in 1764.[5]

The rhetoric of Sarkar's prose suggests that he worked with a strong sense of being a new kind of historian of his time in India. Writing about the fall of the Mughals, he would sometimes refer to himself as "the reflective historian" or "the critical historian." The adjectives would mean, to use his own words, "dispassionate" or, sometimes, "impartial."[6] In criticizing V. K. Rajwade in the controversial obituary that he published in the *Modern Review*, Sarkar described his ideal picture of a true historian this way: someone who is endowed with "wide synthetic power, the passionless voice of superiority [as]to time and place, supreme common sense and select and well-digested reading." These were qualities, wrote Sarkar, to be found not only in the exalted Gibbon but even in "a second-rate European historian," but they were sadly "denied to Rajwade."[7] But what did a "passionless voice" mean to Sir Jadunath? "Impartiality," it was once remarked of Ranke, "must have been all the more difficult for an historian who felt as keenly as did Ranke."[8] One could say the

4. Jadunath Sarkar, *Fall of the Mughal Empire*, vol. 2, *1754–1771* (1934: New Delhi: Orient Longman, 1971), 171n, 218n, 220n, 253n.

5. Ibid., 363n, 370.

6. Ibid., 255, 257, 265; Sarkar, *Fall of the Mughal Empire*, vol. 3, *1771–1788* (1938; Calcutta: Orient Longman, 1975), 260.

7. Jadunath Sarkar, "The Historian Rajwade," *Modern Review* (February 1927), p. 187.

8. Edward Armstrong, introduction to Leopold von Ranke, *History of the Latin and Teutonic Nations (1494–1514)*, trans. G. R. Dennis (London: George Bell, 1909), p. xii.

same of Sarkar. He could not have meant by the use of word like "dispassionate" or "impartial" that his own narratives were bereft of passion. There was, as his readers can easily see, plenty of passion in his work. Nor was he afraid to pronounce judgment. Describing the expansive and warring Marathas in the eighteenth century as "locust swarms from the south" or "blood-sucking leeches of the south" or opium as "so indispensable to the Rajputs" could not have won him friends among contemporary regional historians who often wanted to express pride in their regional identities.[9] Sarkar obviously thought that his own passions, whatever they were, were all there to strengthen his commitment to truth in the writing of history. What then was Sarkar opposed to?

"False" Patriotism in Bengal

In his writings and correspondence, Sarkar gave many examples of the patriotism that, in his judgment, was false. "A false provincial patriotism," wrote Sarkar in one of his contributions to the second volume of the *History of Bengal: Muslim Period, 1200–1757*, which he edited,

> has led modern Bengali writers to glorify the Bara Bhuiyas [lit., "twelve landlords," meaning a group—more than twelve, since "twelve" stood for an indefinite number—of Afghan and local landlords and warriors who fought against Mughal control of the province] of Bengal as the champions of national independence against foreign invaders. They were nothing of the sort. Firstly, they were nearly all of them upstarts, who had grabbed at some portion of the dissolving Karrani [Afghan ruler] kingdom of Bengal and set up as masterless Rajas . . . in the inaccessible regions of the sea-coast in Khulna and Baqarganj or beyond the mighty barrier of the Brahmaputra in Dacca and the still remoter jungles of North Mymensingh and Sylhet.

It was absurd, Sarkar contended, to compare these "mushroom captains of plundering bands" to "the hereditary chieftains of the Sisodia and Rathor clans of Rajputana who fought the Mughals in defence of homes they had bought with the blood of their ancestors through centuries of struggle."[10]

9. Sarkar, *Fall*, 2:136, 158. One should note, though, that Najib-ud-daulah, who more or less ran Delhi between 1761 and 1770, when the emperor was in exile, described the Marathas as "more numerous than ants and locusts" (2:293n). Contemporary Marathas would not, I suppose, have endorsed this analogy.

10. Jadunath Sarkar, "Transformation of Bengal under Mughal Rule," in *The History of Bengal: Muslim Period, 1200–1757*, ed. Sir Jadunath Sarkar (Patna: Academica Asiatica, 1973; first published by the University of Dacca, [1947?]), p. 225.

He reserved special fire for destroying the image of Pratapaditya, a sixteenth-century landlord who had become the darling of many early-twentieth-century Bengali nationalists. They lauded him as a key figure in the heroic resistance to the Mughals that native Bengali leadership, with the Bengals' innate love of freedom, was supposed to have offered as the Mughals tried to annex the region to their empire. Much of this imagination was itself inspired by the way James Tod's stories of Rajput valor were appropriated by Bengali nationalists, who looked for Rajput-like heroes in the annals of the province.[11] Sarkar considered it his duty as a historian to fight this myth—and the general tendency that underlay it—tooth and nail. "The height of absurdity is reached," he wrote, "when our dramatists call Pratapaditya of Jessore . . . the counterpart of Maharana Pratap Singh of Mewar. It is therefore necessary to debunk the Bengali 'hero' by turning the dry light of history on him."[12]

What naked truth did the dry light of history reveal? That the aforesaid Pratapaditya was not the scion of "any old and decayed royal house." "His father was Srihari, a Kayastha writer in the service of Daud Khan Karrani [Afghan ruler of Bengal, r. 1573–76], who rose to be that chief's confidant after the murder of the worthy *wazir* Ludi Khan." On the fall of Daud, Srihari "built a safe refuge for fugitives from the advancing tide of [Mughal] invasion" in the "extreme south of the Khulna district." "The ex-*'amla* took the grandiloquent title of the Indian Charlemagne—Maharaj Vikramaditya, and could give his son and heir no lesser title than Pratapaditya,—reminiscent of the official designations of the great Gupta Emperors of antiquity." But this later Pratapaditya "never once defeated any Mughal army in pitched battle; his son . . . took flight at the first sign of a losing naval battle" and the father himself "submitted to the Mughal general without holding out till he was assured of life and honour." Such heroes, as Sarkar's scathing prose put it, "were at best bloated zamindars . . . [who] had their brief day in the twilight between the setting Afghan kingship and the rising Mughal empire in Bengal; and when the Mughal power came out . . . in full splendour, they vanished into the obscurity from which they had arisen." The evidence led up to his insis-

11. For an excellent account of the "apotheosis" of Pratapaditya in Bengali history and literature, see Clinton B. Seely's essay "Raja Pratapaditya, Problematic Hero," in his *Barisal and Beyond: Essays on Bangla Literature* (Delhi: DC, 2008), pp. 208–230. For an up-to-date history of Pratapaditya that also takes note of the relevant historiography and is critical of Jadunath Sarkar on certain points of facts and interpretation, see Anirudhha Ray, "Case Study of a Revolt in Medieval Bengal: Raja Pratapaditya Guha Ray of Jessore," in *Essays in Honour of Prof. S. C. Sarkar*, comp. Barun De et al. (Delhi: People's, 1976), pp. 135–164.

12. Sarkar, *History of Bengal*, p. 225.

tent and pointed question to "false patriots": "But where was the nation in all this?" For if "the Mughals who came in 1574 must be called foreign invaders, so were the Karranis who came in 1560."[13]

Sarkar may have been right on the "facts" about Pratapaditya (though not always right, as later research has shown), but clearly a certain kind of nationalist imagination that in turn assimilated to itself some other long-standing Indian genres of writings about the past—genres that blended the factual with the fabulous—was simply illegitimate in Sarkar's judgment.[14] It was, in his terms, "false patriotism." The extravagant claims made on behalf of the Jessore landlord Pratapaditya are a case in point. They involved formations of memory that in part antedated the coming of British rule. Long before there was any talk of modern nationalism, the battle between the Mughal general Man Singh (and his successors) and the Hindu landlords of Bengal (the class that Pratapaditya represented) had become part of eighteenth-century genealogical literature that sought to explain the rise and fall of well-known landed Hindu families in Bengal by recourse to stories that mixed the mundane with the miraculous. One such text was the *Kshitishvamsavalicharitam*, a Sanskrit genealogy of the family of the maharaja of Krishnanagar. This was the text

13. Ibid., pp. 225–226. However, Sarkar's student Tapan Raychaudhuri maintained that Mughal rule in Bengal "preserved its character of a foreign conquest. The viceroys and officers came and went without taking any real interest in the life of the province." Tapankumar Raychaudhuri, *Bengal under Akbar and Jahangir: An Introductory Study in Social History* (Calcutta: A. Mukherjee, 1953), p. 43. It is possible, though, that the idea of a "foreign conquest" in the context of late-sixteenth- and early-seventeenth-century Bengal was itself a instance of anachronistic thinking, an application of a later nationalist understanding of the word "foreign."

14. For recent criticisms of Sarkar, see Ray, "Case Study." The "first" mention of Pratapaditya was in Persian histories having to do with his submission to Islam Khan. He merited no mention in the *Akbarnama* or *Ain-i-Akbari*. See Sudhindranath Bhattacharya, "Conquests of Islam Khan, 1608–1613," in Sarkar, *History of Bengal*, p. 248n1. Bhattacharya also writes there: "The fanciful achievements of Pratapaditya and the halo of romance, valour, and glory that gathered round him as a great national hero, and the confusion regarding his career, particularly, his fall from power, have been fairly cleared by Sir Jadunath Sarkar (articles in Bengali in *Prabasi*, 1326, 1327, 1328) and Dr. N. K. Bhattashali (. . . *Bengal Past and Present*, 1928)." Some of Sarkar's Bengali essays on Pratapaditya published in *Shanibarer chithi* have now been reprinted in Guha and Pal, *Jadunath Sarkar*. For a critical history of the frenzied nationalist prose that was written on Pratapaditya by many Bengali writers the early 1900s—inspired by European researches of the late nineteenth century (published mostly in the journal of the Asiatic Society of Bengal), see N. K. Bhattasali, "Bengal Chiefs' Struggle for Independence in the Reign of Akbar and Jahangir," *Bengal Past and Present* (1928), pp. 25–39. As Bhattasali shows, most of Jadunath's researches debunking the Pratapaditya myth were published in Bengali in the 1920s, at the time when he was involved in his debates with Poona historians of Shivaji.

that Bharatchandra Ray Gunakar (1712–1760), an eighteenth-century poet of the maharaja's court, drew upon to describe the glory of Pratapaditya in the first part of his long erotic poem *Vidyasundar*, and the king's defeat in the final part of his *Annadamangal* (c. 1752–53), an account in verse of the power of the goddess Annada, to whose blessings the prosperity and preeminence of the ancestor of Maharaja Krishnachandra Ray, Bharatchandra's patron, were attributed.[15] Factually speaking, these accounts were not right, for they had Pratapaditya fighting the Mughal *subahdar* (provincial governor) Man Singh, and not Man Singh's successor Islam Khan, who actually fought and defeated Pratapaditya in 1612.[16] But facts did not matter to this prenationalist memory, just as they did not have much of an impact on later, early-twentieth-century popular-nationalist imaginations of the past. Fabulous memories of Pratapaditya—with some historical elements thrown in—became the subject of one of the very first books published in Bengali, by a Fort William College pundit—Ramram Basu's *Raja Pratapaditya charitra* (1801).[17] Ramram Basu also claimed to be from the same social group as Pratapaditya—the Bengal-born Kayasthas (*Bangja kayastha*).

The already existing legends about Pratapaditya's prowess became the subject of patriotic imaginings in the nineteenth century, when a librarian of the Asiatic Society in Calcutta, Pratapchandra Ghosh, wrote a two-volume historical romance about the king, *Bangadheep parajay* (The defeat of the king of Bengal), which was used by the young Rabindranath Tagore in the early

15. "Annadamangal," in *Rai Gunakar bharatchandrer granthabali* (Calcutta: Basumati Sahitya Mandir, n.d.).

16. See Dr. Kshetra Gupta and Dr. Bishnu Bosu, eds., *Bharatchandra rachanabali* (Calcutta: Bhoumik, 1974), pp. 180–181, 317–329. The Basumati edition of Bharatchandra's works has these sections in a different order—see "Vidyasundar" and "Annadamangal" in *Rai Gunakar bharatchandrer granthabali* (Calcutta: Basumati Sahitya Mandir, n.d.), pp. 10, 136–140. See also the discussions in Sanatan Goswami, *Kabi bharatchandra* (Calcutta: Pustak Bipani, 1978), pp. 87–91; Kumkum Chatterjee, *The Culture of History in Early Modern India: Persianization and Mughal Culture in Bengal* (Delhi: Oxford University Press, 2009), pp. 32–33; and Dilwar Hossain, *Bangla upanyashe mughal itihasher baebohar* (Dhaka: Bangla Academy, 1984), pp. 14–17. On the defeat of Pratapaditya by Islam Khan, see Sarkar, *History of Bengal*, section entitled "Pratapaditya of Jessore Crushed, 1612," pp. 264–270.

17. Ramram Boshu [Basu], *Raja pratapaditya charitra with a Short Biography of Ramram Boshu by Brajendranath Bandyopadhyay* (1801; Calcutta: Ranjan, 1941). Bhattasali gives Basu credit for "deviating" from "the poetical account" of Pratapaditya "given half a century before him in the *Annada-Mangal* by the poet Bharat Chandra," who named Mansingh as "the Subadar in whose hands Pratapaditya fell." "Basu correctly gives the name as Islam Khan." Bhattasali, "Bengal Chiefs' Struggle," p. 27.

1880s to write his first novel, *Bou-thakuranir haat*.[18] In the early twentieth century, the story of Pratapaditya became grist for the mill of Hindu-Bengali nationalism when the well-known writer Kshirodprasad Bidyabinod (1863–1927) wrote a play called *Bonger Pratap-aditya* (Bengal's Pratap; also meaning "Bengal's prowess"). In the Bengali historian Nalinikanta Bhattasali's words, "no drama had a greater success" in Bengal. "It continued to draw packed houses night after night and soon the drama was staged and re-staged in every mofussil town and in every considerable village."[19] Here is a sample of the play, act 5, scene 1, in which the emperor Akbar and his son Selim (the future Jahangir) discuss Bengali valor (in reading the excerpt, the reader has to understand that the invocation of "seventy million Bengalis" [*saat koti bangali*] was, from Bankimchandra to Rabindranath, a coded reference for the entire population of Bengal, inclusive of Muslims and Hindus, thought of as one people, but with the Muslims immediately forgotten to project a point of view that was mainly Hindu):

SELIM: *Jahanpana* [Lord of the world], may I ask why you sent for this slave?

AKBAR: I sent for you to discuss some very special business. . . . Have you heard about what's happening in Bengal?

S: I have—some small landholder has turned rebellious.

A: Yes, that's how it's been reported in Agra. . . .

S: I cannot believe that the Emperor of Hindusthan would be so worried about the rebellion by an insignificant Bengali landlord. . . .

A: Have you seen Bengalis?

S: I have. They are very smart but very weak when it comes to physical and mental strength. They are peaceful, polite, patient, soft-spoken, and full of love—and yet very weak. . . . Bengalis lack in their commitment to truth, they are quick to find fault in others, suffer from envy, and are selfish. As individuals, Bengalis are endowed with great capacities—in the spheres of knowledge, education, intelligence, speech, and second to none in the world in efficiency at work . . . . But together, even ten Bengalis make an insignificant lot, and are the lowest of the low. . . .

A: But do you know that Bengalis now realize what their shortcomings are? Do you know what a force they could be if they acted on the basis of that realization? . . . A sense of unity has come over Bengalis. Bengalis have become a nation. Bengali rebellion is not the insignificant rebellion of a landlord. It is the great national uprising of seventy million Bengali

18. See the discussion in part 2, chap. 3, of Hossain, *Bangla upanyashe mughal*, pp. 252–297.

19. Bhattasali, "Bengal Chiefs' Struggle," p. 28.

people. Tell me Selim: isn't that something that should worry the Emperor of Hindusthan?[20]

Even if such absurd dramatizations were a matter of the past by the middle of the twentieth century, the fact remains that Pratapaditya continued to linger on in the political memory of the Bengali *bhadralok* (gentlefolk).[21] The Calcutta Corporation—once it came under nationalist control in the 1930s and later—named two major streets after Pratapaditya and his uncle Raja Basanta Roy in 1931 and 1932, respectively.[22] The second chief minister of West Bengal, the nationalist leader Dr. Bidhan Chandra Roy, was said to be a direct descendant, nine generations down, of Pratapaditya.[23]

Sarkar had nothing but contempt for this breed of patriotism. In his bibliographic essay at the end of the *History of Bengal* volume edited by him, he remarked how he had, in the interest of time and space, deliberately ignored "heaps of dead leaves and the vapourings of ignorant national pride" such as "the assertions made *in 1947* that Pratapaditya had conquered Assam and brought all the Rajas and Sultans of Bengal under his vassalage, or that Mohan Lal [a Kashmiri] who was wounded at Plassey was a Kayastha of Bengal and [that] the Lal Paltan [lit., red army] of Clive was composed of Bengalis by race."[24]

Taking the Fight to Maharashtra

Pratapaditya, whatever Bengali nationalists may have made of him, was after all a minor figure among the many "heroes" Indian nationalists sought in their precolonial pasts. One of the most important such figures was Shivaji

20. Kshirodprasad Bidyabinod, *Banger pratap-aditya* (17th reprint; Calcutta: Gurudas Chattopadhyay, 1957), 5.1.152–153. On such theatrical and nationalist uses of the past in early-twentieth-century Bengal, see the discussion in Partha Chatterjee, *The Black Hole of Empire: History of a Global Practice of Power* (Princeton, NJ: Princeton University Press, 2012), chap. 8.

21. Tagore's first novel, *Bou-thakuranir haat*, was centered on the figure of a cruel and stony-hearted Pratapaditya. For a discussion of the intellectual influences on the novel, see Prabhatkumar Mukhopadhyay, *Rabindrajibani o rabindrashahitya-probeshok* (1934; Calcutta: Visva-Bharati, 1961), 1:142–143. Both Mukhopadhyay and Tagore point out that the hero-making activity took off in the early twentieth century as a post-*Swadeshi* phenomenon. Rabindranath Thakur [Tagore], "Beginnings" to "Bou-thakuranir haat," in *Rabindrarachanabali*, centenary ed. (Calcutta: Government of West Bengal, 1962), 9:3.

22. P. Thankappan Nair, *A History of Calcutta's Streets* (Calcutta: Firma K. L. Mukhopadhyay, 1987), pp. 682, 711.

23. Ibid., p. 682.

24. Sarkar, *History of Bengal*, p. 508, emphasis original.

(1630–1680), Shivajirao Bhonsle, an inveterate thorn in the Mughal emperor Aurangzeb's side. Shivaji's exploits and adventures were celebrated not only in Marathi ballads and legends but also in the works of many early-twentieth-century Marathi historians, in particular those connected with the Bharat Itihas Samshodhak Mandal of Poona. Sarkar's two books on Shivaji, *Shivaji and His Times* (first published 1919) and *The House of Shivaji* (first published in 1940), were both embroiled in debates about what was factual and what was mythical about the Marathi hero. His expression "dispassionate history" actually occurs in a sentence where this abstract affect is invoked to oppose the "chauvinistic claims" of Maratha historians who, "since the days of Viswanath K. Rajwade," appeared to "belittle the result of the battle of Panipat [1761] as no disaster to the Marathas": "But a dispassionate . . . history would show how unfounded this chauvinistic claim is."[25] Similarly, with regard to the "long" north Indian expedition of Raghunath Rao and Malhar Rao Holkar in 1758, Sarkar would comment on how this episode "caused the wildest exultation among the ignorant sycophants of the Maratha Court" and how "their baseless praise has been echoed by equally ignorant historians of that people in our own days, as 'carrying out the Hindu paramountcy (*Hindu-pat-Padshahi*) up to Attock.'" A "calm" examination, Sarkar said, exposed "Raghunath's vaunted achievement" to be "politically hollow a show and financially barren."[26]

The Maratha search for a hero and statesman in their history culminated in the revival of the figure of Shivaji and led to the publication of books that represented a heady mix of legends, memories, myths, and historical facts. Two such typical titles published by the Bharat Itihas Samshodhak Mandal, Poona, were *The Deliverance or the Escape of Shivaji the Great from Agra* (1929), by Baba Saheb Deshpande, once a police officer with the Government of India, and *Shivaji: The Founder of Maratha Swaraj* (1931), by C. V. Vaidya. Deshpande was a member of the Mandal of which Vaidya was the president. Both books had introductory notes by Datto Vaman Potdar, the honorary secretary of the Mandal, who eventually led a rival camp in the Indian Historical Records Commission that was implacably opposed to Sarkar down

25. Sarkar, *Fall*, 2:255.

26. Ibid., 2:111–112. Sarkar seems to have modified his opinion when the Poona Mandal published some documents relating to the Maratha advance into Attock in 1758. He wrote to Sardesai in 1945: "This evening I have received the Mandal Traimasik, 24th year, no. 1, which prints the Persian *akhbarats* that throw a new light on the subject [the Maratha advance into Attock in 1758]. My sole interest is the discovery of truth from unassailable sources, and I am not so vain as to feel hurt if any statement in a book of mine is contradicted by *later* discovered (or published) sources. For unless such continuous supersession is welcomed, progress in human knowledge would be impossible." NL, JSP, letter no. 770, Sarkar to Sardesai, Calcutta[?], 25 August 1945.

to the 1940s.[27] The opposition, while consistent and sometimes vicious, was, however, never total.[28]

Deshpande and Vaidya extolled the heroic qualities of Shivaji. To Deshpande, Shivaji was "one of the greatest or rather the greatest man of his times"; he had to "recover, reinstate and reform the [Maratha, Hindu] empire snatched from and lost by his own ancestors." "The eyes of the whole of Hindu India were, therefore riveted, on Maharashtra and prayers had been offered to Heaven by all the persecuted and down-trodden Hindus to grant the 'Champion of the Hindu cause' all success in his holy passion."[29] Vaidya's book began by describing Shivaji as "undoubtedly" "the greatest figure in the modern history of India." He was "the founder of Maratha independence in the seventeenth century." Like Washington and Garibaldi, wrote Vaidya, "Shivaji . . . delivered his people from the oppression of an alien [Mughal] rule and religion [Islam] and he may be on a par with these two unquestionably great men" or even "greater," as, unlike the American and the Italian, Shivaji had for his army the Mawlas [Malves] who were "illiterate and unwarlike." Even if institutions, kings, and nations disappeared, wrote Vaidya, quoting Carlyle, "this will always remain, namely the certainty of heroes being sent us and their being worshipped when sent."[30] That much of the modern Marathi extravagant rhetoric about the heroic status of Shivaji owed itself to European ideas of the "hero as king" may also be seen in what S. R. Sharma, "sometime Professor of History" at Fergusson College, Poona, wrote in praise of the Maratha hero in his book *The Founding of Maratha Freedom*, first published in 1934: "Shivaji was a titanic creator in the realm of politics and nation-building. He had the vision of Mazzini, the dash of Garibaldi, the diplomacy of Cavour, and the patriotism, perseverance, and intrepidity of William of Orange. He did for Maharashtra what Fredrick [*sic*] the Great achieved for Germany or Alexander the Great for Macedonia."[31]

27. Baba Saheb Deshpande, *The Deliverance or the Escape of Shivaji the Great from Agra* (Poona: By the author from Vishramdham D. G., Post, Poona no. 4, under the auspices of Bharat Itihas Samshodhak Mandal, 1929); C. V. Vaidya, *Shivaji: The Founder of Maratha Swaraj* (Poona: C. V. Vaidya, 314 Sadashiv Peth, Poona, for Bharat Itihas Samshodhak Mandal, 1931). Deshpande's membership of the Mandala is mentioned in Potdar's introduction to his book (p. 3). For more on Potdar's opposition to Sarkar and Sardesai, see chapter 7.

28. Sarkar's translation of Abbe Carre's French biography of Shivaji, for instance, was published in *Historical Miscellany*, ed. Datto Vaman Potdar and Gangadharrao Narayanrao Mujumdar, M. L. C. (Madras: Bharat Itihas Samshodhak Mandala, 1928), pp. 36–63.

29. Deshpande, *Deliverance*, p. 3.

30. Vaidya, *Shivaji*, pp. 3, 5.

31. S. R. Sharma, *The Founding of Maratha Freedom* (1934; Bombay: Orient Longmans, 1964), p. 137. This book introduces Sharma as "sometime Professor of History" at Fergusson College.

Sarkar was not opposed to the idea of the hero as such, or even to Shivaji's being made one. On the contrary, as chapter 5 will demonstrate, he himself looked for heroes and statesmen in all his writings on Indian history. His point was that—as in the case of the Bengali "minor" hero Pratapaditya—such searches for heroes should be grounded in "unquestionable facts." This is what often pitted him against the political use made of myths in colonial and postcolonial India, and it sometimes left him in a minority of one. Sarkar thought of the Maratha king Shivaji in laudatory terms, though his views changed over the decades. Even at the height of the Shivaji cult, when Sarkar's and Sardesai's intellectual and institutional battles with Poona-based nationalist historians were at their most intense (in the 1920s and 1930s), Sarkar acknowledged that it was Shivaji's "creation of a National state" that, along with some other factors, led to the "fusing" of a "tribe"—the Marathas—"into a nation." He quoted from the introduction to a collection of Maratha ballads, *powadas*: "The Marathas are a nation, and from the Brahman to the ryot they glory in the fact."[32] Yet in his book on Shivaji, Sarkar acknowledged the "hindrances to true nationality" that existed "in Shivaji's age," such as caste, the fragmentation of attachment to one's own land (*watan*), the "impassable chasm between Hindus and Muslims," Maratha "neglect" of "economic factors" and their alleged love of "intrigue," and so on.[33]

Sarkar returned to some of these questions in his later book, *House of Shivaji*, first published in 1948. He acknowledged the statesmanship of Shivaji, defined, as Sarkar said, by "the greatest of Italian statesman and patriots, Count Cavour, . . . as *tact des choses possibles* or the instinctive perception of what is possible under the circumstances," as well as by his spirit of religious toleration and openness to talent, irrespective of caste. But, asked Sarkar, "did he [Shivaji] succeed in creating a nation?"[34] His complex answer, avoiding a simple "yes or no" dichotomy, shows how much he shared with his opponents (such as Vaidya) a Carlylean inspiration in thinking about national politics through figures of heroes and statesmen. Accepting that Shivaji was "not only the maker of the Maratha nation but also the greatest constructive genius of medieval India," Sarkar wrote, clearly echoing not just Carlyle but even Vaidya's citation of Carlyle, showing once again—if proof indeed were needed—how critically important the Scottish writer's texts on heroism were

32. Jadunath Sarkar, *Shivaji and His Times*, 3rd ed. (Calcutta: M. C. Sarkar, 1929), pp. 12, 13, 13n.

33. Sarkar, *Shivaji*, 3rd ed. (1929), pp. 391–398.

34. Jadunath Sarkar, *House of Shivaji: Studies and Documents on Maratha History—Royal Period*, "greatly enlarged third edition" (Calcutta: M. C. Sarkar, 1955), pp. 102–114, quotes on p. 104.

to the nationalist imagination of a certain generation of Indians: "States fall, empires break up, dynasties become extinct, but the memory of a true 'hero as king' like Shivaji remains an imperishable historical legacy for the entire human race." Sarkar then went on to quote from Tennyson's *In Memorium* to describe the appeal of Shivaji to later generations: "The pillar of a people's hope,/The centre of a world's desire."[35]

So, if making a national or regional hero out of Shivaji was not, as such, a point of contention between Sarkar and his opponents in Poona, what was? Why did Vaidya's book, published long after Sarkar's *Shivaji and His Times* (1919, 1920, 1929), studiously avoid any explicit references to Sarkar except by beginning the book with a pointed salvo against those who sought to "minimize the [historical] value" of the poem *Shiva-bharat* (on which, more follows), and why did Deshpande's book ignore—one would think deliberately—all the critical remarks Sarkar made about the Maratha hero and his reign?

The answer lies in the conflicting views that rival forms of nationalism encouraged about the very idea of a historical fact. True, most historical researchers spoke in terms of "facts" and "scientific history" at the level of rhetoric. The doyen of Poona historians and the founding father of the Bharat Itihas Samshodhak Mandal (1910), Viswanath Kashinath Rajwade (1864–1926), had declared a long time earlier that "the method of writing history which is considered scientific in Europe is considered equally so India" and that "faithfulness [to sources] and the scientific method are the two essences of the life of history."[36] In his foreword to Vaidya's book and his introduction to Deshpande's, Datto Vaman Potdar, the leader and secretary of the Poona Mandal, emphasized the importance of "facts." "We must," wrote Potdar in his foreword to Vaidya's volume, "constantly go on ascertaining with the utmost scientific rigour, facts and [*sic*] at the same time attempting to present and interpret the same in a broad, sympathetic and honest spirit."[37] "A bed-rock of facts," he said, was what Deshpande's romantic narrative of Shivaji's escape from Agra was based on.[38]

In an essay published in 1924, Sarkar observed that one only had to "travel in Maharashtra or keep in close touch with modern Marathi newspapers and books to realize the fact that the personality of Shivaji excites even to-day a

35. Ibid., p. 115.

36. Rajwade excerpted in A. N. Surve, "Rajwade's Contribution to Maratha History," in *Shivaji Souvenir*, ed. G. S. Sardesai (Girguam, Bombay: Keshav Bhikaji Dhawale, n.d. [1930?]), p. 110.

37. Potdar, foreword to Vaidya, *Shivaji*, p. 2.

38. Potdar, introduction to Deshpande, *Deliverance*, p. 3.

degree of love and veneration comparable only to that which the great founders of religion command among their followers." "The Maratha intellect"—though not its "better trained" representatives—he wrote, "had devoted itself with astonishing industry and personal sacrifice to search for every scrap of new or neglected information about him [Shivaji] . . . drawing from it all the historical deductions it can yield,—and often more than what it can reasonably yield."[39] There is in fact a passage in Sarkar's preface to the first edition (1919) of *Shivaji and His Times* that he retained in the 1920 and 1929 editions of the book but omitted from the preface to the 1952 edition. The later deletion of the passage may very well suggest a subsidence in the 1940s and 1950s of the conflict—over facts relating to the history of Shivaji—between Sarkar and the Poona historians. The conflict seems to have peaked in the late 1920s and the early 1930s. This is what Sarkar wrote in the prefatory passage: "From the purely literary point of view, the book would have gained much by being made shorter. But so many false legends about Shivaji are current in our country and the Shivaji myth is developing so fast (attended at times with the fabrication of documents), that I have considered it necessary in the interests of historical truth to give every fact, however small, about him that has been ascertained on unimpeachable evidence and to discuss the probabilities of others."[40]

The Murder of Chandrarao More in 1655

A good historical example of how "facts" got embroiled in identity politics in Maharashtra would be the killing in 1655 by Shivaji of Chandrarao More. Sarkar's opinion that Shivaji did not treacherously murder the Bijapuri commander Afzal Khan but only "acted in self-defence" in 1659 when, after agreeing to meet as "friends," the latter "struck the first blow" gladdened the hearts of many Maratha readers. Invoking Burke, Sarkar described Shivaji's act as "preventive murder."[41] But this upset many Muslims.[42] However, exactly op-

39. Jadunath Sarkar, "Sources of the History of Shivaji Critically Examined," *Journal of the Bihar and Orissa Research Society* 10, parts 1 and 2 (March 1924), pp. 70–87, quote on p. 71.

40. Jadunath Sarkar, "Preface to the First Edition," reprinted in *Shivaji and His Times*, 2nd ed. (London: Longman, Green, 1920), p. 7; Sarkar, *Shivaji and His Times*, 3rd ed. (Calcutta: M. C. Sarkar, 1929), preface dated December 1928, p. v.

41. Sarkar, *Shivaji*, 2nd ed. (1920), pp. 79, 81.

42. A young lawyer from Sultanpur in Ayodhya published a book called *The Real Sevaji* in 1935 criticizing this particular claim of Sarkar while using Sarkar's own research to refute Sarkar's point. The book was forgotten after the few disturbing ripples it caused in the political waters of colonial India but was reprinted by a Pakistani publisher in 1980. See Saiyid Tafazzul

posite was the case with the murder of Chandrarao More. The sultan of Bijapur had elevated the Mores into the position of the *jagirdar* of the state of Javli in the Sahayadri mountain ranges sometime in the sixteenth century. Acquisition of Javli was central to the founding of Shivaji's kingdom, but a fierce debate raged between Sarkar and the Poona historians on the motive that led the Maratha king to kill the jagirdar of Javli. After examining the documents available to him, Sarkar came to a clear and—to Maratha nationalists—unflattering conclusion that "the acquisition of Javli was the result of deliberate murder and organised treachery on the part of Shivaji."[43] This statement was unacceptable to those wanting to make a completely moral, Hindu, and nationalist hero out of Shivaji. They had to absolve their hero of the charge of deliberate treachery and murder. Polemical passages that made their way in and out of the various editions of *Shivaji and His Times* indicate both the intensity and the variety of controversy on this point. From early on in the history of Shivaji—and possibly more intensely since the publication of Sarkar's book in 1919—Poona historians claimed that the killing of Chandrarao More was no ordinary treacherous murder; it was undertaken in the interest of Shivaji's larger project of founding a Hindu *swaraj* when More, an agent of the Muslim ruler of Bijapur, simply stood in the way.[44] Sarkar, on the other hand, insisted that "the only redeeming feature of this dark episode in his [Shivaji's] life is that the crime was not aggravated by hypocrisy. All his old Hindu biographers are agreed that it was an act of pre-meditated murder. . . . Even Shivaji never claimed that the murder of the three Mores was prompted by a desire to found a 'Hindu *swaraj*,' or to remove from his path a treacherous enemy beyond the chance of reform."[45]

From this point on followed a debate on what constituted "proper" sources on Shivaji, and the different editions of *Shivaji and His Times* suggest that Sarkar kept battling different challengers who denounced his work at different points in the decade of the 1920s, culminating in political questions in the Bombay Legislative Council that anticipated many of the ideological strands

---

Daud Sayeed Khan, *The Real Sevaji* (Karachi: Indus, 1980; first pub. in 1935 by Popular Printing Works, Allahabad). Sarkar commented on this "disgusting volume" called "'The True Sevajee' written by a Muhammadan graduate from Aligarh" in a letter to Sardesai: "It shows you to what lengths malignity and ignorance can go. It is, I consider, the natural reaction against the chauvinistic brag of Savarkar—and even Rajwade, about the purely imaginary Hindu Pad Padshahi." NL, JSP, letter no. 432, Sarkar to Sardesai, Darjiling, 20 October 1936.

43. Sarkar, *Shivaji*, 2nd ed. (1920), p. 46. Sarkar maintained this position in the subsequent editions of the book.

44. Ibid., p. 47.

45. Ibid., p. 46.

of identity politics in India today. "Some Maratha writers," remarked Sarkar in the first two editions of the book, "have recently 'discovered' what they vaguely call 'an old chronicle'—written nobody knows when or by whom, based nobody knows on what authorities, and transmitted nobody knows how,—which asserts that Chandra Rao . . . had ungratefully conspired . . . to imprison Shivaji. Unfortunately for the credibility of such convenient 'discoveries,' none of the genuine old historians could anticipate that this line of defence would be adopted by the twentieth century admirers of the national hero: they have called a murder a murder."[46] Historians defending Shivaji's role in this episode questioned the sources Sarkar used in coming to his conclusions.[47]

The early editions of *Shivaji and His Times* carried a whole appendix titled "The Murder of the Mores." Sarkar's polemical target, initially, was the historian Rao Bahadur D. B. Parasnis, a well known collector and publisher of historical documents, who based his claims on "the so-called *Mahabaleshwar Bakhar*, which exists in a single anonymous undated MS.—discovered some 20 years ago among the papers of the modern Rajahs of Satara." This manuscript, wrote Sarkar, "has not been shown to the public even in Maharashtra, nor examined by experts with a view to judging its date and authenticity. A critic, evidently in the confidence of the Rao Bahadur, now writes that the MS. contains a statement that it was written by the order of Rajah Shahu. We do not know the authority for this entry, nor whether the colophon was contemporaneous with the body of the MS. or is a modern addition." Sarkar dated the *Mahabaleshwar Bakhar* back to the 1740s or "even later"—"i.e., more than 80 years after the murder of the Mores"—and asked, somewhat rhetorically, "What were its nameless author's means for knowing the truth better than Shivaji's own courtier?" His deeper point was about the proper constitution and evaluation of historical evidence: "The *Mahabaleshwar Bakhar*, . . . even if written in Shahu's time, had no other basis than unreliable oral tradition or deliberate invention. To accept such a work against Sabhasad and Chitnis is to defy the most elementary laws of historic evidence."[48] He made the same point against the use of *Mahabaleshwar Bakhar* in C. A. Kincaid and D. B. Parasnis's *History of the Maratha People*, volume 1. "I trust," wrote a sarcastic Sarkar, "the astonishing method of appraising evidence and drawing legitimate inferences exhibited by the learned ex-judge of Satara . . . will not be taken by scholars abroad as typical of the way in which amateur Judges of

46. Ibid., pp. 46–47.

47. Sharma, *Founding*, pp. 147–153.

48. Sarkar, *Shivaji*, 2nd ed. (1920), pp. 51–52.

the Indian civil service deal criminal justice in India." He added: "The historian who cares for his reputation has, unfortunately, to place truth above popularity."[49] Historical methods thus were very much a part of the clash between competing forms of patriotism.

Evaluating Sources

Sarkar dropped the appendix on More from the third edition of *Shivaji*, which was published in 1929, and added a new appendix to the fourth and fifth editions, of 1948 and 1952, that did not discuss Parasnis anymore. In 1929, in place of the earlier appendix, he added a new footnote to the sentence "Even Shivaji never pretended that the murder of the three Mores was prompted by a desire to found a 'Hindu *swaraj*' . . . etc." The footnote as it was phrased in later editions simply said, "For the desperate and fantastic special pleading of Mr. C. V. Vaidya, LLB, the reader is referred to the *Mahratta* (31 Aug. 1924)."[50] Privately, in a letter to Sardesai in 1932, when the latter was preparing to write a review of Vaidya's book, Sarkar wrote: "Yes, you can send me C.V. Vaidya's *Shivaji* and I shall send back to you a list of glaring mistakes in it with *evidence* (for incorporation in your review)." Letters in *Shiva-charitra-sahitya* (Biographical literature on Shivaji) "establish the importance of Shahji in 1620–1627 as a landholder" and "throw light on Shivaji's doings about 1646." But they did not, wrote Sarkar, show that Shahji (Shivaji's father) "was an *amir wazir* or supreme divisional commander before 1628, or that Shivaji's doings in 1646 were those of a sovereign prince. There were hundreds of contemporary men of exactly the same status and power as Shahji during 1620–1627 . . . and Shivaji in 1646 was a mere *rising* rebel chieftain—not a sovereign Rajah. These two facts are forgotten or muddled with later history by the Poona School. . . . Your Poona friends are reading the history of 1674 *backwards* into the events of 1620–1627 and 1646."[51]

Vaidya, as we have seen, was the president of the Bharat Itihas Samsodhak Mandal in Poona. His "special pleading" was based on his reading of the *Shiva-bharat*, "a poetical life of Shivaji, written by Paramanand, his court-poet and by his order" and made available in a Marathi translation in 1927.[52] Sarkar had described this book *Shiv-bharat* in the 1929 edition of his *Shivaji*

49. Ibid., pp. 53–54.

50. Sarkar, *Shivaji*, 3rd ed. (1929), p. 45n.

51. NL, JSP, letter no. 187, Sarkar to Sardesai, Calcutta, 4 February 1932.

52. Preface to Vaidya, *Shivaji*, p. i. For the date of the Marathi translation, see Sarkar, *Shivaji*, 3rd ed. (1929), p. 415.

as characterized by "nauseating flattery of his [the poet's] patron and absurd exaggerations," giving specific instances substantiating his charges. Sarkar concluded that "such a work cannot be taken literally as history."[53] Sarkar's private views, expressed in a letter to Sardesai in 1927, were not as hard-line. He even considered using some parts of the poem in his history and was prepared to grant that "certain . . . parts [of the poem] (especially about Shahji) are so natural and plausible that I am inclined to accept them if those parts . . . on which we possess parallel light from Persian sources are found correct on comparison with the latter." But "certain passages are purely fictitious, and some (I suspect) are modern interpolations,—viz. Shivaji's education and encyclopaedic knowledge, the details of hand to hand combats &c., Shahji's overpowering love for Jija and Shiva." "A poor Brahmin scholar," he added, "could not have burdened himself with histories of Bijapur, Ahmadnagar, the Mughal empire, &c., during a long journey from Deccan to North India, nor could he have burdened his memory with the names of *yavanas* [in Nagri, meaning "Muslims"] who fought fifty years ago! Therefore, he must have made these lists from his imagination or recollection of more recent battles—or the poem was composed in *Tanjore* in the late 18th century when Persian histories of the above Muhammadan dynasties were *all* available. It is not a contemporary record even in the narrative portion."[54] In 1952, he went further to say that *Shiva-bharat* was "merely a laudatory poem written by a Court flatterer" and that it had been hailed by the ignorant as a historical source of first-rate authenticity written by a contemporary [of Shivaji]." Some Marathi scholars, added Sarkar, even suspected it "of being a very late Tanjore fabrication." It was, however, "very useful for [the documentation] of Tantrik influence on Shambhuji."[55]

Vaidya's book was a direct assault on Sarkar's position, without naming Sarkar. "Though a poem, especially one called *Bharata*," wrote Vaidya, "exaggerates many things, there are some facts which can never be invented." "Thus

53. Sarkar, *Shivaji*, 3rd ed. (1929), p. 415. "The poem was narrated in the form of a dialogue between the poet and the Brahmans of Benares, where Paramanand had come on a pilgrimage (between 1664 and 1673)." Sarkar comments: "A Hindu priest-pilgrim to far-off Benares could not in those days of difficulty of transport and unsafe travelling, have burdened himself with history books, and yet our poet, writing about 1670, professes to give minute details and long lists of generals (sometimes on three sides) for battles that were fought in 1624 and even earlier! This holy Brahman must have had a prodigious memory for non-Scriptural matters!" (p. 415). See also Sarkar's criticism of the text on p. 145n.

54. NL, JSP, letter no. 71, Sarkar to Sardesai, Tonga Rd, Darjeeling, 3 October 1927.

55. Sarkar, *Shivaji*, 5th ed. (1952), pp. 394, 396. See also Sarkar's extended remarks on this text in his *House of Shivaji*, chap. 22, entitled "Shivaji's Poet Laureate."

Shiva-Bharata may exaggerate the beauty of Shivaji's mother or the prowess of Shivaji in battle. But it cannot invent a new date or a new name or even a new incident. Especially we may bear in mind that Paramanand was a contemporary poet writing at Shivaji's suggestion and had thus at command the assistance of reliable papers and persons." And, then, as if in a direct reference to Sarkar, Vaidya laid down his charge: "Those who seek to minimize the value of this work because it is a poem are really mistaken in their view and *may be said to be inexpert in the appreciation of evidence*." For, "events, dates or names cannot be questioned when noted by contemporary writers."[56]

History and the Politics of Recognition

Debates over the heroic exploits of Shivaji got complicated in the 1920s and 1930s as a Brahman–non-Brahman conflict erupted in Maratha history, making the seventeenth-century Maratha king Shivaji a key symbol in this conflict.[57] When the liberal Maharashtrian Brahman politician M. G. Ranade wrote his *Rise of the Maratha Power* at the end of the nineteenth century, he treated Shivaji (a Maratha king coupled with a Brahman guru, Ramdas) as a national symbol for all castes, including Brahmans. This was indeed the Shivaji that Bengalis celebrated during the Swadeshi movement (1905–1907).[58] As the non-Brahman movement in Maharashtra gathered momentum, however, in the late nineteenth and early twentieth centuries, Shivaji, a Shudra king with aspirations to Kshatriya status, was claimed as a symbol of non-Brahman pride in public life.[59] Caste conflicts over interpretations of the past were endemic in Indian modernity. One important reason that V. K. Rajwade left his own Itihas Samshodhak Mandal forever around 1917–18 had to do with a historical spat with Keshav Sitaram Thakre, more popularly known as Pabodhonkar Thakre, who was the father of Bal Thakre, the founder of the modern political party Shiv Sena in Maharashtra. Rajwade read a paper entitled "Gagabhattakrut shivarajprashasti va kayasthdharma pradeep" (A panegyric on Shivaji by Gagabhatta, or the lamp of Kayastha-dharma) at a meeting of the Mandal in 1916. The paper came as an affront to the Prabhus, Chandraseniya kayasthas, a caste group that was heavily involved in the

56. Preface to Vaidya, *Shivaji*, pp. i–ii, iii, emphasis added.

57. See Laine, *Shivaji*; Jasper, "Commemorating Shivaji"; and Rosalind O'Hanlon, "Maratha History as Polemic: Low Caste Ideology and Political Debate in Late Nineteenth-Century Western India," *Modern Asian Studies* 17, no. 1 (1983), pp. 1–33.

58. See Gautam Bhadra's essay on Sakharam Deuskar, "Janaparishare itihash: 'Desher katha'" [in Bengali], *Charcha* (Calcutta) (July 2012), pp. 47–72.

59. O'Hanlon, "Maratha History as Polemic."

emerging non-Brahman movement and that claimed to have enjoyed a close relationship to Shivaji during the latter's reign. Thakre, a leader of the CKPs (as the Chandraseniya Kayastha Prabhus were called), soon came out with a reply, "Kodandacha tanatkar" (the twang of a bow), which targeted Chitpavan Brahmans, a group to which Rajwade belonged. At this, Rajwade broke all his associations with the Mandal.[60]

Sarkar's book *Shivaji and His Times* (1919) appeared in this maelstrom of politics over Maratha identity. His book was criticized on publication by Poona scholars for, among other things, his supposed failure to even mention *maharashtradharma* [roughly translated as "the spirit of Maharashtra"]—a term "fully symbolic of the great movement of uplift that Ramdas [Shivaji's guru], and Shivaji . . . had carried on during the seventeenth century, . . . a term which is the key to unlock the mystery of the Marathi Swarajya [self-rule]."[61] This criticism, mainly from Brahman sources (since Ramdas was seen as a Brahman favorite), was only to be supplemented by more intense complaints as the Brahman-non-Brahman conflict unfolded in Maharashtra.

Sarkar, Sardesai, and Their Non-Brahman Critics

Krishnarao Arjunrao Keluskar, a teacher at Wilson High School in Bombay, wrote a biography of Shivaji in 1907, entitled *Kshatriyakulabatangsha chhatrapati Shivajimaharajanche charitra* (A life of Shivaji maharaj, lord of the royal umbrella and the pride of the Kshatriya lineage). The book was dedicated to the king of Kolhapur, Shahu Maharaj, who himself had just managed to upgrade his status from Shudra to that of being a Kshatriya.[62] N. S. Takakhav, a teacher at Wilson College, in Bombay, translated the book into English in 1921. In 1924 the Shri Shivaji Literary Memorial Committee was founded in Bombay, as part of the growing non-Brahman movement. Keluskar, the author of the original Marathi version, was a member of this commit-

60. The story is told in Dr. Suresh R. Deshpande, *Maratheshahiche adhunik bhashyakar* (Pune: Gokul Masik Prakashan, 1994), pp. 66–67. The story of the conflict between Chitpavan Brahmans and C. K. Prabhus is detailed in Prachi Deshpande, *Creative Pasts: Historical Memory and Identity in Western India, 1700–1960* (New York: Columbia University Press, 2007), pp. 181. For Thakre's reminiscences of these incidents, see his "Majhi jeevan gatha," in *Probodhankara Thakare samgra vangmaya* (Mumbai: Maharshtra Rajya Sahitya ani Sanskriti Mandali, 1997), 1:191–193.

61. See the review by "Junata Purusha" [Common man], *Mahratta* 17 (August 1919).

62. I have used an English translation of this book: N. S. Takakhav, *The Life of Shivaji Maharaj, Founder of the Maratha Empire* (adapted from the original Marathi work written by K. A. Keluskar) (Bombay: Manoranjan Press, 1921), foreword.

tee. The committee decided to publish an "authentic life story" of Shivaji, with a view to removing "unfounded prejudices and misunderstandings unfortunately perpetuated in . . . Maratha history written by irresponsible writers who chiefly gathered their information from Mahomedan sources," a reference to the likes of Sarkar. Keluskar's Marathi book was selected for this purpose. The ruler of the Holkar dynasty—another pillar of the non-Brahman movement—gave twenty-eight thousand rupees to get four thousand copies of this book distributed gratis to libraries and institutions. One copy of the book ended up in the Regenstein Library of the University of Chicago.[63]

In his preface to the translation of Keluskar's volume, Takakhav referred to Sarkar's *Shivaji and His Times* (1919) directly to say: "His [Sarkar's] sympathies are with Moguls and the commanders of the Mogul empire. His sympathies are with the British factors in Surat and Rajapur. His sympathies are anywhere except with Shivaji and his gallant companions. . . . Shivaji is at best patronized here and there with a nodding familiarity and spoken of as if a familiar underling with the name of 'Shiva.'"[64] It was no small irony that the new non-Brahman history warriors would thus make the self-described admirer of Ranke, Jadunath Sarkar, out to be a partisan, Muslim-influenced, and deliberately anti-Hindu historian, while some Muslim intellectuals had already taken exception to Sarkar's exposition of Islam and of Aurangzeb's religious policies, particularly in the third volume of his *History of Aurangzib*.[65] Even today, as we saw in the introduction, several scholars regard Sarkar as a "Hindu communal" historian.[66]

The anti-Brahmanic history war over Shivaji reached a crescendo around 1930–31. Much of it had to do with the question of access to the Peshwa Daftar, the records left by the pre-British rulers, the peshwas, in western, central, southern, and northern India that the first governor of Bombay, Lord Elphinstone, acquired and gathered at the Alienation Office in Poona. This material attracted the attention of the Indian Historical Records Commission, mainly because of "the great revival of interest in the Maratha period of Indian History" that was "a feature"—as Sir Leslie Wilson, the governor of Bombay, put it in opening the 1925 meeting of the commission—"of the last quarter of

63. Ibid. The copy at the Regenstein Library at the University of Chicago has all this information printed on a sheet of paper attached to the back cover. Non-Brahman leaders from Gwalior and Baroda too helped with the publication and distribution of this book.

64. Takakhav, *Life*, preface, p. 6. For more criticisms of Sarkar, see pp. vi, ix, 16n1, 268n3, 478n1, 566, 569n1, 620n1.

65. See Zahiruddin Faruki, *Aurangzeb & His Times* (1935; Delhi: Idarah-I Adabiyat-i Delli, 1972).

66. See the discussion in note 28 to the introduction.

a century."[67] The 1921 meeting of the commission had passed a resolution "urging upon the Government of Bombay the importance of scientific investigation of the . . . Peshwa Daftar."[68] (Sarkar would have had a hand in introducing the word "scientific" into the resolution.) The 1925 meeting passed a further resolution recommending to the government of Bombay "that an expert be placed on special duty to prepare a handlist of the unsorted and unclassified *rumals* (bundles of documents) in the Poona Daftar."[69] The motion was reaffirmed at the meetings of 1926 and 1927, and the upshot was the appointment of Sarkar's friend G. S. Sardesai to the task.[70] Sardesai worked on this project under the official guidance of Sarkar and eventually produced a series known as the *Selections from the Peshwa Daftar*, in forty-five slim volumes. Sir Roger Lumley, the governor of Bombay who opened the commission's meeting at Poona in 1938, devoted a long paragraph of paean to Sardesai for having published selections from the Peshwa Daftar: "The work has been completed and 46 [*sic*] volumes, covering some 8000 pages, have been published. . . . Future generations of students . . . will owe an immense sense of gratitude to . . . Sardesai for this great work."[71] With active assistance from the bureaucracy, Jadunath Sarkar and G. S. Sardesai later took up the editing and selection of the records of the East India Company official who served as the resident at the Poona court in the eighteenth century.[72]

All hell broke loose in the non-Brahman political circles—as well as among the Mandal historians of Poona who themselves wanted access to the records of the Peshwa Daftar—on Sardesai's appointment to this position. Prachi Deshpande has described how once the report of the Inam

67. *IHRC Proceedings*, vol. 7, *Seventh Meeting, Held at Poona, January 1925* (Calcutta: GOI, Central Publishing Branch, 1925), p. 3.

68. The Government appointed a committee with Professor H. G. Rawlinson, principal of Deccan College, Poona, as chair, and with B. K. Thakore, D. V. Potdar, G. S. Sardesai, D. B. Parasnis, and Jadunath Sarkar as members. Ibid., p. 4.

69. Ibid., p. 105.

70. Ibid., p. 33.

71. *IHRC Proceedings*, vol. 15, *Fifteenth Meeting, Held at Poona, December 1938* (Delhi: Manager of Publications, GOI, 1939), p. 5.

72. A note circulated at the 1937 meeting of the IHRC said: "As a result of the various resolutions passed by the Commission at earlier sessions the cream of the Maratha records of the Peshwa Daftar has been published by the government of Bombay in 45 volumes under the editorship of Rao Bahadur G. S. Sardesai. The selections from the Poona Residency are also being published under the joint editorship of Sir Jadunath Sarkar and . . . G. S. Sardesai. Four volumes of this series [have] already been published." *IHRC Proceedings*, vol. 14, *Fourteenth Meeting, Held at Lahore, December 1937* (Delhi: Manager of Publications, GOI, 1938), p. 148. Sarkar said at this meeting that the project took four years (1930–1933) to complete at a cost of Rs. 10,000 per year.

Commission—set up to inquire into records kept by village accountants and district officers in the peshwa period immediately preceding the establishment of British rule—was submitted in Bombay in 1873, "the Peshwa Daftar in Pune became the focus of a new historical imagination for the Western-educated Marathi middle class."[73] But of critical importance to this part of the story were larger political developments in the Bombay Presidency. The non-Brahman movement of the presidency had achieved new strengths by the mid-1920s. The well-known non-Brahman leader B. D. Jhadav was appointed the first non-Brahman education minister of the Bombay government for 1924–26. He stayed on as the agriculture minister for the next few years. The non-Brahman leaders of the Bombay Legislative Council raised many questions over the appointment of Sardesai (a Karhare Brahman) as the editor of a proposed set of selections to be made from the eighteenth-century Maratha records now held by the British.[74] They said many mean things. For instance, they described histories written by Sardesai as "story books." They asked, insultingly: What experience of research did he have? Did the government know that he had been dismissed [not true] by the Baroda state?[75] Their questions and motives—turning around whether or not a Brahman could write the history of non-Brahmans (such as the Marathas)—would not sound new to us. But they show how deep the connection between history and identity politics is on the subcontinent. I cite here some of the questions asked and answers given in the Bombay Legislative Council. The questioners of 13 March 1930 were Rao Bahadur S. K. Bole, N. E. Navle, and others. W. F. Hudson supplied the answers on behalf of the government. The questions were aimed at the Brahman Sardesai and his Brahman assistant, K. P. Kulkarni:

RAO BAHADUR S. K. BOLE [SKB]: Were applications invited for the post? . . .
HUDSON [WFH]: No.
SKB: Were there no fit persons to do the work from the backward communities?
WFH: Not as far as I know.
SKB: May I bring to the notice of the Honourable Member names of persons from among the backward castes who have done historical research work?

73. Prachi Deshpande, "Scripting the Cultural History of Language: Modi in the Colonial Archive," in *New Cultural Histories of India: Materiality and Practices*, ed. Partha Chatterjee, Tapati Guha-Thakurta, and Bodhisattva Kar (New Delhi: Oxford University Press, 2014), p. 81.

74. See Maureen L. P. Patterson, "A Preliminary Study of the Brahman versus non-Brahman Conflict in Maharashtra" (M.A. thesis, University of Pennsylvania, 1952), pp. 113, 115.

75. S. R. Tikekar, *Jadunath Sarkar yani Riyasatkar Sardesai: Toulonik charitmatmak abhyas* (Mumbai: Popular Prakashan, 1961), pp. 37–40.

WFH: Thank you. . . .

SKB: How many non-Brahmin readers and how many Brahmin readers are employed?

WFH: Three Brahmins and three non-Brahmins.

N. E. NAVLE: Is it not a fact that the backward classes, especially the Marathas and the allied communities[,] apprehend that damage would be done to their history at the hands of the Brahmin officers whom the government have appointed?

WFH: Government are not aware of it.

SKB: Are not the government aware that manipulations are being made to give more importance to Ramdas [a Brahman saint] and less importance to Shivaji? . . .

WFH: Does the question arise, Sir? . . .

SKB: My question points out the apprehension of the backward classes that history might be tampered [with]. I was going to point out how they have begun to [distort history].[76]

It was also at this time that much was made of the fact that Sarkar could not read the Modi script in which old Marathi documents were written. Sardar G. N. Mujumdar, a Maratha member of the Legislative Council and an office-bearer of the Itihas Mandal, asked: "Is it not a fact that Sir Jadunath Sarkar and Professor Rawlinson [the recently retired principal of the Poona Fergusson College] do not know the Modi script?"[77] Bole intervened in the council debates again to ask if the government was aware "that much discontent is felt among the non-Brahman communities because no trained [non-Brahman] man, although available, was taken [by] Daftar to protect their [the non-Brahmans'] own interests in their history and that they have shown their distrust in the personnel appointed."[78]

A book published by Shri Shiva Charitra Karyalaya in Poona in 1931, *English Records on Shivaji*, edited by D. V. Kale, who later wrote a biography of Shivaji as well in Marathi, was full of complaints about Sarkar. Here is one typical example: "There is a good deal of first-class material published in Marathi. . . . Sir Jadunath has used not more than half a dozen letters from Marathi and he claims that though based as it is on English and Persian records his biography of Shivaji 'so far as existing material goes is definitive.'

76. *Bombay Legislative Council Proceedings* (Bombay: Government of Bombay, 1931), vol. 39, *Questions and Answers, 13 March 1930*, pp. 1320–1321.

77. Ibid., p. 1323.

78. Ibid., 18 March 1930, p. 1476.

This claim is fantastic even for Sir Jadunath's self-complacency. First-class historical material from Marathi sources he has not used, probably because he cannot use it properly."[79]

Faced with these history wars, the idea of "scientific history" as understood and promulgated by Sarkar had to beat a hasty retreat. It was clear that history, the discipline, was not going to acquire the kind of public life that Sarkar once dreamed for it. On being told that his histories were untrue to the real spirit of non-Brahman Maratha history because he could not read the Modi script, Sarkar could now fume only in private, for he recognized that the space for the kind of historical "truth" that he pursued had shrunk in the "public life" that populist politics had created in India. He wrote privately to his friend Sardesai:

> Potdar's statement in large type [in the *Purandaré Daftar*, vol. 2] directed against me is a piece of dishonest misrepresentation, characteristic of an infernal liar like him. I have said that I have used all the Maratha materials on Shivaji available. Now, the only materials available are the printed ones, which are *all* in *Balabodh* [Marathi in Devnagari script] and therefore can be read by me. In addition, the Modi shakhavali presented in ms. in the library of the B[om]bay branch of the R[oyal].A[siatic].S[ociety]. has been transcribed in *Balabodh* for me and used by me. No material, besides these, *known* to refer to Shivaji exists in ms. in Modi. I reject the *nibadpatras*, *mazharnamas* and worthless private documents of which thousands have been printed and many thousands are lying in ms. in Modi. My claim therefore is true to the letter, while Potdar is making a lying suggestion that *historical* papers relating to Shivaji are definitely known to exist in unprinted Modi. If so, where are they? My ignorance of Modi does not handicap me in the least, in view of the known condition and extent of Shivaji sources.[80]

Not by Facts Alone

How deep ran the lines of fissure between Sarkar's stringent demands regarding historical "facts" and the needs of Marathi historians for whom the past was a matter of regional pride may be gauged from the disagreements that surfaced privately even in the correspondence between Sarkar and his closest friend Sardesai, who, in public debates having to do with the veracity of par-

79. D. V. Kale, ed., *English Records on Shivaji (1659–1682)* (Poona: Shri Shiva Karyalaya, 1931), p. 44. The reference to Kale's biography is given in Sharma, *Founding*.

80. NL, JSP, letter no. 118, Sarkar to Sardesai, Darjiling, 16 March 1930. See also Hari Ram Gupta, ed., *Life and Letters of Sir Jadunath Sarkar* (Hoshiarpur: Punjab University, 1958), pp. 151–152.

ticular sources, sided with Sarkar all his life. But Sardesai, the older of the two scholars, remained a historian who understandably identified with the pride of the Marathas. After all, restoring Marathas to their rightful place in history was one of the major reasons why he undertook the work he did. As he himself said in the last volume of his English work *New History of the Marathas*: "The Marathas have long been misjudged by their rivals . . . as if they had no single good point to their credit."[81]

My point is not to ascertain whether either Sarkar or Sardesai was right in every pronouncement he made. But one can see how it was through debates like theirs—caught here in the intimate web of friendship—that rules of historical objectivity received their value in the history of historical writing in India. Sarkar was famously against partisan reading of sources (which is not to claim that his own readings were always nonpartisan). Thus, he wrote to Sardesai in 1940 against the excesses of nationalist historiography: "The writings of K. P. Jaysawal, though containing a few original documents, are ninety-nine per cent pure nationalist brag and moonshine, and you would be well-advised to keep clear of his theories."[82] His criticisms of sources popular with many of the historians based in Maharashtra were of the same nature. Yet Sardesai turned to some of the same sources when it came to writing *New History of the Marathas*, and partly out of motivations similar to those of Rajwade, Parasnis, and the like. Take the case of the text *Shivadigvijay* (Shivaji's conquest of the directions), allegedly "written by Khando Ballal (the son of Shivaji's secretary Balaji Avji) in 1718" and edited and published by P. R. Nandaburkar and L. K. Dandekar from Baroda in 1895.[83] Sarkar had decided as early as 1917 that this text was of no value as historical evidence. "Dear Govind Rao," he wrote to Sardesai in 1917, "I am now convinced that the *Shiva-Digvijay* is a modern forgery, probably based upon some old materials."[84] In his bibliographical essay appended to his *Shivaji* (1920), Sarkar dismissed the claim that this text was written by the son of Shivaji's secretary as "false." "The kernel of the book" may have been some "lost Marathi text composed about 1760–'75," but "the published version," Sarkar was convinced, "was evidently

81. Cited in Vasant D. Rao, "Govind Sakharam Sardesai," in Sen, *Historians*, 230.

82. NL, JSP, letter no. 632, Sarkar to Sardesai, Calcutta, 30 July 1940. Sarkar made a similar point when approached in 1957 by the president of India about chairing a committee for writing a national history of the country. He said: "The historian will not suppress any defects of the national character, but will add to his portraiture those higher qualities which, taken together with the former, help to constitute the entire individual." Cited in Jagadish Narayan Sarkar, "Thoughts on Acharya Jadunath Sarkar," *Indo-Iranica* 24, nos. 1–2 (March–June 1971), 13.

83. Sarkar, *Shivaji*, 2nd ed. (1920), p. 451.

84. NL, JSP, letter no. 14, Sarkar to Sardesai, Jail Rd, Darjeeling, 12 June 1917.

fabricated at Baroda by a writer familiar with the style of modern vernacular novels written by imitators of Bankim Chandra Chatterji. Too much gush . . . , rhetorical padding, and digression. The author speaks of an English general being present at Shivaji's coronation . . . and of goods from *Calcutta* [founded in the 1690s] used in decorating his hall in 1674 . . . !!! Shiva bows to his mother two years after her death . . . ! Tanaji Malusre visits Haidarabad seven years after his death!"[85]

Such scathing criticism of Marathi sources often made Sardesai squirm in private. Deccan College in Poona now holds his library. The collection, thankfully, and unlike the Sarkar collection at the National Library in Calcutta, has not been dispersed. If one reads through the marginal comments that Sardesai made on reading what Sarkar and other Bengali historians wrote about the Marathas, his private discomfiture about several of the claims these historians made becomes palpable, and they speak of the deep pride that he took in the history of his own people. There are many polemical question marks that litter, for instance, the margins of his copy of Surendra Nath Sen's *The Military System of the Marathas*, published in 1928. When Sen adduced a document to question Ranade's proposition that the Marathas protected "chauth [tribute]-paying countries from external aggression other than their own," Sardesai noted on the margin that the document in question "entirely supports Ranade's theory."[86] More telling are his private responses on reading the 1929 (third) edition of Sarkar's *Shivaji and His Times* (1929 was a year when Sarkar and Sardesai's battles with the Poona School were at their peak). For reasons of space, I will quote only one of Sardesai's marginal remarks on Sarkar's chapter 16 on the "excess of finesse and intrigue" in Shivaji's rule. "Writing about Shivaji," Sardesai remarks astringently, "one should not bring in all the Marathas; one should first study and then write."[87]

It is not surprising, therefore, that there should be letters dating from the early 1930s and the 1940s suggesting Sardesai's discomfiture over Sarkar's lofty dismissal of some of the texts valued by Maratha historians. He wrote to Sarkar on 28 December 1933 about a letter from Shivaji to his brother, cited in

85. Sarkar, *Shivaji*, 2nd ed. (1920), p. 451. Sarkar maintained virtually the same opinion in *Shivaji*, 3rd ed. (1929), p. 413. *Shivadigvijay* does not even rate a mention in the 1952 edition of his book.

86. Deccan College Library (DCL), Sardesai Collection, Surendra Nath Sen, *The Military System of the Marathas* (Calcutta: Book, 1928), p. 48n31. See also pp. 1, 4, 5, 47–48.

87. DCL, Sardesai Collection, Sarkar, *Shivaji*, 3rd ed. (1929), p. 398. See also Sardesai's comments on pp. v, 1, 5, 7, 8, 13, 14, 15, 17, 20, 24, 26, 27, 29, 30, 31, 32, 35, 38n, 44, 60, 61, 63, 64, 72, 89, 105, 112, 230, 388, 390, 404, registering some mild to strong disagreements mixed in with some praise as well.

Shivadigvijay, that seemed "entirely authentic." Hence, he thought that, "shorn of its flourishes, which can be easily detected, [*Shivadigvijay*] has a great substratum of truth in it and cannot be rejected as worthless." Sarkar, in his letter of 13 January, "dissented" from this view but added, somewhat despairingly, "but it would take a long time to argue the matter—and argument would probably be fruitless."[88]

This private debate continued into their letters of the 1940s. In public, Sarkar had always praised his friend and comrade-in-arms, Sardesai, in their battle against the Poona group, as a historian who made "tireless strivings after accuracy," whose "cool balance of judgment and unfailing commonsense in interpretation" had "marked him off from the common herd of popular rhetoricians and platform orators with their sole stock in trade of effervescent verbiage and cheap claptrap."[89] Things were different in private. Sardesai never quite accepted Sarkar's harsh judgment on some of the sources he really valued.

> You have summarily rejected *Shivadigvijaya* and Shivaji letters to Maloji Ghorpade . . . These letters have been fully translated in my Shivaji souvenir. It is a genuine document and explains incidentally the object of Shivaji's whole undertaking as nothing else does. I should request you to read it carefully over again and tell me why you reject it. Similarly, *Shivadigvijaya* throughout quotes genuine original letters that passed between Shivaji and his brother Ekoji. . . . The author of *Shivadigvijaya* appears to have been of Shivaji's inner circle. Of course, this *bakhar* has many worthless imaginary portions, but that must not prevent us from accepting what is palpably genuine.[90]

Sarkar's reply was unambiguous: "It would be a fatal mistake for you to depend on any point on *Shivadigvijaya*. It is opposed to the principles of historical evidence." Sarkar then referred Sardesai to authorities on the rules of historical evidence: "Borrow . . . George's *Historical Evidence* and read it through. The legal principle is 'False in one, false in all' and such witnesses are totally rejected."[91]

88. NL, JSP, letter no. 292, Sardesai to Sarkar, Kamshet, 28 December 1933; letter no. 294, Sarkar to Sardesai, Ghoramari, Rajshahi, 13 January 1934.

89. Jadunath Sarkar, "Govind Sakharam Sardesai," in *Sardesai Commemorative Volume*, ed. Shripad R. Tikekar (Bombay: Keshav Bhikaji, Dhawale, 1938), p. 299.

90. NL, JSP, letter no. 804, Sardesai to Sarkar, Kamshet, 13 June 1944.

91. NL, JSP, letter no. 807, Sarkar to Sardesai, Calcutta, 4 July 1944. The point is continued in another letter of Sarkar's: "It was no trouble to me to revise your ms at Kamshet last April. . . . My only sorrow was that I differed from you so fundamentally on the law of historical evidence; you know I reject as spurious—the letter to Jai Singh, the Hindavi Swaraj and *bel bhandar* of Jedhe; the *Shivadigvijaya* and most of the *Chitnis Bakhar*—also the letter to Venkoji after 1678,

The book that Sarkar referred Sardesai to—Hereford Brook George's *Historical Evidence* (1909)—was not an original work of scholarship. It mainly summarized a series of propositions relating to rules of evidence for historians that were gaining popularity in England in the second half of the nineteenth century after the publication of the two volumes of the scholar-politician and aristocrat George Cornewall Lewis's *An Inquiry into the Credibility of Early Roman History*.[92] George (1838–1910), who was a fellow of the New College at Oxford, followed and actually cited Lewis in characterizing historical evidence in the following terms: "Historical evidence, like every kind of evidence, is founded on the testimony of credible witnesses . . . [and] all original witnesses must be contemporaneous with the events," which was exactly the point that Sarkar made in all his correspondence and public statements on the matter.[93]

But the story did not end there. As the different volumes of *New History of the Marathas* came out, through the 1940s, the debate between Sarkar and Sardesai continued in private. Faced with Sarkar's insistent criticism of his use of sources, Sardesai sometimes took refuge in the thought that what he was writing was not scientific history, but a text in some other older genre, a *kaifiyat* (a traditional narrative; a local village collection of historical documents), for example. "I have on purpose put in Shivaji's estimates by foreign writers," he wrote in July 1944: "The Marathas have long suffered from foreign attacks on all sides. My work is essentially the Maratha *kaifiyat*."[94] Sarkar wrote back

---

as contradicted by unimpeachable contemporary evidence." NL, JSP, letter no. 815, Sarkar to Sardesai, Calcutta, 25 August 1944.

92. George Cornwall Lewis, *An Inquiry into the Credibility of Early Roman History* (London: John W. Parker, West Strand, 1855).

93. Rev. H. B. George, *Historical Evidence* (Oxford: Clarendon, 1909). See pp. 48–49 in particular.

94. NL, JSP, letter no. 809, Sardesai to Sarkar, Kamshet, 22 July 1944. Rama Mantena describes *kaifiyats* as "particulars of a place . . . collection of disparate documents that a village accountant kept as a historical record and transmitted from one generation to another. They come to occupy a prominent place in the late-eighteenth-century South India." Mantena, "The Question of History in Precolonial India," *History and Theory* 46 (October 2007), p. 404. The noted Marathi historian A. R. Kulkarni describes *kaifiyat* as "apologia" in his essay "Marathas in History," in A. R. Kulkarni, *Explorations in the Deccan History* (Delhi: Pragati and the Indian Council of Historical Research, 2006), p. 21: "I propose to present in this article, to borrow a phrase from the Riyasatkar Sardesai, 'a true kaifiyat (apologia)' of the Maratha people for the consideration of historical scholarship." Raja Dixit, "Historical Writing and Research," in *A History of Modern Marathi Literature*, ed. Rajendra Banhatti and G. N. Jogalekar (Pune: Maharashtra Sahitya Parishad, 2004), 2:239, defines it as "family accounts." H. K. Sherwani, "Contemporary Histories of the Qutb Shah Dynasty of Golkonda," in *Historians of Medieval India*, ed. Mohibbul

in December 1945 to say that he did not "approve of [the] tone or style" of Sardesai's draft introduction. "It is too much like modern political platform oration from some political aspirant, and does not breathe the calm judicial spirit of a true historian," he admonished, offering to rewrite it "wholesale."[95] Sardesai politely refused: "I did not to wish to put you to so much labour."[96]

Sarkar continued with his criticisms into the following two years. On 6 April 1947 he wrote humorously: "I have consulted a *Joshi* [astrologer] and he tells me that your chapter . . . on 'The Contingent in History' was born under the planet *shanichar* [Saturn]. . . . Please reduce it to one short paragraph. A historical book meant for a permanent place on the library shelf is not a table talk."[97] He was filled with "despair" on reading drafts of "the last chapters of your volume III"—in particular to read Sardesai "on the 'heroic' role of the Pindharis" (groups that used to attach themselves to Maratha troops and engage in looting and plunder in the wake of their actions)—"and I have therefore made no attempt to modify or correct them from *my* point of view."[98] Again in August 1947: "What pained me most was your attitude to historical evidence and certain political theories."[99]

The Fusion/Confusion of Genres

The conclusion to this story suggests how closely intertwined were the two modes of history writing, the one involving one's pride in a particular identity, and the other aspiring to some principle of impartial objectivity. It is interesting to see that till the very end, Sardesai retained the wish to clothe his historical claims about the Marathas in some genre that resisted objective history—*kaifiyat*, table-talk, and so on—even after Sarkar had explicitly warned him that a "historical book meant for a permanent place on the library shelf is not . . . table talk."[100] He sent Sarkar a draft "farewell to [his] last

---

Hasan (Meerut: Meenakshi Prakashan, 1968), pp. 96–97, explains the genre *kaifiyat* in this way: "We have a number of village accounts called *Kaifiyats*. These originated in the *dandakaviles* or *kaviles* which were kept by the village *karnam* or revenue office (*patwari*), and contained information about the political, religious, social and economic conditions of the village, including an account of the contemporary events which had bearing on the locality. . . . These *kaifiyats* are an 'admixture of legends and history.'"

95. NL, JSP, letter no. 864, Sarkar to Sardesai, Calcutta, 30 December 1945, night.

96. NL, JSP, letter no. 867, Sardesai to Sarkar, Kamshet, 13 January 1946.

97. NL, JSP, letter no. 925, Sarkar to Sardesai, Calcutta, 6 April 1947.

98. NL, JSP, letter no. 934, Sarkar to Sardesai, Calcutta, 27 July 1947.

99. NL, JSP, letter no. 938, Sarkar to Sardesai, Calcutta, 19 August 1947.

100. NL, JSP, letter no. 925, Sarkar to Sardesai, Calcutta, 6 April 1947.

volume" for the correction of a particular sentence he was unhappy with. He initially described his work as "table-talk"—precisely something Sarkar said history was not—and then deleted that word. It is a tribute to the quality of the friendship of these two men that Sarkar, who drastically revised that particular sentence at Sardesai's request, let the expression "table-talk" stand. Sardesai had originally written: "I do not claim to be a scholar or even a trained historian but an eager tireless student. Call this my final work, if you like it, the endless table-talk of a garrulous old man." He then himself took out the expression "table-talk" and changed it to read: "I do not claim to be a scholar or even a trained historian but an eager tireless student. Call this my final work if you like it, the endless outpourings of an ardent heart." But see how Sarkar revised the sentence while restoring—perhaps with a mixture of feelings—the expression "table-talk" to its original position:

> I do not claim to be a scholar or even a trained historian but only an *eager* [circled by JS] *~~tireless~~* [crossed out by JS] *earnest* [inserted by JS] worker. Call *this* [circled by JS in pencil] my final work, *if you like it* [crossed out and then restored by JS], the *~~long~~* [inserted and then crossed out by JS] *~~endless~~* [crossed out by JS] table-talk of a *~~garrulous~~* [crossed out by JS] *~~student~~* [underlined by GSS, crossed out by JS] *lifelong seeker after knowledge* [inserted by JS].[101]

It is this version, revised by Sarkar, that now stands in Sardesai's book.

This mutual accommodation between Sarkar's positivist position and Sardesai's stance that was partisan to Maratha national sentiments, I suggest, may be read as a compressed allegory of the process through which the principles of academic history were born in colonial India—always distinct from, and even opposed to, the popular, but also always in conversation with the latter. Popular struggles for historical recognition—whether it was for Indians as a nation or for the caste or religious identity of some group or other—left their birthmarks, as it were, even on the works of those committed to produce academic history.

The Remaining Problem of Vernacular Pasts

Sarkar's commitment to academic history was, as we have seen, also a commitment to the global republic of letters, where European scholarship set the standards. His friend and contemporary Rabindranath Tagore, the poet, could see that histories written in Indian languages and meant to address the

101. NL, JSP, letter no. 973, Sardesai, Kamshet, undated; Sarkar noted on the letter: "posted Kamshet, 3 September '48; recd. 17 September 1948."

feelings of different groups of Indians often issued from a wounded psychology, in this case the psychology of the colonized who needed to compensate for the ways in which Indians were often depicted in the histories that the Europeans, especially the British, wrote about them. (Lower castes would similarly extend the argument to cover the wrongdoings of the upper castes.) When the Bengali historian Akshaykumar Maitreya (1861–1930) published his Bengali history of Siraj-ud-daulah (1898), challenging imperial accounts of the "Black Hole tragedy," Tagore wrote an admiring but critical review of it. Tagore's criticisms had little or nothing to do with any violation of the usual rules of evidence that historians were supposed to abide by, but with the point that Maitreya's prose displayed a degree of impatience and emotion that Tagore thought distracted from the spirit of calmness called for in historical judgments, thus giving rise in the reader's mind to an "unnecessary anxiety about partisanship."[102] But he maintained an understanding attitude toward Maitreya's aggrieved emotions, for he saw them as the products of the "wounded heart" of the oppressed.[103] "We are forced to study statements by foreigners that damn us, for we have to learn them by rote in order to pass examinations," wrote Tagore. There was, besides, the question of the colonized's admiration for the colonizer: "The English are our powerful masters. Their power and influence are excessively attractive [for us]. They are indeed so powerful that weak individuals would just be too overcome with fear, surprise, and a [sense of] blind attachment to be able to respond even if some injustice or oppression were committed." On the other hand, "only a few among the English could even imagine the resentment born out of humiliation in the minds of the educated public." Hence, "to doubt that which brings us only calumny in the conflict of the East and the West and to present proofs to the contrary," as Maitreya had done in his book on Siraj-ud-daulah, was to tend to the most urgent needs of "our lowered heads and wounded hearts."[104]

Tagore also contrasted the dryness—the word he used in Bengali was *nirosh* (Sanskrit *Nirasa*, without *rasa* or juice, desiccated)—of the English histories of India with the way that Indian stories about Indian heroes touched readers' hearts. "Whoever has had to commit history to memory in school

102. Rabindranath Thakur [Tagore], "Sirajuddoula," in *Rabindrarachanabali* [Collected works of Rabindranath] [in Bengali], 13:473–474.

103. On the larger question of the relationship between identarian histories and what I call "historical wounds," see my essay "History and the Politics of Recognition," in *Manifestos for History*, ed. Keith Jenkins, Sue Morgan, and Alun Munslow (London: Routledge, 2007), pp. 77—87.

104. Tagore, "Sirajuddoula," p. 475. Chatterjee, *Black Hole of Empire*, chap. 8, has a rich discussion of the cultural processes and institutions that helped Bengalis assimilate the story of Siraj-ud-daulah into their twentieth-century nationalism.

will have to acknowledge that descriptions of English rule in India form the driest part of Indian history," wrote Tagore. One reason for that was that "one could not see clearly the play of human nature in these descriptions." "A governor arrives, a battle takes place, victory and defeat are handed out, laws are made, five years go by, and the governor leaves." Mughal rule expressed the likes and dislikes of individual emperors, something that gave "Indian history a variety of *rasas* at every step." "But England's India was ruled by [the constitutional] monarchy of England." The play of passions was a very minor factor compared to "policy." "No people, no king, only a policy that has in place a relay of runners covering its long path, runners who are replaced every five years." This is how Tagore described this history. The network of policy was like "a cobweb" that "extended as far as Gibraltar and Egypt while covering India from head to toe." Mr. Lyall's book *Indian Empire*, added Tagore, was distinguished by a brief and pleasant account of its subject. But this history lacked "the *rasa* of the historical novel"—or "what is called romance in English"—that one could find, for instance, in accounts of the rule of the East India Company before the Crown took over.[105]

Knowledge of history—or the lack of such knowledge—was where the gap between the literate and the nonliterate assumed its most visible form in India, argued Tagore in an essay entitled, significantly, "Itihaskatha" (The story of history). History had to be taken to "the people" in the shape of genres of performance they were most familiar with: *jatra* (traditional forms of play) and *kathakata* (performative storytelling). "My proposal is this," he wrote: "that we adopt the means needed to propagate history by enlivening its stories . . . with colorful descriptions through the forms of *jatra* and *kathakata*." Even "imaginary stories"—perhaps accounts that Sarkar might have called "false"—might serve this purpose, argued Tagore. In conclusion, he asked: "If the story of *Bidyasundar* could be disseminated by *jatra*s, why wouldn't stories of Prithviraj, Guru Govind, Shivaji, Akbar and others be of interest to people? And why wouldn't novels like *Aanadamath* and *Rajsingha* be delightfully enjoyable, coming from the lips of a storyteller [*kathak*] who also sang well?"[106]

What Tagore wrote went to the heart of the distinction between the public and the cloistered lives of history in the subcontinent. English became the language of Indian academic history, thus cutting it off from the masses that

105. Tagore, "Sirajuddoula," p. 472. Perhaps the book by Lyall that Tagore referred to was Alfred Comyn Lyall's *The Rise and Expansion of the British Dominion in India* (London: John Murray, 1893).

106. Tagore, "Itihaskatha," in *Rabindrarachanabali*, 13:490–491.

had no access to that language. Academic history in India, thus, would find it very difficult to be what Nietzsche once called "history for life." Sarkar respected Tagore's writings on history and even translated some of his essays on the subject. But one doubts that Sarkar's imagination would have traveled this far with his more famous and gifted contemporary. Tagore's points, however, continue to resonate with South Asian scholars for whom, as for Sarkar, English remains a "second language," a "foreigner's tongue," however proficient they might be in handling it. The point was taken up about a decade ago by Ranajit Guha in his *History at the Limit of World-History* and has been elaborated upon in some recent and significant publications on histories "in the vernacular."[107] The spirit of Sardesai's struggle against Sarkar, one might say, continues to haunt even the cloistered life of the subject called "Indian history."

107. See Ranajit Guha, *History at the Limit of World-History* (New York: Columbia University Press, 2002); and Partha Chatterjee, "Introduction: History in the Vernacular," and Sudeshna Purakayastha, "Restructuring the Past in Early-Twentieth-Century Assam," in Aquil and Chatterjee, *History in the Vernacular*, pp. 1–24, 172–208. See also my essay "Itihasher janajibon" [The public life of history] [in Bengali], in Dipesh Chakrabarty, *Itihasher janajibon o onyanyo probondho* [The public life of history and other essays] (Calcutta: Ananda, 2011).

5

The Statesman as Hero: An Imperial Aesthetic for a National History

Why would "unquestionable facts" signify true patriotism for Sir Jadunath? One way to understand what Sarkar could have meant by "true"—as opposed to "false"—patriotism would be to examine his use of the word *tragedy* with regard to the fall of the Mughal empire. The use of this word was not original with him. He may have owed it to the historiography developed by colonial officials. He was not even the first person to speak of the "rot" of the empire that allegedly set in in the concluding decades of Aurangzeb's reign. For Sidney Owen argued precisely that point in his *The Fall of the Mogul Empire*, published in 1912. Owen remarked in his preface: "A common impression is, that, as it is so often the case in the East, the decline and fall of the Mogul Empire were due to the degeneracy of its Sovereigns. But it is the object of this book to show that it was irretrievably ruined in the reign of Aurangzib, a monarch of great ability, energy, and determination, but lacking in political insight, and a bigoted Mussulman."[1]

But Sarkar's use of the word *tragedy* also marked a departure from the way European writers had used it to describe the fall of the Mughals. The word connected his sentiments of patriotism, his aesthetics of historical prose, and his training in literature. More importantly, it let him express a particular view of the political that we will discuss in this and the following chapters. We will not understand Sarkar's ideas regarding historical methods unless we see that for him, politics turned around the question of virtue and thus around the idea of character. The imperial literary canon supplied him with the tropes necessary for such an exercise, the tropes of heroism and tragedy. Readers will recall that Muslim historians and chroniclers of the eighteenth

1. Sidney J. Owen, *The Fall of the Mughal Empire* (London: John Murray, 1912), p. v.

century also spoke of vices and virtues of the sovereign and used the image of "rot" to describe the disintegration of the Mughal Empire over the eighteenth and early nineteenth centuries. We need to understand both what Sarkar's political imagination owed, and what it did not owe, to the late Mughal and the imperial British traditions, respectively, in order to see what may have been distinctive about his political and historical imagination. That exercise will also help explain a point about his method: why the category of "character" was so important to his historical analysis, a topic that we take up in chapter 6.

Why Political History Was Literary

Sarkar's political sensibility could not be separated from his literary sensibility, nor the latter from his sense of what historical writing was. He saw his historical prose, ideally, as literature, and he referred to his authorial endeavors, throughout his life, as his literary work. "Literary grace is the *sine qua non* for my Foreword, as for an essay in the *Edinburgh Review*," he wrote to Sardesai in 1931 after the latter made some complaints about a foreword Sarkar had penned for the multivolume selections from the Peshwa Daftar records that Sardesai had edited.[2] Or, in his old age, he would write thus to Sardesai in 1943: "In my growing years of accumulation of unfinished literary work, I must husband my time and energy in future."[3] And later, in 1948: "I have been passing my days in a sort of living death in the damp heat of Calcutta since my return. . . . I can do no literary work in the climate, but have to pass my days like a bullock or a dog."[4] Or even more depressingly in 1955, when his old age had been troubled by a series of bereavements and losses in personal life: "I am facing my 86th birthday without any joy and without that serene look at the future which is the highest reward of a well-spent life. I do not share your happy lot in standing on the brink of Eternity, as an absolutely detached creature, free from every earthly entanglement and ready to drop into eternal slumber at a moment's notice. . . . I see only darkness before me. This distracting thought is sapping my vitality and has put an end to my literary activity."[5]

Given that historical writing was a "literary activity" for Sarkar, matters of style and presentation were naturally of the utmost concern to him. Once, in January 1943, when Sardesai was working on his three-volume English-

2. NL, JSP, letter no. 168, Sarkar to Sardesai, Darjiling, 14 August 1931.

3. NL, JSP, letter no. 779, Sarkar to Sardesai, Calcutta, 22 November 1943.

4. NL, JSP, letter no. 960, Sarkar to Sardesai, Calcutta, 25 June 1948.

5. NL, JSP, letter no. 1194, Sarkar to Sardesai, Calcutta, 7 December 1955.

language *New History of the Marathas*, he approached Sarkar for help with "choosing appropriate [English] words," remarking: "Sir Richard Temple's writings strike me as splendid particularly in point of happy phraseology. McMordie was common in my school days."[6] Sarkar's response shows how seriously he took the role of the historian as a writer. There was a "new and greatly improved edition of Roget's *Thesaurus*," he said; and McMordie was indeed "very useful in teaching us how to avoid *errors* of grammar or idiom," but it was "not helpful in showing the way to elegant writing."

> In fact [wrote Sarkar], the surest means of acquiring a good style is (1) to read *aloud* the best English prose—avoid ornate and involved author[s], such as Dr. Johnson and Macaulay—for half an hour *every morning*; (2) to avoid trashy authors, except when it is necessary to pick facts out of them, and (3) to pause and revise frequently in the course of our own writing. . . . You write too long and too diffusely, and hence your style is bound to suffer. I compress as much as I can, and hence I have the time to revise and polish my words,—or rather, as I meditate before writing, the words flow well-chosen out of my pen. This would have been impossible if I had to write 50 or 60 foolscap folios of English prose everyday.[7]

A couple of years later, when Sardesai mailed him a copy of a draft "introduction" to his *New History*, Sarkar wrote back disapprovingly of its tone or style." "It is too much like modern political platform oration from some political aspirant, and does not breathe the calm judicial spirit of a true historian." He referred Sardesai to the American writer John Lothrop Motley's *Rise of the Dutch Republic* (1855), which told of "the struggle of a small beauty-loving nation against a tyrannical empire" and was "one of the most elevating examples of human endeavour."[8] Perhaps Motley could provide a model for Nana.

Style, therefore, was of crucial concern to Sarkar; it helped to convey the drama of history. "Many years ago," he wrote somewhat proudly to Nana in 1935, "a European critic called me 'a master of the miniature' style of history writing—i.e. of the art of putting many things into a small readable compass, where nothing of use is omitted."[9] The following year, while working on the third volume of his *Fall*, he spent a lot of time thinking about how to present the historical material he had collected: "The style is the thing that has given me most trouble, and not the facts. I long racked my brain over the problem of how to make this sickening story of decadence, intrigue and misery read-

6. NL, JSP, letter no. 754, Sardesai to Sarkar, Kamshet, 22 January 1943.
7. NL, JSP, letter no. 755, Sarkar to Sardesai, Calcutta, 29 January 1943.
8. NL, JSP, letter no. 864, Sarkar to Sardesai, Calcutta, 30 December 1945.
9. NL, JSP, letter no. 389, Sarkar to Sardesai, Calcutta, 30 December 1935.

able to the modern world. But the back of the difficulty has now been broken, thanks to judicious omission, arrangement and turning around things, and the rest of the volume will be more speedily written."[10] Sardesai received advice along similar lines a few years later: "Don't clutter your canvas by going into details about our countless minor dynasties. . . . Try to lay your emphasis on the great dynasties—and only on the great personages in them and . . . [on] reflections on the characteristics of the periods, culture and great characters and their influence on Indian life and society—so as to leave a *clear* impression on the reader and to make your presentation memorable."[11]

Sarkar may have thought of Macaulay's prose as "ornate" and "involved," but there is no question that the great English writer was an important point of reference in Sarkar's own erudition. Consider how, in the third volume of his *History of Aurangzib*, Sarkar sets the scene of the beginnings of Aurangzeb's rule. He describes how, having disposed of the brothers who had given him trouble before and during his coronation in 1658, the emperor sought to impress "foreign" ambassadors at his court by making "that lavish display of his wealth and pomp which 'dazzled even eyes which were accustomed to the pomp of Versailles.'"[12] Sarkar cited no source for that fragment of a quotation about dazzling "even eyes which were accustomed to the pomp of Versailles." These unacknowledged words that Sarkar seamlessly wove into his own sentence were actually Macaulay's, taken from the latter's famous essay "Lord Clive," published in the *Edinburgh Review* in January 1840.[13] Sarkar assumed a degree of familiarity on his reader's part with Macaulay's prose. He saw himself in the tradition of modern (English) historiography that existed before the rise of what toward the end of the twentieth century came to be known in the Anglophone world as "social history," that is to say, before history became a softer version of the social sciences and a handmaiden, mainly, of sociology.[14]

Imperial Heroism

History shaped by a powerful literary sensibility is, then, what Sarkar aspired to write. His prose is sprinkled with quotations from literary sources—Burns,

10. NL, JSP, letter no. 432, Sarkar to Sardesai, Darjiling, 20 October 1936.

11. NL, JSP, letter no. 632, Sarkar to Sardesai, Calcutta, 30 July 1940.

12. Sarkar, *History of Aurangzib*, vol. 3 (1916; Delhi: Orient Longman, 1972), p. 4. The publisher wrongly gives 1928 as the date for the first edition.

13. See Thomas Babington Macaulay, "Lord Clive," in his *Essays on Lord Clive and Warren Hastings* (New York: Charles E. Merrill, 1910), p. 34.

14. Here I refer mainly to the dominant historiography in the Anglophone world in the 1950s, 1960s, and 1970s, before the emergence of "new cultural history" and postmodernism.

Tennyson, Shakespeare, Coleridge, and others—but they remain mostly unnamed. Himself a professor of English literature, he perhaps expected his reader to know the literary canon of the empire. His own relationship to this canon was deep. He had absorbed to a great degree the imperial lore of the British. This literary universe not only molded a large part of Sarkar's moral-political and even military imagination; it acted as the very incubator of his political thought. It cannot be without significance that for a man steeped in Persian sources, many of which—letters and histories, for example—often had nuggets of Persian poetry embedded in them, Sarkar's imagination of the human condition was strangely uninflected by this literature to which he was exposed every day. Of far more profound influence was the literature of the imperial world the British created. The intellectual heritage of the British Empire in India provided him with the raw materials with which to forge the image of the nation. Why else would he use the form of imperial history—with Gibbon as its master artist—to create a possible past for the nation?[15]

Consider how Sarkar conveys his sense of military heroism while discussing the Maratha disaster on the battlefield of Panipat against the Afghans (Ahmed Shah Abdali) in 1761 in the second volume of his *Fall*. Sarkar accuses "Maratha writers" of judging harshly the military leader of the Marathas in that campaign, Sadashiv Rao Bhau, by making him a "a scapegoat of the Maratha debacle." Sarkar did not condone Bhau's military policy: "His conduct on the last day no student of the military science can justify," for "a generalissimo who has led into ruin half a lakh [50,000] of fighters and eight times that number of non combatants entrusted to his care, and made no provision for their orderly retreat . . . in the event of an almost certain defeat" was unpardonable.[16] But the fact that Bhau courted a soldier's death, "half a mile from the front," fighting, after having been wounded in the thigh by a musket shot and a spear by "five Durrani horsemen" who had been "lured by his splendid dress and rich jewels," earned him the historian's praise: "The wounded lion turned at bay and struck three or four of his assailants . . . before he was killed and his head cut off."[17]

This instance of valor reminded Sarkar of Tipu Sultan: "The historian's memory goes forward to the day 38 years later, when, under a dark gateway of Seringapatam, another heroic Indian prince, after the wreck of his army

15. I have benefited from discussions with Faisal Devji on this point.

16. Jadunath Sarkar, *Fall of the Mughal Empire*, vol. 2, *1754–1771* (1934; New Delhi: Orient Longman, 1971), p. 253.

17. Ibid., p. 247.

and cause, came to his end in resisting an alien spoiler's hand on his person."[18] "When a soldier makes the supreme sacrifice, there may be sorrow for it, but not regret," wrote Sarkar of Sadashiv Rao Bhau's death at the hands of the Durranis. The ethics that underwrote this statement was a British-imperial one, and it came indeed from the imperial lore on heroism at war. "The young hero," Sarkar continued, "who fell into the arms of victory on the Heights of Abraham after a life-span only two years longer than that of Bhau's, was fond of singing,"

> Why, soldiers! Why
> Should we be melancholy, boys?
> Why, soldiers! Why,
> We whose business 'tis to die?

To such a hero, it was not victory or defeat that mattered. "It would have made no difference," wrote Sarkar of this hero on the "Heights of Abraham," to his outlook on life "if he had changed places with his gallant French rival and closed his eyes amidst the darkness of defeat."[19] It was the ethical nature of his death that made the hero a hero.

A small mistake in Sarkar's prose suggests that he wrote these lines and reproduced the song from memory and without research. For someone who was such a stickler for going to the original sources, a minor lapse only shows how steeped he was in the heroic military lore of the empire. Major General James Wolfe (1727–1759) defeated the French in Quebec on the *Plains*, and not the Heights, of Abraham in 1759, a battle in which he died from enemy gunfire. It is said that he refused treatment at the final moment and died content, "like a noble Roman," when told that the enemy had been defeated. Wolfe's death became a part of the imperial military legend and was profoundly romanticized, his final utterances having been glorified by the historian Francis Parkman and the scene of his death made the subject of songs and a painting (1770) by Benjamin West that now hangs in the National Gallery of Canada.[20]

18. Ibid.

19. Ibid., p. 253.

20. "James Wolfe," Wikipedia, http://en.wikipedia.org/wiki/James_Wolfe. The painting may be viewed at "File: Benjamin West," http://en.wikipedia.org/wiki/File:Benjamin_West_005.jpg. For the 1759–60 song "The Death of General Wolfe," see "The Death of General Wolfe," www.musicanet.org/robokopp/english/genwolfe.htm. All sites accessed 18 November 2010. A book that is very useful on the ironies of the historical process through which General Wolfe emerged as a lionized hero of the British empire but has nothing on "General Wolfe's Song"—perhaps confirming how apocryphal the song is—is Alan McNairn's *Behold the Hero: General Wolfe and the Arts in the Eighteenth Century* (Montreal: McGill-Queen's University Press, 1997). His chapter 6, "A Coat and Waistcoat Subject," traces the history of paintings devoted to portraying

The lines quoted by Sarkar come from a song that became known as "General Wolfe's song." It is said that Wolfe wrote it the night before his death. It is actually an old song that existed in print as early as 1710–19.[21] The song had even featured in an opera of the 1720s. Scholars surmise that "some enterprising music-seller in 1759 slightly altered the meter of the fifty-year old song, added the first verse, and cashed in on the enormous fame and popularity of the dead Wolfe by inventing the pathetic story of Wolfe composing this song before he died."[22]

Similarly, Sarkar captures the outcome of the Lalsot campaign of the Mahadji Sindhia against Rajputs by comparing it to the inconclusive 1715 Jacobite rebellion in England and Scotland, on the subject of which Robert Burns wrote a poem, "Battle of Sheriff-muir."[23] "The Maratha dispatch writers and Mahadji himself," wrote Sarkar, "boasted that on the field his army [had] been victorious. That in one sense they had been; but the impartial historian must say that, as at Sheriffmuir, so here too 'none wan.'"[24] It is hard to overlook the Scottish diction of the word "wan."

Most telling in this respect—that is, with regard to the question of how the imperial literary canon influenced Sarkar's imagination—are his comments on Rajputana in the eighteenth century, when the "the Emperor in Delhi became a lifeless shadow confined within the harem" and all "unifying bond and common controlling authority was dissolved." In the absence of a "superior power [in Delhi] to enforce lawful rights," wrote Sarkar, with

"the death of General Wolfe." The first such painting was by George Romney and was exhibited in London in 1763 (p. 91). Benjamin West's painting was exhibited first by the Royal Academy in 1771 and "was elevated to the status of a national icon for the English, who saw it as a symbol of their right to dominion over North America, their military virtue, and the triumph of Protestant righteousness over Catholic perfidy" (p. 109).

21. The words occur in the Duke of Marlborough's *Deloght or His Honours Cordial Advice to His Fellow Soldiers* (1712), available at the Bodleian at Oxford, http://bodley24.bodley.ox.ac.uk/cgi-bin/acwwweng/ballads/image.pl?ref=Firth+b.21%28118%29&id=16153.gif&seq=1&size=1, accessed 18 November 2010.

22. Anon., "What Was Hamilton's 'Favorite Song'?," *William and Mary Quarterly*, third series, 12, no. 2 (April 1955), p. 304n11. "The song gained instant popularity, was repeatedly reprinted and used in such plays as Shield's The Siege of Gibraltar. While Wolfe's close friends and family knew the truth, the public did not; it was only in the mid-nineteenth century, long after Hamilton's death, that this successful advertising fraud was exposed. Even so, Schuyler Hamilton and Greybill in the 1890's still believed that Wolfe wrote the song." Ibid.

23. The poem is available on the web at "The Battle of Sheriff-Muir," http://literaryballadarchive.com/PDF/Burns_1_Battle_Sheriff_Muir.pdf, accessed 26 December 2013.

24. Jadunath Sarkar, *Fall of the Mughal Empire*, vol. 3, *1771–1788* (1938; Calcutta: Orient Longman, 1975), p. 260.

shades of Hobbes coloring his prose, Rajputana resembled a land where an established order had come undone: "a zoological garden with the barriers of the cages thrown down and the keepers removed." "The fiercest animal passions raged throughout the land, redeemed only now and then," said Sarkar, now resorting to Burkean diction, "by individual instances of devotion and chivalry which had not yet totally disappeared from [the] human bosom."[25] "The wounds" of these "long suffering" people, the Rajputs, were not healed until "British peace" was established and "British suzerainty" accepted, creating conditions—as Sarkar would argue—for the birth of an Indian nation. Until then, "the martial manhood of Rajputana ha[d] sunk into the placid sleep of opium," wrote Sarkar, who went on to quote a couple of unattributed lines from Oliver Goldsmith's long poem *The Traveller; or, A Prospect of Society* (1764), to describe the condition of Rajputs in the eighteenth century: "Unknown to them, when sensual pleasures cloy,/To fill the languid pause with finer joy."[26]

Empire, Literature, and the Imagination of the Political

This little nugget of English poetry from *The Traveller*, left anonymous in Sarkar's narrative, serves as a small monument to his colonial education and as a reminder that he was, after all, a teacher of literature. It is also a clue to the larger political imagination that influenced Sarkar. While steeped in Persian sources and even sharing in their moods on occasion, Sarkar's sense of drama about eighteenth-century Indian history owed little, it seems, to the narrative spirit of historians or writers of the Mughal period. His reflexes were trained more by the literature of Victorian and imperial Britain than, say, by the Persian literature on Mughal decline. That the "tragic drama," for instance, of "murder, suicide and the untimely death of the young" that unfolded in Maratha history after the death of Peshwa Balaji Rao in 1761 should remind him of "Theban horrors" was symptomatic of the Victorian nature of his literary dispositions.[27] Or think of his response to the "Maratha debacle" at

25. Jadunath Sarkar, *Fall of the Mughal Empire* (1932; Delhi: Orient Longman, 1971) (hereafter cited as vol. 1), p. 146; see also p. 215. Compare Burke's use of the word and the idea of "chivalry" in his lament: "The age of chivalry is gone. That of sophisters, economists, and calculators, has succeeded; and the glory of Europe is extinguished for ever." Edmund Burke, *Reflections on the Revolution in France*, ed. Frank Turner (New Haven, CT: Yale University Press, 2003), p. 65.

26. Sarkar, *Fall*, 1:147.

27. Sarkar, *Fall*, 2:259. "Theban drama" and "Theban horrors" were popular Victorian expressions for entangled and unhappy relationships. Matthew Arnold used them in describing Percy

Panipat, which, wrote Sarkar, "was a nation-wide disaster. . . . There was not a home in Maharashtra that had not to mourn the loss of a member, and several houses their very heads." "It was, in short," he suddenly said, "like Flodden Field"—an appeal to the memory the Scottish-English battle of 1513.[28] But this memory, again, was strongly mediated through imperial literature; immortalized by Sir Walter Scott's long verse narrative on Flodden Fields, *Marmion*.[29]

The use of Goldsmith in describing Rajputs also reveals a very nineteenth-century and imperial reading of this eighteenth-century poem. Oliver Goldsmith (of Irish origin) was a hardy perennial of the canon of English literature in the colony. His works were included in the syllabi of Indian universities for a very long time and read continuously from at least the 1880s to the mid-1960s, when I was in high school, and probably even later.[30] Arthur Barrett, professor of English Literature at Elphinstone College in Bombay, published an edition of *The Traveller* and *The Deserted Village* as one book—with an introduction and notes—in 1888. The book was reprinted in 1891, 1899, 1904, 1906, 1920, 1926, and 1931 (the last edition I could consult) without a single word replaced.[31] Every year, from at least the 1890s on (when Sarkar went to college), university examinations in Calcutta would contain questions about Goldsmith's writings, with particular reference to the two poems *The Traveller* and *The Deserted Village*. The questions and the expected answers did not change very much, either, as one can tell from reading the editor's notes to an

---

Bysshe Shelley's involvement with the family of William Godwin. See Mathew Arnold, "Shelly" (1888), in *The Portable Matthew Arnold*, ed. and with an introduction by Lionel Trilling (New York: Viking, 1949), p. 388. For an older use of the expression, see Burke, *Reflections*, p. 61, where he speaks of "Theban and Thracian orgies."

28. Sarkar, *Fall*, 2:252.

29. See Sir Walter Scott, *Marmion: A Tale of Flodden Field*, ed. Zelma E. Clark (New York: Charles E. Merrill, 1919), canto 6.

30. Goldsmith was of course Irish by birth, but I describe his poetry as "English" advisedly. Arthur Barrett makes the following—and not entirely unprejudiced—comment in his introduction to *The Traveller* and *The Deserted Village*: "There are but few indications in these poems that Goldsmith was an Irishman apart from the description of the evictions and the emigration [in *The Deserted Village*] which are readily associated with Irish troubles. If Goldsmith ever used any provincialisms, or expressions characteristic of Ireland, his long absence from his native land and his association with educated Englishmen had nearly removed them before the poems were published. Still in l. 323 of the *Deserted Village* his use of the word 'sure' is perhaps Irish—'Sure, scenes like these no troubles e'er annoy.'" Arthur Barrett, ed., *The Traveller and The Deserted Village* (London: Macmillan, 1891), p. xvi.

31. I say this on the basis of a comparison of the 1891 edition with that published in 1931. See Barrett, *The Traveller and The Deserted Village* (1891, 1931).

Indian edition of *The Traveller* and *The Deserted Village* that was put together in Calcutta in the early part of the twentieth century to help university students prepare for their examinations.[32]

Goldsmith's lines quoted by Sarkar in his description of the fallen, opium-induced slumberous state of the once-valorous Rajputs were actually meant to describe the Swiss, of all people, the "bleak Swiss" who, from the fifteenth century onward, had often supplied mercenaries to the fighting armies of Europe—in France, Italy, and elsewhere.[33] And Goldsmith's words did not represent a wholesale condemnation of the Swiss. The lines cited by Sarkar belonged to a section where Goldsmith discussed the virtues and vices of the rugged Swiss. And his words, while mindful of the miseries of the lives of the Swiss, also spoke of their simple but passionate patriotism and of their republican virtues:

> No product here the barren hills afford
> But man and steel, the soldier and his sword;
> No vernal blooms their torpid rocks array,
> But winter lingering chills the lap of May:
> No zephyr fondly sues the mountain's breast,
> But meteors glare, and stormy glooms invest.
>
> And e'en those hills that round his mansion rise
> Enhance the bliss his scanty fund supplies.
> Dear is that shed to which his soul conforms,
> And dear that hill which lifts him to the storms;

32. See Oliver Goldsmith, *The Deserted Village and The Traveller*, ed. N. Mookerji (Calcutta: Chuckervertty, Chatterjee, n.d.), section entitled "Important Topics. Questionnaire," pp. lxxxiv–xcv. I have used a copy that belonged to an aunt of mine who was in her first year of college sometime in the late 1920s or the early 1930s. The exact year is difficult to ascertain, as she committed suicide a few years later (while studying for her master's degree in Bengali literature); her history was suppressed in the memories of my family. My copy bears the signature "Sneha Lata Chakravarty, First Year Science, Bethune College" and has copious notes in pencil on its pages, indicating how this book, meant to help the student in Calcutta develop an appreciation of English poetry, may have been actually taught and read in the classroom.

33. Frederick Tupper Jr., PhD, professor of rhetoric and English literature at the University of Vermont around 1900 and author of a book entitled *Goldsmith's The Traveller and The Deserted Village* (New York, 1900), commented: "For three hundred years before Goldsmith, they [the Swiss] had served for pay in the armies of Europe, but the greatest and the most fatal triumph of Swiss mercenaries was to come in the palace of Louis XVI, nearly twenty years after Goldsmith's death. Thorwalsden's 'Lions of Lucerne' is the noblest tribute to this feat and to Helvetian fidelity and honor" (p. 84). William J. Rolphe, another nineteenth-century commentator on the poem, reminds us of "*Hamlet*, iv, 5: 'Where are my Switzers?'" in *Select Poems of Oliver Goldsmith*, ed. William J. Rolphe (New York: Harper, 1894), p. 116.

And as a child, when scaring sounds molest,
Clings close and closer to the mother's breast,
So the loud torrent and the whirlwind's roar
But bind him to his native mountains more.
Such are the charms to barren states assign'd;
Their wants but few, their wishes all confin'd.[34]

So what made it possible for Sarkar to use Goldsmith's half-admiring description of the Swiss to portray the Rajput as simply subject to "animal passion"? Hidden in this apparent reversal of the intended meaning of Goldsmith is a history of how *The Traveller* was received and read in the nineteenth century, as the British Empire consolidated itself as a world phenomenon. Sarkar's use of the poem was, I want to argue, an instance of a complex imperial-nationalist reading of *The Traveller*. Let me briefly explain this point, for that will help to unravel some of the complicated strands of Sarkar's own nationalism.

Sarkar, a Child of the Empire

At the center of Goldsmith's poem, composed in the 1760s, was a very eighteenth-century, Montesquieu-like, political question: If different climes and histories produced different forms of government, with the British being, of course, at the top as "the lords of humankind," did different nations enjoy different degrees of happiness as a result?[35] Goldsmith's answer was unambiguous: "I have endeavoured to show," he said in dedicating the poem to his brother, Rev. Henry Goldsmith, "that there may be equal happiness in states that are differently governed from our own; that every state has a particular principle of happiness, and that this principle in each may be carried to a mischievous excess." The poem, discussing the Dutch, the Swiss, the Italians, the French, and the British, was intended to "illustrate" "these positions."[36] Each of these peoples had their own principle of happiness that, paradoxically, was often the cause of the peculiar miseries that each suffered. Thus the "independence" that the Britons "prize[d] so high" could also keep "man from man" and break "the social tie."[37] Several commentators have pointed out that Goldsmith was also very mid-eighteenth-century in "abhorring mountains"

34. Goldsmith, *The Traveller* (1764), in Rolphe, *Select Poems*, pp. 58, 60.

35. "The lords of humankind" is Goldsmith's expression for the British in line 328 of *The Traveller*.

36. Tupper, *Goldsmith's The Traveller and The Deserted Village*, p. 35.

37. Ibid., p. 47.

when it came to describing the Swiss.[38] As William Rolphe observed in his commentary of 1894, Goldsmith's description of Switzerland displayed "no appreciation of the wild beauty and the grandeur of the scenery which attracts the throngs of tourists in our day." Rolphe also pointed out that this was remarked on by Macaulay in chapter 13 of his *History of England*: "He [Goldsmith] was disgusted by the hideous wilderness, and declared that he greatly preferred the charming country round Leyden, the vast expanse of verdant meadow, and the villas with their statues and grottoes, trim flower beds and rectilinear avenues."[39] Such "indifference to, indeed shrinking from, wild nature, . . . [was] characteristic of Goldsmith's time," observed Tupper in his commentary. "As Ruskin points out, even Shakespeare abhorred mountains; and to Thomas Gray is usually assigned the distinction of being the first Englishman to appreciate their beauties." Rolphe's notes on Goldsmith further clarify, referring again to Ruskin's *Modern Painters*, that this attitude was part of the Homeric tradition—where to possess natural beauty was to be composed of "a fountain, a meadow, a shady grove." It marked the "mediaeval mind" and showed up in Dante's *Divina Commedia*. In a recent and insightful reading of this poem, Ingrid Horrocks has suggested that the poem both uses and departs from the tradition of "prospect poems" in developing "the figure of the wanderer or the traveler"—"Rather than standing and surveying from on high [as was customary in prospect poems], this new observer is imagined as moving through the world, assembling a view of society from multiple fragmentary sights and interactions." It represents the "viewpoint of a wanderer who moves through the landscape as the only basis on which sympathy, and so a new community, can be developed." Horrocks goes on to show how this move could be critical and subversive of imperial ideals.[40]

The Goldsmith lines that Sarkar quotes thus belong to a very particular eighteenth-century combination of aesthetics and politics that allowed the poet not to condemn the Swiss in any out-of-hand fashion for their rugged climes and temperament but to use them only as examples of his considered position that—as Macaulay put it in his biography of Goldsmith: "our happiness depends little on political institutions, and much depends on the temper

38. Ibid., p. 83.

39. Rolphe, *Select Poems*, p. 115.

40. Tupper, *Goldsmith's The Traveller and The Deserted Village*, p. 83; Rolphe, *Select Poems*, p. 116; Ingrid Horrocks, "'Critical Eye' and 'Houseless Stranger': The New Eighteenth-Century Wanderer (Thomson to Goldsmith)," *English Literary History* 77, no. 3 (Fall 2010), pp. 665–687, quotes on pp. 665–666. See also the discussion in Megan Kitching, "The Philosophical Traveller as Social Critic in Oliver Goldsmith's *The Traveller, The Deserted Village* and *The Citizen of the World*" (master's thesis, University of Otago, Dunedin, New Zealand, 2011), chap. 2.

and regulation of our own minds."[41] What, then, made it possible for Sarkar to misread Goldsmith, as it were, and to use him to convey his own sense of the unmitigated "tragedy" that he saw as unfolding in eighteenth-century India?

Even a thumbnail sketch of the history of the reception of Goldsmith shows that his position did not go unchallenged in the eighteenth century; but as the British Empire developed a strong faith in its civilizing mission, readers of *The Traveller*—not so much as of his other works such as *The Deserted Village*—began to find fault with Goldsmith's politics and increasingly separated his aesthetics from his politics, until such separation became routine in the early part of the twentieth century. Eighteenth-century critics sometimes quibbled with Goldsmith's political positions, finding them logically confused. A review published in January 1765 argued: "It is certain that every individual has a peculiar principle of happiness; but does it therefore follow, that a state composed of these individuals should have the same? Rather the contrary." Dr. John Aikin (1747–1822), a naturalist and chemist of "considerable distinction," found Goldsmith's "political opinions" marred by "confused notions and a heated imagination." Writing in 1796, he said: "Though it is probable that few of Goldsmith's readers will be convinced . . . that happiness of mankind is every where equal," there was more philosophical force to the argument that "man's chief bliss is ever seated in his mind . . . and that a small part of real felicity consists in what human government can bestow or withhold." An 1803 German edition of *The Vicar of Wakefield*, *The Traveller*, and *The Deserted Village*, in English with German footnotes, reproduced memoirs of the poet by Robert Anderson (Goldsmith's physician), containing some disagreements with Goldsmith's political opinions as expressed in *The Traveller*. The disagreements did not have much to do with the civilizing mission of the empire: "The description of the people of Italy [is] not less just than that of their country is picturesque and harmonious; but the moralist may object to the conclusion as unfavourable to the interests of virtue. . . . . The characteristics of the different nations are just and ingenuous but the descriptions are neither full nor perfect. He has contented himself with exhibiting them in those points of view in which they are generally beheld; but the lights are much strengthened by the powers of poetic genius."[42] Leigh Hunt (1784–1859), a critic and poet, writing in critical

41. Thomas Babington Macaulay, "Oliver Goldsmith," in his *Biographical Essays* (Leipzig: Bernhard Tauchnitz, 1857), p. 125.

42. John Langhorne in *Monthly Review* (January 1765), reproduced in *Goldsmith: The Critical Heritage*, ed. G. S. Rousseau (London: Routledge and Kegan Paul, 1974), p. 37; John Aikin, "A

appreciation of *The Traveller* in 1846, faulted Goldsmith's logic: "The fact is that GOLDSMITH thought he was reasoning finely, when he was writing fine poetry only. It is the fault of the poetical argument that the reasoner is apt to forget his logic in his fancy. . . . If *The Traveller* had been written in prose . . . it would allure no readers at all."[43]

Such formal or logical criticism of *The Traveller* gave way to a mode of criticism that was decidedly political in substance as the nineteenth century progressed and utilitarianism and liberalism—for all their contradictions—came to supply the ruling doctrines of the British Empire.[44] An 1879 edition of *The Traveller* and *The Deserted Village* published in London had this to say by way of editorial comment: "It is assuredly not true that there is no relation whatever between the government of a country and the happiness of its inhabitants. A government can, as it pleases, or according to its enlightenment, make circumstances favourable or unfavourable to individual development and happiness. So *a priori* one would assume; so *a posteriori* one sees that it is. The political indifferentism set forth in *The Traveller* is in fact merely paradoxical. Fortunately, one's enjoyment of the poem does not depend upon the accuracy of the creed it professes." This challenge to the cosmopolitanism of Goldsmith or of Samuel Johnson (Goldsmith's mentor and promoter) fell on sympathetic years in the age of John Stuart Mill, and *The Traveller* found its place in the literary canon in the colony only on the condition that students were taught to separate Goldsmith's aesthetics from his politics, so that the poem could be enjoyed for its literary qualities alone. A "model" examination question in N. Mookerji's notes meant to help students at the University of Calcutta read *The Traveller* quoted two lines from the poem—"How small, of that human hearts endure/That part which laws or kings can cause or cure"—and asked: "Whose dictum is this and what is its precise meaning? How far is it right? Does the poem depend for its success on the correctness of this theory?" And this is how the model answer read in part (notice its similarity

---

Critical Dissertation Describing Goldsmith's Poetic Achievement in Relation to His Contemporaries" (1796), in ibid., pp. 226, 233–234; Oliver Goldsmith, *Select Works of Oliver Goldsmith* (Berlin: G. C. Nauck, 1803), pp. xliii–xliv. I have modified the punctuation in this passage. Anderson's criticism appears to have reproduced, almost verbatim, opinions expressed in the Langhorne 1765 critique excerpted in Rousseau, *Goldsmith*, p. 39.

43. Leigh Hunt, excerpted in Rousseau, *Goldsmith*, p. 31.

44. These contradictions have been the object of recent analyses in Thomas Metcalf, *The Ideologies of the Raj* (Cambridge: Cambridge University Press, 1994); Uday Singh Mehta, *Liberalism and Empire: A Study in Nineteenth-Century British Liberal Thought* (Chicago: University of Chicago Press, 1999); Karuna Mantena, *Alibis of Empire: Henry Maine and the Ends of Liberal Imperialism* (Princeton, NJ: Princeton University Press, 2010).

to the 1879 argument cited above): "These are among the lines contributed by Dr. Johnson to the poem. . . . This theory is of course wrong. Forms of government cannot but influence the happiness of society. . . . [Dr. Johnson] was forgetting that the opportunities for individual freedom and development are in too great a degree under the control of government to make such a generalization valid. . . . Happily the poetry of [*The Traveller*] does not depend for its success on the correctness of the political theory."[45]

Sarkar's Goldsmith was thus a poet whose eighteenth-century thesis that happiness was indifferent to forms of government had been filtered out by readings that came after the rise of liberalism and the simultaneous consolidation of the British Empire, whereby the question of human happiness came to be connected to particular political choices: an oppressive government could not be conducive to happiness. It was this history of the reception of *The Traveller* that enabled Sarkar to read Goldsmith's description of the Swiss as a negative judgment on their character and apply it to the Rajputs. Sarkar's allegory of the zoological garden—that Rajputana in the eighteenth century resembled a zoological garden where the animals had been let out of their cages and the keepers were nowhere in sight—clearly spoke of a dramatic decline in what used to be a pleasant and happy order, the once-organized "zoological garden"—a decline brought about by a corresponding and original decrease in the quality of governance that the ailing Mughal Empire could provide to the country. His lament over the disappearance of heroism from the annals of the Rajputs in the eighteenth century was ultimately a point about the decline of the State. Sarkar's citations from the literary canon of the British Empire throughout his texts were no mere literary flourishes used simply to embellish his historical prose. His very historical imagination was deeply shaped by the way the political was conceptualized and celebrated in this literature. Politics itself was the material for literature, and vice versa. How else could one come to write up the story of the decline of the Mughals as a national—and a nationalist's—tragedy?

Mughal Decline as Tragedy

This close connection between history and literature—or, more properly, this identification of history and politics as a single domain of activity amenable to literary treatment—is the key to understanding Sarkar's conception of his-

45. Oliver Goldsmith, *The Traveller; or, A Prospect of Society and The Deserted Village*, new ed., with notes philological and explanatory by J. W. Hales (London: Macmillan, 1879), p. 27; Goldsmith, *Deserted Village*, ed. Mookerji, pp. lxxxv–lxxxvi.

torical methods, his ideal of a disinterested commitment to the truth of facts and hence to a more obviously metaphysical ideal of truthfulness on the part of the historian. History was thus in the main a human drama driven by the passions, strengths, and weaknesses of human character, be it that of the nation or of significant groups or individuals. History was definitely not about the clash of impersonal forces—of the market or of class structures or of other abstract institutions. The drama of characters was also the moral drama of politics. Politics, in other words, was something that lent itself profoundly to literary—rather than socioeconomic—analysis. I will come back to the question of character, but for now let us turn to the main literary trope—that of tragedy—through which Sarkar looked at the fall of the Mughal empire, a process that began, for him, in the final decades of Aurangzeb's reign.

"Our immediate historic past," wrote Sarkar, introducing the very first edition of the first volume of his *Fall of the Mughal Empire*, "resembles a tragedy in its course," one that was "no less potent than a true tragedy to purge the soul by exciting pity and horror."[46] Sarkar's reference to tragedy—not an Indian narrative genre until the coming of British rule—and its soul-cleansing functions expresses the vein of European classicism that, though seldom deep, is ever present in Sarkar's understanding of why the empire fell. All this is obvious to a degree. However, while there was indeed a long European tradition of seeing the conflicts of the post–Shah Jahan Mughal order as tragedy, Sarkar's use of the same term, *tragedy*, signaled a significant departure from that tradition.

But let us first do a quick survey of the European tradition of seeing Mughal decline as tragic before returning to Sarkar's use of the trope of tragedy. Bernier, a seventeenth-century French traveler in India, sought leave from his ideal "early-modern" European reader, who might have expected a "formal" account of "the Manners and Customs, the Learning and the Pursuits of the Mogols and the Indians," to describe what he called, using terms drenched with recent European history and thus familiar to his reader, "a Civil War and Revolution in which all the leading Statesmen of the nation took a part."[47] One can only agree with Nicholas Dew that Bernier, as his use of the term "civil war" suggests, looked on Mughal India "as a form of

46. Sarkar, *Fall*, 1:iii.

47. François Bernier, *Travels in the Mogul Empire AD 1656–1668*, trans. and ed. Archibald Constable, rev. Vincent A. Smith, 2nd ed. (1934; Delhi: Munshiram Manoharlal, 1992), "To the Reader," p. xlvii. The European tradition of describing Mughal wars of succession as "civil war" or "civil broil" continued into what European observers of the regime wrote after Bernier. See Father Francis Catrou, S.J., *History of the Mogul Dynasty in India from Its Foundation by Tamerlane, in the Year 1399, to the Accession of Aurengzebe, in the Year 1657*, trans. from French (The

allegory on what is usually thought of as the nascent 'absolutism' of Louis XIV—which is to say, once again, that Bernier foreshadows the author of the *Persian Letters*."[48]

The "civil war" in question was the battle of succession that broke out in the Mughal empire in 1657–58, and the "Statesmen" were none other than the Mughal princes themselves—Dara (b. 1615), Shuja (b. 1616), Aurangzeb (b. 1618), and Murad (b. 1624)—and their partisan kings and nobles, many of whom actually switched sides when the battle turned decisively in favor of Aurangzeb. This was neither a civil war nor a revolution, as war between contending princes was one method by which the Mughals settled issues of imperial succession, though the question of a son, Aurangzeb, claiming the throne while his father, the emperor (in this case Shah Jahan), was still alive remained a thorny political and theoretical question.[49] A few pages into his text "The History of the Late Rebellion in the States of the Great Mogol," however, Bernier describes the story as a "tragedy." It is also clear that Dara is the tragic hero of his narrative, for he simply describes Aurangzeb as "the hero of this history and the future King of India."[50] If anything, this was a domestic tragedy, for Dara had some "good qualities"—"he was courteous in conversation, quick at repartee, polite, and extremely liberal." But he also had some fatal flaws, such as entertaining "too exalted an opinion of himself" and speaking "disdainfully of those who ventured to advise him," thus

Hague, 1708; London: J. M. Richardson, 1826), p. 165, where Prince Khurram's rebellion against his father, Jahangir, is described as "civil broil."

48. Nicholas Dew, *Orientalism in Louis XIV's France* (Oxford: Oxford University Press, 2009), p. 134. See also the comment on p. 17: "By the mid-seventeenth century, absolutist political philosophy called for a powerful prince to maintain order against the mutability of human society, particularly after the religious and civil wars of the mid-century." The role of humanist educators in this part of Europe was not just that of "scholars holding up a mirror for princes, but [providing] a reflection of a Catholic and absolute conception of royal government which entailed the weeding-out of heresy and superstition, and the education of the populace as good Catholic subjects." See also the discussion in Joan-Pau Rubiés, "Oriental Despotism and European Orientalism," *Journal of Early Modern History* 9, nos. 1–2 (2005), 109–180; Stanley J. Tambiah, "What Did Bernier Actually Say? Profiling the Mughal Empire," *Contributions to Indian Sociology* 32, no. 2 (1998), pp. 361–388; Franco Venturi, "Oriental Despotism," *Journal of the History of Ideas* 24, no. 1 (January–March 1963), pp. 133–142.

49. As Jorge Flores remarks, "Aurangzeb's revolt, in truth, was not very original. It was in the end the history of all Mughal princes who fought for the throne as soon as they felt the authority of their father, the emperor, to be waning." Jorge Flores, "'I will do as my father did': On Portuguese and Other European Views of Mughal Succession Crises," *e-Journal of Portuguese History* 3, no. 2 (Winter 2005), pp. 1–23.

50. Bernier, *Travels*, p. 16.

deterring "his sincerest friends from disclosing the secret machinations of his brothers."[51] Aurangzeb, the hero of his narrative, is not a figure of tragedy and is portrayed in unflattering colors: "[He] was devoid of that urbanity and engaging presence, so much admired in Dara" and, though possessed of "sounder [political and military] judgments," remained a "complete master of the art of dissimulation."[52]

When it came to John Dryden's dramatization (and bowdlerization) of Bernier's narrative into his rhymed play *Aureng-Zebe—A Tragedy* (1675), the tragedy at issue was still a domestic or personal one—though Dryden spoke of the "tragedy of wit" in his prologue—but with Aurangzeb, not Dara, as the tragic hero.[53] And the "tragedy," as Shawn Lisa Maurer has pointed out, had more to do with the issue of masculinity and patriarchy in the constitution of royal power in Dryden's England than with the historical actualities of Mughal India.[54] Aurangzeb's virtues are established through a statement of the fictional character Arimant, the governor of Agra, in the very first scene where the four brothers are discussed for their qualities:

> But Aureng-Zebe, by no strong passion swayed
> Except his love, more temp'rate is, and weighed.
> This Atlas must our sinking state uphold;
> In council cool, but in performance bold.

51. Ibid., p. 6.

52. Ibid., p. 10.

53. That Dryden borrowed his narrative primarily from Bernier while adding characters of his own and imagining Aurangzeb in a novel way is a well-attested fact. Vincent A. Smith wrote in an appendix to his edition of Bernier's text: "Dryden founded his play on the English translation, 1671–72, of Bernier's *Travels*, and even a cursory perusal of his *Tragedy* will show many passages which are mere paraphrases, so to speak, of Bernier's text." Bernier, *Travels*, appendix 1, "Regarding Dryden's *Tragedy of Aureng-Zebe*," p. 468. See also the discussion in Frederick M. Link's introduction to John Dryden's *Aureng-Zebe* (Lincoln: University of Nebraska, 1971), pp. xvi–xvii. Some scholars also suggest that Dryden's "playing fast and loose" with the historical facts about the real Aurangzeb had something to do with the point that the latter was already the reigning emperor of India, on whose whims and pleasures depended the fortunes of the growing India trade of the East India Company. See Peter Craft, "Dryden's Transformations of Bernier's *Travels*," *Restoration Studies in English Literature* 38, no. 2 (Fall 2009), pp. 47–55. For a nuanced discussion of Dryden's relationship to history, see Achsah Guiborry, "Dryden's Views of History," *Philological Quarterly* 52, no. 2 (April 1973), pp. 187–204.

54. Shawn Lisa Maurer, "Fathers, Sons, and Lovers: The Transformation of Masculine Authority in Dryden's *Aureng-Zebe*," *Eighteenth Century* 46, no. 2 (Summer 2005), pp. 151–173. See also the discussion of *Aureng-Zebe* in George McFadden, *Dryden: The Public Writer, 1660–1675* (Princeton, NJ: Princeton University Press, 1978), chap. 6, pp. 187–188 in particular. McFadden's views are critiqued in David B. Haley, *Dryden and the Problem of Freedom: The Republican Aftermath* (New Haven, CT: Yale University Press, 1997).

He sums their virtues in himself alone,
And adds the greatest, of a loyal son;
His father's cause upon his sword he wears,
And with his arms, we hope, his fortune bears.[55]

And Aurangzeb's tragic sense of life is suggested by the famous words he speaks in the first scene of act 4:

When I consider life, 'tis all a cheat,
Yet, fooled with hope, men favor the deceit,
Trust on, and think tomorrow will repay,
Tomorrow's falser than the former day,
Lies worse, and while it says we shall be blest
With some new joys, cuts off what we possessed.[56]

It was not Aurangzeb but his descendant Muhammad Shah who formed the tragic subject in the little known and little-remembered play *The Fall of the Mogul, a Tragedy*, by Rev. Thomas Maurice (1754–1824)—Byron's "Dull Maurice."[57] One subject of this tragedy was "the subversion of a mighty Empire effected by the well-known irruption into India of Nadir Shah in the year 1738 [*sic*]."[58] "So great and sudden a revolution," wrote Maurice, introducing the play, "so vast and awful a vicissitude in human affairs, I considered sufficiently interesting and important, both in a moral and political point of view, to become the subject of Imperial Tragedy." For it demonstrated "the important truth, that the proudest fabric of human glory and grandeur is baseless, when energy and virtue are wanting to its support."[59]

Muhammad Shah, who sat on the throne of Delhi between 1720 and 1748 and on whose watch Delhi suffered the destruction and ignominy of the invasion of Nadir Shah of Persia in 1739, illustrated Maurice's point about the "want of [public] virtue." Shah, "whose sufferings this Drama records" and who, "having annihilated his enemies" in claiming the throne, fell into "all the excess of Eastern luxury and intemperance" and "immersed [himself]

55. Dryden, *Aureng-Zebe*, p. 20.

56. Ibid., p. 75.

57. Thomas Maurice, *The Fall of the Mogul, A Tragedy, Founded on an Interesting Portion of Indian History, and Attempted Partly on the Greek Model with Other Occasional Poems by the Author of "Indian Antiquities"* (London: J. White, 1806). For an extended discussion of the histories of India written by Maurice, see Michael Dodson, "Thomas Maurice and Domestic Imperialism, 1790–1820," in *Knowing India: Colonial and Modern Constructions of the Past: Essays in Honor of Thomas R. Trautman*, ed. Cynthia Talbot (New Delhi: Yoda, 2011), pp. 54–83.

58. Maurice, *Fall of the Mogul*, introduction, p. i.

59. Ibid., pp. ix, xvi.

in every species of voluptuous dissipation," with his intellect "impaired" in consequence, constituted a tragic subject for Maurice.[60] In Maurice's judgment, Shah was a good subject for evoking sentiments related to the feeling of tragedy, for while he was possessed of many "private virtues"—he had a benign deposition and was a good husband and parent—he was "neither deeply criminal nor wholly innocent." His sufferings rendered him "an object of our deepest commiseration . . . *pity*," to produce which, Maurice reminded his reader, "is one great end of Tragedy."[61] A fictional character in the play, Sadi, "an Indian chief," exclaims about the emperor:

> Such was Mahommad! What a strange reverse!
> His martial spirit and each princely virtue
> Lost in luxurious indolence, and sunk in torpid inactivity.[62]

Curiously, another tragic subject for Maurice "was the miserable fate of the patient, oppressed Hindoo" who had for long seen his "beloved native region" alternately made a desert or "deluged with blood."[63] Maurice therefore "ventured"—"after the manner of the ANCIENT CHORUS"—to present a "band of Brahmin priests" as the chorus for the play, supplemented in part—of all peoples—by a group of Parsi priests, representatives of "another injured race," the two groups together allowing the author to display his knowledge of their respective myths.[64]

Maurice's expression "imperial tragedy," which appears to have been in vogue anyway, turns up in *The Fall of the Moghul Empire—An Historical Essay* (1876), by Henry George Keene, once a judge of the District and Sessions Courts of Agra and a fellow of the University of Calcutta.[65] Keene did not explain his use of the word *tragedy*, but his language suggests a close relationship between themes of virtue and of vice in an emperor—in a word,

60. Ibid., pp. iii, iv.

61. Ibid., p. xvii.

62. Ibid., p. 26.

63. Ibid., p. xiv.

64. Ibid., pp. xv, xix, xx.

65. Henry George Keene (1826–1915) served in the civil service of the East India Company and then the Raj from 1847 to 1882. He is included in *Pillars of the Empire: Sketches of Living Indian and Colonial Statesmen, Celebrities, and Officials*, ed. T. H. S. Escott (London: Chapham and Hall, 1879) See K. K. Sharma, "Henry George Keene," in *Historians of Medieval India*, ed. Mohibbul Hasan (Meerut: Meenakshi Prakashan, 1968), pp. 271–273. Sharma quotes Keene as saying: "I have not yet met with a Hindu who has one good quality; and honest Musalmans do not exist" and comments: "It appears that Keene could neither forget nor forgive the events of 1857" (p. 273).

character—and their connection to changing fortunes of his rule. Early in the book, preparing the reader for the structure of his narrative of the "fall" of the mighty Mughals, Keene writes: "During the long reign of Mohammed Shah, [r. 1719–1748] foreign violence [a reference mainly to Nadir Shah's invasion in 1739] will be seen accomplishing what native vice and native weakness have commenced; and the successors to his dismantled throne will be seen passing like other decorations in a passive manner from one mayor of the palace to another." "One by one the provinces fall away from this distempered centre. At length we shall find the throne literally without an occupant, and the curtain will seem to descend while preparations are being made for the last act of this imperial tragedy."[66]

By the beginning of the twentieth century, the tendency to look on the fall of an empire that had held together for centuries as a "tragedy" was common. Sidney J. Owen, who was for some time a professor of history at Elphinstone College in Bombay and then reader in Indian history at Oxford at the beginning of the century, remarked in his *The Fall of the Mogul Empire* that "the decline and dissolution" of the empire was indeed "a remarkable and tragic phenomenon," in short, an "Imperial tragedy."[67]

The Tragedy of the Patriot

Sarkar also thought of Aurangzeb's life as tragic; the final volume on Aurangzeb begins with the statement: "The life of Aurangzib was one long tragedy,—a story of a man battling in vain an invisible and inexorable fate, a tale of how the strongest human endeavour was baffled by the forces of the age."[68] His descendant, Shah Alam, presented a sad spectacle. The 1770s and the 1780s were the period when the Mughal royal family began to become impoverished as their vassal states refused to send the imperial share of revenues to Delhi. The crucial years were the last seventeen years (1789–1806) of Shah Alam's rule, the really tumultuous period from 1772, when he came into Delhi, "to the bloody tragedy of 1778 which turned the Mughal monarch into a mere shadow and transferred his government to a perpetual vicar." In concluding his preface to the third volume of the *Fall*, Sarkar wrote: "The author is cheered by the prospect of bidding farewell to unrelieved bloodshed

66. Henry George Keene, *The Fall of the Moghul Empire—An Historical Essay* (London: Wm. H. Allen; Calcutta: Brown & Co., 1876), p. 33.

67. Owen, *Fall of the Mogul Empire*, pp. 134, 236.

68. Jadunath Sarkar, *History of Aurangzib*, vol. 5 (1924; New Delhi: Orient Longman, 1974), p. 1.

and treachery and making his acquaintance with revenue and administration, agriculture and industry, social changes and cultural growth in a part of India not yet under British rule."[69]

This history was meant to produce an affect:

> As the historian plods his painful way through these thousand and more pages of daily reports of Najaf Khan's regency [c. 1780], he feels that he is visiting the world of shades, by a dolorous path, through a murky air, with the hopeless shrieks and agonized groans of the living . . . [whose] calling for death [is] ever ringing in his ears. He wonders not why the Delhi empire fell but how it could continue even after this. He understands the nature of the burden which Mahadji Sindhia took upon his shoulders and which all but crushed him.[70]

And the death of Ghulam Qadir, the Afghan Rohilla chief who blinded Shah Alam in an extreme act of cruelty, brought an end to this tragic drama with almost a Shakespearean mixture of magic and evil:

> Ghulam Qadir's dead body was to have been sent to Delhi for public exposure, but according to popular belief his Infernal Master to whom he had sold his soul, took it away. Khair-ud-din tells a gruesome tale of how, when his headless trunk was hung upside down from a tree, a black dog with white rings round its eyes sat below it and lapped up the blood dripping from the neck; the beast returned to his horrid meal again and again though driven away with stones, and after two days both corpse and dog disappeared, never to be seen again by any human eye!

Sarkar's third volume of the *Fall* ends with the following sentence: "With this weird and ghastly scene the most tragic drama in the history of the Timurid sovereigns of India closes."[71]

However, there was clearly a distinction between a contemporary Mughal historian and the "modern historian," a patriotic Indian, of British times.

> The torture and dishonour inflicted by Ghulam Qadir Khan on the Delhi royal family . . . fills, in my manuscript of Khairuddin's Persian history, 33 foolscap folio pages with 20 lines to the page, and drags on from day to day for two months. But a modern historian cannot conduct his reader through all the agonized circles of this inferno of the living; he must pass over the horrid details and give only a brief general sketch of the kind of suffering borne by the Timurid royal house, not a hundredth part of which was endured by the house

69. Sarkar, *Fall*, "Preface to First Edition," 3:iii, v.

70. Ibid., 3:138.

71. Ibid., 3:321.

> of Cappet, whose misery too found a mercifully speedy end of the guillotine, four years later.[72]

The tragic thus occurs in two registers with Sarkar, and this is where he departs from the European tradition of using the word *tragedy* with regard to the Mughals. The Mughals in themselves may or may not have been tragic; the more important point was that it was the patriotic (and male) twentieth-century Indian historian for whom the "fall" of their empire was a real tragedy. The subjects of this second tragedy were the historian himself and the ideal Indian reader he had in mind. "On this occasion of your 86th birthday," Sarkar wrote to Sardesai on the night of 15 May 1950, "I have given the finishing touches to the last chapter of my *Fall of the Mughal Empire* and sent it to the press." The letter is well known to Sarkar scholars but is worth quoting at some length, for it expresses the tragic passion that moved Sarkar's narrative along:

> I can say that I have written it, not with ink, but with my heart's blood. In saying so, I am not thinking of personal sorrows and anxieties—which have clouded the evening of my day, nor of the minute study and exhausting labour that had to be devoted to the subject in this terrible summer heat,—but of the subject-matter of the last chapters,—the imbecility and vices of our rulers, the cowardice of their generals, and the selfish treachery of their ministers. It is a tale which makes every true son of India hang his head in shame. But, at last, my task is done, and I am free again.[73]

The split suggested by the last line of this letter between the quotidian personhood of Sarkar—signified by the use of personal pronouns in "*my* task is done" and "*I* am free"—and the self of the historian, the "true son of India," is telling. The fall of the Mughals is a story that makes every "true son" of the motherland "hang his head in shame." One would not be a "true son" if one did not feel this sense of shame on being told the story. The historian in Sarkar aspires to be a "true son" of India, and he writes, clearly, from within a horizon of a very particular kind of nationalism, one that lost out to the popular anticolonial variety of mass politics that Gandhi created and led.

72. Ibid., 3:308. The contrast Sarkar draws between the voice of the Mughal narrator and that of "the modern historian" is reminiscent of Gibbon's prose. Referring to the "ancients" who "dazzled the extensive sway" of the Roman Empire and "usurped the licence of confounding the Roman monarchy with the globe of the earth," Gibbon wrote: "But the temper, as well as the knowledge, of a modern historian requires a more sober and accurate language." Edward Gibbon, *The Decline and Fall of the Roman Empire*, vol. 1, *180 A.D.–395 A. D.*, based on Everyman's Library Edition, ed. Oliphant Smeaton (New York: Modern Library, n.d.), pp. 24–25.

73. NL, JSP, letter no. 1034, Sarkar to Sardesai, Calcutta, 15 May 1950, "night."

Sarkar's patriotism is never in question. He takes care to document the steps the British actively took to impoverish and humiliate the royal family in Delhi from around the middle of the eighteenth century. He tells how the Company protected the Wazir of Oudh when the latter refused to pay "the customary fine on succession and the annual surplus revenue of his fertile subah [province], and even to share with him the imperial jagirs in Rohilkhand which he usurped with British aid." In addition, "the English Company secured from him [Shah Alam] a grant of the diwani of Bengal, Bihar and Orissa, which legitimized their enjoyment of the revenue of his richest provinces in India; but they [soon] . . . stopped paying him the tribute of 26 lakhs of Rupees a year which was the condition of that grant." After serving the emperor with many excuses over the years, Warren Hastings "gave the soothing assurance that he had made a representation about this tribute to his masters in London, and was only waiting for their commands." And Sarkar comments: "The poor deluded Shah Alam did not know that the representation was for stopping the tribute altogether, but he felt all the same that he would never see English money again." Sarkar's patriotism flares up at this point: "These grievous wrongs could be righted only by force, but where was that force to be found?"[74] This is where the Marathas failed both the Mughal Empire and its historian, Sir Jadunath. For in 1784, we find "the two masters of low cunning and underground intrigue," "the dead Mir Bakshi's diwan Narayandas and his ally the unscrupulous Gosain Himmat Bahadur" planning to "bribe the Emperor with twelve lakhs of Rupees . . . to devour the revenue of his jagirs," while "Major Browne was working desperately to revive Warren Hastings's abandoned plan of turning the Emperor into an English puppet and governing the empire through a Muslim regent who would be under the dictation of the British Resident at the capital, as the Nawab of Oudh already was."[75]

Sarkar's Nation

It is true, as some modern historians have complained, that Sarkar's patriotic voice—the voice of "the true son of India"—is sometimes hard to distinguish from other kinds of patriotism that may have been actually present in the eighteenth century. Thus, when Mirza Muhammad Shafi, a *mir bakshi* (army minister) to the emperor and "the last fighting army chief of the empire," was slain through "the blackest treachery" by Muhammad Beg Hamadani, a

74. Sarkar, *Fall*, 3:151.

75. Ibid., 3:199.

Mughalia sardar (chief), on 23 September 1783, Sarkar has the Maratha envoy "aptly describing" the situation: "Muhammad Shafi is dead. All Hindustan is lying bare. No sword for fighting is left in India."[76] But Sarkar is also being a ventriloquist here. The deliberate mixing of his authorial voice with that of the Maratha envoy produces a cultivated ambiguity, but the two types of patriotism can be analytically separated. The Maratha envoy's anguish would not have been tied in any way to a modern sense of, or a desire for, the nation. But then again, we should also be aware of the ambiguity of the word *nation* that allowed Sarkar to thus mix up sentiments belonging to very different historical periods. He would say of the "Jat state" during the "prudent reigns of Badan Singh and Suraj Mal" that its prospects of enjoying "a period of peaceful recuperation and progress" were destroyed by factors internal to the community: "A nation's greatest enemy is within, not without." Similarly, "internal quarrels and lack of statesmanship and even of intelligent self-interest among their leaders . . . so often ruined the national cause of the Marathas."[77]

It is such ambiguous use of the word *nation* that leaves Sarkar vulnerable to the charge of anachronism: did the Marathas themselves think of a "national cause," or was it national only in the eyes of the beholder? But that ambiguity should not blind us to the fact that much of Sarkar's lifelong absorption in Mughal, Maratha, and Rajput histories was devoted to a quest for a measure of the potential India had for creating from within pre-British history a united and modern nationhood. Recall his question to other historians in his discussion of the affairs of the Bengali hero Pratapaditya that we discussed in chapter 4: "But where was the nation in all this?" The fall of the Mughal Empire was a tragedy for Sarkar because, in his view—and here Sarkar sounds a little like our contemporary "early modernists"—the Mughals laid the initial groundwork needed to make India into a modern nation-state and yet failed to push the process to its logical conclusion.

The 1932 foreword to the first edition of the first volume of *Fall of the Mughal Empire* described that empire as having "broke[n] down the isolation of the provinces and the barrier between India and the outer world, and [having] thus [taken] . . . the first step necessary for the modernization of India and the growth of an Indian nationality in some distant future."[78] "It must be admitted," he wrote as he brought his multivolume *Fall* to a conclusion, "that the Mughal Emperors united many provinces of India into one political unit, with uniformity of official language, administrative machinery,

76. Ibid., 3:179–180.

77. Ibid., 3:2, 9.

78. Sarkar, *Fall*, foreword, 1:iii.

coinage and public service, and indeed a common type of civilization for the higher classes. They also recognized it as a duty to preserve peace and the reign of law throughout their dominions."[79] Yet the Mughals missed their chances through Aurangzeb's orthodoxy, which was followed by a series of inept rulers in the eighteenth century. Sarkar's idea of the fall of the Mughals as a national tragedy makes no sense until we see him as a votary of some kind of "modernity"—an economically and politically united nation-state that advances education, welfare, and science for all. What was remarkable for Sarkar about the Mughals was that it was their rule that initially prepared the country for a movement in this direction: "Administrative and cultural uniformity was given to nearly the whole of this continent of a country; the artery roads were made safe for the trader and the traveler; the economic resources of the land were developed; and a profitable intercourse was opened with the outer world. With peace, wealth, and enlightened Court patronage, came a new cultivation of the Indian mind and advance of Indian literature, painting, architecture and handicrafts, which raised this land once again to the front rank of the civilized world. Even the formation of an Indian nation did not seem an impossible dream."[80]

Yet, Sarkar wrote at the end of his study of Aurangzeb, "Aurangzib did not attempt such an ideal [of nation-making], even though his subjects formed a very composite population . . . and he had no European rivals hungrily watching to destroy his kingdom. On the contrary, he deliberately undid the beginnings of . . . a national and rational policy which Akbar had set on foot."[81] Akbar had successfully converted "a military monarchy into a national state"—not constitutionally but in effect—by remaining open both to talents of the Hindu Rajputs and to the "right type of recruits" from among the fortune seekers who came from "Bukhara and Khurasan, Iran and Arabia."[82] Aurangzeb in particular failed precisely on this score. Whereas the "liberal Akbar, the self-indulgent Jahangir, and the cultured Shah Jahan had welcomed Shias in their camps and courts and given them the highest offices, especially in the secretariat and revenue administration," the "orthodox Aurangzeb . . . barely tolerated them as a necessary evil."[83] The latter's conflict with the Rajputs and "the hated poll-tax (*jaziya*)" lent Shivaji the aura of a Hindu "national" leader in the eyes of his contemporaries. Sarkar

79. Jadunath Sarkar, *Fall of the Mughal Empire*, vol. 4, *1789–1803* (1950; Calcutta: Orient Longman, 1975), p. 338.

80. Sarkar, *Fall*, 1:2.

81. Sarkar, *Aurangzib*, 5:378.

82. Sarkar, chap. 11, in Irvine, *Later Mughals*, 2:308, 309.

83. Ibid., 2:310.

wrote: "To the Rajputs and Bundelas, who had so long been the staunchest supports of the Mughal cause, the Mahratta hero [Shivaji] appeared as their heaven-born deliverer,—a Rama slaying Ravana or a Krishna slaying Kansa. This feeling breathes in every line of the Hindu poet Bhushan's numberless odes on Shivaji." Sarkar then makes "Bhushan kavi" (as he was known) speak for all Indian Hindus: "He really voices in smooth and vigorous numbers the unspoken thoughts of the millions of Hindus all over India. At the end of the 17th century they had come to regard the Mughal Government as Satanic and refused to co-operate."[84]

Thus, to revert once again to the prose of the *Fall*, a "natural progress" toward nationhood "was arrested," and "after a quarter century of heroic struggle by that monarch," decline "had unmistakably set in." Sarkar restated his disappointment in the Mughals in what he added to William Irvine's *Later Mughals* when he edited the book for publication in the 1920s: "The profuse bounty of Nature to this country, its temperate climate which reduces human want, and the abstemious habits of its people, all combined to increase the national income of India in the sixteenth and seventeenth centuries. . . . The wealth of Ind[ia] was the wonder and envy of other nations. But the Mughal court and Mughal aristocracy had not the sense to insure this wealth by spending a sufficient portion of it on efficient national defence and the improvement of people's intellect and character by a wise system of public education."[85]

So what was the ideal state the Mughals might have created? Sarkar's ideals were all derived from the professed ideals of the British Empire. These ideals, it has to be remembered, were valued by many members of the intelligentsia—not of all them Western-educated—in the India of the nineteenth century in which Sarkar grew up. They came to be questioned in the twentieth century as a new and vigorous anti-imperial nationalism gained ground in India. Thus, securing unity and peace, that is, order, for the population was in Sarkar's eyes the sine qua non of good government. The years 1754–1772, covered in the second volume of his *Fall*, saw the Afghans and the Marathas vie for Delhi

84. Ibid., 2:309. On Bhushan Kavi, see Allison Busch, *The Poetry of Kings: The Classical Hindi Literature of Mughal India* (New York: Oxford University Press, 2011), where she actually shows how much the *riti* poets, of whom Bhushan was one, owed to Mughal patronage. See also Allison Busch's thesis, "The Courtly Vernacular: The Transformation of Brajabhasha Literary Culture (1590–1690)," (PhD diss., University of Chicago, June 2003), p. 215n29, where she cites R. S. McGregor, "The Progress of Hindi, Part 1: The Development of a Transregional Idiom," in *Literary Cultures in History*, ed. Sheldon Pollock (Berkeley: University of California Press, 2003), to show that Bhushan's earlier patron, Indrajit, called even Akbar "the king of *daityas* [demons]."

85. Sarkar, *Fall*, 1:2; Sarkar, chap. 11, in Irvine, *Later Mughals*, 2:315.

and the Jats "forming a kingdom within the space of a decade." But this was also a period when emperors were in turn deposed, banished, blinded, and murdered. But as the narrative got close to the end of the period, "the worst [was] over," commented Sarkar, "and we begin to emerge into light." What was this "light"? It had to do with the securing of peace and order. "The Sikhs have now established their rule over much of the Punjab," he wrote, "and given to the people of that province internal security and the promotion of agriculture in a degree unknown for sixty years past." At the same time he praised the "British peace" that was established in "Bengal, Bihar and Oudh up to Allahabad"—"a misty dawn, . . . of which the noontide splendour was to be seen in the 19th century." For the British *pax* brought about "unprecedented revival" of the "indigenous culture" that had been "quenched in blood in the capital cities of the [Mughal] empire" and led to a "new birth"—literally, a renaissance—of "Indo-Persian historical literature" under "alien patronage" (such as in the case of Ghalib).[86]

Anachronism?

Was Sarkar being anachronistic? His admittedly ambiguous use of the word *nation*, his blaming Aurangzeb and his successors for not carrying the unity of the country achieved by their predecessors to its "natural" conclusion, the nation—was not all this simply a case of the historian projecting backward his strong desire to see India grow into a nation? Ironically, it would seem, if anyone was ever truly disappointed with the Mughals for their failure to produce an early-modern India, it was their preeminent modern historian, Sir Jadunath Sarkar! Add to this the criticism that has been registered by several important and respected scholars of Mughal India of our times—that historians like Sarkar or his mentor Irvine often reproduced the sentiments and biases of their eighteenth-century sources to create an image of "decline" and "decay"—and the charge of anachronism is compounded. Did Sarkar fail to maintain a critical distance between his own time and the times he studied?

There is something to these criticisms—see below—but they need to be seriously nuanced if we are to develop some sense of what it was that Sarkar himself wanted the discipline of history to do for him. Now, to the simple

86. Sarkar, *Fall*, 1934 preface, 2:iii. For more on Sarkar's appreciation of the benefits of British rule, see Jadunath Sarkar, "Our Immediate Future," *Modern Review* (October 1948), pp. 273–275. On Ghalib as a product of British-Mughal Delhi, see C. M. Naim, "Ghalib's Delhi: A Shamelessly Revisionist Look at Two Popular Metaphors," in his *Urdu Texts and Contexts* (New Delhi: Permanent Black, 2004), pp. 250–273.

charge of anachronism first. I think it would be a posthumous and gratuitous insult to Sarkar's intelligence to think that he would not have been intellectually aware of the problem of anachronism. He himself accused some of the Poona historians of reading history backward because they looked to glorify Shivaji and his father by portraying them as more powerful in their early years than they actually were. For example, in a letter to Sardesai in 1932, when the latter was preparing to write a review of C. V. Vaidya's book on Shivaji, Sarkar wrote: "Yes, you can send me C.V. Vaidya's *Shivaji* and I shall send back to you a list of glaring mistakes in it with *evidence* (for incorporation in your review)." Evidence, Sarkar commented, did not show that Shahji (Shivaji's father) "was an *amir wazir* or supreme divisional commander before 1628, or that Shivaji's doings in 1646 were those of a sovereign prince. There were hundreds of contemporary men of exactly the same status and power as Shahji during 1620–1627 . . . and Shivaji in 1646 was a mere *rising* rebel chieftain—not a sovereign Rajah. These two facts are forgotten or muddled with later history by the Poona School. . . . Your Poona friends are reading the history of 1674 *backwards* into the events of 1620–1627 and 1646."[87] The word "backwards" in the expression "reading backwards" was underlined by Sarkar himself; so there is no question that he very well understood what the problem of anachronism was. He made the same point again in a letter of 1940: "It is pure moonshine to suggest that Baji Rao and Jai S. planned to cooperate in founding a Hindu Pat-Padshahi. We make ourselves ridiculous when we read the ideals and thoughts of the 20th century English educated nationalists into the lives of the sectarian or clannish champions of the 17th and 18th centuries."[88]

We also have to acknowledge, however, the additional problem that the word *nation* lent itself to plural uses and that this led to certain ambiguities. Sometimes, Sarkar would use the word *nation* in an unexceptional way, as it was used in the nineteenth century and before—to mean an ethnos, a people, and not necessarily a political formation or consciousness. The nineteenth-century colonial historian John Clark Marshman, for instance, wrote of the Maratha "national standard" (meaning the flag), using the word "national" in an ethnic sense.[89] But Sarkar would often use the word "national" as if to suggest that, in addition to there being a Maratha "ethnos," there could be a Maratha "imperial" or even "national" project as well. Thus he would write of the peshwa's flag as "the national flag" of the Marathas and speak

87. NL, JSP, letter no. 187, Sarkar to Sardesai, Calcutta, 4 Feb 1932.

88. NL, JSP, letter no. 621, Sarkar to Sardesai, Calcutta, 8 May 1940.

89. See John Clark Marshman, *The History of India*, vol. 2 (London: Longmans, Green, Reader and Dyer, 1871), p. 55.

of the "stringency in public expenditure" of Nana Fadnis—"the Chitpavan Machiavel (as his modern admirers in Puna like to call him)"—as a factor that ensured that money was never spent "in strengthening the *national* defence and or improving the people's lot."[90] In fact, section 2 of Sarkar's chapter 42, in volume 4 of *Fall*, carries a title that speaks not so much of Maratha desires as of Sarkar's own vision of what the Marathas could have achieved. The section is headed: "Nana Fadnis ruins Maratha national interests by selfishness and want of a statesmanly vision."[91] Sarkar would sometimes see the rivalry between the Holkars and the Sindhias as "civil war" and see the families as lacking in the "spirit of patriotic self-sacrifice"—as though it entirely escaped him that it was also possible that Maratha polity may not have been based on the idea of a united nationhood or an even an empire but rather on warring families of Maratha sardars that came together on occasion and pragmatically, without ever losing their interest in internecine struggle for rank and status among themselves.[92]

Sarkar, of course, knew all of this factually.[93] His own material points to the possibility that the Marathas may have seen themselves as in charge of a certain territory that was properly their own and as a raiding polity with regard to other regions that they dominated but only as raiders.[94] Surely, they accepted the fiction of the Mughal Empire, even if they sought to control its treasury. Sarkar himself described how General Gerard Lake's victory in 1803 and his assumption of power in Delhi "brought a crowd of Hindustani chiefs competing for Lake's favour to rise against the oppression and avarice of their late rulers, the Marathas and their French agents." Why, then, would he see an unbridled conflict between the Sindhias and the Holkars as producing "anarchy" and costing the Marathas their "independence"?[95] What, then, could

90. Sarkar, *Fall*, 4:28, 205, emphasis added.

91. Ibid., 4:130.

92. Ibid., 4:190, 214.

93. Thus Sarkar would write—with regard to the Peshwa Baji Rao II—that "the life of the Maratha empire depended on the solution of the hereditary rivalry between Sindhia and Holkar," but also recognize that imposing such a solution would have been "opposed to the *traditional* Puna policy of never settling a dispute finally, but keeping two separate and rival authorities in the same locality so as to weaken both of them and make both dependents on the central Government, and thus increase the chance of the Puna Court exacting as much money as possible from the two." Ibid., 4:194, emphasis added.

94. Rosalind O'Hanlon's current research, when completed, will give us a more nuanced understanding of the multiple senses of region with which Marathas and others operated in early modern India. See her forthcoming paper "Performance in a World of Paper: Puranic Histories and Social Communication in Early Modern India."

95. Sarkar, *Fall*, 4:313, 193.

have been the status of the question of "national liberty" that he wrote about with such a strong sense of grief?

As Sarkar once said in a letter to Sardesai, the subject of the fourth volume of his *Fall* was "even more truly the fall of the Maratha Empire."[96] The very first chapter describes Nana Fadnis's jealousy of Mahadji Sindhia and his encouragement of conflict between the Sindhias and the Holkars as "unpatriotic."[97] The "anarchy" was brought to an end only when the British ushered in the "modern age." He wrote in the following vein on Holkar's raid on Malwa: "The classic land of Malwa had once been the fountainhead of Hindu culture . . . [of] Sanskrit poetry and drama, science and the fine arts. . . . But in the year 1798 the dark cloud of anarchy, rapine and popular suffering descended on the unhappy land." "This anarchy," he said, "did not end with the crushing of the Pindharis by the British in . . . 1817, but continued to smoulder till the suppression of the Mutiny of 1858 and the dawning of the modern age." "Malwa's misery," Sarkar thought, could be blamed squarely on "Jaswant Holkar's unpatriotic ambition and . . . on Daulat Rao's insane desire to extinguish the power of the House of Holkar."[98] Sarkar disagreed with Rajwade's assessment that dissensions among Marathas were created by "neighbouring superior Power[s]," blaming the English East India Company by implication. Sarkar responded: "*Perfide Albion* once more and everywhere; yes, *we* are not to blame for our national downfall, but the hated English!"[99] But who was this "we"? Sarkar painted a very similar picture of wanton destruction for the Desh districts of Maharashtra and for "Maratha penetration into other provinces of India" generally. "The last fruit of civil war is the loss of national liberty," wrote a grieving Sarkar, and he added, "Holkar's triumph [over Sindhia] made the Peshwa an English vassal."[100]

Was all this mere anachronism? Did Sarkar fail to judge the Marathas by the reigning moral standards of their own times?

The Statesman as Hero

While it is clear that Sarkar did not do what we would do today—judge historical political leaders by the standards they set for themselves—we would not understand Sarkar's project without asking why he felt free to judge the

96. NL, JSP, letter no. 1034, Sarkar to Sardesai, Calcutta, 15 May 1950.

97. Sarkar, *Fall*, 4:4–5.

98. Ibid., 4:167.

99. Jadunath Sarkar, *House of Shivaji: Studies and Documents on Maratha History—Royal Period*, 3rd ed. (Calcutta: M. C. Sarkar, 1955), p. 289.

100. Sarkar, *Fall*, 4:215.

politics of, say, Shivaji's time and later by standards that appeared to be universal. Consider how Sarkar granted that Shivaji was a "statesman," "a king among men" ("as the ancient Greeks would have called him") and that he had founded a "sovereign State."[101] According to Sarkar, Shivaji established the three main principles of a "good State": he gave to his dominions "peace and order"; he "threw careers open to talent" (Sarkar adds: "the motto of the French revolution of 1789"); and he gave people "freedom in exercise of religion" and "respected the *Quran* no less than his own scriptures."[102] Besides, he was "free from all vices and indolence in his private life"; and even though he was himself a "devout Hindu," he could recognize true sanctity in a Musalman. . . . All creeds had equal opportunity in his service." Thus, says Sarkar, his "political ideals were such that *we can accept them even today without any change*. He aimed at giving his subjects peace, universal toleration, equal opportunities for all castes and creeds, a beneficent, active and pure system of administration, a navy for promoting trade, and a trained militia for guarding the homeland."[103] Clearly, Sarkar's standards were universal. But then comes his next and perhaps the most critical question: "Did he succeed in creating a nation?"[104] "No," was Sarkar's answer, loud and clear. However, it was not Shivaji's fault that he failed to create a nation. For it was the prevalence of caste, "kulinism" (rules of endogamy among Brahmans), and "personal jealousies" among Maratha rulers that ensured that the Marathas did not have "the *sine qua non* of a nation."[105]

Sarkar's thinking on statesmanship and nationhood was guided by his reading of European history—especially but not exclusively the history of the English. He thought these ideals of statesmanship had universal validity in an age of modernizing nations. The understanding of "statesmanship" was something he clearly owed to the English historian-cum-politician H. A. L. Fisher (1865–1940), and one of the greatest statesmen in the world, in his reckoning, was the Italian Count Cavour.[106] Sometimes he would rue the absence of a Bismarck in Indian history: thus, Ahmad Shah's empire "could only have been saved by a wazir [prime minister] of Bismarckian capacity and dictatorial power."[107] Following Fisher, this is how Sarkar painted his ideal statesman, while analyzing Shivaji's success: "The true statesman does not grumble when

101. Sarkar, *House*, 3rd ed., pp. 102–104, 111.

102. Ibid., pp. 111–112.

103. Ibid., pp. 113, 114, emphasis added.

104. Ibid., pp. 102–104.

105. Ibid., pp. 106, 109.

106. Sarkar, *Fall*, 1:217.

107. Sarkar, *House*, 3rd ed., pp. 102–103.

he cannot find the materials for his purpose ready to his hand. . . . Statesmanly wisdom consists in taking correct stock of the available human material around us, . . . so as to enlist them *all* in the service of the grand aim and understanding of the statesman. That aim must be the paramount object of his pursuit. . . . His success proves his divine gift of genius, which baffles our analysis."[108]

Caste, for Sarkar, was an obstacle to nationhood, for "without the completest freedom of marriage within a population . . . that population can never form a nation." Why could Indians not accept the mixture of many races that made them one people?—"Englishmen of today do not consider their blood as defiled when they say in the words of their late poet laureate [Lord Tennyson, "A Welcome to Alexandra," written on the occasion of the marriage of the Prince of Wales to Princess Alexandra, eldest daughter of Christian IX of Denmark, in 1863]: "Saxon and Norman and Dane are we."[109] "Where caste and kulinism reign," wrote Sarkar, "merit cannot have full and free recognition and the community cannot rise to its highest possible capacity of greatness." And without the principle of equality in action, "democracy is inconceivable there, because the root principle of democracy is the absolute equality of every member of the *demos*—the belief [and here Sarkar quotes, without naming the author, from Robert Burns's 1795 poem "A Man's a Man for A' That," which was popular among many educated Bengalis] that '*The rank is but the guinea's stamp./A man's the gold for all that* [*sic*].'"[110]

The plethora of references to European literature and history will show that the principles by which Sarkar measured the readiness of a people for nationhood were ones deeply connected to the history of nation-formation

108. Jadunath Sarkar, "Shivaji: His Genius, Environment and Achievement," *Modern Review* (May 1927), p. 618.

109. Sarkar, *House*, 3rd ed., p. 108. Sarkar here almost echoes a commonplace contemporary self-understanding of the English in the nineteenth century. See, for instance, the discussion of this line from Tennyson (again slightly misquoted in Sarkar), [C. L. W. Powlett], *History of Battle Abbey* (London: William Clows, 1877), p. 70. The Bodleian library copy of this book is available on the Internet.

110. Sarkar, *House*, 3rd ed., p. 108. Rabindranath Tagore, writing in the early 1930s, returned to the same poem of Burns to express India's political and intellectual debt to Europe. "That today in spite of all our weaknesses we can attempt to change the situation of our nation and the state is due to our taking a stand on the ground of [a European] theory. . . . It is on the strength of this theory that we fight clamorously with such a powerful government over demands we would never been able to dream of raising with the Mughal emperor. . . . This is the theory expressed in the poet's line, 'A man is a man for all that.'" Rabindranath Tagore, "Kalantar," in *Kalantar* [Changing times], in *Rabindrarachanabali* [The collected works of Rabindranath], translated from Bengali (Calcutta: Government of West Bengal, 1968), 13:212.

in Europe; but he obviously attributed to them a universal validity. He stated some of these principles with great passion at the end of the final volume on Aurangzeb, first published in 1924, when he spoke of the "eternal truth" that "there cannot be a great or lasting empire without a great *people*." And "no people can be great unless it learns to form a compact *nation* with equal rights and opportunities for all,—a nation the component parts of which are homogeneous . . . but freely tolerating individual differences in minor points and private life, recognizing individual liberty as the basis of communal liberty—a nation whose administration is solely bent upon promoting national, as opposed to provincial or sectarian interests,—a society which pursues knowledge without fear, without cessation, without bounds."[111]

The vision of a polity that recognized and created opportunities for talent irrespective of the differences of caste or creed may have been something of a reaction to the way the politics of identity—though it was not known by that name then—was becoming an enduring feature of the emerging political scene in India, with electoral seats, and eventually employment, being reserved for particular social groups. In the William Mayer lectures that he delivered at the University of Madras in 1928, Sarkar denounced "the [official] policy of splitting up the nation" by "public exaltation of caste differences among the Hindus." "Men to whom all blacks had been pariahs," he wrote, "now began to show a heart torn by anguish for the lot of the depressed caste Hindus. In Bombay and Madras, non-Brahmans were set up against Brahmans."[112]

Of course, Sarkar's understanding of the actual nature of the politics of affirmative action as they developed in India in the colonial and postcolonial periods will seem seriously deficient to many today. On the other hand, it has

111. Sarkar, *Aurangzib*, 5:378. A note in Sarkar's *India through the Ages* (1928; Calcutta: Orient Longman, 1993), pp. 82–83, explains what he meant by "homogeneity" or "uniformity" in this context:

> We already see the beginnings of . . . a sense of oneness among all the Indian people. The victory of a Bengali football team over a British regiment at Simla now causes Punjabi spectators to rejoice. The sufferings of Tamil emigrants in South Africa or Fiji are keenly resented in Calcutta and Puna. There is a notorious sameness in the agenda paper and procedure of an orthodox Hindu caste conference and, say, an all-India Muslim Education Conference. Both have stolen their programme from the hated Europeans! Our nationalists denounce the West with the very arguments and methods borrowed from the West. The Muslim League has stolen its thunder from the Indian National Congress who had stolen it from the Irish.

See also Jadunath Sarkar, "The Unity of India," *Modern Review* (November 1942), pp. 377–380.

112. Sarkar, *India through the Ages*, p. 96.

to be recognized that his vision of the nation was not peculiarly his own. It represents a particular variety of nationalism that jostled with and eventually lost ground to other, more aggressive, varieties. Writing to Prasantachandra Mahalanobis in September 1928, the poet Rabindranath Tagore expressed very similar sentiments: "The psychology of politics in our country is naturally the psychology of division."[113] And students of Mughal history will remember that the historian Makhanlal Roy Chowdhury, in 1941, praised Akbar for exactly the same reason that made Sarkar praise Shivaji:

> With Akbar, the dicta were, "recognise merit wherever ye find it," "right man in the right place," "intellect is not the monopoly of the believers." He unhesitatingly chose Rajput princes as his generals and raised Tansen (originally a Hindu) to be the first musician of the court. Daswa Nath, son of a Kahar (palanquin bearer) was appointed the first painter of his court; Mahadev became the first physician and Chandrasen the first surgeon. . . . Among the famous Nine Jewels of his court no less than four were Hindus. . . . Akbar appreciated merit and he knew how to pick it up and recognise it.[114]

We can now see this talk of "merit" as part of a contemporary tussle—not quite dead even in our times—between an imperial-liberal vision of how the Indian nation was to be built and a more populist-democratic vision of the same. Needless to say, the latter prevailed in Indian history, but that is precisely why we have to make a conscious effort to understand how Sarkar's variety of patriotism worked and how it may have been connected to the methods and philosophy guiding his historical research.

Apart from the issue of merit being given its due, at the center of Sarkar's vision of modernity was also the question of India accepting modern European disciplines, both in the sense of "scientific knowledge" and in institutions such as the army. The two points were often connected. European military discipline, for instance, plays a very strong part in Sarkar's narrative in the *Fall*. Such discipline was a "classic example of the superiority of science over muscles," and Sarkar saw Benoît de Boigne (1751–1830), the famous French military adventurer who commanded Sindhia's army in the 1780s and 1790s, as the embodiment of such military science. Europe's military

113. Tagore to Mahalanobis, 13 September 1928, in *Kalyaniyeshu Prasanta: Rabindranath-Prasantachandra Mahalanobis patrabinimoy*, ed. Prasantakumar Pal (Kolkata: Pashimbanga Bangla Akademi, 2005), p. 68. For an extended discussion, see my Bengali essay "Politikser buli, democrasir buldojar" [The cant of politics, the bulldozer of democracy], *Desh* (17 November 2013), pp. 24–27.

114. Makhanlal Roy Chowdhury's *The Din-i-Ilahi; or, The Religion of Akbar* (1941; Calcutta: Dasgupta, 1952), pp. 83, 85.

superiority symbolized for Sarkar that which made Europe modern and successful.[115] This was a melding of rational sciences, institutions, and technologies coupled with statesmanship and character on the part of the rulers. Sarkar's ideas about modernity underlie what he wrote in praise of European armies and in criticism of their Indian counterparts: "The true superiority of the European armies lay in the education of the intellect and development of character, and not primarily in their more efficient weapons. These two qualifications were utterly wanting in our indigenous armies; most of our old style officers were illiterate and proud of their ignorance; even the few who could read, never improved themselves by studying new books as the European soldiers and civilians in India very often did. After all, there is no escape from the truth, emphasized in Elizabethan England, that *Knowledge is Power*."[116]

His modernizing patriotism shines even more clearly through what he said a page later: "The new system [of appointing European heads for some sections of Indian armies] was a valuable military growth no doubt; but it . . . could not take root in the Indian soil so long as the Indians did not heartily accept and universally spread western knowledge and the western spirit. From this fact [*sic*] follows the further need of modern India adopting western industrial methods and producing *on the soil* modernized officers and modern munitions, so as to possess within her own bosom an inexhaustible reserve of all that a New Model Army requires."[117] Indeed his main complaint about the "Rajput warrior class" in the second volume of *Fall* was that their "isolation within narrow and obscure nooks of their homeland" prevented them from "acquiring the new knowledge" of the "European military system" and thus "moving with the times." Unlike the "famished Scottish laird" for whom "salvation came in the course of the expansion of the British empire in this very second half of the eighteenth century," the Rajputs "supplied not one lieutenant in England's conquest of the East."[118] This was indeed the problem of the Rajput that he sought to capture by citing Goldsmith.

Sarkar's unhesitating and often misunderstood admiration of British-imperial ideals was thus really a measure of what he desired for India and Indian leaders. When Daulat Rao Sindhia fought with the British in 1803, his war preparations only invited scathing criticism from the historian: for they were "marked by folly, indecision and delay, as if mere deception and

115. Sarkar, *Fall*, 4:106.

116. Ibid., 4:110.

117. Ibid., 4:111.

118. Sarkar, *Fall*, 2:374–375.

theatrical demonstration could decide the fate of nations." The governor general Marquess Wellesley, on the other hand, was described by Sarkar as "a statesman of marvellous vision, organizing power, and skill in choosing the fittest instrument for his purpose." Sarkar thought the military preparations the British undertook immediately before the war with the Marathas entirely "worthy of a race that deserves to win an empire, because it provides for everything that can be thought of beforehand and leaves very little to be clumsily improvised under the stress of actual conflict."[119]

It remained his perpetual lament that in the Mughal court "no attempt was made by any Indian noble or scholar to learn European languages, arts or military system." "A modern Indian nationalist will best realise how blindly selfish and autocratic the Mughal Emperors and the Indian aristocracy of the 16th and 17th centuries were, if he considers that while they spent lakhs every year in buying European objects of luxury or art, not a single printing press, not even a lithographic stone was imported, either for popular education or public business."[120] The complaint was repeated almost verbatim in concluding the four volumes of the *Fall*: "Ever since the middle of the 17th century, there had been close commercial exchange between India and England, but our royalty and ruling class imported only European articles of luxury; none cared for European knowledge; no printing press, not even the cheapest and smallest lithographic stone was installed by the Mughal Emperors or the Peshwas. They imported only what catered to their luxury and vice." This was not an aristocracy that could have produced the seminaries, the academies, or the universities of early-modern Europe. "During the decline of Mughal civilization," continued Sarkar in the last chapter of the *Fall*, "education died out in India; the only schools that survived devoted themselves to the low but useful work of preparing clerks and accountants."[121] Clearly, Sarkar was not thinking of the centers for higher education in logic, grammar, or rhetoric that several scholars of our times have focused on.[122] His sights were firmly trained on knowledge that might have contributed to the process of modernization *before* British rule. This explained, he writes, why Indian kings were

119. Sarkar, *Fall*, 4:264, 265, 268.

120. Sarkar, *Aurangzib*, 5:355. Sarkar adds in a footnote that at the Mughal court "interpretation was done for European visitors by Armenians or by Europeans who knew Persian. Only one Muhammadan (Mutamad Khan, c. 1703) is spoken of in Aurangzib's letters as knowing the English language."

121. Sarkar, *Fall*, 4:345, 344.

122. I have in mind the current researches of Sheldon Pollock, Christopher Minskowski, Rosalind O'Hanlon, Janardan Ganeri, Gary Tubb, Yigal Bronner, Allison Busch, Whitney Cox, Lawrence McCrea, Daud Ali, and others.

so keen to employ European and Eurasian mercenaries to lead their armies, for "no Indian could be found with the least knowledge of *modern* arts and sciences."[123]

The shadow of Bernier hovers over Sarkar's prose in these moments. In the concluding chapter of the final volume of *Aurangzib*, Sarkar quoted the colonial administrator-scholar William Crooke to describe how the Mughals had never been able to develop something like the "modern Cabinet" system of government—"the monarch was obliged to fall back on the mob of adventurers who crowded round his *darbar* . . . whose function was more to amuse their master than to act as a modern Cabinet. It was never the Mughal policy to foster the growth of a hereditary aristocracy."[124] This criticism was originally Bernier's, though parts of it were reproduced in the nineteenth century by other European observers (including Marx) of India's institutions. Sarkar distinctly alluded to Bernier in the final chapter of the *Fall*, volume 4, in thinking about why the Mughals failed to usher India into the beginnings of "modernity": "Bernier had noticed in the middle 17th century that the Mughals had no hereditary peerage like that of England or France, but only an official and military aristocracy, personal in theory, but tending to be renewed in each generation with decreasing rank."[125] It is worth remembering what Bernier had actually said. Proceeding from the assumption that all land in Mughal India was held by the Crown, and thus the formation of an independent hereditary aristocracy was discouraged, Bernier remarked that "the *Omrahs* [nobility], therefore, mostly consist of adventurers from different nations who entice one another to the court; and are generally persons of low descent, some having been originally slaves, and the majority being destitute of education. The *Mogol* raises them to dignities, or degrades them to obscurity, according to his own pleasure and caprice." "A profound and universal ignorance," Bernier continued, "is the natural consequence of such a state of society. . . . Is it possible to establish in *Hindoustan* academies and colleges properly endowed? Or, should they be found, where are the scholars? Where [are] the individuals whose property is sufficient to support their children at college? Or, if such individuals exist, who would venture to display so clear a proof of wealth?"[126]

Bernier's critique of the absence of academies and colleges stemmed, as Nicholas Dew and others have pointed out, from his experience of and sup-

123. Sarkar, *Fall*, 4:344.

124. Crooke cited in Sarkar, *Aurangzib*, 5:368.

125. Sarkar, *Fall*, 4:338.

126. Bernier, *Travels*, "Letter to Colbert," pp. 212, 229.

port for the absolutist rule of Louis XIV, 1661–1715, when several new institutions of learning were founded, including "several new royal academies," and when Bernier's correspondent, Jean Baptiste Colbert, enjoyed his "ministerial preeminence." By Bernier's time, comments Dew, "absolutist political philosophy called for a powerful prince to maintain order against the mutability of human society, particularly after the religious and civil wars of the mid-century"—it is interesting that the battles for succession in seventeenth-century India should be understood by Bernier as constituting "civil wars"—and "humanist educators" were expected not just to hold up "a mirror for princes," but to produce "a reflection of a Catholic and absolute conception of royal government which entailed the weeding-out of heresy and superstition, and the education of the populace as good Catholic subjects."[127] It is not clear that Sarkar would have wanted his ideal Mughal rulers to be absolutist monarchs of the European kind, but the Mughals and the Marathas did lack in his eyes the vision or the character or the institutions that could have led India's population to the path of exact and scientific knowledge. India had to wait for the coming of a British-imperial *pax* that produced the nineteenth-century interest among Indians in modern science and literature—the so-called renaissance.[128] He was also always aware that in describing certain policies of Shivaji or Akbar as characterized by an "openness to talent," he and Makhanlal Roy Chowdhury and others were invoking "the motto of the French Revolution of 1789," or, as Sarkar put it to himself in an undated note on Shivaji:

"Indian nationality possible and enduring only when there are equal rights for all and a fair field and no favour, or as the French Revolution of 1789 declared, 'careers open to talent' only. . . . This is the supreme ideal of a modern state—Shiva[ji] realised it 250 years ago."[129]

All of this was no simple anachronism. Sarkar's works were a particular variety of patriotic history that had been brought up on a diet of the British-imperial literary canon, which disseminated some classical themes of virtue and heroism in politics. Sarkar thus looked for an openness in the empirical world by having recourse to two particular categories of profoundly European provenance: providence and character.

127. Dew, *Orientalism*, pp. 16–17.

128. Sarkar, *India through the Ages*, the chapter "The English and Their Gifts to India."

129. Sarkar, "Shivaji," p. 621; NL, JSP, "Miscellaneous" File, handwritten undated "sketch" by Sarkar.

6

Between Providence and Character: The Historian Himself

Providence and Indian History

Sarkar's critique of Mughal India was deeply anchored in a theory of Providence. We might call the associated mode of thinking "providentialism." Rooted in Christian thought, the idea of Providence and its importance to human history was championed in the nineteenth century by none other than Leopold von Ranke.[1] "History when rightly read," wrote Sarkar, opening the concluding paragraph of his five-volume study of Aurangzeb in 1924, "is a justification of Providence, the revelation of a great purpose fulfilled in

1. It is well known that Ranke's ideas on Providence and world history evolved, but a basic distinction between two rather different ideas of Providence may be illustrated by reference to Ranke's and Hegel's works. Ranke mostly worked with the Lutheran idea that while God did design human history, His intent was not open to scrutiny by humans. It is in this context that scholars quote Ranke's famous 1831–32 statement "God alone knows world history; we know the contradictions." Ranke cited in Leonard Krieger, *Ranke: The Meaning of History* (Chicago: University of Chicago Press, 1977), p. 136. See also Leopold von Ranke, "On Progress in History," and in particular his dialogue with King Maximilian II of Bavaria (1854) in his *The Theory and Practice of History*, ed. Georg Iggers, trans. Wilma A. Iggers (London: Routledge, 2011), pp. 20–23; and the discussion in Frederick C. Beiser, *The German Historicist Tradition* (Oxford: Oxford University Press, 2011), p. 264. Hegel, on the other hand, famously argued (against the likes of Niebuhr and Ranke) that "world history is governed by an ultimate design, that it is a rational process, whose rationality is . . . but a divine and absolute reason" and hence could be accessed "from a knowledge of reason itself." Georg Wilhelm Friedrich Hegel, *Lectures on the Philosophy of World History: Introduction: Reason in History*, trans. H. S. Nisbet, with an introduction by Duncan Forbes (1975; Cambridge: Cambridge University Press, 1996), p. 28. See also pp. 19, 22, 26, 30. This Christian theological disputation about the accessibility or obscurity of God's intent with respect to human history is totally absent from Sarkar's thoughts.

time."[2] What was this purpose? It was for India to become a self-governing modern nation. Ideally, Sarkar would have liked it if the process had completed itself *before* British rule—in the seventeenth and eighteenth centuries. His wish for the eighteenth century was that Indians had been rational, nationalistic, and united enough to learn from Europeans (in areas where the latter were genuinely superior), so as to foil their attempt to take control of India. It was a matter of profound and lasting sorrow to him that "a union of hearts between Sindhia and Holkar [the two leading Maratha leaders], which alone could threaten danger to British Power and disturbance to the British protectorate of Haidarabad, was an impossibility."[3] The charge of helping India realize her destiny then fell to the British. Sarkar returned to this thought in 1950 while composing the last few sentences of the fourth volume of his *Fall*: "Modern India has become an independent, fully sovereign state. That political evolution has been made possible only by British imperialism. This is the reason why the noblest sons of India, like Bankim Chandra Chatterji, Dr. Prafulla Chandra Roy, and Gopal Krishna Gokhalé, have recognised a divine dispensation in the fall of the Mughal Empire, as looked at from before and behind."[4] It should be mentioned, however, that as late as 1928, Sarkar thought that the process for creating the "necessary basis for nationality" had "just begun" in India and "its completion [was] yet far off."[5]

As he himself indicated, Sarkar was by no means alone in taking a providentialist view of British rule. The tradition of providentialist thinking by Indians goes back at least to the early part of the nineteenth century. Rammohun Roy (1772/4–1833), the putative "father of modern India," expressed his hope that "through Divine Providence and human exertions" the "advocates of idolatry" would one day "avail themselves" of a "true [and nonidolatrous] system of religion."[6] Decades later, Rabindranath Tagore, writing at the height of the Swadeshi movement (c. 1905) in Bengal, underlined the idea again by referring to the greater purpose that revealed itself through the Brit-

2. Jadunath Sarkar, *History of Aurangzib*, vol. 5 (1924; New Delhi: Orient Longman, 1974), p. 378.

3. Jadunath Sarkar, *Fall of the Mughal Empire*, vol. 4, *1789–1803* (1950; Calcutta: Orient Longman, 1975), p. 261.

4. Ibid., 4:350.

5. Sarkar, *India through the Ages* (1928; Calcutta: Orient Longman, 1993), p. 58.

6. Roy said this in his introduction to his English rendering of the *Kathoponishad*. See Stephen Hay, ed., *Sources of Indian Tradition* (New York: Columbia University Press, 1988), p. 23. For a suggestive recent discussion of Rammohun Roy's thoughts and their relationship to liberalism, see C. A. Bayly, *Recovering Liberties: Indian Thought in the Age of Liberalism and Empire* (Cambridge: Cambridge University Press, 2012), chaps. 2 and 3.

ish domination of India: "Like the ambassador of the lord of all ceremonies [*jaggeshvar*], England has forced herself right into our homes by breaking down our old and creaking doors in order to stir up in us a spirit of initiative that [would make us realize] that we also were needed in the world, . . . that [it was only] our growing and varied connections to the world in the spheres of knowledge, love, action, and multifarious inventions that would awaken and keep alive in us this sense of being needed." Tagore did not think independence was even possible until this destiny had been fulfilled: "We will not have the strength to expel the English by force until we have responded to their invitation, until our union with them has achieved its results. England has been sent for the sake of the India that, having germinated in the past, is now sprouting towards the future."[7]

Or consider the point that the twentieth-century nationalist leader and writer Chittaranjan Das made as part of his presidential address to the Indian National Congress's annual session held in Gaya in December 1922. Das spoke on "Non-Co-Operation and Council Entry." "Throughout the pages of Indian history," he said, "I see a great purpose unfolding itself. Movement after movement has swept over this vast country, apparently creating hostile forces, but in reality stimulating the vitality and moulding the life of the people into one great nationality."[8]

In the secular form in which the originally Christian idea of Divine Providence circulated among Hindu-Indian nationalist thinkers, it became deeply tied to another originally European idea: that of civilization, the idea that there was a specific, Indian civilization and that India's historic destiny was to give it the form of the nation.[9] Listen, again, to Chittaranjan Das:

> Now what is nationalism? It is, I believe, a process through which a nation expresses itself and finds itself, not in isolation from other nations, not in opposition to other nations, but as part of a great scheme by which, in seeking its own expression and therefore its own identity, it materially assists the self-expression and self-realisation of other nations as well. . . . I contend that each nationality constitutes a stream of the great unity, but no nation can fulfill itself unless and until it becomes itself and at the same time realizes its identity

7. Rabindranath Tagore, "Purba o poshchim" (1315; c. 1908–9), in *Samaj* collected in *Rabindrarachanabali*, centenary ed. (1368; Calcutta: Government of West Bengal, 1962), pp. 53–54.

8. Rajen Sen and B. K. Sen, comps., *Deshbandhu Chitta Ranjan Das: Brief Survey of Life and Work[,] Provincial Conference Speeches, Congress Speeches* (Calcutta: Karim Bux, [1926?]), pp. 190–191.

9. My essay "From Civilization to Globalization: The West as a Signifier in Indian Modernity," *Inter-Asian Cultural Studies* (Taiwan) 13, no. 1 (2012), pp. 138–152.

with Humanity. The whole problem of nationalism is therefore to find that stream and to face that destiny.

Since destiny was civilizational, a nation's "becoming itself" was also a matter of being able to infuse its own distinct sense of a being a civilization into the very process of becoming modern. Das therefore concluded: "If you find the current and establish a continuity with the past, then the process of self-expression has begun, and nothing can stop the growth of nationality."[10] Tagore made a very similar point in the essay cited above, invoking Rammohun Roy: "The main reason why Rammohun Roy was able to absorb Western thoughts was that he was never overwhelmed by the West. There was no weakness on his side. He stood on a firm ground of his own in order to acquire from the outside [world]. He knew where Indian treasures lay and had made them his own. He therefore possessed the measures and the balancing instrument with which to judge whatever he found."[11]

Sarkar's providential position, then, was that India was destined to become a nation, for that was the way peoples in the world had been moving since the seventeenth century. Nationalism, properly constituted, could act as the vehicle that took the nation to its tryst with destiny. The later Mughals failed in this mission in spite of their forebears' having laid down the basis of nationhood. They were either incurious about the scientific spirit of modern Europe, or their interest in this new knowledge was superficial. "The mere copying of the externals of European civilisation, without undergoing a new birth of spirit, cannot produce a renaissance," wrote Sarkar.

> It only led to the growth of the Anglo-Muslim culture of the Oudh Nawab's Court, which was a bastard sprout producing no flowers or fruit. In it the inner spirit of modern civilization was wanting. . . . No modern literature took its birth at the Lucknow royal court; the picture and poetry it produced were mostly pornographic; Asaf-ud-daula used to eat 64 grains of the strongest Turkish opium every day. His successor, Sadat Ali, knew English and a little French too, but turned out on the throne to be such a drunkard that he had to be assisted to his bed almost every night.[12]

"The Indian Renaissance" of the nineteenth century under British rule was possible "only because a principle was discovered" that had not been discovered in Mughal times. It was one by which "India could throw herself

10. Sen and Sen, *Deshbandhu*, pp. 189–190.

11. Tagore, "Purba o poshchim," p. 56. See also the discussion in C. A. Bayly's *Recovering Liberties*.

12. Sarkar, *Fall*, 4:349.

into the full current of modern civilization in the outer world without totally discarding her past." True, she was an "impoverished cousin of Europe," but "India was not called upon to plume herself in the borrowed feathers of European civilization,"—all she had to do was "to assimilate modern thought and modern arts into her inner life without any loss of what she had long possessed."[13]

Not Anachronism

Providential thinking, as observed before, was not the same as anachronistic thinking; nor was it deterministically teleological. There was no provision in it, for example, for something like the Hegelian "cunning of reason" that triumphed over human folly and ignorance and set the world right in the end. While the "great purpose" of national history revealed itself through historical events, the purpose depended on self-conscious human action for its realization. The Mughals, the Rajputs, and the Marathas and their likes in the seventeenth and eighteenth centuries needed to be more curious about the sciences and the institutions of Europe, but they lacked the requisite character, both collectively and in their individual leaders. "India had ceased to produce leaders, with the sole exception of Mahadji Sindhia." The task was unfinished even in 1947, when India became a sovereign nation-state but—to Sarkar's mind—not yet a nation. For a "necessary condition" of "democratic government or true nationhood" was "a long course of preparation or practical education and a surging up of the masses in search of a new political ideal." This process, interrupted since Aurangzeb, was restarted by the British, but even England "failed to form a nation in India" while unwittingly putting in place much of the basic framework needed to make it successful. "When the British resigned their trusteeship for India in 1947," writes Sarkar, expressing the idea of Providence again through the word "trusteeship," "they had failed to give the Indian people a political education which would enable them to stand on their own feet," for "two successive deluges of world-wars within 30 years of each other upset all former political speculations and prophecies, and forced the hands of the rulers and the ruled in India."[14] And, needless to say, Sarkar had little faith in the mass politics or in the run-of-the-mill leaders that the nationalist movement had generated. "A class of professional politicians has risen to power and are only held back from doing incalculable mischief by the few giants at the top," he wrote in the early years of independence while add-

13. Ibid., 4:348.
14. Ibid., 4:344, 342–343.

ing a chapter to a reprint of his 1928 William Mayer lectures. "A false sense of values has been taught to the electorate: to have been held by the English in political detention is proclaimed as a qualification for a ministership; a coat without a collar is the symbol of true patriotism. (A tie? Good God! It is the badge of a slave of the English.) Patient constructive workers for the nation's uplift are taunted with having made no sacrifice compared with the white-cap patriots. Patriotism of this type is sometimes cashed in to found bogus joint-stock banks." "But all this," he consoled himself, "will pass away, if only we are vouchsafed by the kind heaven fifty years of peace and strong and wise hands at the helm of India's government. Then England's marvelous achievement in India will be appraised in a just balance, in peace of mind, all passion spent."[15]

In 1945, asked by "Sir Tej Bahadur Sapru, Dr. Arundel, Allama Mashriqi and other all-India leaders" about his views on a possible constitution for independent India, Sarkar, while describing himself as "a nobody, a non-party non-leader non-follower individual unit of the population, an old man," a "mere Featherless Biped (the old Greek definition of man)" or—"in the more elegant idiom of Persia"—a "*zerra-e-bemiqdar* (this worthless atom), this *faqir-e-haqir* or poor beggar," repeated many of his disagreements with contemporary forms of mass politics. With "an eye on the future evolution of our State and not to the immediate gains of the moment," he felt that "a unitary legislature (and consequently ministry) in the provinces and at the Centre, elected *solely* by a general constituency proportioned to the population is theoretically possible in India, but it will do more harm than good if set up before Nineteen-hundred and *ninety-five*." For the need of the hour was the development of a "solid core . . . of truly national character in . . . the various fields of State activity, which will stand absolutely free of all considerations of religion, rank, wealth or race and similar disintegrating factors."[16]

15. Sarkar, *India through the Ages*, pp. 99–100.

16. Jadunath Sarkar, "A Scheme—Or a Dream?," *Modern Review* (June 1945), pp. 263, 264. Before we dismiss Sir Jadunath's ideas as emanating from the reactionary brain of a lover of the old empire, we should remember that even someone as radical as B. R. Ambedkar saw no guarantee in Gandhian street-politics involving the masses for a successful transition to democratic self-rule in India. Writing to A. V. Alexander, a member of the Cabinet Mission sent to India to discuss arrangements for the transfer of political power to Indians, Ambedkar said on 14 May 1946:

> To my mind, it is only right to say that the Hindus and Muslims are today mentally incompetent to decide upon the destiny of this country. Both Hindus and Muslims are just crowds. It must be within your experience that a crowd is less moved by material profit than by passion collectively shared. It is easier to persuade a mass of men to sacrifice itself collectively than to act upon a cool assessment of advantages. . . . It is moved by

Character Mediates Destiny

What mediated between the "destiny" of a people and the contingency of their empirical reality, in Sarkar's view, was something called "character," the sheer capacity in humans for leadership, discipline, effort, reason, mastering passions, and self-cultivation. It was what separated destiny from fate and left the former open to multiple possibilities. Take away the question of character, and the revealed greater purpose in human history remains unfulfilled. "Character" is a keystone concept in the architecture of Sarkar's political thought. It determined a country or kingdom's success or failure at embracing the modern world created by the expansion of Europe. Character was thus both a moral and a political word, signifying a zone of human freedom within the structure of Providence, creating space for human drama and action. It was therefore also a literary device. The centrality of "character" to Sarkar's texts takes us back once again to the question of his intimate relationship to the imperial literary canon.[17]

"Shah Alam's character *alone* was responsible for the fate that now overwhelmed him and his house," wrote Sarkar, referring to the situation in Delhi months before the Afghan Ghulam Qadir invaded the royal residence in Delhi to torture and blind Emperor Shah Alam II, violate women of the royal family, and loot their wealth. The emperor, in Sarkar's judgment, "had no strength of character, energy or even personal courage, [and] was bound to pass his life under the tutelage of some cleverer brain or stronger will."[18] Later

---

> motives which may be high or low, genial or barbarous, compassionate or cruel, but it is always above or below reason. The common sense of each is lost in the emotion of all.

Vasant Moon, ed., *Dr. Babasaheb Ambedkar: Writings and Speeches* (Bombay: Education Department, Government of Maharashtra, 2003), vol. 17, pt. 2, pp. 199–200, cited in Faisal Devji, *Muslim Zion: Pakistan as a Political Idea* (London: Hurst, 2013), p. 172.

17. Sarkar was not alone in thinking of character as something that determined the destiny of an individual. In a letter he wrote in 1908 to Arabindamohan Basu, son of the nationalist Anandamohan Basu, Rabindranath Tagore spoke of character in the same vein: "You have read in [*The*?] *Creed of Buddha* that Buddhadev said that 'conduct moulds character and character in [is?] destiny.' Whether it is an individual or a nation, destroying one's own character to achieve a short-term objective dissipates one's capital and leads to bankruptcy." See *Rabindra biksha*, no. 40, 23 December 1908, p. 7. Tagore's biographer Prabhatkumar Mukhopadhyay writes that Edmond Holmes's *The Creed of Buddha* was a favorite book of Tagore's. Prabhatkumar Mukhopadhyay, "Tukro tukro chhobi" [Vignettes], in *Nanajoner Rabindranath* [Rabindranath as he appeared to many], ed. Bishnu Bose and Ashokkumar Mitra (Calcutta: Punashcho, 2003), p. 110.

18. Jadunath Sarkar, *Fall of the Mughal Empire*, vol. 3, *1771–1788* (1938; Calcutta: Orient Longman, 1975), pp. 305, 60.

Sarkar said, in a more nuanced voice, that while "the Padishah was extremely weak and inconstant, . . . [he] was not treacherous nor incapable of right thinking. He only lacked firmness of purpose and the capacity for action. . . . Hence with all his intelligence, his daily study of scripture and history, and his life of piety and abstinence (except in making additions to his harem), he only proved another example of how cowards die many times before their death."[19]

That quotation from Shakespeare in the last sentence of this quote—obviously too familiar to be acknowledged—is a key to Sarkar's thinking on character. It is true that he borrowed much from contemporary sources when it came to describing individuals. But "character" for Sarkar belonged to a liberal form of thought the British empire in India had encouraged. In that, it was probably different from what historians of Mughal times may have understood by corresponding words in Persian that European scholars translated as "character." Potentially, anybody could acquire strength of character, for "character" implied sovereignty over self. It was like virtue: it needed to be cultivated. It was a measure of sovereignty because in it lay one's destiny; one became the maker of one's own fate by imbibing character. As Sarkar said—again, of Shah Alam—and with further unacknowledged but obvious debt to Shakespeare: "No man can rise above his destiny as the wise of the ancient days have truly said. Destiny is only another name for character, and Shah Alam's character alone was responsible for the fate that now overwhelmed him and his house."[20] The idea that character was destiny belonged, as Sarkar said, to the ancients, one source of it being the philosophy of Heraclitus, who said, in the much discussed 119th of his *Fragments*, "Man's character is his daimon [sometimes translated "destiny"]."[21] Heraclitus may not have been unknown to Sarkar and other Indian thinkers, for Aurobindo published six commentaries on Heraclitus in the journal *Arya* between 1916 and 1917, responding not only to Nietzsche's discussion of the philosopher but also to a "small treatise" that the Indian philosopher Professor R. D. Ranade had pub-

19. Ibid., 3:305. See also 3:117.

20. Ibid., 3:304–305.

21. Heraclitus, *Fragments*, Fragment B119: "A man's character is his guardian divinity," cited in Friedrich Nietzsche, *The Pre-Platonic Philosophers*, trans. and ed. Greg Whitlock (Urbana: University of Illinois Press, 2001), p. 73. See also the discussion in Shirley Darcus, "'Daimon' as a Force Shaping 'Ethos' in Heraclitus," *Phoenix* 28, no. 4 (Winter 1974), pp. 390–407. For a modern and fascinating discussion that traces connections between the idea of "ethos" and "dwelling" and etymologically connects "daimon" to "that which lacerates," see Giorgio Agamben, "*Se: Hegel's Absolute and Heidegger's *Ereignis*," in his *Potentialities: Collected Essays in Philosophy*, trans. and ed. Daniel Heller-Roazen (Stanford, CA: Stanford University Press, 1999), pp. 117–118.

lished in India on the ancient Greek philosopher.[22] But it is more likely that Sarkar, being a teacher of English literature, got the idea more immediately from his readings of Shakespeare—from famous lines such as "Our faults lie not in our stars but in ourselves" that Indian students were often expected to commit to memory.[23] Sarkar's own expectation that his reader would be familiar with the bard comes through even in the way he explained the expression "*domni-bachcha*"—"son of the lowest caste dancing girl"—with which Ghulam Qadir abused Prince Akbar Shah, "the heir to Shah Alam's throne." Sarkar described the invective to his reader as something similar to "Falstaff's favourite epithet."[24]

As readers make their way through the first volume of Sarkar's *Fall*, "character"—or the lack of it in late-Mughal India—dominates the props with which Sarkar sets the scene, as it were, for his larger narrative to unfold. The book opens with a short note entitled "What Goes Before," that begins by mentioning that while its narrative began in 1738, the "unperceived origin and gradual spread of the moral decay" and a "step by step" account of "how the poison worked in the body politic of the Delhi empire" had been detailed in Sarkar's earlier multivolume work on Aurangzeb and elsewhere. But the "dry rot" that destroyed the empire from within in the eighteenth century clearly had something to do with the run of "weaklings and imbeciles" on the throne of Delhi. At the root of this "moral canker" was the question of the character of the ruler: "A nemesis worked itself out inexorably on the destiny of the Empire from the character of the Emperor and his leading ministers."[25]

Sarkar's indictment of Muhammad Shah, who ascended the throne in Delhi in 1719 at age seventeen, is all about the emperor's lack of a statesman-like character:

> He possessed natural intelligence and a good deal of foresight; but . . . [events] crushed any desire that he might have once had to rule for himself and to keep his nobles under control. He . . . plunged into a life of pleasure and amusement . . . of inactivity and sexual excess [that] soon impaired his constitution and he became a confirmed invalid by the time he was only forty.

22. Aurobindo's essays, reprinted in his *Essays in Philosophy and Yoga*, are available at www.aurobindo.ru/workings/sa/16/0033_e.htm, accessed 4 September 2012.

23. *Julius Caesar*, 1.2.140–41; also 2.2.32–33. Sarkar's discussion of destiny and providence suggest that he was not aware of the distinction Nietzsche made in his discussion of Heraclitus between "destiny" and "fate," destiny being what happens to man from within, and fate from without. Nietzsche, *Pre-Platonic Philosophers*, p. 73.

24. Sarkar, *Fall*, 3:312.

25. Jadunath Sarkar, *Fall of the Mughal Empire* (1932; Delhi: Orient Longman, 1971) (hereafter cited as vol. 1), pp. xvii, 2, 4.

> The evil was aggravated by his taking to opium. . . . When we read how Muhammad Shah spent his morning hours not in doing public justice or holding State councils . . . but in viewing a wrestling match between two bears, or a fight by "three pairs of bears, a goat, a ram, and a wild boar, which was wrapped up in tiger skins and trained to attack an elephant" (as he is recorded to have done on 25th April 1743), we wonder whether such spectacles would be considered a worthy diversion by any one outside a nursery unless he were a country clown, and whether the lord of a hundred and fifty million souls at the ripe age of 41 had no more serious use for his time and no more refined tastes.[26]

Sarkar's "facts" about, say, the slothfulness or diligence of particular rulers came, naturally, from the sources he used. For instance, while writing of the "nemesis that worked itself . . . on the destiny of the Empire," Sarkar referred, though only just, to a text by Muhammad Bakhsh, a foster brother of the emperor—*Tarikh-i-Shahadat-i-Farrukhsiyar wa Jalus-i-Muhammad*—preserved at the India Office Library.[27] Even the image of the "dry rot" through which Sarkar attempted to convey something of his assessment of Mughal rulers in the eighteenth century did not originate with him. For example, *Seir Mutaqherin*, the well known Persian history written in the early 1780s by a Syed Gholam Hossein Khan, "a Moslem Nobleman, who used, with his father, to reside at the Court of the Nawabs of Bengal, Behar and Orissa," used this image to describe the weakening of "foundations of the Delhi monarchy" under the rule of the emperor Muhammad Shah (1702–1748; r. 1719–1720; 1720–1748). Gholam Hossein's expression (at least in translation) was "really rotten."[28] Hossein also blamed the failure of Bahadur Shah—the son of Aurangzeb who followed his father to the throne—to get others to accept his respect for Shia Muslims on the king's lack of political will (it has to be remembered, of course, that Hossein himself belonged to this sect): "An affair of so much importance required a power absolute, and a great firmness of

26. Ibid., 1:5.

27. Ibid., 1:4.

28. Preface (1902) to "Nota-Manus," in *A Translation of the Seir Mutaqherin or View of Modern Times, Being an History of India from the Year 1118 to the Year 1194 (This Year Answers to the Christian Year 1781–82) of the Hedjrah; Containing in General the Reigns of the Seven Last Emperors of Hindostan, and in Particular, An Account of the English Wars in Bengal with a Circumstanstial Detail of the Rise and Fall of the Families of Seradj-ed-Daowlah, and Shudjah-ed-Dowlah to Which the Author has Added Critical Examination of the English Government and Policy in Those Countries Down to the Year 1783. The Whole Written in Persian by Seid-Gholam-Hossein-Khan., an Indian Nobleman of High Rank, Who Wrote Both as an Actor and Spectator*, vol. 1 (Lahore: Sheikh Mubarak Ali, 1975; first published in Calcutta in 1789) (hereafter *Seir*). Sarkar cites *Seir*, 3:25, in his *Fall*, 1:6–7.

mind, qualities, which were never eminent in the characters of the Princes of the House of Timur, especially in those of the later times."[29]

It was not only Sarkar who owed his damning facts about weaknesses in the ruler's character to his Persian sources; so did his mentor and predecessor, the colonial administrator-historian William Irvine, in his book *Later Mughals*, edited and published by Sarkar after Irvine's death.[30] Could one argue, then, that more than being influenced by European ideas about character, Sarkar and Irvine derived their judgment from the very Persian sources they used? There is no question that they sometimes did so. Thus, Gholam Hossein's criticism of Farrukhsiyar—Aurangzeb's grandson (1683–1719) who occupied the throne between 1713 and 1719—was scathing; it could easily have found a place in Sarkar's narrative (if Sarkar had covered the period) or in Irvine's. "Feroh-syur had neither the extent of genius, nor the firmness of temper, nor the keenness of penetration, requisite in an Emperor. . . . He was low-spirited, and homely-minded, as well as sordidly inclined," wrote Hossein. Irvine's judgment was not much different: "He was strong neither for evil nor for good . . . feeble, false, cowardly, contemptible."[31] Similarly, Gholam Hossein said of Prince Azim-ush-shan, the second son of Bahadur Shah, who dillydallied at critical junctures in battles: "Whilst he was so much inclined to dilatory measures, he took none to gain the hearts of his troops. . . . Whenever any bolder advice was proposed, he was sure to mar it, by answering in those very words of his—*wait a little more*." Irvine repeats the charge: "It was a saying that the coldest place to be found was Azim-us-shan's kitchen. To every report that was made his only reply was the unchanging *andak bashid*, 'Wait a little longer.'"[32]

29. Hossein, *Seir*, 1:20. It would be interesting to find out what the Persian word was that Nota-Manus translated here as "character." Irvine wrote: "His great fault was over-generosity and an inability to say no to any one." William Irvine, *Later Mughals*, ed. and augmented with *The History of Nadir Shah's Invasion*, by Jadunath Sarkar (Delhi: Munshi Manoharlal, 1996; first published in Calcutta by M. C. Sarkar in two volumes in 1921–22), 1:138.

30. See chapter 1 for the history of the publication of *Later Mughals*.

31. Hossein, *Seir*, 1:65; Irvine, *Later Mughals*, p. 397. This echo of eighteenth-century sources in Irvine (or, for that matter, in Sarkar) should not blind us to the fact that Sarkar and Irvine were not unaware of the problem of bias in their sources. Irvine points out, for example, that the *Siyar* [*Seir*] reproduces "an apocryphal story" about "the mode of Farrukhsiyar's death, by which the direct blame for it is removed from the shoulders of the Saiyyids [the Saiyad brothers of the Mughal nobility]" and then remarks: "The evidence for this story seems insufficient, and the author's animus, as a Sayyid and Shia defending other Sayiids and Shias, is sufficiently obvious here as elsewhere" (pp. 392–393).

32. Hossein, *Seir*, 1:26; Irvine, *Later Mughals*, p. 167.

Character as an Abstraction

The category "character" in Sarkar or Irvine thus had the nature of a palimpsest.[33] There was no question that Sarkar or Irvine often shared the mood and sometimes even the biases—as Muzaffar Alam and others have observed—of their sources. But, historiographically speaking, they were also heirs to an English tradition of historical narratives that included separate sections on the "character" of particular kings and queens, a tradition that appears to go back to the seventeenth century. Sir Richard Baker's *Chronicle of the Kings of England* (1643), which combined "native chronicle traditions" with "the newer politically oriented approach that reached England through Machiavelli and continental historians and ultimately through Tacitus," is said to have followed Suetonius in including discussions of the kind under sections like "Of his personage and condition" or "Of men of note in his time."[34] By the end of the eighteenth century, an author named John Holt published a large compendium of sketches of royal "characters" culled from a variety of historical narratives (including those produced by Smollett and Hume) for use in schools for the benefit of youth.[35] On top of this tradition, one can identify—as we shall soon see—a surface layer of a Victorian vision of character as something one could acquire through sheer dedication and effort, a vision reminiscent of Samuel Smiles. The layers in the composite category "character" do not always sit easily with one another, for the early-modern preference for "birth and nobility" did not jibe with the Victorian idea of "self-help." But even after taking all these different qualifications into account, one can identify at least four features that distinguished Sarkar's use of the word "character" in his narratives from the way early-modern Indian historians used it.

1. A MOTIVE FORCE OF HISTORY

For Sarkar or Irvine or others writing in the traditions of European historiography, "character" was an abstract but determinate motive force of history.

33. I am grateful to Daniel Woolf for a very illuminating discussion on the issue of "character" as a historiographical category. I owe to him the metaphor of the palimpsest and leads to some of the references I have used here.

34. Martine Watson Brownley, "Sir Richard Baker's *Chronicle* and Later Seventeenth-Century English Historiography," *Huntington Library Quarterly* 52, no. 4 (Autumn 1989), pp. 481–500.

35. J[ohn] Holt, *Characters of Kings and Queens of England, selected from different histories; with observations and reflections chiefly adapted to common life; and particularly intended for the instruction of youth. To which are added, notes historical* (Dublin: J. Moore, 1789).

What I mean is something like this: just as Marxists would aver, long before they researched any particular history, that the economy must have played a determining role in it, Sarkar and Irvine would have held that that the character of rulers and of members of the ruling households determined, causally, the course of their histories. In other words, if we could imagine, anachronistically, Sarkar or Irvine teaching a graduate seminar on "Theory and Methods" in a doctoral program in history in their time, "character" would have been featured as an abstract theme in their syllabi in the same way that questions relating to "the base," "superstructure," "real and formal subsumption," and "ideology and misrecognition" would have been featured in the syllabus of a seminar on Marxist approaches to history.

India's precolonial historians would not have held this kind of sociological and abstract view of character. This is not to say that precolonial Muslim historians did not see individuals as characters. They did, and they sometimes even saw a particular person's character as contributing to the person's rise or downfall. They often saw, and not without reason, particular administrative or strategic gains or lapses as emanating sometimes from the strengths or weaknesses of an individual king's character; and historians such as Keene, Owen, Irvine, and Sarkar were happy, in such instances, to borrow those earlier historians' opinions and observations. Sarkar, for example, consciously echoes Gholam Hossein, the author of *Seir* (also called the *Siyar*), when he writes of Nasir Khan, a faujdar (garrison commander) of Jamrud who was appointed subahdar (provincial governor) of Kabul around 1709/10, that he was a "simple-minded and indolent man" whose "chief business was hunting" and who was therefore unfit to defend Kabul against Nadir Shah's aggression.[36] Or Irvine himself would mix his language with that of late-Mughal historians to write: "Contemporaries concur in asserting that, although Muhammad Murad had liberality (*sakhawat*) and kindliness (*maruvvat*), he had not the talent (*hausla*) required in a *Wazir*, or even a great noble. Nor was he valorous."[37] So the point is not that Mughal historians did not work with ideas about character. But their comments were embedded in discussions of particular individuals and situations; they did not see character itself as an abstract and motive force of history in general.

That character in the European classical sense of rulers embodying in themselves public virtues was not a necessary category in Mughal appraisal of personnel may be seen in the entries of the three volumes of the *Maathir-ul-umaraa*, the compendium of biographies of officers who served the Mughals

36. Jadunath Sarkar, chap. 11, in Irvine, *Later Mughals*, 2:323.

37. Irvine, *Later Mughals*, 1:345.

from Akbar's time to about 1780, begun in the 1740s by Nawab Samsam-ud-daula Shah Nawaz Khan Khawafi Aurangabadi and later completed in 1780 by his son Abdul Hayy.[38] While more than seven hundred individual biographies are assembled in the three volumes of the *Maathir*, seldom—perhaps nowhere—is something like the character of an individual discussed in the abstract, whereas particular stories of valor, of military and political cunning and skills, and even involving gratuitous cruelty, abound.[39] Even when we come to the discussion of character, as in the case of the author Hayy discussing his father, the original author of the *Maathir*, the words used are meant to function as a eulogy (or a denunciation, as the case may be) rather than as a historian's considered judgment: "The virtues of [t]his incomparable Amir are beyond the powers of the pen to delineate, nor could a wide expanse of parchment contain them. Truly the eye of the world never beheld another Amir with such a combination of excellencies, nor have the ancient heavens over weighed in the balance of a vision a statesman of such an universality of talents. From the beginning of his development the marks of rectitude appeared on his forehead, and lights of future excellence shone on the brow of his actions."[40]

The European tendency to misread such a eulogy as a description of someone's character shows up very clearly in Sidney Owen's use of Mughal historian Khafi Khan in his chapter on "The Emperor Bahadur Shah" (r. 1707–1712) (Shah Alam I) and his "character and policy." He quotes Khafi Khan as sketching the "character" of the king. While it would be interesting to know what the original Persian word was that Elliott and Dowson—Owen's source—translated into English as "character," it is clear that the very first sentence of the quote aimed at no rhetoric of objective or analytical description and instead produced the hyperbole typical of courtly writing in Persian: "For generosity, munificence, boundless good-nature, extenuation of faults, and forgiveness of offences, very few monarchs have been found equal to Bahadur Shah—and especially in the race of Timour." The rest of the quote ac-

38. Nawaab Samsam-ud-daula Shah Nawaz Khan and his son Abdul Hayy, *Maathir-ul-umara, being biographies of the Muhammadan and Hindu officers of the Timurid sovereigns of India from 1500 to about 1780 A.D.*, trans. H. Beveridge, rev., annotated, and completed by Baini Prashad, 2nd ed., vol. 1 (Patna: Janaki Prakashan, 1979; first published by the Asiatic Society of Bengal in 1887). On the history of the text, see Baini Prashad's 1941 preface to this edition.

39. Baini Prashad writes: "The first [volume] was prepared by the author, and later restored to with a few editions by Mir Ghulam Ali Azad; it consisted of 261 biographies. The second edition was the work of the son . . . [of the author]. . . . The biographies in the second edition are 731 in number." Baini Prashad, preface to Khan and Hayy, *Maathir*, p. v.

40. "Author's Preface," in Khan and Hayy, *Maathir*, p. 15.

tually reproduces popular criticism of Bahadur Shah's rule—"the protection of the state" and "the government and the management of the country" were so badly neglected that "sarcastic people found the date of his accession in the words *Shah-i-be-khabr*—'Heedless King.'" But this, Khafi Khan actually pointed out, was in spite of the king's having "no vice in his character."[41] The difference from the European use of the word *character* (which often went with a certain degree of heroism) could not, perhaps, be clearer.

Or consider the text *Tarikh-i-Dilkasha*, its second part translated by Sarkar himself under the title *Nuksha-i-Dilkasha*, by Bhimsen Burhanpuri (Saxena).[42] It is not that Bhimsen does not discuss the character of individuals. Murad Baksh is described as a simpleton quite early on in the book.[43] Of Mughal officers like Mahabat Khan, Bhimsen observes: "He . . . had the temperament of kindness. He . . . looked after his forces very affectionately." Or about Mir Razi-ud-din, the *darogah* of the "writer's [Bhimsen's] department": "He was a trustworthy man but a little selfish. He actually entrusted all the responsibilities of his appointment to me and would never come to *kacheri* for office work." Or here, in a more self-regarding manner, is Bhimsen on himself: "He is a polite man with decent habits and he treats big and small alike in a sincere manner. He deals with his friends and companions nicely and respects their status and station. With whomsoever he comes in contact, he attracts that man in a friendly manner. None bears any grudges against him. . . . May God award him His greatest blessings." This was praise, albeit self-praise in the last instance, but it is clear that character here was a matter of the writer being polite or critical about others (or even himself), or sometimes even philosophical, as in this assessment of Aurangzeb: "I have found men of the world very greedy, so much so that an Emperor like Alamgir, who is not in want of anything, has been seized with such a longing and passion for taking forts that he personally runs about panting for some heaps of stone (i.e. hill-forts). What shall I say about the men of weak intellect, who are the majority of people? I have never found any man free from greed and desire by looking at whom one may gain composure of mind."[44] This was some kind

41. Sidney J. Owen, *The Fall of the Mogul Empire* (London: John Murray, 1912), p. 128. Owen was the reader in Indian history at Oxford at this time, having served as a professor of history at Elphinstone College, Bombay.

42. [Bhimsen Burhanpuri], *Tarikh-i-Dilkasha* (Memoirs of Bhimsen relating to Aurangzib's Deccan Campaigns; Sir Jadunath Sarkar Birth Centenary Commemoration Volume), English translation (second part translated by Jadunath Sarkar), ed. V. G. Khobrekar (Bombay: Department of Archives, Government of Maharashtra, 1972).

43. Ibid., p. 15.

44. Ibid., pp. 96, 114–115, 146, 223.

of a philosophy of history, to be sure, but there was no conception here of a historical process in which character itself was an independent and abstract determining force. Miracles and curses, in fact, work as a much stronger force of history than character in Bhimsen's text. Shivaji is described as a "straight forward man and matchless soldier . . . [and a master] of the art of cunningness and shrewdness." But see what he dies of: Shivaji "harassed" a religious man, Jan Muhammad, a *Darwesh*, and "it is probable that due to the curse of that saint that Shivaji fell ill and after bearing the said trouble for some days, he died."[45]

2. AN ANALYTICAL CATEGORY

Character, then—and this is a proposition that simply follows from the first—was also an independent analytical category for colonial historians of Sarkar's or Irvine's ilk. The tendency to see character as a separate theme of historiography comes out in two ways. First, historians like Irvine would actually set aside a section in nearly every chapter under the heading "character" and thus abstract characterological comments from the flow of particular narratives. *Later Mughals* has sections explicitly devoted to the discussion of the "characters" of different emperors and nobles of Delhi: Bahadur Shah, Jahandar Shah, Farrukhsiyar, the Sayyid brothers, and so on.[46] Sarkar would do the same. He would say of the Rajput rajas of Jaipur and Marwar: "A study of the characters of the chief actors in this tragic drama will help us to understand the course of events better."[47] Chapter 7 of his *Fall of the Mughal Empire*, "Ahmad Shah's Reign: Events up to 1752," began with a section entitled "Emperor Ahmad Shah: His Character," and many other chapters either began in a similar way or contained a separate section for discussing a person's character.[48] His *History of Aurangzib* had pages devoted to discussing the character of Dara Shikoh, Murad Baksh, and others. Sarkar said in writing about the *Wazir*

45. Ibid., p. 127. For more instances of miraculous forces in human history, see pp. 81–82, 92. Rumors about witchcraft causing the death of Mahadji Sindhia were also reported in contemporary reports. See Jadunath Sarkar, "Mahadji Sindhia's End," *Modern Review* (March 1944), pp. 177–179, in which Sarkar summarized what was reported in Fakir Khair-ud-din Allahabadi's *Ibratnamah*. The curious details of this incident may be found in Sarkar's notes titled "Sindhia Affairs (1789–1791 A.D.) as Described in Ibrat-Namah (Asiatic Society of Bengal Ms.)," typescript, pp. 2–4, NL, JSP.

46. Irvine, *Later Mughals*, 1:133, 240, 394; 2:95–98.

47. Sarkar, *Fall*, 1:150.

48. Ibid., 1:205–206; but also 1:69 on Bengali character; 1:146 on Rajput character; 1:251 for Sarkar's characterization of Naga *sannyasis*—"utterly naked savages."

Intizam-ud-daulah's conflict with the Bakshi Safdar Jang that ultimately undid the rule of Emperor Ahmad Shah (r. 1748–54): "Delhi [meaning Mughal] historians have charged Intizam with treachery to his master for this failure; but there is no valid ground for this view. The character of these two chiefs made such a catastrophe as inevitable as the working of destiny."[49]

In completing William Irvine's *Later Mughals* and writing the final few chapters, Sarkar stated the point as a general principle. He asked: "Why did the seemingly flourishing State of Aurangzeb fall down like a house of cards only 31 years after his death?"[50] His answer, firstly, was "a startling decline in the character of the nobility" (leading to an inefficient army), but this decline "of the Mughal nobility" was "mainly due to the decline in the character of the Emperor." Sarkar does not rest there. The remainder of the sentence actually shows why the idea of character, taken in abstraction, was such an important category in Sarkar's histories of Mughal India: it was a shorthand for a certain theory of sovereignty that provided the mainstay of Sarkar's narrative.

On this point, Sarkar was different from Irvine, while sharing with the latter an analytical investment in the category of character. Sarkar's nationalism shows; Irvine, after all, was a colonial official. Consider how the connection between "character" and "sovereignty" works itself out in Sarkar's logic. The character of the nobility in late Mughal times suffered because of a decline in the quality of the character of the emperors. Why? "Because," Sarkar explains, "it is *the first duty of a sovereign*, to choose the right sort of servants and give them opportunities for developing their talent and acquiring experience by instructing and supervising them during administrative apprenticeship." The very crisis of the late-Mughal empire lay in the nobles' finding that "career was not open to talent, that loyal and useful service was no security against capricious dismissal and degradation."[51] The theme of character in Sarkar thus leads back to his ideas about modernity that we encountered in chapter 5. Throughout his entire writing career, Sarkar judged the Indian kings he wrote about—Aurangzeb, Shivaji, the later Mughals, Maratha leaders like Mahadji Sindhia—by this standard of sovereignty. A good sovereign

49. Sarkar, *History of Aurangzib: Mainly Based on Persian Sources*, vols. 1 and 2 (1912; New Delhi: Orient Longman, 1973), pp. 170–172, 182–183 (vols. 1 and 2 are continuously paginated in the 1973 ed.); Sarkar, *Fall*, 1:332. The original title of vol. 2 of *History of Aurangzib* (1920 ed., published by Longmans, Green, of London) had this for its subtitle: "Based on Original Sources." A copy of this edition held by the University of California Library can be consulted on the Internet.

50. Sarkar's chap. 11 in Irvine, *Later Mughals*, p. 307. The word "seemingly" in Sarkar's prose was deliberate, for he went on to argue in his five-volume *History of Aurangzib* that the roots of this decline go back to some of the bigoted policies of Alamgir.

51. Sarkar, chap. 11, in Irvine, *Later Mughals*, 2:311, 312, emphasis added.

ran a government open to talents and did not cater to the prejudices of any single religious group or caste or an ethnic collectivity. Sarkar considered this particularly important in the case of a country as diverse internally as India.

3. AS SOCIAL STATUS

Another major difference between Sarkar's or Irvine's use of the word "character" and its use by earlier historians was that "character" signified a high-low distinction of social status in what Mughal or precolonial Muslim historians wrote about political rule.

However pragmatic and "liberal" Akbar or Jahangir or Muslim emperors before them may have been in their recruitment of nobles, they lived and ruled in a society where all Muslim theorists of sovereignty emphasized the difference between the low-born and the high-born and claimed the capacity to rule for the high-born only. This is not to say that in reality only the high-born ruled, but the distinction between the high and the low remained of critical importance to the theorists of rule in precolonial Muslim India. Thus, Zia al-din Barani's *Fatawa-i Jahandari* (c. 1358–59) claimed:

> *As excellences have been put into those who have adopted the nobler professions, they alone are capable of virtues*—kindness, generosity, valour, good deeds, good works, truthfulness, keeping of promises, protection of other classes, loyalty, clarity of vision, justice, equity, recognition of rights, gratitude for favours received and fear of God. . . . These groups alone are worthy of offices and posts in the government. . . . *On the other hand, the low-born, who have been enrolled for practicing the baser arts and meaner professions, are capable only of vices. . . . The promotion of the low and the low-born brings no advantage in this world, for it is impudent to act against the wisdom of Creation.*[52]

Muhammad Baqir Najm-i Sani's *Mau'izah-i Jahangiri*, a book of advice for kings, produced in Jahangir's time—around 1612/13—expressed similar sentiments: "Rulers should not place incompetent and low-born (*bad-gauhar*) people on the same footing with a high-born [person] (*asil*) and prudent persons of pure extraction. They should regard the maintenance of this hierarchy as a true principle in the laws of the empire and the covenants of kingship."[53]

52. Mohammad Habib and Afsar Umar Salim Khan, *The Political Theory of the Delhi Sultanate (Including a Translation of Ziauddin Barani's "Fatwa-i Jahandari," Circa, 1358–9 A.D.* (Allahabad: Kitab Mahal, [1960]), pp. 97–98.

53. *Advice on the Art of Governance, Mau'izah-i Jahangiri of Muhammad Baqir Najm-i Sani, an Indo-Islamic Mirror for Princes*, trans. and introduced by Sajida Sultana Alvi (Albany: SUNY Press, 1989), p. 65.

In fact, as we shall see, in much of the mourning that accompanied the eclipse of Mughal power in the eighteenth century, the lament had to do precisely with the breakdown of this hierarchy between the high and the low.

Take the case of Jahandar Shah (1664–1713), a grandson of Aurangzeb, who was the Mughal emperor for about ten months until he was defeated and killed by his nephew—his brother's son—Farrukhsiyar in 1713. Jahandar Shah receives bad press in the hands of both Mughal and post-British historians because, by all accounts, he was an ineffective and effete ruler. Gholam Hossein repeats the familiar charges: that the king was too given to pomp and pleasure—and too attached to his favorite mistress/wife Lal Kunwar (spelled "Lal-coar" in *Seir*)—to be worthy of historians' praise. But it becomes clear in reading Gholam Hossein's text that the real problem with Jahandar Shah's fondness for Lal Kunwar was that she was of lowly origin and others of lowly origin took advantage of her closeness to the emperor to dislodge the "natural" rulers, the Mughal "nobility," to which Gholam Hossein himself belonged. Nota-Manus writes in a footnote to the *Seir*: "This title of *Coar* alone would prove that she was a dancing-woman or a public dancer, and a courtesan."[54] Gholam Hossein complains that such a commoner "was decorated with the title of Imtiazmahal-begum, or the Exalted Princess of the Sanctuary or Seraglio, and distinguished with the privilege of riding close to her master on an elephant covered by an umbrella, an honour [Hossein does not forget to mention] affected to the Imperial person only."[55]

Not only was Lal Kunwar thus elevated to a status usually reserved for members of the nobility, but her "milk-brother" was raised to "the office of Emir-ul-omrah, or Prince of Princes, which was now the third dignity in the Empire." Jahandar Shah, complains Hossein, was "so very fond" of this man that "he would add everyday something to his influence and emoluments." The emperor seemed "solely intent on pleasing her [Lal Kunwar]." Her brother, "Qhoshall-qhan," was "made a Hest-hezary, or a Commander of Seven Thousand Horses; and her uncle, Naamet khan, received the command of five thousand." "Not content with that," the king proceeded to "dispossess an illustrious Nobleman of the Viceroyalty of Ecbar-abad, in order to bestow it on Qhoshall-khan."[56] For Hossein, as for many of his ancestor nobles some seventy years before him, this was a world turned upside down, where overnight, thanks to the king's perverse preferences, the lowly suddenly enjoyed the status of the high. The former nobles could sense a change in the quality of

54. Hossein, *Seir*, 1:31n42.

55. Ibid., 1:35–36.

56. Ibid., 1:36.

the times, when upstarts (a word used by Hossein) ruled; and noblemen like "Chin-kylydj-khan" (later the Nizam-ul-Mulk), reports Hossein, "abstained from coming to the court, finding that the times did not agree with [them]."[57]

Lal Kunwar, "when yet a common dancer," was "intimately connected" with Zohra, a woman "who sold greens about the streets." Now Zohra was "the channel of favours and graces, an office by which she was able to appear in the streets with a retinue equal to that of the greatest Lord," and her people became "exceedingly insolent and overbearing."[58] The same was true of Lal Kunwar's brother—an "upstart" in Hossein's description—who was "unable to contain himself in his sudden elevation" and committed "excesses of all sorts," including one day forcing himself on the wife of a "gentleman" who happened to live in the same neighborhood as the Minister Zulfikar Khan, a well-known member of the Mughal aristocracy. What saved the woman from "that upstart's violence" was the intervention of the minister, who was "naturally," says Gholam Hossein, "a great lover of justice and man of vigour."[59] This brother of Lal Kunwar received his comeuppance when he applied to the Vazir for the ratification of his appointment to the "Viceroyalty of Ecber-abad." The Vazir asked for a fee of "five thousand guitars" (*sarangis* in some descriptions) and "seven thousand timbrels!" The explanation that the Vazir offered to the emperor for such a strange demand spoke volumes about how topsy-turvy the world now seemed to the nobility. The Vazir said: "The custom of your Imperial ancestors has been only to amuse themselves with dancers and singers, whose merits it was customary to reward only by pensions and bounties; so soon as these last shall aspire to dignities and Governments, . . . there shall remain no other party for your nobility but that of betaking themselves to the profession just forsaken by the dancers and singers"—hence the need to distribute guitars and timbrels among the aristocracy![60]

Apocryphal or not, this last story captures the resentment the nobility felt at the elevation of "commoners" to exalted positions in the bureaucracy, and Gholam Hossein both partook of the sentiment and was its historian at the same time. This is indeed what he identifies as the "disease that had fastened itself on the vitals of the state"—the rise of commoners to positions of power and prestige and the "strange" neglect of "the administration of the most important affairs . . . by the very persons at the head of the Empire."[61]

57. Ibid., 1:38.
58. Ibid., 1:37.
59. Ibid., 1:39.
60. Ibid., 1:36–37.
61. Ibid., 1:66.

Farrukhsiyar was wanting as an emperor because he was "fond of keeping company with common street-sharpers" and because he promoted someone like "Emir-djemlah" (Mirjumla), a man "unfit for any higher office" and who yet "wanted to overtop all the grandees of the Empire." But there was also the neglect of duties by the Vazir, "Abdollah-khan"—"a man of abilities" but "so passionately addicted" to women, "feasting, music, and dancing" that he left all administrative decisions in the hands of his Diwan, Ratan Chand, "a man who had been once a shop-keeper, but who by all means was too enthusiastic in his false religion to discharge decently all the duties . . . ; yet too narrow-minded likewise to feel his own consequences and to act with a temper suitable to it." Yet it was "such a man" who now "carried everything with a high hand, and enjoyed an uncontrolled influence all over the Empire of Hindostan."[62]

Gholam Hossein's diagnosis would have been shared by many members of the nobility that served the empire from the time of Akbar to that of Aurangzeb. The "rot" they described was administrative. Emperors after Aurangzeb promoted "commoners" to positions that the nobility saw as exclusively its own preserve. This was what was destroying the empire from within: "In consequence of so much incapacity on one side, and so much sloth and supineness on the other, enmities gained daily ground, and daily fuel was added to attentive rancour; and these enmities in their consequences rose to such an amazing height, as to overtop the sublime columns of the Timurian throne, which they crushed down at last under their weight, involving in its downfall the families of the two Seids [aristocratic brothers], which they demolished entirely, and ultimately altering the very constitution of the Empire."[63] The times were thus bad: this is why Gholam Hossein called his book *Seir Mutaqherin* (or *Siyar-ul-Mutaqherin*, as it is sometimes written), meaning "a review of modern times" or, in alternative translation, "the manners of the modern." The moderns were disturbingly different in their ways from all that symbolized the continuity and grandeur of the imperial tradition, a sign of the decline in the quality of the times. Discussion of the characters of the different emperors was thus central to Hossein's analysis, for the rot of the empire started with the patronage that successive kings gave to commoners, dislodging in the process the nobility, in whose hands the administrative reins of the empire had resided for generations.

Sarkar undoubtedly sometimes sympathized with the "hereditary nobility"—for he also saw the fall as having been caused in major part by

62. Ibid.

63. Ibid.

the incompetence of rulers who did not have the requisite training and background that might have enabled them to rule and who, therefore, gave too much power away to "upstart" parvenus. It is also true that for such information Sarkar was dependent upon chronicles that echoed the points of view of the nobility. More than that, he sometimes even shared the sentiments of contemporary historians who had decidedly partisan sympathies. Witness his reference—in the course of his discussion of the all-powerful eunuch Javid Khan, who for a while exercised a stranglehold on the mind of the emperor Ahmad Shah—to a passage from *Chahar Gulzar-i-Shujai*, a 1784 manuscript by a Harcharan Das, found in Patna: "Well might a Delhi historian of the time reflect with sadness," wrote Sarkar in introducing the following lines from Harcharan Das's manuscript: "Never since Timur's time has a eunuch exercised such power in the state; hence the Government became unsettled. The hereditary peers felt humiliated by having to make their petitions through a slave and to pay court to him before any affairs of the state could be transacted."[64] Another vein of sentiments similarly shared between the twentieth-century historian and an eighteenth-century court-chronicler can be traced through the lines that Sarkar wrote on the "riotous disturbances" caused by unpaid and rebellious troops that rocked Delhi toward the end of Ahmad Shah's reign, when the exchequer was running on empty. Notable, in particular, is his sentimentalization of a piece of history written by a "devoted and hereditary servant of the house of Babur." "The monotonous tale of such riots . . . in almost every month, with its sickening details," wrote Sarkar, "runs through the entire history of the reign of Ahmad Shah written by a loyal courtier[,] . . . the terse *Delhi Chronicle*. Shakir Khan of Panipat, a devoted hereditary servant of the house Babur, thus describes the tragic situation."[65]

But what Harcharan Das or Shakir Khan wrote were contemporary complaints, fragments of conversations that must have occurred among members of the classes that lost power and limelight in the eighteenth and nineteenth centuries. For many of these Mughal historians, administrative lapses on the part of the emperor were correctable errors; all that needed to happen to set things right again was for the losing nobles to be reappointed to or reinstated in their positions. They wrote in a manner of blaming their contemporaries. For the author of *Tarikh-i-Ahmad Shahi*, for instance—an "anonymous author" who "was present at all times and saw with his own eyes the utter misery of the Emperor Ahmad [Shah] and wept"—the observation that "this wazir [Safdar Jang] was a desolator of the realm and an impoverisher of his

64. Sarkar, *Fall*, 1:ix, 212.

65. Ibid., 1:216–217.

master" or that the "wickedness of the Irani and Turani nobles" had made the sovereign "weak" were indeed expressive of the frustrations felt by many of the older court nobles in the eighteenth century, but it was not necessarily a part of a stated framework in which character was an explicit explanatory or interpretive key to history in general.[66] Sarkar, while sometimes sharing these sentiments, had nevertheless a distinct though implicit theory about why character remained a main guiding factor in the history of the rise and fall of empires.

4. A GENDERED CATEGORY

The category "character" also worked as a modern, liberal, but imperial and "manly" (i.e., gendered) category in Sarkar's prose.[67] The point relating to gender is not hard to prove. Sarkar's "gender politics"—to speak in a somewhat anachronistic manner but not to put too fine a point upon it—were plain awful. He described eighteenth-century battles as "the manly game of war" in which the Holkar queen Ahalya Bai's virtues, for instance, "counted for nothing," because "she could not command in the field."[68] Of Shah Jahan's loss of Qandahar to Persians in 1649, he wrote (mimicking Napoleon): "In war it is not men but *the man* that counts."[69] When Aurangzeb's forces invaded Golkonda in 1656, Sarkar described the local king, Qutb-ul-mulk or Qutb Shah, as "more helpless than a child and more unnerved than a woman." When the Maratha captain Santa Ghorparé was killed in 1697 by some machinations on the part of the wife of Nagoji Mane—for Ghorparé had killed her brother—Sarkar saw her behavior as marked by "a woman's unquenchable vindictiveness." And here is how he described Begum Samroo's dismissal of the Irish mercenary George Thomas from her service on charges of "wenching": "The Irish youth must have wearied of the faded charms of the old hag and consoled himself among the younger beauties of her large mestizo household. So, she dismissed him."[70]

Some elements that went into the making of Sarkar's ideas on gender and manliness definitely appear Victorian and prudish when looked at today.

66. Ibid., 1:x, 276n.

67. One of the best recent discussions of liberal imperialism is in Karuna Mantena's book *Alibis of Empire: Henry Maine and the Ends of Liberal Imperialism* (Princeton, NJ: Princeton University Press, 2010).

68. Sarkar, *Fall*, 4:76.

69. Sarkar, *Aurangzib*, 1:76.

70. Sarkar, *Aurangzib*, vols. 1 and 2 (continuously paginated), p. 128; 5:98; Sarkar, *Fall*, 4: 232–233.

"It was a most painful surprise for me," he wrote in a footnote to the fourth volume of the *Fall*, "to learn from the Marathi despatches that many of the Rajput Rajas, nobles and ministers were infected by the filthy unmentionable disease which is Nature's punishment for gross licentiousness." There are several places where he writes with severe moral disapproval of anybody's love of "wine and women." Even of his favorite Najaf Khan in 1780, he said: "Excess in wine and women quickly sapped Najaf Khan's vitality." Or consider his harsh judgment of the character of the Kachhwa (Rajput) Raja Sawai Pratap Singh, who, as Sarkar put it, had "no brains, but was not harmless and quiescent like most other imbeciles. . . . Anticipating the decadent Nawabs of Oudh, he used to dress himself like a female, tie bells to his ankles and dance within the harem."[71]

Sarkar's anathema of "amorousness and epicureanism" may have owed something—but only something, for one cannot imagine the Mughals to have been very strongly anti-epicurean—to the misogyny of his sources.[72] Muhammad Qasim, who worked for the sons of Shah Alam (Bahadur Shah) and eventually became *Bakshi* in the army of the Nizam-ul-Mulk, wrote thus of the emperor in *Ahwal-ul-Khawaqin*, based on "personal observation": "The king is sitting like a woman within the four walls (of the palace). If the king follows the manners of women and acts on what the effeminate say, then it is the more necessary that the Muslims should take up the path leading to Mecca and Madina, and if they do not have traveling expenses, in that case, they should, it is better, commit suicide by taking poison." Long before him, there was Khusrau, who commented in his *Tughlaq-Nama*: "Wine and love, lust and youth, pleasure and enjoyment, dominion and success. How can one whose mind is filled up with such . . . air currents give thoughts to, and feel concerned with, the future? It does not behoove the ruler to become immersed in love and lust. A king is the constant protector of God's creatures. It would be wrong for such a guardian to remain intoxicated . . . for the enemies [would then take over]."[73]

But Sarkar's misogyny also had a strong code of modern military honor attached to it, and this becomes evident in his choice of the kind of violence

71. Sarkar, *Fall*, 4:72n; Sarkar, *Fall*, 3:133, 230.

72. The quoted phrase is from Alan McNairn's *Behold the Hero: General Wolfe and the Arts in the Eighteenth Century* (Montreal: McGill–Queen's University Press, 1997), p. 5.

73. Muhammad Umar, "A Comparative Study of the Historical Approach of Muhammad Qasim and Khafi Khan," in *Historians of Medieval India*, ed. Mohibbul Hasan (Meerut: Meenakshi Prakashan, 1968), pp. 156, 158; Amir Khusrau, *Tughlaq-Nama*, ed., Syed Hashim Faridabadi (Aurangabad, 1933), p. 16, cited by Mohibbul Hasan in *Historians of Medieval India*, ed. Mohibbul Hasan (Meerut: Meenakshi Prakashan, 1968), p. 30.

he took pleasure in relating. As readers of Sarkar would know, he exulted in describing regular battles, paying detailed attention to military formations, weapons used, and strategies executed. This was moral violence of a sort, for military discipline had to do with character. But he would desist from taking any pleasure in describing the violent cruelties that marked life in the royal and courtly circles of late-Mughal India, often reducing pages-long accounts in his sources into a few, sometimes colorful, sentences. Thus, in describing the "torture and dishonour" inflicted by Ghulam Qadir Khan on Shah Alam II and his family, including women, children, "servant-girls, eunuchs, petty store-keepers and humble valets," Sarkar mentions that the account in his "manuscript of Khairuddin's Persian history [*Ibratnamah*]" filled up "33 foolscap folio pages with 20 lines to the page, and drags on from day to day for two months."[74] Now *Ibratnamahs* were meant to do just that, for, rhetorically speaking, they belonged to a "poetic genre of lamenting social and political chaos (*shahr ashobs*) or books of warning (*'ibrat namahs*)."[75] But Sarkar would include none of that in his description: "A modern historian [can]not conduct his reader through all the agonised circles of this *Inferno* of the living; he must pass over the horrid details of suffering borne by the Timurid royal house, not a hundredth part of which was endured by the house of Capet, whose misery too found a mercifully speedy end on the guillotine, four years later."[76] It is not only Sarkar's reluctance to describe these gory and "unmanly" cruelties that speaks of his modern military relation to violence, and thus of his chivalry (to use a Burkean term); it is also his brief references to European literature and history, to Dante (note the spelling of "inferno" with a capital "I") and the French revolution that do the same.

The popularization of the idea of character, as discussed, went back to the early-modern times in Europe, to the second half of the seventeenth century. Though an English word of fourteenth-century vintage, "character" in the sense of "a person in a play or novel," says the *Online Etymology Dictionary*, dates from the 1660s "in reference to the 'defining qualities' he or she is given by the author." The word was obviously in popular use in what European observers wrote of the late Mughal world. Francklin's well-known account of

74. Sarkar, *Fall*, 3:308.

75. *Advice on the Art of Governance*, p. 2. See also Alvi's comment on p. 104n7: "The tradition of historiography changed in eighteenth-century India. The historians, unlike their predecessors, criticized the shortcomings of the government and named their works *'Ibrat Namahs*. Notable among these historians are: Muhammad b. Mu'tammad Khan, Sayyid Muhammad Qasim Husayni, and Maulawi Khayr al-Din."

76. Sarkar, *Fall*, 3:308, emphasis added.

the rule of Shah Alam that was published in 1798 described Rohillas and the Afghans as a "hardy warlike race, equally capable of arms and husbandry," "Shuja o Dowla" as "active and vigorous in his mind," the "Raja of Jynaghur," "Pertaub Singh," as of "weak capacity" and as "enervated by a long interval of effeminate pleasures." Shah Alam himself, the "nominal emperor of Hindustaun" who was "now in his 75th year," appeared "irresolute and indecisive in his measures." "His excessive love of pleasure, and infatuated attachment to unworthy favourites, contributed to degrade him in the eyes of his neighbours and allies." Long before Francklin, the Jesuit priest Francis Catrou's 1708 description of Aurangzeb was also fundamentally a description of the emperor's character: "Nature seemed . . . to combine, in the person of this prince, the perfection of mind and body. . . . From his tenderest years, he was observed to have a turn for policy and dissimulation. Though affecting in his discourse the most retired sentiments, Aurengzebe concealed an ambitious mind."[77]

But Catrou's history clearly belonged to the "universal history" of the Enlightenment tradition. His aim was to give "the Public a General History of the Mogul Empire" based on Manucci's Portuguese manuscript (1697), for "the History of the Mogul Dynasty was wanting [a] universal history" that would show "that the human passions, which are the soul of great events, are the same in Asia as in Europe; that the people of France might acquire instruction from the example of Indian virtues, as did formerly the people of Greece from the models of genuine integrity and true generosity furnished them by the Scythians."[78]

I do not know exactly when "character" ceased to be a gift from nature and became something that one could inculcate in oneself through discipline and effort. Henry George Keene, the colonial historian of Mughal India, cites [Harry] Verelst, the governor of Fort William in Bengal from 1767 to 1769, who wrote to the Court of Directors of the East India Company on 28 March

77. *Online Etymology Dictionary*, www.etymonline.com/index, accessed March 5, 2012; W. Francklin, *The History of the Reign of Shah-Aulum, the Present Emperor of Hindustaun* (1798; Allahabad: Dr. L. M. Basu, M.B., Panini Office, Bahadurganj, 1934), pp. 61, 67, 147, 201; Father Francis Catrou, S.J., *History of the Mogul Dynasty in India from Its Foundation by Tamerlane, in the Year 1399, to the Accession of Aurengzebe, in the Year 1657*, trans. from French (The Hague, 1708; London: J. M. Richardson, 1826), pp. 200–201.

78. Catrou, *History*, author's preface, pp. ix–xi. Sarkar, in editing Irvine's book, suggested that Catrou had plagiarized from Manucci. Catrou's cavalier treatment of Manucci's text receives detailed commentary in Irvine's introduction to his translation of Manucci. See William Irvine, *Mogul India 1653–1708 or Storia do Mogor by Niccolao Manucci, Venetian*, 4 vols. (London, 1906–7; New Delhi: Atlantic, 1989), 1:xviii–xxxii, xxxviii–xl.

1768 about the Afghan "premier [Mughal] noble" Najib-ud-Daulah in the following terms: "He is the only example in Hindostan of, at once, a great and good character." Verelst's description suggests that the idea of "character" had already achieved a degree of democratization; for one did not have to be born in a noble family in order to have a noble character. Continuing, Verelst wrote: "He raised himself from the command of fifty horses to his present grandeur entirely by his superior valour, integrity, and strength of mind. Experience and ability have supplied the want of letters and education, and the native nobleness and goodness of his heart have amply made amends for the defect of his birth and family."[79] The fact that Holt's 1789 collection, mentioned above, of sketches of "royal characters" was compiled for the "instruction of youth" suggests a further movement toward the view that character was something one could acquire through disciplined effort; one did not have to be born to it.

Character and the Cultivation of Discipline

Very closely tied to Sarkar's idea of character, then, was the idea of discipline, both self-discipline and the discipline that modern military regimentation inculcates in the individual. This is also what made this particular strand of thinking fundamentally *liberal*—in that anyone, even a low-born person, could aspire to be disciplined—and national, for a nation's future depended on a disciplined citizenry. Discipline, statesmanship, military heroism, and valor are what Sarkar admired in the likes of General Lake, the European mercenary Benoît de Boigne, Mahadji Sindhia, and the army minister of Shah Alam, Mirza Najaf Khan.[80] De Boigne and Pierre Cuillier-Perron act as each other's foil in Sarkar's narrative, but they embody, in the first place, the discipline and character Sarkar considered integral to statesmanship. "The aim of these two French officers was to do their duty of collecting money smoothly, and they took care to save the peasantry from plunder or molestation by their soldiery. We possess a Persian letter in which Perron takes legitimate pride in the discipline of his troops, and assures the addressee, 'Dear Rao Sahib, these are *campo* [indigenous term for European-controlled] troops, not Maratha

79. Henry George Keene, *The Fall of the Moghul Empire—An Historical Essay* (London: Wm. H. Allen; Calcutta: Brown, 1876), p. 93.

80. Sarkar, *Fall*, vol. 4, has extensive and admiring discussion of the character of de Boigne; see pp. 33, 82, 84, 88, 90, 92–94, 107, 134, 145, 146, 149, 187. On General Lake's heroism, see pp. 308–309.

light horse (*fauj*). If my soldiers extort one rupee from your kingdom, I shall pay you two rupees as compensation.'"[81]

There was a special aspect to Sarkar's emphasis on military discipline in eighteenth-century Mughal India. Sarkar was convinced, with good reason, that the increasing introduction of European battle practices in eighteenth-century India through European mercenaries fundamentally put more premium on disciplined military training and in time would lead to a more general adoption of scientific reasoning.[82] "True discipline in the army," Sarkar wrote once, "is impossible without discipline at home and regular habits in daily life. These are utterly wanting among the indigenous population of India."[83] He made a similar point in his obituary of Rajwade: "Rajwade, with an insane hatred of modern Europe, could not realise, in spite of his omnivorous reading, that behind a modern European army there are years of self-control, hard training, exact co-ordination of individual effort, and the brain power of the General Staff—that discipline is a moral product and not a matter of long-range guns—that an honest law court implies something different from a knowledge of physical science or even of jurisprudence."[84]

Mirza Najaf Khan, the Persian *mir bakshi* (army minister) of the emperor Shah Alam, was admirable to Sarkar because "he possessed that cool leadership, that power of co-ordination and that skill in the choice of fitting instruments which were indispensable for success in the new system of war that the Europeans had introduced into India. He easily realized that the mobile field artillery and disciplined foot-musketeers were the decisive factors in this new warfare."[85] Sarkar also admired Najaf Khan's ability to make use of European mercenaries—Rene Madec, Walter Reinhard, and the Comte de Modave—without becoming, unlike the Maratha Daulat Rao Sindhia, "the helpless slave of his foreign mercenaries." Indeed, in a section on the "Character of

81. Ibid., 4:52. Sarkar's gloss on the word "campo" runs as follows: "For the sake of convenience I use the word *campo* for . . . European-trained [Indian] brigades, and the word *fauj* for the old type of Indian troops, mostly cavalry. Words like *campo*, *paltan* (battalion), *kumedan* (Fr. Commandant), *manjar* (major), *jarnal* (General) have come from the French and have become naturalized in our indigenous histories and despatches written in Persian and Marathi" (4:103n). It is not clear what French or English word the word *campoo* was trying to mimic (camp? company?). Why Sarkar connects it to "brigade" is unclear as well.

82. This theme is ubiquitous in Sarkar, *Fall*, vol. 4.

83. Jadunath Sarkar, "India's Military Discipline: What It Implies," *Modern Review* (October 1929), p. 374.

84. Jadunath Sarkar, *House of Shivaji: Studies and Documents on Maratha History—Royal Period*, "greatly enlarged third edition" (Calcutta: M. C. Sarkar, 1955), p. 288.

85. Sarkar, *Fall*, 3:155–156.

Mirza Najaf Khan," Sarkar remarked: "When we contemplate the career of Najaf Khan we do not know what to admire most—his military capacity, his political insight, or his humanity."[86]

Character, thus conceived, did not have to run in one's family. Sarkar did not at all take to Afrasiyab Khan, "a Hindu grocer's boy Mirza Najaf Khan had captured as an orphan, converted to Islam and made his favourite slave and his adopted son in all but name." For this Khan had "none of the master's military capacity, power over men, or passion for strenuous endeavour." Sarkar's dislike comes through powerfully in cryptic, shorthand notes he had probably written to himself while reading different sources on Afrasiyab Khan's life—he nevertheless published these notes as part of a footnote in the third volume of his *Fall*: "*Character: Afrasiyab*,—bania boy, no soldier (*HP*. 323), slave (*Ibr*., ii, 87, 34), had temper (*Ibr*., 36, 78, 69, 34), demands Najaf's daughter."[87] A "baniya boy, no soldier"—the preferences of Sarkar's liberal-imperial patriotism are clear.

Sarkar's admiration of the military discipline of some European mercenaries in late-eighteenth-century India was not without its blind spots, however. These European officers had a certain kind of race consciousness—a sense of European superiority—that Sarkar actually documents but does not himself recognize in his analysis. It is clear from the examples of Perron and de Boigne that they created and protected a racialized market for European military skills. Europeans, for instance, considered Armenians Asiatic and would not let them into their mess: "We know of two Armenians in Sindhia's army—Jacob—whom Perron could not create a Captain in 1795, because his European officers refused to admit an Asiatic to their mess, . . . and Aratoon."[88] When faced with the British (in 1803), all of Perron's English and Scottish officers resigned, "refusing to bear arms against their own country."[89] Perron, or de Boigne for that matter, never developed "an indigenous body of commanders."[90] The East India Company's efforts to "seduce" the European officers of the Sindhia's army on the eve of the battle of 1803 were conducted through ethnic connections or lines of marital ties that only show how tightly the European-Eurasian community was knitted (pace all contemporary writings about "white Mughals"): "The Marquess [of Wellesley] very early discussed with General Lake a plan for making personal con-

86. Ibid., 3:30.
87. Ibid., 3:159, 159n.
88. Sarkar, *Fall*, 4:245.
89. Ibid., 4:250, 255.
90. Ibid., 4:257.

tact with Perron through Sutherland (a Scotsman in Sindhia's service who was married to the daughter of Madame Perron's brother)"; "George Hessing, who held the fort of Agra, was to be seduced through . . . Sutherland (his maternal uncle's son-in-law), and Mr. Thomas Longcroft, an English indigo-planter settled in Aligarh district since de Boigne's time, was sent to Aligarh fort to seduce Col. Perron."[91] The fort of Agra fell to the British in part because "its defence had been left to Colonel George Hessing, Dutch mestiche, and Colonel Sutherland, both related to Perron by marriage. Their one aim was to save their personal wealth and earn Wellesley's promised reward by deserting to the English."[92]

The point is not that these European mercenaries were not rational in trying to escape with their personal fortunes—they were mercenaries, after all; the point is that they retained this military market for themselves, by not training their Indian subordinates well enough for the latter to be able to take up the reins of leadership when the Europeans abandoned Sindhia.[93] Maratha leaders, except for Mahadji Sindhia, were happy to use European military skills but did not care to train their Indian soldiers to be independent of the Europeans, a point that supports Sarkar's critique of them. Their calculations of the loyalty or disloyalty of their European officers would have been drawn up according to the cultural grammar of Mughal India: instances of personal loyalty shining amid an ever-changing terrain of shifting alliances. But the role that European race-consciousness played in structuring the market for European military skills escaped Sarkar's analytical framework, which focused so much on the question of character.

Character as Method

Later historians have mostly missed the intellectual significance of the category of character in the historiographical tradition that Sarkar both drew on and enriched. It has recently been said, partly in criticism of Sarkar, that those who "look for causes of decline in the character of the reigning emperor and

91. Ibid., 4:273.

92. Ibid., 4:294–295.

93. True, Sarkar could come back with the example of Ambaji Ingle, who took charge of Sindhia's troops as European officers like "Chevalier Dudrenec deserted to the English with two other European officers, Smith and Larpent" and whose "one object in life was to create a State for himself in independence of Sindhia, as Sindhia had carved out a kingdom independently of his master, the Peshwa." In fact, a person "of lesser rank," Sarwar Khan, had to force their remaining French commanders "to give battle to the English at Patparganj." Ibid., 4:296. See also Sarkar's remarks on 4:307–308 and on the fall of the Ahmednagar fort on 4:316n.

the alleged moral degeneration of Mughal aristocracy" end up "over simplifying . . . the complex issues and factors involved in the discussion of the collapse of the Mughal empire."[94] I hope I have shown that character was no simple matter in Sarkar's thinking.

Character was what made the logic of Providence open to the historical foibles of human beings. By the same token, the imperial-liberal idea of character helped to open up an imaginary and utopian space for a politics of will: as in the case of the individual, a nation also could enjoy its tryst with destiny, provided it had the will to develop character. What was the nature of this will? It was the capacity to face up to one's defects and not allow the temptation to glorify an identity—be it of the individual, a caste, a region, an ethnic group, a religious community, or a nation—to stand in the way. This is where Sarkar found a moral place for the historian. As he said about his researches on Maratha history: "At the end, it is the impartial historian's duty not to conceal the defects of the Maratha racial character. They have been strong, they have been free, but they have not been united. Like the Afghan tribes or the clans of the Scottish highlands, Maratha family has fought Maratha family, clan has fought clan, in selfish personal feuds. The result has been disastrous to the interests of the nation as a whole."[95] Or again: "The Maratha failure to create a nation even among their own race and in their small corner of India, requires a searching analysis on the part of the Indian patriot and the earnest student of Indian history alike." For "we cannot blink at the truth that the dominant factor in Indian life—even to-day, no less than in the 17th century,—is caste, and neither religion nor country." He stated the principle again at the very beginning of his *Fall*: "The headlong decay of the age-old Muslim rule in India and the utter failure of the last Hindu attempt at empire-building by the new-sprung Marathas, are intimately linked together, and must be studied with accuracy of detail as to facts and . . . causes if we wish to find out the true solutions to the problems of modern India and avoid the pitfalls of the past."[96]

And the point was reinforced famously in a letter Sarkar wrote on 19 November 1957, about a year before his death, to his former student and the then president of the Republic of India, Dr. Rajendra Prasad, who had written to him about the idea of a "national" history of the country. Sarkar insisted on this quality of truthfulness: "National history must be comprehensive, true,

94. Zahir Uddin Malik, *The Reign of Muhammad Shah 1719–1748* (New Delhi: Icon, 2006), preface, p. x.

95. Sarkar, *House*, 3rd ed., p. 339.

96. Ibid., pp. 106–107; Sarkar, *Fall*, foreword, 1:iii.

accurate and impartial. . . . It will be national not in the sense that it will try to suppress or white-wash everything in our country's past that is disgraceful, but because it will admit them and at the same time point out that there were also other and nobler aspects in the stages of our nation's evolution. . . . [The historian] will not suppress any defects of the national character but add to his portraiture those higher qualities which, taken together with the former, . . . constitute the entire individual."[97]

The importance of the idea of character made the historian himself (or herself) into a part of the research methods. For a patriotic but "impartial" historian would have to be able to face facts, even unpleasant, unwelcome, and, as Ranke said, "unattractive" facts; he would, in fact, seek them out in an effort to acknowledge and help rectify the defects of his nation's character. But this exercise could be carried out only by a historian who himself had a certain strength of character. Building a character was therefore part of the preparation the historian had to undertake in order to be a seeker of the truth about the past. Sarkar's colonial-Victorian and pro-Brahmo upbringing no doubt helped him in nurturing such an idea of truthfulness and in his pursuit of the necessary self-discipline.[98] His diaries, unfortunately, have not been preserved or are not accessible. A few loose and torn pages from the time when he was about twenty, c. 1889–90, have survived and are available among his papers at the National Library, Calcutta. Even from these, we get a glimpse of his very Victorian struggle to acquire strength of character early in life. He would keep accounts of how he spent his hours—reading Macaulay's essays "for recreation" one day, spending a whole weekend "epitomizing" [William Edward Hartpole] Lecky's "[*History of*] *England vol. III*," reading "Carlyle's *Cromwell* to cheer up" on another occasion, and making calculations about how many days it would take him to read a list of authors including Burke, Spenser, Fawcett ("By the end of January finish these").[99] Even his scrupulous recording of the tribulations of his soul speaks of a determination to face up to issues that were deeply personal and, for a young man, deeply troubling. On 3 October 1889, during the Durga Puja festivals, we find him taking the vow of banishing all sinful thought—*papachinta parityajyam*—but he con-

97. Sarkar's letter of 1957 cited in Moni Bagchi, *Acharya Jadunath: Jibon o sadhana* (Calcutta: Jijnasa, 1975), pp. 192–193.

98. Sarkar attended Brahmo Samaj religious ceremonies in the 1890s. See NL, JSP, file titled "Gifts of the Centre for Studies in Social Sciences, Calcutta," Personal Diary, entry for January 23 [1891?], 11th *Magh* on the Bengali calendar, a day of Brahmo festivities. "Walk[ed] to Brahmo Samaj. Hear[d] sermons and songs there."

99. Ibid., entries for 11 February [1889?], 21 January 18[90?], 3 February 1890, 11 and 12 January 1891.

fessed to his diary that the vow "was soon disregarded."[100] On another occasion around this period, he bared his soul to himself in a way that the older Sir Jadunath probably never did again, not at least in writing, the third-person description here possibly enhancing the objective tone of his self-diagnostic prose:

> A weakness has seized homo after the examination, brought on no doubt by the relaxation of spirit and . . . he feels weak and cannot work. . . . He cannot be careful and keep an eye on everything for his loneliness and a memory of past sorrows and future hopelessness make him reluctant to exert himself[.] He likes to pass his time in lethargy—he lets things take their course. So long ambition has had mastery over him and given him strength. Now it seems powerless to stir him up—he feels deeply the want of love—man cannot be moved all his life by ambition—there are terrible reactions after the exertions prompted by ambition and homo is [suffering] one of these. Ambition rules the mind; but love rules the heart, it consoles and refreshes after fatigue. . . . It is [a] perpetual but quiet and uniform motive power. The want of it is dreadful and leaves the heart vacant and my mind . . . becomes deplorably aimless—such is homo. For whose sake is he pursuing the path of fame, for whose sake is he flogging himself to death [?]—these are questions which painfully and irresistibly suggest themselves to this labourer's mind.[101]

Throughout his life, Sarkar kept up this intensely moral and austere relationship between his personality, his everyday comportment, and rectitude, so much so that, as we have seen, his students and admirers could not make a distinction between his research methods and his character (see the introduction). All memories of Sarkar revolve around the question of his personality, which was no doubt quirky but very formidable. He would stage himself in everyday life as a "character." Niharranjan Ray, the celebrated author of *Bangalir Itihash* (A history of the Bengali people, 1941) for which Sarkar wrote a foreword, thus remembered "acharya [the teacher] Jadunath" in a preface he wrote in turn for Sarkar's biography by Moni Bagchi: "There is an image of *acharya* Jadunath that people who knew him carry before their mind's eye. It is the image of a man of erect, unbending personality, strong as thunder but yet governed by rules and self-control; someone who was straight, simple and measured in his speech; who was puritanical in character and lived a life of strict routine; someone indifferent to pleasure and unmoved by suffering."[102] Ray believed with many others that this external appearance of Sir Jadunath

100. Ibid., entry for 3 October [1889?].

101. Ibid., entry for Wednesday, 22 May, year uncertain.

102. Niharranjan Ray, foreword to Bagchi, *Acharya Jadunath*, p. 9.

FIGURE 9. Jadunath Sarkar in Patna, year unknown. Photographer unknown. Courtesy of the Archives, Centre for Studies in Social Sciences, Calcutta. Used with permission.

hid an inner and softer core.[103] But his words, ending with an invocation of the *Gita*—"indifferent to pleasure and unmoved by suffering"—capture the public persona of the historian, the fact that he cultivated in his own life "the character" he sought in the history of his people.

Much of this is best captured in the very erect bodily posture Sarkar tried to assume all his life. There is photograph of him, discovered in a pile of rubbish in his house at 10 Lake Terrace, Calcutta 29, after it became the home for the Centre for Studies in Social Sciences, Calcutta, founded in 1973, and now preserved in the Centre's archives. It perhaps dates from the time he taught in Patna College [1889–1900, 1902–1917, 1923–1925]. It shows a young Sarkar, his profile to the camera, sitting completely erect—his spine artificially and willfully held absolutely straight, probably by years of self-conscious effort and habit (fig. 9).

This photo says it all. There are no commentaries available on this picture, neither from Sarkar nor from anybody else. One can only make sense of it by reading what Sarkar himself wrote in admiration of the erect spine when he encountered it in others whom he judged endowed with the strength of char-

103. He writes, "This image was true but not the whole truth." Ibid.

acter. This is how Sarkar described his meeting with the Marathi historian Kashinath Narayan Sane:

> His [Sane's] grown up and distinguished son . . . died of the terrible influenza epidemic which swept all over the world just after the First World War. Sane's heart was made desolate, but his back was unbent. He kept up his regular habit of taking daily exercise by a morning walk. When, in 1924, I paid him a visit to Kalian solely for the purpose of seeing him again, I found the old man returning on foot from the Durgadi side, a slim, vigorous, perfectly erect figure, who struck even a stranger as a commanding personality. Indeed, he reminded one most of the late Justice Sir Chandra Madhav Ghosh, whose aged thin but stiff and distinguished form could be seen taking his customary walk on the *maidan* of Calcutta every morning almost to the day of his death."[104]

Sarkar could have written this of himself. For character was not something to be sought only in the pages of the past. One did not find out the truth about the past until one had oneself imbibed the strength of character. When the nationalist leader Surendranath Banerjee died in 1926, Sarkar gave a lecture praising his qualities as a statesman. It is interesting to see the traits in Banerjee that Sarkar chose to praise: "The first trait of his character was his boundless courage and hopefulness." The second was his "long and patient preparation," so that "he could be worthy to serve our great Mother." Third were his "methodical habits and orderly industry." And finally, his "intense patriotism and ceaseless industry combined with an ascetic simplicity of life and taste." According to Sarkar, Banerjee "never drank or smoked, he never even read a novel. The modern craze for the sex element in literature would have horrified him."[105] These words could have described Sarkar just as well. Of the historian Jadunath Sarkar, then, it could truly be said that his goal as a scholar was to make himself an integral part of his method of researching and writing history. His scholarly persona *was* part of his method as well.

104. Sarkar, *House*, 3rd ed., pp. 207–208.

105. Jadunath Sarkar, "In Memoriam: Surendra Nath Banerji," *Modern Review* (December 1926), pp. 619–621.

7

Archiving the Nation: Sarkar's Fall from Grace

"Such in brief is the history of the National Archives of India. It has no politics."[1] So declared in 1948 the concluding paragraph of a book that was, inter alia, an official account of the history of the Imperial Record Department of the Government of India. The department, which had been set up in 1891 in Calcutta and moved to Delhi in 1937, was renamed the National Archives of India after India gained independence in 1947.[2] The irony was, of course, that the transition from a department of record established primarily for internal use by government officials to a "national" repository of historical material serving researchers and officials alike was a process that—contrary to the claim of the official history—was nothing but political.

There was, as we have seen, a tussle between the conservative political instincts of a colonial bureaucracy wary of giving Indian scholars free access to government records and the growing "national" demands for such access on the part of historians in Indian universities and learned societies. But equally critical were sharp and divisive conflicts—both personal and ideological—that existed between Indian scholars themselves. These conflicts too molded the history of "national" and "provincial" archives in India. The main parties to the conflicts I discuss here were Sir Jadunath Sarkar and Dr. Surendra Nath Sen (1890–1962), a younger scholar we have met before. Sen made his name in the 1920s as a researcher of the history of the Marathas in

1. *IHRC Retrospect*, p. 67.

2. For a recent history of the department, see Syamalendu Sengupta, *Experiencing History through Archives: Restoration of Memory and Repair of Records* (Delhi: Munshiram Monaharlal, 2004), pp. 61–95.

the seventeenth and eighteenth centuries.[3] Sen was an ally of Mahopadhyay Datto Vaman Potdar, who, to recapitulate, was a leader of the Bharat Itihas Samshodhak Mandal in Poona in their fight against Sarkar in the 1930s and the 1940s. Sarkar, Sen, and Potdar were all intimately involved in the life of the Indian Historical Records Commission (IHRC) in the decade leading to India's independence in 1947. Much of the politics that the official history denied pertained to this story, the story of an often-personal struggle between Sir Jadunath and his younger contemporaries for control of the commission. But, personalities aside, this struggle and its outcomes afford us distinct insights into a process that saw two rather different approaches to the question of archives come into conflict.

For Sarkar, archives were mainly of interest as a collection of primary or original documents that ought to form the basis for "scientific history." He used the platform of the Historical Records Commission to propagate this message. It is the status of these documents as "original" that interested him in the first place. Sarkar dreamed of a public records act that might by the fiat of law "nationalize" and gather all records relating to the state—both at the regional and central levels—into a single official structure. For historians such as Sen or Potdar, who belonged to a younger generation, however, archives were more about issues having to do with the preservation of, and access to, documents. They sought to establish a more federal network of archives that left the question of access to documents in different regions (eventually provinces) of India in the hands of historians from those regions. Sarkar's line of thinking, if pursued, would have produced a centralized, "nationalizing" archive for India. The victory of the likes of Sen and Potdar ensured, however, that the political control of access to documents at provincial levels remained firmly in the hands of the powerful historians of the provinces. When India received independence, the "Imperial Record Department" became the "National Archives of India," but only in name, for there was nothing "national" about it: as in British times, it contains the files of the "central" government, located initially in Calcutta and then, after 1911, in Delhi. What makes the Sarkar-Sen conflict a significant story is the context of transition from the colonial to the postcolonial India in which it played itself out.

3. Sen's two major books, *Administrative System of the Marathas* (Calcutta: K. P. Bagchi, 1976), and *The Military System of the Marathas* (Calcutta: Orient Longmans, 1958), were first published in 1923 and 1928, respectively.

Politics in and of the Indian Historical Records Commission

The first two Indian historians nominated to the commission were Jadunath Sarkar (who was still with Patna College, Bihar, but was soon to join, in 1919, Ravenshaw College in Cuttack, Orissa) and B. K. Thakore of Deccan College, Poona. The two Englishmen nominated as historian-members were Archdeacon W. K. Firminger from Calcutta and L. F. Rushbrook Williams, the inaugural professor of history at the University of Allahabad. None of the historians appointed to the commission had a research degree.[4] In the 1920s and 1930s (except for the years 1931 to 1936, when, for financial reasons, the commission was held in "suspended animation"), Jadunath Sarkar remained the intellectual center of the commission and a vital force behind its activities and annual meetings.[5] Patriotic but, as we have seen, a subscriber to something of a liberal vision of the empire, he commanded a certain degree of respect and acceptance in the colonial administrative circles. Sir Frank Noyce, the president of the commission, opened his remarks at the 1929 meeting of the commission, for example, by congratulating "Sir Jadunath" on his recent knighthood: "Sir Jadunath has shown that India can produce historians worthy to rank with the greatest names of the West."[6] Sarkar routinely received assistance from the staff of the Imperial Record Department in locating or copying records relevant to his own research.[7] His term of three years on the

4. See *IHRC Proceedings*, vol. 1, *First meeting, Held in Simla,* [19–20] *June 1919* (Calcutta: Superintendent of Government Printing, 1920), p. 1; and Anil Chandra Banerjee, *Jadunath Sarkar* (Delhi: Sahitya Akademi, 1989), p. 7.

5. The expression "suspended animation" was Sarkar's. He used it in welcoming delegates to the 1937 meeting of the commission: "Today, the . . . Commission meets again after seven years of suspended animation due to the financial difficulties of the Government." *IHRC Proceedings*, vol. 14, *Fourteenth Meeting, Held at Lahore, December 1937* (Delhi: Manager of Publications, GOI, 1938), p. 7. See also the discussion in NAI, IRD, January 1937, Proc. no. 18, note by "S.D.U" dated 10 September 1936: "The meetings of the . . . Commission were held in abeyance in 1931 as a measure of retrenchment. It has not yet been possible to revive them though the question is raised by the K[eeper of] R[ecords] from year to year. Last year efforts were made for their revival but they proved unsuccessful. The question will be taken up again shortly in connection with the budget estimates for 1937–38."

6. *IHRC Proceedings*, vol. 12, *Twelfth Meeting, Held at Gwalior, December 1929* (Calcutta: GOI, Central Publications Branch, 1930), pp. 10–11. Sir Frank went on say: "I speak of what I know, for one of Sir Jadunath's works has been by my bedside for months. I hasten to add that it has not been the same one all the time!"

7. See, for example, NAI, IRD, June 1933, Proc. no. 7; March 1934, B Proc. no. 47; August 1936, Proc. no. 3; (Research Branch) January 1937, Proc. no. 57. Sarkar continued to receive such cooperation from the staff of the Imperial Record Department even after Dr. Surendra Nath Sen, otherwise instrumental in the removal of Sarkar from the IHRC, became the Keeper of

commission as an ordinary member was renewed until 1940. In recommending an extension of his term in 1930, A. F. M. Abdul Ali, the keeper of records, described Sarkar in terms that spoke of the high esteem in which he was held by the administration: "Jadunath Sarkar, whose reputation as an historian is well-known to the Goverment of India, has been a member of the Commission ever since its establishment and has materially helped the Commission attain its present degree of efficiency." Ali just barely managed to stop short of recommending an indefinite tenure for Sarkar by striking out the following sentence: "It will, in my opinion, be a distinct advantage so long as he remains directly associated with the Commission."[8] Sarkar's preeminence is also attested by the official history of the commission:

> The *ex-officio* President . . . the Secretary to the Government of India in the Department of Education was a busy official with heavy pre-occupations and he could not always attend the annual session of the Commission. . . . In the absence of the permanent President, the deliberations of the Commission were generally conducted under the chairmanship of the seniormost ordinary member. For four sessions, from 1923 to 1925, Sir Evan Cotton was, for all practical purposes, the *de facto* President and from 1926 till the reconstitution of the Commission in 1940, Sir Jadunath Sarkar was called upon to play that important role.[9]

Sarkar's closeness to the colonial officials did not mean, however, that he merely echoed the bureaucracy in his own thinking. When Sardesai suggested a change of venue—from Poona to Bombay—for the 1938 meeting of the commission, so that more officials could attend, Sarkar chided him privately by saying, "Why hanker for state dinners and lunches?"[10] If anything, he was closer to Ramsay Muir's vision of what I have called "imperial liberalism" in chapter 2, an outlook the government never fully adopted. Sarkar's enthusiasm for the role that the IHRC could play in the development of a culture of historical research and criticism in India was in some ways even greater than that of Muir, for he believed himself capable of playing the role of the teacher that Muir had reserved for an English historian (see the discussion in chap-

---

Records for the Government of India. See NAI, IRD, February 1940, B Proc. no. 53; July 1940, Procs. nos. 44 and 61.

8. NAI, IRD, IHRC Branch, August 1930, Proc. no. 41, draft letter from secretary, IHRC, to the secretary, Department of Education, Health and Land, Government of India, dated Calcutta, 24 March 1930.

9. *IHRC Retrospect*, p. 12.

10. See NL, JSP, letter no. 541, Sardesai to Sarkar, Kamshet, 10 November 1938; and Sarkar's reply, letter no. 543, Calcutta, 15 November 1938.

ter 2). It was, it would seem, mainly on Sarkar's urging that the commission quickly developed into a public forum for discussing problems of research.

Slowly, a small but discernible research community of historians gathered around the annual meetings of the commission. The importance of research as a "public" activity was underlined early in the commission's career by Sir Henry Sharp, who presided over the second meeting of the commission in 1920. In his speech, Sir Henry pointed out that the first meeting of the commission had been held "so to speak *in camera*" and added: "It was borne in upon me at the time if the work of the Commission was to get known . . . , it ought not only to hold its meetings at different places, but also to hold some of them publicly . . . meeting with people who have been considering the question of research."[11] To the public session was also added the attraction of an exhibition of historical artifacts and documents in order to encourage families with historical records in their custody to make such records public.[12] In addition, the commission created in the midtwenties a category of "co-opted" members that allowed it to involve interested scholars and persons associated with learned societies and universities to enlarge the number of participants for any particular meeting. And in 1924 a further category was added: "corresponding members," who also enjoyed a three-year appointment with no voting rights.[13] The number of delegates enrolled to attend the meetings of the commission increased from 9 and 12 in 1919 and 1920, respectively, to about 52 and 51 in 1929 and 1938 (including the few who failed to attend). In 1942, after the reconstitution of the commission in the preceding year—of which, more later—the number swelled to 110.[14]

Scholars from different parts of the country applied to the Government of India to be considered for membership of—or even to be associated with—the commission. Thus Lt. Col. H. Bullock, of Head Quarters, Eastern Command, Naini Tal, U.P, wrote to the secretary of the commission and the keeper

11. *IHRC Proceedings*, vol. 2, *Second Meeting, Held at Lahore, January 1920* (Calcutta: Superintendent of Government Printing, 1920), p. 4.

12. See speech by Jadunath Sarkar in *IHRC Proceedings*, vol. 13, *Thirteenth Meeting, Held at Patna, December 1930* (Calcutta: GOI, Central Publication Branch, 1932), p. 7.

13. *IHRC Proceedings*, vol. 6, *Sixth Meeting, at Madras, January 1924* (Calcutta: GOI Central Publication Branch, 1924), p. 159. NAI, IRD, August 1937, Proc. no. 48, thus explained the membership categories: The IHRC had a "nucleus of . . . permanent members who would be the managing body of the Commission, the co-opted members who would be co-opted for particular meetings of the Commission, and corresponding members who would not be invited to meetings and have no voice in the affairs of the Commission but would give their help by correspondence and would receive the publications of the Commission as a compliment. Such members might do much to keep alive local interest in records."

14. The figures are taken from the *IHRC Proceedings* for the individual years.

of records, A. F. M. Abdul Ali, in November 1930, inquiring about the possibility of cooperation with the commission.[15] Similarly, Muhammad Nazim, a Cambridge PhD in history employed in Patna as an assistant superintendent of the Archaeological Survey, applied with testimonials in 1937 for the position of corresponding member of the commission.[16] A more illustrious case is that of Dr. Surendra Nath Sen, who was to be appointed the keeper of records from 1939 and who stayed on to be appointed the first director of the National Archives of India after independence. He was still a lecturer in history at Calcutta University in 1930 when he attended the thirteenth session of the IHRC at Patna.[17] Promoted, within a year of his attendance at Patna, to the prestigious Ashutosh Professorship in History at Calcutta, he "made a request" in 1937 to the Imperial Record Department "that he . . . be offered a seat on the [Records] Commission as a regular (ordinary) member." "It appears," noted a departmental officer, "that Dr. Sen will have no objection to serve as a corresponding member pending settlement of the question of his appointment as an ordinary member"; the keeper of records, unaware of the historical irony that Dr. Sen would actually be his replacement in the very near future, commented: "There is at present no vacancy for ordinary membership of the Commission."[18] The commission, in thus involving historians from universities and elsewhere in its own governance, played a very important role in the creation in India of what might be called a history bureaucracy, a necessary ingredient of the process by which the discipline became a profession.

The Nationalist Challenge to Colonial Conservatism

So long as the different uses of the commission did not threaten them, colonial officials were happy to support such research as was represented by the work of Sarkar and his close friend and collaborator G. S. Sardesai (as, for instance, in the case of the Peshwa Daftar). But there was still much official nervousness about letting Indian research students in on the records that were in the possession of government bodies, particularly at a time when the nationalist movement was reaching a crescendo under Gandhi's leadership and producing different kinds of tensions among Indians themselves. The rules permitting "*bona-fide* research students of history" to examine the

15. NAI, IRD, February 1931, Proc. no. 15, letter from Bullock dated 3 November 1930. Ali invited Bullock to attend the Patna session, but Bullock could not.

16. NAI, IRD, August 1937, Proc. no. 71.

17. *IHRC Proceedings*, 13:1.

18. NAI, IRD, June 1937, B Proc. no. 53, note dated 23 March 1937 by "H. S. D." and note by A. F. M. Abdul Ali, dated 20 April 1937.

Bombay government's records in the Alienation Office at Poona were, for example, seriously restrictive. A research student was required to specify the period for which he or she needed permission and had to "make a fresh application" to extend this period. The student was also required to prepare her or his notes in duplicate and submit a copy for scrutiny, along with English translations of them.[19] Even Sardesai was stopped by the commissioner of the Central Division from using in a paper he proposed to present at the IHRC's meeting in 1929 "such information as [he] might have gathered during [his] recent work at the Alienation Office."[20]

The nationalist movement further unnerved the officials. The state of affairs in the case of the records in possession of the Imperial Department may be gauged from the fact that in 1937, no records were absolutely open to the researcher. The poor Indian scholars had to get their notes screened by the keeper of records and for that purpose were charged an "examination fee of Rs 2 per 10 typed pages (double spacing) with a minimum of Rs 15 . . . charged before permission is given to take or make use of . . . [the] extracts from records." All extracts, in addition, had to be submitted in typescript. The rules also stipulated that, if necessary, "the Keeper of Records will arrange to have them typed at a cost of one anna for every 50 words."[21]

Some of these measures appear to have been a part of the official response to the fact that Indian scholars, in larger numbers than ever before, were becoming interested in researching the past of their country. For all his admiration for the idealistic sides of the Raj, Sir Jadunath Sarkar was compelled to remark at the IHRC meeting of 1937: "Formerly the rules were simpler, but recently they have been so drawn up as to make it practically impossible for Indian students to make use of the records in India, while it is much easier and cheaper to get copies from the India Office typed."[22] There was an understandable howl of protest against these rules at this meeting; several attendees objected to the official restrictions under which the Indian scholar had been placed.[23] They knew that "the India Office did not charge anything

19. NAI, IRD, August 1938, B Proc. 15, letter no. 0/10557-F, M. J. Desai, I.C.S., deputy secretary to the government of Bombay, Revenue Department, to the secretary, Indian Historical Records Commission, dated Bombay, 26 May 1938, and appendixes. For more on this, see *IHRC Proceedings*, 14:149.

20. NL, JSP, letter no. 113, Sardesai to Sarkar, 2 December 1929.

21. *IHRC Proceedings*, 14:272.

22. Ibid., 14:161.

23. Ibid., 14:159–164. Nilakanta Shastri (Madras), R. C. Majumdar (Dhaka), O. P. Bhatnagar (Allahabad), D. N. Banerji, Nandalal Chatterjee, Krishnaswamy Aiyangar (Madras), B. S. Baliga (Madras), and Father Heras (Bombay) were among those who protested.

for checking copies and there was no reason why they should pay for copies from Imperial Records in India."[24]

The inherently nationalist demand for opening up records for use by Indian students of history marked a generational shift from the attitudes of Sarkar and Sardesai. Both Sarkar and Sardesai had a certain proneness to be sympathetic to the reasons officially given for restricting access of private Indian researchers to government records. Thus, even when he acknowledged that the British government at home was "more liberal" than the colonial Indian government in making home and foreign office records after 1853 available to the public "without reserve," Sarkar went to some trouble in explaining why this may have been so: "Indian [Native] States are far more touchy than the Continental Powers with whom England fought in the past. . . . In the official circles it was feared that access to these records might [revive] . . . boundary disputes, claims of land . . . by one jagirdar against another jagirdar."[25] At its core, this was not much different from what Sardesai had said at Gwalior in 1929. The Bombay government, he had then said, was "not . . . unwilling" to open up their Marathi records, but they had to wait until "all the records were sifted"—presumably by Sardesai's research—to decide "how far and under what conditions these records should be made available to the public." For the trouble was that "most of the records at the Alienation Office" were "inextricably intermixed with current administrative papers." He saw his own work as trying to produce "an arrangement suitable for historical research." "The authorities," he wrote, "recognise the intensity of feeling in Maharshtra over these records and I am sure as soon as a workable arrangement is completed, the Government will be able to throw open these records for the purpose of legitimate study."[26]

This was precisely the kind of argument that would no longer satisfy the younger generation of scholars in India. Sen directly countered this conservative-seeming sympathy with the logic of official thinking in a paper he presented to the members of the commission in 1937. He asked, "Does it matter much if it is discovered that a public servant of eminence, long deceased, committed an indiscretion one century or two centuries ago?" and continued, as if in direct response to Sarkar and Sardesai: "A responsible public man once told me that the Peshwa Daftar of Poona could not be thrown open to the research scholar, because his industry may one day reveal some records that may help to revive some inconvenient claims. . . . I believe

24. Ibid., 14:163.
25. Ibid., 14:161.
26. *IHRC Proceedings*, 12:26.

most people will recognise that this objection is not frivolous but . . . , is not insuperable, and the problem may be easily solved by passing an Indemnity Act."[27] Some of the delegates at the 1937 meeting of the commission argued against the very practice of bringing out selections of documents without opening up the records to others at the same time. This led to a discussion of "how far Government would allow non-official historians access to the records for editing selections and preparing calendars." Sarkar's presumptuous comment that "when calendaring was done by competent scholars, most historical inquirers could satisfy all their needs from these calendars and only in 2 or 3 per cent of the cases was a reference to the original document found necessary," could not have made him popular.[28] Nilakanta Shastri said that he "had no objection to . . . selections being printed if that was to be in addition to the systematic scheme of calendaring as the latter was the proper way of presenting records to students."[29] Sarkar's response only reinforced his patrician image. He said that for it to be done "correctly," calendaring "must be done by a competent scholar trained in history who could judge the needs of historical students of different types."[30] S. N. Sen made a criticism in his paper that was related to Shastri's point. "No selection," he said, "however exhaustive, can altogether preclude the necessity of a fresh examination of the published records and a scrutiny of papers deemed unworthy of publication."[31]

Sen's remarks were in tune with the mood of the meeting, where many raised the question of opening up all records pertaining to a period before a certain date—1800 or 1859—free of charge to all Indian researchers irrespective of their "competence."[32] The force and impact of this debate may be inferred from the fact that the following year the Government of India "abolished the inspection fee of Rs. 5 . . . and the minimum fee of Rs. 15 for the examination of papers" and extended the period—from two months to six—for which permission to consult records in Delhi was valid.[33]

Yet the problem of accessibility of sources remained and may have been further complicated by the exigencies of the war, for we hear Sarkar himself

27. S. N. Sen, "A Few Observations on the Record Rooms of India," in *IHRC Proceedings*, 14:189–191, quotes on 14:190.

28. Ibid., 14:154.

29. Ibid., 14:153.

30. Ibid.

31. Ibid., 14:190.

32. Ibid., 14:159–164, 167–172.

33. *IHRC Proceedings*, vol. 15, *Fifteenth Meeting, Held at Poona, December 1938* (Delhi: Manager of Publications, GOI, 1939), p. 189.

ending his speech at the 1939 meeting of the commission on an uncharacteristically strong note of protest. The Indian Historical Records Commission, he said, had "long been recognized as the connecting link between the Government of India and the wider public interested in Indian history. It is our duty to voice the feelings of the students of history in respect of the Government of India records." He sounded like a younger nationalist. Maybe he had seen the point of the nationalist demand for access to sources. Maybe he was also trying to bend to the sentiments of the young. Or maybe he had read the writing on the wall, for this was the year that Abdul Ali was replaced by Sarkar's bête noir Dr. S. N. Sen as the new permanent secretary of the commission. In any case, his statement bears witness to the growing strength of nationalist resentment over barriers to access to the historical records of the government. This is what Sarkar said: "Our students complain that it is easier, quicker, and less harassing to secure the transcripts of any document from the India Office than from Delhi; only it is far more costly. . . . Is it not safer that after [a] sterilising lapse of time, the old secret should become an ascertained public fact, correctly founded on documentary evidence? In England all historical documents have been thrown open to scholars if they are at least 70 years old. Here in India we have been crying for the same liberality in respect of documents 120 years old, but without success."[34]

Old Conflicts Revived

The seventeenth meeting of the IHRC, in 1940, turned out to be the last meeting of the commission that Sarkar ever attended or chaired. Sen was now the keeper of record and therefore the secretary to the IHRC. For a few years, Sarkar had had forebodings of certain crucial shifts in his relationship to the bureaucracy of the Imperial Record Department. As early as 1936, the impending retirement of Abdul Ali and the removal of records to Delhi in 1937 had filled him with anxiety. In a personal letter to Sardesai, he had said: "You hardly realise what a stunning—nay, annihilating—blow to our cause is the compulsory retirement of Abdul Ali in disgrace, . . . and the enforced removal of the records (in defiance of the recommendations of the Indian [Historical] Records Commission) to Delhi from July next."[35] He tried to get for Sardesai

34. Speech by Jadunath Sarkar in *IHRC Proceedings*, vol. 16, *Sixteenth Meeting, Held at Calcutta, December 1939* (Delhi: Manager of Publications, GOI, 1940), pp. 3–4.

35. NL, JSP, letter no. 412, Sarkar to Sardesai, Darjiling, 2 June 1936. See also Sarkar to Sardesai, letter no. 341, Darjiling, 4 April 1936: "When the pre-Mutiny records go to Delhi we shall be quite at sea, and a single document will cost us *four* times our present expense in picking it out and getting it copied."

a "permanent" berth in the commission as one of its "ordinary" members, but this was not to be.[36] Sen became the supreme power in the commission soon after Sarkar made this attempt.

One overdetermining factor influencing the history of what became the National Archives of India was the long-standing feelings of rivalry and hostility that characterized the relationship between Sarkar and Sardesai—less Sardesai and more Sarkar—on the one hand, and Surendra Nath Sen, Shafaat Ahmad Khan, Datto Vaman Potdar, and many other scholars associated with the Poona Itihas Samshodhak Mandal, on the other. The Mandal collectors and publishers of historical documents had long looked down upon Sardesai's effort to synthesize their "discoveries" into connected historical narratives; Sardesai, employed until 1925 by the Baroda state, was not a "discoverer" of documents. They therefore denied his claims to be a historian and called him a *sankalankar*, a mere compiler of narratives. They did not like it at all that Sarkar considered Sardesai to be "the greatest living historian of Maharashtra." We have taken note of this conflict before. Readers will recall that Potdar became the leader of the Poona Mandal from the mid-1920s. He began as an assistant secretary of the Mandal in 1915 and served as its secretary (a position he shared with Sardar G. N. Mujumdar) between 1918 and 1942, when he was elevated to the chairmanship of the Mandal's Executive Council.[37] The conflict reached its peak after 1926. Sardesai wrote to Sarkar in 1927: "It is the extremely hostile attitude of these Poona people which has retarded the progress of history in the university and with Government. They are extremely jealous of other workers and would rather damage all other work in the hope of pushing on their own hobbies."[38]

Many Marathi scholars took umbrage at Sarkar's *Shivaji and His Times* the very first time it was published in 1919. They acknowledged—sometimes grudgingly—his industry and scholarship and his expertise in working with Persian sources but took an intense dislike to his tendency to attack as unreliable or as "forgery" versions or sources of history that they had long treasured. They resented Sarkar's treatment of revered figures such as V. K. Rajwade or D. B. Parasnis when he wrote notices on them in the *Modern Review*

36. See Jadunath Sarkar to the Keeper, Imperial Records, Delhi, dated Darjiling, 21 May 1937; and the Keeper of Records, Government of India, to Jadunath Sarkar, dated 22 June 1937, in NAI, IRD, July 1937, B Proc. no. 2. Also see the general discussion contained in this file.

37. See Surendra Nath Sen, ed., *Mahamahopadhyaya Prof. D. V. Potdar Sixty-First Birthday Commemoration Volume* (Poona: D. K. Sathe B.Sc. for M. M. Potdar Sixty-First Birthday Celebration Committee, 1950), "Mahamahopadhyay Prof. D. V. Potdar, B.A: A Brief Chronology of Events of Life," p. 1.

38. NL, JSP, letter no. 64, Sardesai to Sarkar, Girgaum, Bombay, 14 April 1927.

after they passed away in the mid-1920s. Furthermore, it hurt the Maratha intellectuals' regional pride that Sarkar's book on Shivaji (1919) should refer to the Maratha king in the diminutive form "Shiva."[39] A review published in the *Mahratta* found this way of referring to "Shivaji Maharaj"—"following perhaps his Persian authorities"—disrespectful. "What would he think," it retorted, "if he himself be referred to as 'Jadu'?" "We take this opportunity to inform the Bengali savant that the whole Maratha world would take an insult at their greatest hero being referred to in this contemptuous way!" They found fault with his Marathi and accused him of failing to understand "Maharashtradharma," the spirit of Maharashtra, an expression they claimed was "the key to unlock the Marathi Swarajya [self-rule]."[40] A review in the *Times of India* repeated these charges. He was described as "ignorant of Marathi" and unable to spell Marathi names properly—"Singhgarh for Sinhgad" and "Raigarh for Raigad" were "just as irritating as if a writer were to refer to London as Londres and the Thames as the Tamise."[41] A writer in the *Mahratta* of 17 October 1926 described Sarkar as "a Shivaji-hater and Moghal-lover" while lampooning him also as someone "who thinks that he is the only man in India who has a knowledge of Mahomendan sources" and claiming that "no more scurrilous attempt to decry a book can be conceived" than Sarkar's review of C. V. Vaidya's *Downfall of Hindu India* in the same magazine.[42] Hostile sentiments flared up when Sarkar's obituary notices on Rajwade and Parasnis were published in the *Modern Review*, since both had sections that offended individuals in the Poona literati. An unsigned article titled "Prof. Jadunath Sarkar's Attack on the Late Mr. Rajwade" claimed that while Sarkar might have been able to read "the [Marathi] letter," he could "hardly follow the idiom[;] much less can he enter into the spirit of classical Marathi." The writer also sought to add salt to injury by stating that, had Rajwade been "so minded," he could have, "like Prof. Sarkar—by mere compilation and translation—posed as a great historian, and [the] hard worker [that] he was he would have doubled if not trebled the volume of his [Sarkar's] out-put."[43] Sarkar's statement that D. B. Parasnis had been wise to "keep aloof" from "the Poona School of Historical Students whose mutual wranglings have almost

39. See the discussion in Vasant D. Rao, "Govind Sakharam Sardesai," in *Historians and Historiography in Modern India*, S. P. Sen (Calcutta: Institute of Historical Studies, 1973), pp. 222–233, and pp. 227–228 in particular.

40. Review of *Shivaji and His Times*, in *Mahratta*, 17 August 1919, by "Junata Purusha" [People's man]. See also the discussion in Rao, "Govind Sakharam Sardesai."

41. Anonymous review of *Shivaji and His Times* in *Times of India*, 15 October 1919.

42. "Downfall of Hindu India," *Mahratta* (17 October 1926), pp. 521–522.

43. *Mahratta* (13 February 1927), pp. 69–70.

sterilized their intellects and some of whom have degraded past history into an instrument of present-day political agitation" prompted another writer's riposte: "The Professor should rest assured that the wranglings are certainly not mean quarrels but the usual conflicts of intellect that take place when persons of equal study, equal devotion, and equal acumen come together. Such clashes of intellect with intellect do never sterilize intellects . . . but sharpen them and make them more useful."[44] It was claimed by yet another writer that the Bharat Itihas Samshodhak Mandal set up the Shiva Charitra Karyalaya, a workshop for disseminating facts about Shivaji's life, in part to combat precisely "the inherent defects" of, among other texts, Sarkar's *Shivaji and His Times*.[45]

It particularly rankled the Mandal historians when Sardesai, on the recommendation of Sir Jadunath, was put in charge of making selections out of the Peshwa Daftar records.[46] The Mandal had been demanding "greater access to the [Peshwa Daftar] . . . for nearly two decades during which Potdar himself was refused entry."[47] They were upset that Sardesai had been given access through the influence of Sarkar, whom some saw as an interloper in the historical affairs of western India. Readers will remember from chapter 3, on historical sources, that when Sarkar and Sardesai undertook a tour of Maval in 1930 in search of primary documents, it was "preceded by a hostile printed handbill signed by Potdar and one of his tools."[48] In 1930, as we have seen, ugly things were said about Sarkar and Sardesai in the Bombay Legislative Council and outside with regard to their being given permission to handle the Peshwa Daftar. On 3 July 1932 Potdar gave a public lecture in Poona criticizing Sardesai's work on "the history of the Daftar [by] pointing out how higher authorities of the Bombay Government confounded printing of selections with the printing of a handlist of the Peshwa Dafter." The next day the Mandal held a meeting where N. C. Kelkar—the director of *Kesari* and the vice president of the Mandal—moved a series of resolutions criticizing, in all but name, the work being done by Sardesai.[49]

44. "Prof. Sarkar and the Poona School of Historical Research," *Mahratta* (18 June 1926), pp. 301–302.

45. "Shiva-Charitra-Karyalaya"—What It Has Achieved," by "A Student of History," in *Mahratta* (2 March 1930), p. 107.

46. See chapter 5 of this volume.

47. Prachi Deshpande, *Creative Pasts: Historical Memory and Identity in Western India, 1700–1960* (New York: Columbia University Press, 2007), p. 119.

48. NL, JSP, letter no. 168, Sarkar to Sardesai, Darjiling, 14 August 1931.

49. NAI, IRD, October 1932, Proc. no. 5, secretary of BISM to "Nabob Abdul Ali," secretary, IHRC, dated 28 July 1932, 314 Sadashiva [Peth], Poona City.

Sarkar's hostility toward and disrespect for Potdar stemmed from the former's commitment to working critically with primary sources. When it came to the Peshwa Daftar records, Sarkar did not trust the ability of Potdar and his colleagues to handle these historical records. This may have been his prejudice, but a statement by Sardesai in 1929 lets us see how much the work of editing the peshwa records actually called for an ability to work with, and judge, primary sources in the difficult Modi script. According to Sardesai, the Peshwa Daftar records at the Poona Alienation Office were "scattered over some 27,000 *rumals*, divided into various large sections, which would take a long time for a close scrutiny." There was, besides, a difference between the peshwa records and the British archives on the Marathas. "Old English papers invariably contain the date of origin," making the chronology of events obvious, while the "Marathi papers here as a rule bear no date and often not even the name either of the writer or of the addressee." Dates had to be deduced from "circumstantial evidence." But this was a "slow and tedious process"—"one can hardly edit more than 30 papers a day working steadily for six hours."[50]

Sarkar was also cut to the quick by the charge that his ignorance of the Modi script meant that he could not have used Marathi sources in his book on Shivaji. We have noted his private fury before: "Potdar's statement in large type [in the *Purandaré Daftar*, vol. 2] directed against me is a piece of dishonest misrepresentation, characteristic of an infernal liar like him." Sarkar always prided himself on the thought that he had "used all the Maratha materials on Shivaji available. . . . No material, besides these, *known* to refer to Shivaji exists in ms. in Modi." And then followed a lofty gesture of source-criticism typical of Sarkar: "I reject the *nibadpatras*, *mazharnamas* and worthless private documents of which thousands have been printed and many thousands are lying in ms. in Modi. My claim therefore is true to the letter . . . My ignorance of Modi does not handicap me in the least, in view of the known condition and extent of Shivaji sources."[51] Sarkar retained very strong feelings against his detractors in Poona. Thus, in a letter to Sardesai, dated 14 August 1931, he wrote: "The wide world of scholarship knows the difference between my work and that of the Mandal oracles. I have never tried to humour them." He went on to describe the "Mandal oracles" as "the howling mob of Puna."[52]

50. G. S. Sardesai, "Present Needs of Maratha History," *IHRC Proceedings*, 12:22–27, quotes on 12:24.

51. NL, JSP, letter no. 118, Sarkar to Sardesai, Darjiling, 16 March 1930.

52. NL, JSP, letter no. 168, Sarkar to Sardesai, Darjiling, 14 August 1931.

Or, as he wrote to Raghubir Singh in 1937: "The Poona *Itihas Sanshodhak* [*sic*] *Mandal* has pursued a campaign of lies against Sardesai and me for the last 14 years out of envy and I have refused to help them, either with my expert guidance or my MS collection in their projected book on the Persian sources on Shivaji. . . . It is best that men boasting of modern education and patriotism (of the Maratha Brahman type) whose malignity is also equalled by their ignorance, should be left to stew in their own juice."[53]

These were strong words uttered in private, but Sarkar's attitude was well known to those associated with the Mandal. For a long time Sarkar's interpretations of Maratha history upset numerous scholars in Poona. Consider the introduction that the much younger scholar Trayambak Shankar Shejwalkar (1895–1963), a member of the Mandal and reader in Maratha history at Deccan College, Poona, wrote to his 1946 book on the Battle of Panipat, 1761, where the Marathas were forced to concede defeat to the Afghan forces of Ahmad Shah Abdali, the responsibility for which Sarkar had laid, in the second volume of his *Fall*, at the feet of Maratha leaders for their disunity and faulty military tactics. Shejwalkar described his book as "a reply" to the writings of Sarkar and repeated against Sarkar many of the charges we have already encountered: that Sarkar treated Marathas "from a wrong angle" and unfairly; that his knowledge of Marathi was "inexpert," and that his "masterly English" misled the reader into taking a "wrong perspective" and left him or her unaware of "the incorrectness of the conclusions."[54] Shejwalkar's critique did not change Sarkar's mind. While revising, "minutely," the section on the 1761 battle of Panipat in the second volume of his *Fall* in 1950, Sarkar gave Sardesai his assessment of Shejwalkar's achievements: "Shejwalkar, after his 14 years of 'strenuous and exclusive labour' on the Panipat campaign of four months—against the entire North Indian history for 17 years treated in my volume—has been able to correct me in only four small points. . . . So much for Research as practiced by the Puna University at a large cost."[55]

53. Sarkar to Raghubir Singh, 11 February 1937, Calcutta, in *Making of a Princely Historian: Letters of Sir J. N. Sarkar to Dr. Raghubir Singh of Sitamau*, ed. S. R. Tikekar (Bombay: Maharashtra Board of Archives and Archaeology, 1975), p. 41.

54. Trayambak Shankar Shejwalkar, *Panipat: 1761* (Poona: Deccan College Postgraduate and Research Institute, 1946), preface, pp. v–vi.

55. NL, JSP, letter no. 1051, Sarkar to Sardesai, Calcutta, 19 October 1950.

Beyond the Personal: Access and Preservation versus Pedagogy

Potdar and Sen, on their part, accepted Sarkar's hostility as a fact of their lives and were prepared to collaborate to take the fight back to Sarkar. As Sen wrote to the Goan historian Pissurlencar from Lisbon in 1926: "As for Professor Sarkar, you are wrong in thinking that he will make peace with me but I do not mind it if it is necessary."[56] It is not surprising, then, that Sen should lead the popular charge against the conservative attitude of the colonial bureaucracy in 1937 and thus strategically force Sarkar to join in his campaign. Sen now wielded power as the new keeper of records of the Government of India. If anything, he was more powerful than his predecessor Abdul Ali. He now had the authority to co-opt members for particular meetings of the commission and thus put himself in a position to be the benefactor of numerous historians aspiring for recognition in the government circles.[57] Throughout the 1930s, he also made alliances with Potdar and Shafaat Ahmad Khan of Allahabad and was one of the patriarchs—along with those two—of the Indian History Congress (1935), an organization Sarkar shunned because he did not believe the cause of research and source criticism could be served by what he and Sardesai sometimes derisively called a "show" or "hollow trash."[58]

We should not be misled into thinking, however, that the conflict between Sarkar and Sen, Potdar, and company was merely personal. More significant from a historical point of view was the difference between their understandings of the role of the Records Commission in helping the fledgling historical profession in India. What Sen and Potdar stood for was a demand that was both national and democratic: that there should be greater access to and better preservation of government records. It was indeed a limitation of Sarkar's outlook that he gave less importance to this demand than to his own expectation: that the Records Commission would give him a forum to instill in

56. Letter from Sen dated Lisbon, 2 October 1926, in *Bibliography of Dr. Pissurlencar Collection*, ed. B. S. Shastry and V. R. Navelkar (Bambolim: Goa University, 1989), pt. 3, pp. 218–219.

57. NAI, IRD, January 1941, Proc. no. 46; B. A. Saletore's letter (dated Ahmedabad, 22 December 1942) to Pissurlencar: "The Government of India have been pleased to extend my Corresponding Membership of the Indian Historical Records Commission for a further period of five years from June this year. I must thank my good friend Dr. Sen for this act of kindness on the part of the Government." Shastry and Navelkar, *Bibliography*, pp. 107–108.

58. See Datto Vaman Potdar, *Welcome Address to the Indian History Congress, Silver Jubilee Session, Poona* (Poona: N.p., 1963), pp. 4–6. See also NL, JSP, Sarkar to Sardesai, letter no. 586, Calcutta, 8 September 1939: "I always avoid the Indian History Congress and shall do so even when I am here during its sitting. It is a vulgar tamasha started by a drunkard." See also NL, JSP, letter no. 524, Sarkar to Sardesai, Darjiling, 12 July 1938; and letter no. 526, Sardesai to Sarkar, Kamshet, 31 July 1938.

other historians a deep appreciation of—or even enthusiasm for—"primary" sources. He considered the question of preservation of documents a "technical" matter beyond the province of the historian. Sen, additionally, fancied himself as an archivist in touch with the latest methods of preservation and organization of documents. He probably began to take an interest in the "science" of preservation of records from around 1930, when he acted as an honorary assistant adviser on records to the Government of Bengal.[59] One of the first decisions of the reconstituted commission in 1942 was to resolve to bring out "a quarterly or bi-annual archives journal, with a view to disseminating the extant knowledge of the science of preservation and administration of archives."[60] Delivering his presidential address at the 1944 session of the Indian History Congress held in Madras, Sen, who was by then officially designated as the director of archives, Government of India, extolled the role of the archivist in national life in this way: "The archivist has been so long a self-effacing servant of the state, . . . the time has come when he should play his rightful role as the helpmate of the historian along with the archaeologist. Conservative English opinion in the pre-war days held that preservation was the only function of the archivist[;] publication was no business of his. This view has of late undergone a radical change and the archivist is deliberately claiming to be treated as the 'honoured cousin of the historian.'"[61]

It is difficult to say how good an archivist Sen really was in the early 1940s, given that his training had been that of a historian and not of an archivist.[62] But it is clear that both Potdar and Sen looked on the task of rescuing and preserving documents as the main task of the commission. Potdar pushed for provincial commissions that would continue the work of the IHRC at the provincial level and for such things as microfilming of records. His remark, cited below, that the Records Commission should primarily be about records and not "lengthy papers" reflected that interest. In contrast, Sardesai's oppo-

59. See S. N. Sen's letters dated Calcutta 1 July 1930 and 28 June 1934 to the Goa-based historian Pandurang S. S. Pissurlencar, in Shastry and Navelkar, *Bibliography*, pt. 3, pp. 206–209.

60. *IHRC Retrospect* (Delhi: Manager of Publications, GOI, 1948), p. 26.

61. S. N. Sen, "Presidential Address," in *The Proceedings of the Indian History Congress, Seventh Session* (29–31 December 1944) (Allahabad: General Secretary, Indian History Congress, 1945), pp. 7–20, quote on p. 17.

62. Sen's 1940 report on the state of government records in Bombay elicited a negative response from some of the high officials in Bombay government. The commissioner of the Central Division of the Presidency, under whose jurisdiction fell the Poona Alienation Office, reportedly asked Sardesai on 18 January 1941: "What can I do with this unworkable expert opinion of the Keeper of the Imperial Records?" NL, JSP, letter no. 664, Sardesai to Sarkar, Kamshet, 21 January 1941.

sition to microfilming—that "the would-be student would find original files more suitable for personal study than the films" or that "already filmers have most recklessly dismantled the beautiful bound volumes"—sounds positively arcane today.[63]

Sarkar's self-appointed role at these conferences was that of a teacher. For Sarkar, the Indian Historical Records Commission was a pedagogical and intellectual platform from which to propagate a particular vision of historical research and argue for the indispensability of public archives for the cause of writing history. He was, as we have seen in chapter 3, acutely aware that it was the absence of proper archives that hindered the progress of modern historiography in India. In a paper presented at the 1925 session of the commission, Sarkar focused on the question of archives as the condition of possibility for Mughal Indian history. "The problem of Indian history in the Mughal period," he wrote, "is to find out the most original sources of information."[64] We have already discussed some of the arguments he made explaining why it was difficult to build up a national archives in India without a public records act helping the government in Delhi nationalize papers in the informal custody of private, ruling families. "Even a transcendent historical genius like Ranke," he said in one his lectures at a meeting of the commission, "failed to give fullness and finality to his *History of the Popes* because he could not open those closed treasuries of information."[65] What hope would Indian history have without a collective effort to imbibe the Rankean love of primary sources? It was clearly this question that engaged Sarkar's passion. As he said in the very first paper he presented to the commission: "I have come across very few historical letters in Persian for these three [second, third, and fourth] decades of Aurangzeb's reign. . . . The missing materials can be discovered only by the combined search of many men at many places."[66] The idea therefore was to "interest the outer public" in the work of the commission and "to tempt private records out of their seclusion by . . . [having] a public session." To the public session was also added the attraction of an exhibition of historical artifacts and documents. As Sarkar put it in the same speech: "The exhibition has been our most helpful auxiliary for this purpose."[67]

63. NL, JSP, Sardesai to Sarkar, letters nos. 711 and 720, Kamshet, 23 April and 30 June 1942.

64. Jadunath Sarkar, "Historical Records Relating to Northern India, 1700–1817," in *IHRC Proceedings*, vol. 7, *Seventh Meeting, Held at Poona, January 1925* (Calcutta: GOI, Central Publishing Branch, 1925), p. 28.

65. Jadunath Sarkar, "The House of Jaipur," in *IHRC Proceedings*, 12:18.

66. Sarkar, "The Missing Link in the History of Mughal India from 1658 to 1761," in *IHRC Proceedings*, 2:7, 8.

67. See speech by Jadunath Sarkar in *IHRC Proceedings*, 12:7.

Sarkar tried to use the annual meetings of the commission to instill in others a Rankean appreciation of the importance of "eye-witness accounts" to historical research. As we have seen, Sarkar looked upon history as a sort of calling, a call to truth, its objective method something to be practiced as a personal virtue. In speaking of himself in a radio broadcast in 1948, he referred to the "eternal vitality" that was always there in honest efforts and true words.[68] He thought it impossible that someone could be a historian without "the right mental attitude." "Our history of India," he wrote on another occasion, "in order to find acceptance in the wide world of scholarship, must appeal to universal reason by transcending the narrow limits of national prejudices and beliefs[;] it must be scientific in its method, and science knows no barriers of country or race and owes no homage except to truth."[69] He clearly saw the Records Commission as a forum he could use to generate a critical enthusiasm among the students of Indian history for collecting and evaluating "original" records in order to be able to write history from primary sources. Educating Indian historians in the method of what the Germans called *Quellenkritik*, or source criticism, remained his lifelong passion, though he was not much interested in philology.

When Chaudhuri Abdul Hamid, a professor of history at Government College, Lahore, presented his paper "Manuscripts of the 'Tarikh-i-Muzaffari'" at the meeting at Lahore in 1920, Sarkar intervened to point out that this "long history" of "the Delhi empire" in the eighteenth century was "a mere compilation from earlier works and . . . for most parts . . . [was] neither an eye witness's account nor a summary of State papers" and hence could not be seen "as a *primary* authority."[70] At the same meeting, in response to a paper by Maulvi Zafar Hasan, assistant superintendent, Archaeological Survey of India, reproducing an acrimonious and insulting exchange of letters purported to have taken place between Shah Sulaiman Safavi of Persia and the Mughal emperor Aurangzeb, Sarkar hastened to underline the nature of such sources. He doubted whether Aurangzeb's letter "was ever really delivered to the Persian king, as the courier of such a message was sure to forfeit his life." Instead, he pointed out—as a teacher might to a class—that "these letters, as well as acrimonious correspondence between Aurangzeb and his rebel son

68. See Moni Bagchi, *Acharya Jadunath: Jibon o sadhana* [in Bengali] (Calcutta: Jijnasha, 1975), p. 3.

69. Sarkar's speech at the Indian Academy of History, proceedings of the inaugural session at Benares, 30–31 December 1937, pp. 20–23, cited in Raghubir Singh, "Jadunath Sarkar as a Historian of the Marathas" in *History in Practice: Historians and Sources of Medieval Deccan—Marathas*, ed. A. R. Kulkarni (New Delhi: Books and Books, 1993), p. 66.

70. *IHRC Proceedings*, 2:23.

Muhammad Akbar, represent a class of Persian epistolary composition which students in those days were taught as exercises in rhetoric . . . never actually used in diplomatic intercourse, being too full of taunts and retorts."[71]

Over time the public sessions became more crowded, and the published proceedings stopped recording discussions that may have followed the presentation of individual papers. But Sarkar's own contributions never ceased to put the emphasis on the importance of original sources for the writing of modern, "scientific" history. His paper "The Missing Links in the History of Mughal India from 1658 to 1761," presented in 1920, pointed out the crucial role that "original" documents play in modern historical reconstructions of the past. A "modern historian," he said, "cannot be satisfied with . . . Court chronicles, which are, after all, compilations. He wishes to go to their very source, to the raw material out of which they have been constructed." And then, as if trying to enthuse an audience of students by giving them concrete examples of ways in which primary sources helped in illuminating the past, he spoke of how the daily bulletins from the Mughal court provided the reader "with life-like touches . . . on men and manners. . . . We are told of how on [once] hearing reports of Shivaji's raids, Aurangzeb remained silent, . . . how when a dispatch from a province evidently containing [bad] . . . news was handed to him . . . , he read it and put it into his pocket" or how he "tore . . . up in anger" a letter from the Maratha commandant of the Fort of Vishalgarh when the fort was under siege from his own army in 1702.[72]

The Final Blow

The tension between Sarkar and the Sen-Potdar combination was visible soon after the commission resumed its annual meetings in 1937. On the very first day of the meeting in 1940, for example, Potdar brought a resolution asking the IHRC to endorse "in general" a report Sen had prepared on the Peshwa Daftar—the report was available to the commission—and to urge the Bombay government to implement Sen's recommendations. Sen's report, published in the printed proceedings of the meeting, actually contained suggestions made in consultation with Potdar about preservation of records and some additional recommendations from Potdar himself. Sarkar, however, disallowed the motion from the chair, because "it had not been previously circulated," and the meeting resolved to take up the report for discussion the fol-

71. Ibid., 2:18.
72. Ibid., 2:6–7.

lowing year.[73] This "insult" to Potdar was not new. At the fifteenth meeting of the commission, held in 1938 at Poona, Potdar had brought eight resolutions. They were all focused on Bombay government and problems of historical preservation in that province. Sarkar, chairing the meeting, annulled most of them, but one was passed in a modified and milder form.[74]

Sarkar had clashed several times with Sen in the recent past when the latter presented some technical details about methods for preserving documents, in the course of which Sen and Dr. Baliga, from Madras, differed on "the comparative merits of laminating and vacuum fumigation" of records. Sen's detailed and passionate rebuttal of Baliga's argument was interrupted by Sarkar, who said, "You may circulate your note" (at which Dr. R. C. Majumdar pleaded, "Sir, we want to hear him"). The verbal duel raged on until Sarkar brought the debate to a close with an unashamed expression of his lack of interest or competence in the technical problems of archives, for he, as a researcher, focused on the documents themselves. "To be frank," he said, "these things [issues of preservation] are beyond me." Potdar then suggested that both Sen's and Baliga's notes be circulated among the members for their opinions. Sarkar postponed the discussion with the remark, "We are not experts. The British and American opinions are divided on the subject."[75]

However, now that Sen was in power, word must have also gone around that some kind of reorganization of the commission was afoot, for in his welcoming speech at the Baroda meeting of December 1940, Sarkar was unmistakably anxious over the prospect of enmity and reorganization. He described "the scholars and archivists" assembled at the conference as "a band of brothers, united in the search of truth about India's past life experience and ready to help each other . . . , pooling their resources together at the shrine of the Historic Muse." He concluded, significantly it seems, by pointing out how "the knowledge of the dark alleys of Indian record-hunting and of the differences of local conditions which *this* Commission has acquired by this time"—the word "this" referring to the commission *he* more than anybody else had helped to build up—would "prove most helpful in any plan for the future reorganization of the Indian Historical Records Commission that may be contemplated."[76]

73. *IHRC Proceedings*, vol. 17, *Seventeenth Meeting, Held at Baroda, December 1940* (Delhi: Manager of Publications, GOI, 1941), pp. 1, 14 (proceedings of the members' meeting).

74. For details, see *IHRC Proceedings*, 15:194–195.

75. *IHRC Proceedings*, 17:9–10 (proceedings of the members' meeting).

76. Ibid., 17:2.

Nilakanta Shastri shared Sarkar's anxieties. Shastri had come to know only as he was leaving Madras for this meeting that there was "a proposal . . . for the reorganization of this Commission." "May I suggest," he asked, " that we should request the Government of India that no proposal should be taken up without circulating it among the members?" The commission, after all, had "an experience of twenty years." Sen remained quite taciturn in the face of all this anxious questioning. The proposals, he said, were "tentative" and were still being discussed by provincial governments, who had also been "requested to obtain the opinion of local universities and learned bodies." "At present," he repeated in a tone that must have sounded reassuring, "the proposals are only tentative suggestions and the Government of India may or may not put them into action. They may also modify their views in the light of suggestions they receive. It is only then that the time will come for placing their proposals before the Commission."[77]

Sen actually knew more than he was letting on. A note internal to the Imperial Record Department observed on 26 February 1940 that "the Govt. of India have invited K[eeper of] R[ecords] [i.e., Sen] to submit proposal for reconstitution of the Commission." Sen was also waiting for a chance to change the personnel of the commission. He expressed the opinion in a note dated 3 May 1940 that "in view of the proposed reconstitution of the Commission, it is better not to add any fresh names to our list of corresponding members."[78] But he remained tactfully courteous to Sarkar and Sardesai throughout 1940.[79] He was happy to oblige Sarkar whenever the latter approached the Imperial Record Department for historical information. As the new secretary of the commission, he also extended to Sarkar the courtesy of inviting him to "write a paper for the next [1940] session of the I. H. R. Commission," and Sarkar responded saying that he would be "glad to comply with it."[80] This was around March 1940, when the idea of reconstituting the commission had already been mooted.

77. Ibid., 17:1, 14 (proceedings of the members' meeting).

78. NAI, IRD, September 1940, Proc. no. 15, notes by "B. N. B" dated 26 February 1940 and by S. N. Sen dated 3 May 1940.

79. A letter from (the ever guileless) Sardesai to Sarkar written as late as September 1940—barely two months before the meeting of the commission—reads: "I met Sen at Baroda. He presided at my lectures. . . . I found him sufficiently 'humble,' more intent upon making his new job a success than aggravating old acerbities. I feel we should close our chapters without leaving behind any unhealed sores—letting matters end with our lives, good or bad whatever they prove to be." NL, JSP, letter no. 640, Sardesai to Sarkar, Kamshet, 13 September 1940.

80. Sarkar to Sen, dated Calcutta, 7 April 1940, in NAI, IRD, July 1940, Proc. no. 44. For more instances, see Sarkar to Sen, dated Calcutta, 21 June 1940; and Sen's note dated 25 June 1940, in NAI, IRD, July 1940, Proc. no. 61.

Through all this time, Sen had been quietly working on reorganizing the commission. In this he received close cooperation from his friend Datto Vaman Potdar. Potdar wrote a long letter to Sen on 29 March 1940 in which he returned to all the points he had tried to raise at the 1938 Poona meeting of the commission when Jadunath Sarkar, as he put it in this letter, "snubbed" him. The letter began by acknowledging the fact of his recent appointment—under the Sen regime—as a corresponding member of the commission. "So at last this was done!!" exclaimed Potdar. He informed Sen that he had "suggested [Sen's] name as a member of the Selection Committee for the post of the Reader in Marathi History at the Deccan College" and invited him to accompany him (Potdar) on a visit to the Peshwa Daftar in Poona. (This visit occurred in September 1940, when Sardesai met Sen and wrote to Sarkar about Sen's seeming humility.) Potdar then reverted to a topic he felt most passionately about: finding and preserving regional documents and district and High Court records; the question of microfilming ("a microfilming department must be started by the Imperial Record Department as early as possible"); "more dignity and status" to corresponding members; provincial records commissions of which the IHRC would only be a federated expression, and so on. And, finally, in a direct jab at Sarkar's desire to make the commission's meetings into a pedagogical exercise in historiography, Potdar declaimed: "All these matters require very careful consideration & it is these that must be thrashed out at our Commission's meetings as these have prior claims over the Papers which are read and published by us. Our Commission is primarily meant for *Records* and not for learned and lengthy papers." And now that finally Sen was in charge, Potdar saw hope. "This is a very lengthy note," he concluded by saying, "I have tried to write it out for I *now* feel that these matters would *now* receive the attention they deserve at the hands of the Keeper of Imperial Records [Sen]" (fig. 10).[81]

"My dear Dattopant," Sen said in an official but warm and sympathetic letter in response, "the difficulty may be best be solved by the reconstitution of the Commission." Sen was in real earnest—the fact that the letter was dated 1 April 1940 was no reflection on the spirit of its words—for he returned to the theme in a follow-up letter dated 24 April 1940: "It is expected that some of the difficulties referred to in your letter may be solved if the Commission is re-constituted on the lines contemplated." The "contemplation" in question was mainly Sen's, for he writes in the same letter: "I intend to approach the Government of India shortly with a proposal regarding the

81. Datto Vaman Potdar to S. N. Sen, dated Poona, 29 March 1940, in NAI, IRD, October 1940, Proc. no. 11, emphasis added.

FIGURE 10. D. V. Potdar, year unknown. Photographer unknown. Private collection of the author.

Commission."[82] Sen was indeed the author of the changes that followed, and this particular letter allows us to date his proposals for reform. He must have formulated them by May–June 1940, some six or seven months before the 1940 meeting of the commission where, asked about the proposed reconstitution, he deflected discussion by saying it was all still very "tentative."

It is possible, though one can never be sure, that in disallowing Potdar's motion at the December 1940 meeting of the commission on the ground that it had not been circulated before, Sarkar walked right into a trap that had been laid for him. Sen's report (written in consultation with Potdar) was circulated to the members of the commission the evening before the commission met, and yet a discussion of it was not put on the agenda of the meeting because, as Sen said later, the permission to release that document to the commission's members was received only two days before the meeting.[83] Potdar's action of suddenly proposing a new resolution on Sen's report at the beginning of the meeting could have been a calculated move. Potdar had earlier informed officials of the commission that "he would not suggest any subject this year for

82. Sen to Potdar, 1 April and 24 April 1940, in NAI, IRD, October 1940, Proc. no. 11.

83. NAI, IRD, March 1941, Proc. no. 41.

inclusion in the agenda of the Commission's next meeting" (i.e., the meeting in December).[84] Besides, the decision to add something to the agenda as a last-minute move, in all likelihood, would have involved Sen. Sarkar, it would have been obvious to anyone watching his style, depended for power on his prestige and status as a scholar and on his standing with the colonial bureaucracy. His style was more imperial and haughty than wily and tactful. In 1940, his decision to disallow Potdar's motion on a simple procedural ground that it had not been circulated before made him look authoritarian. By that misstep, ironically for someone who retained a lifelong interest in military history, Sarkar won a battle but lost the war.[85]

Potdar lost little time in lodging an official complaint against Sarkar with the secretary of the Education Department, Sir Girija Shankar Bajpai, I.C.S., who was ex-officio president of the IHRC and who had recruited Sen to the position of the keeper of records.[86] Potdar's letter dated 31 December 1940—barely a week after the IHRC session had concluded—began by mentioning his long association with the commission: "At the Poona session in 1938 I was asked to help the Local Secretary and had practically to do a lot of the preliminary work of that session."[87] He then proceeded to state the complaint. Sen's report on his visit to Poona in September 1940, said Potdar, "was circulated to all members of the I.H.R. Commission in the evening of 21st December." As the "report was a pretty long document and required time for reading," Potdar insisted that "any resolution to be submitted thereon could not have been submitted except in the morning of the 22nd."[88]

Potdar's implicit claim that he himself had had no access to the contents of the report before the evening of the 21st is indeed a little suspect in hindsight, since we know that he accompanied Sen during the latter's September visit to the Peshwa Daftar on which the report was based. The report actually contained quite a few suggestions directly attributed to Potdar. But whatever

84. Note by B.N.B dated 18 October 1940, in NAI, IRD, October 1940, Proc. no. 11.

85. In his old age, Sarkar wrote many newspaper articles on the histories of individual battles in Mughal India. These were published posthumously in a book, *The Military History of India.*

86. *IHRC Retrospect*, p. 91.

87. NAI, IRD, March 1941, letter from Datto Vaman Potdar to Sir Girija Shankar Bajpai, Ex-officio President of the Indian Historical Records Commission, dated 31 December 1940. Sarkar was unhappy at the degree of involvement the Poona Mandal had in the organization of the meeting of the commission. He expected Sardesai to preempt this, but Potdar was probably quicker to move: "I understand that Abdul Ali is going to hold an exhibition in the Mandal premises. How was the place chosen without your knowledge? Anyway, I know how I shall act." NL, JSP, Sarkar to Sardesai, Calcutta, 1 December 1938.

88. NAI, IRD, March 1941, letter from Datto Vaman Potdar to Sir Girija Shankar Bajpai, ex-officio president of the Indian Historical Records Commission, dated 31 December 1940.

the merit of this speculative argument, Potdar claimed that since the morning of the 22nd was the earliest his resolution could be brought before the commission, Sarkar's decision to disallow it on that morning was "quite unconstitutional and hence unjust."[89] "The Chairman," he complained, "failed in his duty and adopted an unjust attitude towards my resolution and is guilty of an unconstitutional procedure in disallowing" it. Concluding, he suggested that this attitude on Sarkar's part had a long history. "If I were to go into past incidents it would be a long story, but I refrain. Suffice it to say, that I decided to approach you this time only after things became quite unbearable." His "object would be gained," he added, "if I have succeeded in convincing you that such things would not be repeated."[90] Bajpai wrote back to say he was "calling for a report from Dr. Sen." Sen's report to Bajpai simply described what had happened and did not seek to interpret Sarkar's action. A letter was finally issued to Potdar, but we do not have a copy of that letter. What exists in the relevant file is a draft letter presumably written in the name of Bajpai—for it says "I have received Dr. Sen's report"—but amended in Sen's own handwriting. Here are the final lines that Sen crossed out and rewrote: "I can assure you that all possible efforts were made for the prompt circulation of the report but as it was not included in the agenda it was ~~within the rights of the Chairman to use his discretion in the way he did~~ for the chairman to decide whether it should or should not be placed before the Commission."[91] Sen thus

89. D. V. Potdar, Corresponding and Co-opted Member of the IHRC, 180 Shanwar Peth, Poona City, 31 December 1940, to The Hon'ble Sir Girija Shankar Bajpai, ex-officio president of the IHRC, NAI, IRD, March 1941, Proc. no. 41. There is some confusion of dates here. The piece of paper with a note from Sarkar disallowing Potdar's motion is dated 21 December 1940 in this file. The proceedings of the meeting and Potdar's and Sen's account of it are all clear on the fact that the disallowing happened on the morning of the 22nd and not the evening before. See *IHRC Proceedings*, vol. 17, pt. 3, p. 1. The mistake in the date may have been Sarkar's or of the typist who copied his note for the government file.

90. D. V. Potdar, corresponding and co-opted member of the IHRC, 180 Shanwar Peth, Poona City, 31 December 1940, to the Hon'ble Sir Girija Shankar Bajpai, ex-officio president of the IHRC, NAI, IRD, March 1941, Proc. no. 41.

91. D. V. Potdar, corresponding and co-opted member of the IHRC, 180 Shanwar Peth, Poona City, 31 December 1940, to the Hon'ble Sir Girija Shankar Bajpai, ex-officio president of the IHRC, NAI, IRD, March 1941, Proc. no. 41; draft undated letter to Potdar. The draft itself may have come from Sen's office, for a note (30 January 1941) from John Sargent asks "The K[eeper]. [of] R[records]. [i.e., Sen]" to "put up a draft letter for H.M. to send to Mr. Potdar. In response, there is note from Sen, dated 31 January 1941: "A draft letter is put up for the approval of the H.M."

avoided the question of the chairman's (i.e., Sarkar's) "rights" and instead wrote a letter that was simply correct.

The Denouement

How deeply Sarkar's actions, gestures, and intellectual position as the "senior-most" member of the IHRC wounded Sen (and Potdar) may be seen even in the official prose of the history of the Indian Historical Records Commission that was published in 1948, when Sen was the first director of the National Archives of India, the rechristened Department of Imperial Record.[92] This book as such had no author, but it would not be surprising at all if Sen had had a strong hand in the drafting of the text. The section introducing Sen begins on a certain note of coyness that is unusual for officialese—"To speak of present company is exceedingly embarrassing"—and then goes on to suggest that it was almost the work of destiny that Sen should be the "last Keeper of the Records of the British Indian Government" and the first director of the National Archives. After highlighting some early and serendipitous associations in Sen's life with imperial record-keepers (who were his teachers at Dacca College)—he "must have been infected by his teachers' enthusiasm for archival work"—the passage described Sen in his younger days, when he "visited the records offices of Calcutta, Goa, London, Paris and Lisbon," as "the young man *destined* to be the last Keeper of Records in the British Indian Government."[93]

This official history of the IHRC thus appears to reflect Sen's point of view. It was mainly a narrative of nationalism and democracy. The old commission, said the new history, was "a purely official body, unrepresentative of the provinces and the Indian States, not likely to inspire public confidence or to capture popular imagination." That was "its greatest weakness."[94] Even the "half-hearted device of co-option had proved a failure." Co-opted members "did not bring new strength to the Commission," for they "were nominated *ad hoc*" in a "confessedly indiscriminate" manner.[95] The need was to "infuse fresh blood in the Commission and to associate Indian scholars in a larger number with its activities." The new, reconstituted commission, on the other hand, "sought to convert the close preserve of nominated persons into a

92. *IHRC Retrospect.*

93. Ibid., p. 60, emphasis added.

94. Ibid., pp. 4, 8.

95. Ibid., pp. 5, 7, 8.

widely representative association of historians and archivists." "Co-option was entirely to be done away with."[96] The new constitution came into effect on 3 January 1942.[97] According to this official history, it "inspired the members of the Commission with a remarkable degree of confidence and sense of responsibility." Initiative now lay with the members of the commission and not with the secretary, whose office, it was now said, "retreated within its proper limits," unlike in the past when the "Secretary and the seniormost ordinary member" (a veiled reference, it seems, to Abdul Ali and Jadunath Sarkar) "worked in uninterrupted harmony" and together ran "the machinery of the Commission."[98]

The *Retrospect* thus cast the history of the commission into a story of a change in a particular direction: from a closed, colonial, and unrepresentative institution to an open, representative, and national one; from an era of "nomination" and colonial nepotism to one of being representative and popular; from colonial politicking to, as the last paragraph of this chronicle said, "no politics." Many of the claims made in this document were justified. It is true, as we have seen, that the British bureaucrats of the Imperial Record Department were often unwilling to open up official records for the Indian researcher; it was not until December 1939, and under the pressure of "public opinion," that the Government of India decided to "throw open their [historical] records to *bona fide* research students."[99] While it would not be just to say the old commission was not concerned at all about being representative, it is true that the reconstituted commission had more members and involved the provinces and the universities and learned societies in a more systematic manner.[100] The attendance, as we have noted before, at the 1942 meeting of

96. Ibid., pp. 6, 8, 9.

97. Ibid., p. 10.

98. Ibid., pp. 12, 13, 56.

99. Ibid., p. 61.

100. The official discussion around Sarkar's letter of 1937 proposing Sardesai's name for an ordinary membership of the commission suggests that while in its colonial construction the commission was not meant to have a representative character, it could not in practice avoid the question of representation. Thus, when Sardesai was appointed an ordinary member in 1927, it was partly because the Government was reluctant to have "two official representatives from the Madras Presidency." Father Heras, who came into the Commission "in place of Mr. Rawlinson in 1933," was seen as representing Bombay. Similarly in the case of Dr. Shafaat Ahmad Khan, "it could be overlooked," a departmental official noted, that he was "the only person representing U.P. on the Commission." When R. B. Ramsbotham, then pro-vice chancellor of Aligarh Muslim University, retired back to England in 1935 (and was appointed a corresponding member of the London Centre of the commission), the Government picked Mr. A. B. A. Haleem, a professor of history at the same institution, to replace Ramsbotham as a corresponding member. See letter

the reconstituted commission was nearly double that at the meeting in 1940, the last one that Sarkar chaired. The changes also seem to have been popular and were in tune with the fact that British imperial power was on the wane.[101]

Yet, behind the coldness of the official print and from across the distance of time, the animus against Sarkar that at least in part drove the narrative of this "impersonal" account remains palpable. At some rather significant places in the story, the shadow of Sarkar falls across the text. He is never condemned by name but yet is made to stand in for what was wrong about the old commission. Thus the rhapsodic prose of the *Retrospect* about the new wind of democracy blowing through the portals of the commission—about, for example the secretary (Sen) and his staff "retreating" into their "proper limits," leaving all initiative to the members of the commission—climaxed, rhetorically, with an indirect reference to the memory of Sarkar disallowing Potdar's motion in 1940. Not only was the secretariat's "retreat" hailed as an improvement since 1942, "nor [had] the Chair," emphasized the *Retrospect*, "vetoed or guillotined discussion on any subject." The *Retrospect* also made a reference to the discussion held in 1940 under Sarkar's chairmanship about methods of preserving documents, during which Sen and Baliga took opposed positions. Sarkar, readers will remember, declared at this meeting that the technical subject of preservation was "beyond" his expertise, especially when American and British experts were divided in their opinions. Looking back, the *Retrospect* now blamed it on the preponderance in the commission of "co-opted non-expert" members that the organization was "not competent to deal with complex technical problems of preservation and reference media." The argument is clinched with a direct reference to Sarkar's role at this meeting: "In 1940 the Chairman had actually ruled that the Commission was not in a position to decide upon the comparative merits of two methods of repair."[102]

The reconstituted commission dropped Sarkar altogether and made Potdar one of its nominated "ordinary" members. Sarkar was the only person not to find a place in the expanded and representative entity that the commission now was (except for an associate membership representing a literary academy in Bengal, the Bangiya Sahitya Parishad). He chose not to attend the meeting

---

dated Darjiling, 21 May 1937 from Jadunath Sarkar to the Keeper, Imperial Records, Delhi, NAI, IRD, July 1937, B Proc. no. 2; letter dated 22 June 1937 from the Keeper of Records, Government of India, to Jadunath Sarkar, NAI, IRD, July 1937, B Proc. no. 2. Also see the general discussion contained in this file; NAI, IRD, July 1937, B Proc. no. 2, note dated 5 June 1937 signed "B.N.B."; NAI, IRD, IHRC Branch, October 1937, Proc. no. 9.

101. *IHRC Retrospect*, p. 10.

102. Ibid., p. 7.

of 1942 or meetings thereafter.[103] However, it is not just the fact that Sarkar was dropped that is suggestive of a degree of animus being at work here. It was more *the way* he was dropped. The manner of dismissal was unceremonious, involving no formal or informal notice, and it was perhaps calculated to humiliate the man who, for all his demonstrable faults, was arguably one of the greatest scholars Indian history has ever produced and who had been the intellectual force behind the commission since its inception.

The reforms were announced on 3 January 1942. Sarkar had no inkling of what was looming as late as August the previous year, for in a letter dated 6 August 1941, he asked Sardesai if the latter intended to "visit Mysore for the I[ndian] H[istorical] R[ecords] Commn. December next."[104] Sardesai first broached the topic of the reconstitution of the commission in a letter in October that year. "While in Bombay," he wrote, "I read in the Bombay Govt. Gazette a resolution of the Govt. of India reconstituting the H.R.C. and its functions. It seemed to me that this important change had been effected without your knowledge or consultation and too much centralization had been effected, the secretary of the Commn. alone bossing over everything. . . . Kindly let me know." Sarkar's reply of 16 October simply reported the fact that the commission "would meet in Mysore mid-January 1942."[105]

Sardesai was anxious. On 5 December he wrote: "Yesterday, I received my copy of the [illegible; newsletter of Potdar's Mandal?]—no. 2 of the year 22. Please notice on the backpage cover Potdar's declaration on the subject of the reconstruction of the H. R. C. Joshi has already been deputed to Delhi to help Sen edit and publish Marathi documents of the Imperal Records [*sic*] [Department.]." He passed on the intelligence he had received: "They have planned to drop you out. I wonder what the present position is. Can you not expose the fraudulent manouevres [*sic*] of Sen and Potdar through N. R. Sarkar [the president of the commission in 1942]? It was I think [John] Sargent [the education commissioner] who played into Sen's hands. The plan seems to have been deep laid for the last two years."[106] Sarkar's reply simply stated that he was "planning to retire from the Benares History Board as soon as the Akbar volume (now in my hands) is ready for the press." But he spoke not a word about the commission.[107]

The anxiety of Nana (as Sardesai was affectionately called by many, includ-

103. Sarkar's age was not at issue in his dismissal from the commission.

104. NL, JSP, letter no. 685, Sarkar to Sardesai, Calcutta, 6 August 1941.

105. NL, JSP, letter no. 693, Sardesai to Sarkar, Kamshet, 3 October 1941; and letter no. 695, Sarkar to Sardesai, Calcutta 16 October 1941.

106. NL, JSP, letter no. 700, Sardesai to Sarkar, Kamshet, 5 December 1941.

107. NL, JSP, letter no. 701, Sarkar to Sardesai, Calcutta, 8 December 1941.

ing Sarkar) was growing by the day. "I am not sure," he wrote on 19 December, "how [we] stand in the new constitution of the H.R.C. I am however inclined to think that your absence will be more telling."[108] Sarkar still maintained his studied silence on the matter of the commission's reconstitution. His letter of 28 December speaks simply of the impact of the war on Calcutta and mentions that a well-known lecturer in history—"the Calcutta Ph.D. mentioned by you"—was "unfit to write your chapters in the Benares History of India."[109] Unable to bear this silence, Sardesai came directly to the point: "I was anxious to know something of the developments in connection with the H.R.C. Can you tell me in brief how it affects you and me and whether you would advise me to entirely withdraw from it?"[110] Sarkar's reply was full of warmth. Inviting Nana to stay with him in Calcutta, he said: "There is a room in this my new house, which is spoken of by all as 'Sardesai's room,' and a vegetarian kitchen will also be provided." But it had only one short sentence on the IHRC: "No news has come to me about the Commission."[111] The commission's meeting was now only a few weeks away.

There was a sudden burst of enthusiasm in Sarkar's next letter. On 13 January, he wrote: "A quantity of papers relating to the next meeting of the Commission has been sent to me with a printed note, 'For your use at the Commission.'" But this was no confirmation that he was still the "seniormost ordinary" member of the commission: "But I have received no official intimation as to whether the old and dissolved body of 'ordinary members' still continues to function, or a new body has been approved including myself!" He was too proud to ask, and there was always the fear of humiliation: "I decline to make any such inquiry myself." But clearly this communication from the secretariat of the commission, however impersonal, kindled his hope and enthusiasm, and he excitedly made some quick and provisional plans with Nana: "If, however, I receive a belated message to that effect from the capital, I shall start for Madras on Saturday next, and reach Mysore in the morning of the 20th instant. If I go, I shall wire to you to join me there from your side, provided that your health permits it. At all events, if I am still an ordinary member, I must go, and on my way back from Mysore I shall visit Bombay."[112]

And then, as suddenly as the last flicker of Sarkar's enthusiasm had flared, this drama of humiliation reached its end. No further communication had

108. NL, JSP, letter no. 702, Sardesai to Sarkar, Kamshet, 19 December 1941.

109. NL, JSP, letter no. 704, Sarkar to Sardesai, Calcutta, 28 December 1941.

110. NL. JSP, letter no. 705, Sardesai to Sarkar, Kamshet, 3 January 1942.

111. NL, JSP, letter no. 706, Sarkar to Sardesai, Calcutta, 9 January 1942.

112. NL, JSP, letter no. 708, Sarkar to Sardesai, Calcutta, 13 January 1942.

been received from the commission in Delhi. Sarkar read in newspapers about the new commission soon after his last letter. The new members had been announced. He was not among them. His letter to Sardesai dated 16 January 1942 simply stated the facts:

> *My Dear Nana,*
>
> The five experts nominated by the Government of India as 'ordinary members' [of the IHRC] are
>
> Dr. R. C. Majumdar
> Potdar
> Srinivasachari
> Habib of Aligarh
> Col. Bullock.

And then a few distracting words: "If the war in the Far East does not grow more menacing towards Bengal, I am thinking of visiting you for some weeks' tour together next month. Till then I continue here. Yours sincerely, JNS."[113]

The two old men had been wounded. Sardesai licked his wounds by calling the Research and Publications Committee of the reformed commission "a fad created by Sen and Potdar." It "has done no work . . . and should be no part of the Indian Historical Records Commission."[114] And both men, in their different ways, entertained false hopes of being back in the ring again. Sardesai soon suggested an alliance with "Bisheshwar Prasad of Allahabad." "If he can be weaned away," he wrote to Sarkar in 1942, "Potdar alone will feel helpless. Let us rope in this Bisheshwar Prasad. You can write to him a line asking if he can take up a volume for P[oona] R[esidency] C[orrespondence] and he will feel flattered."[115] Like an old warhorse, he returned to the battle ground in 1946 when he smelled "degeneration" in the commission and thought it "high time the pretensions of Sen, Potdar & Co are thoroughly exposed. . . . If you give me a few points, I will move in the matter."[116] Sarkar, on his part, wrote as late as January 1953—five years before he died—that he would attend the forthcoming Bhopal meeting of the commission only if he were appointed a full member, "otherwise *not*."[117] Unfortunately, none of this was to be. Sen,

113. NL, JSP, letter no. 710, Sarkar to Sardesai, Calcutta, 16 January 1942.
114. NL, JSP, letter no. 1145, Sardesai to Sarkar, Kamshet, 10 August 1953.
115. NL, JSP, letter no. 711, Sardesai to Sarkar, Kamshet, 30 June 1942.
116. NL, JSP, letter no. 906, Sardesai to Sarkar, Kamshet, 12 November 1946.
117. NL, JSP, letter no. 1121, Sarkar to Sardesai, Calcutta, 21 January 1953.

Potdar, and their colleagues had indeed been able to gain control of the commission and consolidate their power.

If there was a tragedy to Sarkar's life as a historian, it lay in his constantly mistaking the very particular and pragmatic British colonial bureaucracy in India for the universal ideals of the empire. He could not see that the colony/empire was an internally fissured formation. The empire spoke of principles; the colonial officials were ruthlessly pragmatic. By the time Sarkar lost out to younger historians such as S. N. Sen and D. V. Potdar in his battle to control the future of historical research in India, colonial officials had silently made room for Indianization of the educational bureaucracy. The Imperial Record Department, named the National Archives after independence, came to be controlled by Sen in the years immediately preceding the transfer of power. Sen and his cohorts pursued a politics of ensuring greater access to official documents for Indian scholars and moved away from Sarkar's emphasis on a national-pedagogical role either for the Records Commission or for the National Archives of India (except in training archivists).

The Indian Historical Records Commission still exists. It still meets every year, and papers are heard. But these academic sessions hardly ever produce any sparkling intellectual discussions about source criticism in history. Nor are they meant to. The commission's constitution was revised again in 1990. The revised text clearly defined the commission's priorities. Its most important task was that of acting "as a forum for exchange between creators, custodians and users of archives and historical documents, of ideas and experiences relating to treatment, preservation and users [uses?] of archives."[118] Sen and Potdar, it would seem, have had the last laugh in this particular story. Sarkar was soon to be—to borrow an expression from A. D. Nuttall—a "man out of his time."[119]

Coda

Sarkar lived on for another eighteen or so years, completing the last volume of his *Fall of the Mughal Empire* in 1950. He died on 19 May 1958. His final years, though productive, were not happy. Readers may remember that he lost his eldest son to the communal frenzy of the late 1940s, his son-in-law to the war on the Singapore front, another son-in-law to ill health, a daughter to suicide

118. See the website for the National Archives of India, http://nationalarchives.nic.in/ihrc.html.

119. A. D. Nuttall, *Dead from the Waist Down: Scholars and Scholarship in Literature and the Popular Imagination* (New Haven, CT: Yale University Press, 2003), p. 97.

while she studied in London, and his remaining son in 1955. And his wife was understandably very low in spirit and health through all these years.

The war years brought some new anxieties. "We are living here," Sarkar wrote to Sardesai in 1941, referring to Calcutta, "in great uncertainty about the future of this town. Though I wish to cling to my library to the last moment possible—as migration elsewhere would enforce idleness on me,—yet the ladies are all apprehensive of the outburst of hooliganism or military licence as soon as a severe reverse to the British arms in the Far East loosens the power of the administration and disorder sets in."[120] Added to this was the trauma of the Hindu-Muslim violence that swept the city on and around 16–17 August 1946. A letter to Sardesai dated 21 August, about a week after the riots, reads: "No port, no public conveyance, no fish or meat, no fresh vegetables except leaves (that too in very small quantities) available since the morning of the 17th. Our faithful milkman and the defense organization (all volunteers) have kept us alive."[121] This was the period in which he supported the idea of partitioning Bengal even though that would mean the loss of his ancestral home: "The administration here is hopelessly inefficient and dishonest and, as no improvement can be expected in the natural course of things, the future for the Hindus here is unquestionably dark. This depression has affected my literary production."[122]

It says something about his self-control and discipline that Sarkar managed to complete his *Fall* in 1950 and, among other things, revise and correct in 1949 the English translation of the second volume of *Ain-i-Akbari*, "a most exhausting and stupendous task—the value of which only some English scholars will appreciate."[123] But age was catching up with him. "I am feeling the touch of old age, in the form of perceptible weakness or desire to take rest," he wrote to Sardesai in May 1954: "My present task is the completion of my *Military History of India*."[124] He complained the next year about "old things" beginning to "escape my memory," but not without a touch of humor when he realized that he had sent a letter meant for the bookseller D. B. Taraporewalla to Sardesai's address instead: "You must have been puzzled." But he reassured Sardesai that "it was due to hurry and not . . . senility."[125] The book on military

120. NL, JSP, letter no. 704, Sarkar to Sardesai, Calcutta, 28 December 1941.

121. NL, JSP, letter no. 892, Sarkar to Sardesai, Calcutta, 21 August 1946.

122. NL, JSP, letter no. 895, Sarkar to Sardesai, Calcutta, 30 September 1946.

123. NL, JSP, letter no. 1008, Sarkar to Sardesai, Calcutta, 18 June 1949.

124. NL, JSP, letter no. 1160, Sarkar to Sardesai, Calcutta, 8 May 1954.

125. NL, JSP, letters nos. 1175 and 1189, Sarkar to Sardesai, Calcutta, dated 1 February 1955, 25 March 1955.

history was published posthumously, perhaps a fitting monument to a man whose interest in matters military was deeply tied to his interest, as we have seen, in modern forms of discipline and character.[126]

Sarkar had a house built for him in the southern part of Calcutta in 1939 on a road named Lansdowne Road Extension. He wrote, with some happiness, to Sardesai on 8 September 1939 that he would now have an "a/c [air-conditioned] room and steel bookshelves up to the ceiling." The land had cost him Rs. 12,050.[127] By the following March, the house had become his residence.[128] The street was given a new name in 1943—Lake Terrace—and his house had a new number, P255.[129] By December 1954, the address had been changed to 10 Lake Terrace, Calcutta 29.[130] This is still the address of the house. In 1973, almost fifteen years after Sir Jadunath's death, the house was bought by the Indian Council of Social Science Research, a federal research-funding body of the Government of India, to establish the Centre for the Study of Social Sciences, which started its life on 1 February 1973. The Centre took possession of the property around July that year, renamed the house Jadunath Bhavan, and put a small tablet outside saying, in Bengali, "In this house lived Acharya [the teacher] Jadunath Sarkar."[131] I mention all this because I started my academic career in history in this house in 1974 when the Centre appointed me a fellow in history for a fixed term of years.

My colleagues and I seldom discussed the house itself and had little awareness of the sad human drama of Sarkar's life that had unfolded there just two decades before the place became ours, though the house in many ways felt like a lived-in upper-middle-class Bengali home. It had not been built to be an office. Now I know that it was from this house, sitting perhaps in his study downstairs, which in our time had become the registrar's office, that Sarkar wrote to his friend Nana about how he felt at the loss of so many of the younger members of his family and the consequent growth in the number of people directly and financially dependent on him: "What robs me of my peace of mind is not grief for loss—which religion or resignation to fate can enable a man to bear—but the worry of having to manage the affairs of those who should, in the normal course of nature, have looked after me in

126. Sir Jadunath Sarkar, *Military History of India* (New Delhi: Orient Longman, 1960).

127. NL, JSP, letter no. 586, Sarkar to Sardesai, Calcutta, 8 September 1939.

128. NL, JSP, letter no. 617, Sarkar to Sardesai, Calcutta, 18 April 1940.

129. NL, JSP, letter no. 769, Sarkar to Sardesai, Calcutta, July 1943[?]

130. See NL, JSP, letter no. 1173, Sarkar to Sardesai, Calcutta, 15 December 1954.

131. Personal communication (dated 25 May 2014) from Mr. Susanta Ghosh, the first registrar of the Centre for Studies in Social Sciences.

my old age, but have gone away so early and left on my shoulders the burden of settling their property troubles, educating their sons, and marrying their orphan daughters. Two widowed daughters and one widowed daughter-in-law are now sheltered in my house and unless I can enjoy ten more years of life and health, how can I set on their feet Abani's sons now aged 16 and 14, or Sudha's sons aged 15, 13, and 11, or provide husbands for Priyambada's seven daughters . . . ? Satyen, my second son, is now in a broken down condition and cannot be expected to lead a robust . . . life."[132] Satyen breathed his last on 8 September 1955. Sarkar had been preparing himself for this loss since at least January of that year, when he wrote to Nana to inform him that there was "no cure" for Satyen's illness. "I now stand entirely son-less like you," he wrote, on Satyen's death, to Sardesai, who also had lost his son: "Only you are free from my anxieties about orphan grandsons coming from my sons and daughters."[133]

The Centre for Studies in Social Sciences that was set up in Sarkar's house in 1973 was a brainchild of Mrs. Indira Gandhi's government, especially of her Marxist minister of state for education, Professor S. Nurul Hasan, once a professor at the Aligarh Muslim University and formerly a student of R. P. Tripathi at Allahabad, one of the first influential academic critics of Sarkar. The Aligarh Marxist school of Mughal history to which Professor Hasan belonged was intellectually close to the world of historical scholarship I was introduced to by my mentor, Professor Barun De, who was my teacher of history at the Indian Institute of Management between the years 1969 and 1971. Barun De was appointed the founding director of this social science center. I owe my interest and early training in history to him. Even though we inhabited his house, Jadunath Sarkar was but a faint whiff of memory in the Marxist intellectual air I breathed at the Centre. Thought of as pro-empire in his sympathies and insufficiently analytical or modern in his approach to history, Sarkar had little or no afterlife in our conversations. All the objects of his house had been removed, and some old papers that were found had been made over to the National Library. It was not until the new millennium that some photos of Sarkar were put up in the building. Sarkar would have enjoyed the irony. This act of wiping memory clean would have reminded him of what he once said to his old student Dr. Bidhan Chandra Roy, the chief minister of West Bengal from 1948 to 1962, when the latter asked him for advice about ridding

132. NL, JSP, letter no. 932, Sarkar to Sardesai, Calcutta, 4 July 1947.

133. NL, JSP, letters no. 1174 and 1189, from Sarkar to Sardesai, Calcutta, 11 January 1955 and 10 September 1955.

the public space of Calcutta of all the statues of British imperial rulers. Sarkar wrote back: "My dear Bidhan, you can remove the statues but can you remove the pages from the history of India?"[134]

Sarkar himself had thus become a part of what I have called the "public life" of history and the politics of remembering and forgetting that it entailed. Stumbling upon excerpts from his letters to Sardesai at the Regenstein Library gave me a glimpse of his struggle (and that of others who joined him in the endeavor) to create a "cloistered life" for the discipline in the very clamor of public life itself, an almost impossible task. I became eager to read the original letters that H. R. Gupta, the editor of the volume that carried the excerpts, had edited to protect individuals. Sarkar had given his consent to the preservation of his and Sardesai's letters for future researchers but had also issued strict instructions: "As for the correspondence between us, kindly go through it slowly but exhaustively and destroy all letters of a purely personal nature, and cut out or black out with ink all the passages that refer to our enemies and their tricks, because the free unrestricted intimacy of private correspondence must avoid the public gaze."[135] I am glad—and grateful—that Sardesai did not follow these instructions strictly. If he had, I would not have been able to tell this story, nor to carry out the conversation with Sarkar that I have now had in my head over the past so many years, in an effort to understand Sir Jadunath and his intellectual project in Indian history, while often finding myself unable to identify with many of his declared academic and political positions.

134. Bagchi, *Acharya Jadunath*, p. 219. Also see Sarkar's essay in the *Hindusthan Standard* of 21 December 1951, where he described as "uncivilized" any plans for indiscriminate removal of statues of imperial rulers without consideration of what they had done for India.

135. NL, JSP, letter no. 763, Sarkar to Sardesai, Calcutta, 10 May 1943.

8

The Author and the Historian: A Conversational Reverie

Time: Early Morning, Place: 10 Lake Terrace, Calcutta 29, India

THE AUTHOR [A]: Please don't shut the door on me, Sir. I did not come by simply to pay my respects so early in the morning. I had some questions as well. Would you mind answering them? I know your time is valuable, but it surely couldn't as precious as it used to be? You don't have to go around looking for sources anymore, nor are you called upon to write books these days. So why would you not speak to me, Sir?

THE HISTORIAN [H]: You seem the precocious type! Well, what did you want to ask me about?

A: Oh, it's about your own work . . .

H: You want to discuss my work? Can you read Persian?

A: No Sir.

H: Marathi?

A: Studied for some time with Philip Engblom at the University of Chicago, but it's all very rusty now . . .

H: Do you have any Sanskrit?

A: Nothing beyond what we were taught at school. And students of science in my generation had an easy time, Sir. In Nehru's India, those studying science were not burdened with anything literary, linguistic, or historical.

H: So what makes you think you are qualified to speak to me? You cannot read the sources on which I based my work. True, the past and the future do not matter to me anymore, but that does not mean I have time to waste . . .

A: I agree, Sir, I don't have those qualifications. But my subject is not Shivaji or Aurangzeb or even the fall of the Mughal Empire. The subject I want to discuss is YOU! You wrote in Bengali and English, and these are languages I may modestly claim to know!

H: You mean you read what I wrote? Truly? But I had heard that people don't read me anymore. I had heard that they all read what's-his-name, this son of Muhammad Habib . . .

A: Irfan Habib, Sir? They do, and he is very good. But not reading you was all part of an era, I think. Didn't people in the 1940s say . . . well, I have read that R. P. Tripathi in his classes at the University of Allahabad used to criticize you for ignoring the role of institutions in history, for writing histories that were too personality-centric. Didn't Faruki criticize you in the 1930s for misunderstanding Islam in what you wrote in criticism of Aurangzeb? See, our teachers—your students' students, you might say—did criticize you. For you overlooked what to them was the most important aspect of Mughal history, the economic one. So I guess it's true that you looked a little dated when we were young. It was a bit like we had forgotten you . . .

H: Why do you say "was"? It's not as though they are discussing me now?

A: I do think you are coming back into view. The influence of Marxism in Indian academic circles is still strong, but generally on the wane, like elsewhere. Besides, some very well-known historians overseas—the late John Richards in his book on the Mughals in Golconda, for example—have begun to acknowledge their debt to your work. Your Bengali essays have finally been collected together in a volume. Even the learned "subaltern" historian Gautam Bhadra, who criticized your Persian in his younger days, says he would like to write something on you. . . . But may I step inside, Sir?

H: Oh, yes, do. But I can't give you more than half an hour, I am afraid. No, no, not in that room. It *was* once my study, but they have now made it into the office of the registrar, Susanta Ghosh, and it's where they all—Dipesh, Partha, and other young people—drop in all the time for idle gossip. I never liked this Bengali addiction to *adda*. There's no atmosphere here any longer for any serious conversation. Let's go and sit in the library upstairs. You see, I live amid these books nowadays. Here, please have a seat. And now tell me, how indeed can I help you?

A: Well, then, let me go straight to the point without wasting your time. Why did you call the fall of the Mughal Empire a tragedy?

H: Where's the problem?

A: Consider this, Sir. Here is an empire that sees wars all the time. There is a quick succession of emperors between 1707 and 1713. Then follow so many rebellions, Nadir Shah's vandalism, the oppression of the Maratha *vargirs*, the revolt of the Rohillas, the blinding of the emperor—what could be tragic about the end of such barbarism? Besides, didn't you yourself say that the coming of the British was fortunate for us Indians?

H: Well, *that* was not a tragedy, no, putting an end to that all that savagery was a good thing. Some deep rot had set in in the empire. Getting rid of that could not be a tragic thing. But that matters had to come to such a pass was tragic.

A: How so?

H: Because it was not inevitable. There was no such chaos in the reign of Akbar, Jahangir, or Shah Jahan. The Mughals had gotten the country together. A huge land, with so much diversity; to bring such a land under the say of one administration, economic system, judicial system, was no small matter. I think the Mughals had created a great historical possibility . . .

A: For what, Sir?

H: For creating a nation where none existed. Most of the advanced countries of the world were making a transition to nationhood at that time; they were laying down the basis for modern societies. It was as though the Mughals, unbeknownst to themselves, had adopted that great historic task as their own. They acted like message-bearers of human history. But they couldn't quite carry it through. Aurangzeb went on a wild goose chase for twenty years in the Deccan and ended up earning the wrath of the Rajputs, the Sikhs, and the Marathas, which only made the empire weak. Rulers who followed him were worthless. So the British had to pick up where the great Mughals left off, and we had to spend two hundred years under the weight of the British. Was that not a tragedy?

A: But you claim that reading about the fall of the Mughals was tragic in a classical sense: you said it was cathartic to read that history. We don't feel any of the feelings that you did. For us, British rule was only another name for modern imperial oppression. We are done with them; good riddance. Neither the Mughals nor the British put India on a genuine path toward modernity, so we have no sense of tragedy about the decline of either of those empires. You know, Sir, many scholars these days are excited about the seventeenth and eighteenth centuries, as a period pregnant with alternative possibilities for development. But since you mention tragedy, let me tell you something. There is a new lament abroad, and you hear it among some Dalit intellectuals. They say that the British came too late and left too early! So they do think of the end of British rule as a tragedy. But maybe partly just to irritate their upper-caste brethren . . .

H: But I never said that. I never thought of the British leaving India as any kind of tragedy. I praised Europeans for their qualities, I said we needed to learn from them, and I know some people thought me a *khair khan* [a flatterer] for that reason . . .

A: I have read you enough to know that that is simply an unjust accusation. I know that. Your lament was rather about the fact that no power in India in the eighteenth century was organized and farsighted enough to be able to beat the British at their imperial game.

H: Thank you. Yes, what seems truly tragic to me is that none of our *badshah*s or *nawab*s or *rajah*s ever felt any serious urge to learn from the Europeans their sense of discipline, punctuality, leadership, military tactics, technology, scientific knowledge, nothing. Even the sight of printed books did not arouse in them any desire to create presses, seminaries, academies, and universities. They had wealth but lacked what they so desperately needed: character. Aurangzeb's obstinacy and orthodoxy alienated the Rajputs, Sikhs, Marathas, and others. The rulers who came after him were weak personalities. And we lost a grand opportunity by failing to use the unity of the country that the Mughals had created, as a base for an independent transition to nationhood. That would have been in keeping with the main trends in world history. Instead, our rulers were blinded by selfish calculations and lost themselves in the pleasures of the flesh—wouldn't all this bring tears to the eyes of anyone who loved this land? Was this not truly sad, young man?

A: Don't you really see, Sir, that to call the fall of the Mughals a "tragedy" from a clearly nationalist point of view would be to engage in anachronistic thinking?

H: Where do you see anachronism in all this?

A: With respect, Sir, aren't you making the same mistake as your critics, like those who find you guilty of neglecting economic forces and institutions? They try to judge you by what you never set out to do. The Mughals, similarly, may very well have united the country and even done so for good reasons, but to prepare the basis of a nationality or nationhood was no part of their conscious goals.

H: Ah, so *that's* the problem? That's what you find anachronistic? The mistake is yours, my friend.

A: How so, Sir?

H: Well, think about it for a minute. Every national history is moving in some direction, while human history as a whole also moves. No one, no country, is outside of what's happening to human history, to world history in that sense. The two must connect somewhere. You would agree, wouldn't you, that the invention of fire, or agriculture—these are parts of a common human history. Similarly, from the seventeenth century on, the most advanced nations of the world began to move toward the formation of modern states and societies. They indicated the general direction in which humans were to proceed. The Japanese traveled that path without having to be subjugated by a foreign power. We could have progressed along that path too, and independently, if our rulers had had more foresight and character, and if Aurangzeb had continued the policy of toleration of his forefathers.

A: So you mean to say, Sir, that the path of history had to be the same for all lands and peoples?

H: No, why should I say that? Nothing of the kind. We all share in the general history of mankind, but how we realize our share depends on the spirit of our own civilization. Nothing requires us to ape the Westerners, though we should, of course, learn from them where needed. The question is about the broad direction of human history, to be able to work out where it is headed. But each civilization has to find its own way to that general history. Nothing about this general history asks of us that we sacrifice what may be distinctive about our civilization. You can be part of the whole while retaining your distinctiveness. If only our precolonial rulers had been far-sighted enough, they could have indigenized European learning; they could have been as efficient as the Europeans in administrative, military, and technical matters and led India to its own destiny. Colonial rule would not have been needed. This constant nagging suspicion we have had within ourselves—are we merely imitating the Westerners?—we would have been spared all that inner agony.

A: Now I see it, Sir. You think nations have destinies, don't you, Sir? You are like Rammohun Roy, or Tagore, or Vivekananda, or even Nehru. So you also have a providential view of history?

H: Meaning?

A: That all national histories are guided by divine Providence . . .

H: Isn't that what von Ranke use to say? And wouldn't you regard him as a pioneer of scientific history?

A: But we don't accept that theory any longer, Sir.

H: What do you mean you don't? Don't you ever sing the Indian national anthem? Don't you ever show respect for it? From where do you think the expression *bharata bhagya vidhata* came? It is even translated as "the keeper of India's destiny." And what about that famous speech of Nehru on the midnight before our independence day—"India's tryst with destiny"? Isn't providential thinking part of modern India too?

A: Not of contemporary India, Sir. Nationalism today revolves around other things, maybe a war or a cricket match with Pakistan, and the media play a very big role in all that. And that speech by Nehru, Sir? That's been torn to shreds by the biting humor of Salman Rushdie. Sorry, you wouldn't know about Rushdie. The point is, Sir, Providence, destiny, *bharata bhagya vidhata*—nobody today will listen to these things.

H: But aren't you all Marxists?

A: Well, sort of. At least in Bengal we have been. But why do you ask, Sir?

H: Remember Marx's statement about British rule working in India as "an unconscious tool of history"—now, wasn't that a providentialist statement if ever there was one? He just gave it a secular varnish. Don't you all accept that statement?

A: Actually, Sir, even Marx is not properly followed these days. There is something called "postcolonial theory" that came from the left field and upset many orthodox Marxists . . .

H: So what do *you* make of the fall of the Mughals?

A: But my subject is you Sir, not the fall of the Mughals.

H: I have absolutely no interest in flattery.

A: I know that. Have read you and about you enough to know that.

H: Are you writing my biography?

A: No, I would have had to raise a lot of personal matters in our discussions then. Besides, Moni Bagchi has written a nice biography of you in Bangla . . .

H: Then are you writing an intellectual biography?

A: No, and partly because Anirudhha Ray, Anil Banerjee, and others have done that, at least to some degree.

H: So what are you after?

A: Well, it's a little difficult to explain, but let me try. I have been reading you and your letters and books and articles and so forth, to find out how history became a researchable academic subject in this country, and to see if one could write a social history of the basic categories and practices of a discipline. So I have been trying to see you as part of an intellectual formation, not quite biography . . .

H: What is an "intellectual formation?" Never heard such an expression!

A: You wouldn't have, Sir. It must have come from structuralism. You see, there was this French Marxist philosopher, Louis Althusser, who used to speak of "social formations" . . .

H: Structuralism? What's that? God, you people are so much in love with jargon these days. I sometimes try to listen to historians who give seminars in this building. Most of it is very hard to understand.

A: It would take a very long time, Sir, to explain structuralism. Let's go back to you instead.

H: Ok, shoot.

A: You explained why "tragedy" was important to you. But why were you so obsessed with character—not only of the historical actors but also of the historian himself?

H: Character is a major motive force in history.

A: But the historians of the Mughal period did not think of character in the abstract like this, did they? Abul Fazl or Badaoni, or Gholam Hossein, and Bhimsen Burhanpuri at a later time.—Of course, they discussed an individual's personality and its strengths and weakness, but they did not create a separate section in their narratives called "the character of so and so."

H: And that is why they are not modern historians. Read Macaulay's essay on Clive or Hastings.

A: I will, Sir. And I guess there was a nineteenth-century Indian side to that story too. I think of Tagore's book of character studies, *chaaritrapuja*. Such books must have also influenced your thinking. But the genealogy of thinking of character as an abstract force in this kind of way probably goes a lot deeper into the past . . .

H: Why do you say that?

A: See, in discussing Shah Alam II, you wrote a line: "Character is destiny," remember?

H: Yes, I took that from Shakespeare. Don't forget that I was a teacher of English literature.

A: Yes, but where did Shakespeare get it from, Sir? Some scholars say he was recycling ancient Greek philosophers who were enjoying a revival in his time. So you can see how the category "character" in your use may indeed be an ancient category . . .

H: But this sounds like intellectual history. Is that what you are doing? Then *I* am not your project; it seems to go right through me to a distant beyond . . .

A: It does and it doesn't, Sir. You set out to write a political history of the Mughal times. But clearly political analysis in your hands is deeply related to analyses of characters. And the category "character" in turn takes us into the realms of literature and philosophy. Obviously, you regarded politics as an expression of virtues and vices of the political actors, and thus amenable to literary treatment—didn't you, Sir?

H: Yes, you could say that. From where else would history get its sense of drama? Don't you make politics into so many dramatic narratives as well?

A: We do. But they no longer amount to an epic drama of any kind; it's neither an epic of the nation nor of a world-historical class; we don't think like that any more. Some people do still look for the epical in Indian politics; but some just think of it as entertainment, a show or *tamasha*, or at worst as a theater of the absurd. And then there are others who . . . but let's not speak of my generation, Sir, I wanted to understand the intellectual environs that sustained your work. Tell me one thing, please—your research methods actually required even the historian to have "character." The historian must be a votary of the Truth, worship at Truth's altar. You even used the very Hindu or Brahmanical word *chittashuddhi*, the purification of consciousness. Why? Nobody says such things any more. Imagine for a moment, Sir, there are hundreds of PhDs in history that India produces these days. If they all had to experience *chittashuddhi*, we would have to teach them the *Gita* before we taught them Bloch or Collingwood! Why did you speak as though there could be a Truth with a capital T?

H: See, everybody in my time talked about "scientific history," even those whose work had nothing "scientific" about it. When we had all these "research societies" coming up in the early twentieth century, they mainly produced histories that pandered to regional, religious, family, or caste pride and still described their method as "scientific." Sometimes they simply tried to prove the veracity of legends with the help of documents, with no discussion of which documents were authentic and which were unreliable or even forged, for that matter. I noticed this when I was working on Shivaji and later on the Bengali hero Pratapaditya. All my life I have tried to possess the strength to face up to facts, even unpleasant facts, facts that did not necessarily make me feel good about being a Bengali or an Indian. The nation, were it to progress, needed true histories and truthful historians.

A: Did you succeed?

H: Don't think so. Even Nana, my closest friend and collaborator, would not always see my point. And Young Turks like Potdar and Sen ganged up on me in the Records Commission and threw me out.

A: But, Sir, don't you realize that those "feel good" histories were also a part of our nationalism? Look at the case of Akshay Kumar Maitreya. Bengalis celebrate him as a pioneer of "scientific history," but he never felt compelled to rail against legends or treasured popular memories in the way you did. His nationalist histories were often built on local patriotic tales. Doesn't his *Rani Bhavani* only add to the pride of the Natore *zamindar* family? Were you opposed to such histories?

H: I would not have considered them fully scientific. But remember, I also had my own sense of nationalism. And I did write to Rajendraprasad about it—that I could take charge of any project of national history only if he would let me speak the truth, even unpleasant truth, truth that puts us all to shame.

A: So you thought of the nation on the model of the individual? Like the individual, a nation could improve its character only if it confronted its own flaws . . .

H: Yes, of course. How would a nation become strong and powerful if it didn't face up to its own shortcomings? And to help in that task, you would need historians who worshipped Truth.

A: Then why did you so dislike Gandhi? He worshipped the Truth.

H: How do you know that I disliked him?

A: Didn't you describe him to Nana as "the demented son of a baniya playing cat and mouse with the British?"

H: You have read that letter? I am shocked. I told Nana to expunge all references to personalities before publishing our letters. I was not a believer in making everything public. Every day of my life, I kept a diary. But nobody has seen them, thank God.

A: But what was your complaint against Gandhi?

H: Look, I was not against Gandhi the man. He was a great man, no doubt. But I did not believe that the form of "mass nationalism" that he created would do the nation any good. Now, here again, I belong to the defeated. But I am not a person to give up my beliefs simply because others have not accepted them. You have to realize that there were many strands within nationalism. We were not all of the same view on the question of how to prepare for nationhood . . .

A: Like?

H: Like many—Tagore and I included—believed in a period of preparation that the masses needed in order to be suitable for democracy. The kind of street politics that Gandhi and the majority of this country favored—that interrupted education and taught people lawlessness—many of use disapproved of such forms of politics. We dreamed of spreading education in the country first—of course, we disagreed on the process; you must know about my criticisms of Tagore's university, for instance—but we wanted to see a process whereby rationalist thinking and scientific temperament would spread throughout the country, fighting superstition and making the nation strong and its citizens disciplined and united. We wanted a genuine rule of law . . .

A: Something like what the absolutist states achieved in Europe? A modern state first, and then, gradually, a democratic one?

H: Well, not exactly, for I always believed that Indian politics ought to be an expression of Indian civilization and its uniqueness. I wrote once that both the Hindu and the Muslim communities would have to experience some sort of rebirth if India were to make progress. But that was not what happened.

A: Yes, I know that you paid a terrible price personally for Hindu-Muslim riots in Calcutta . . .

H: Let's put the personal aside. After all, you are not writing my biography. What I was saying was that there were many Indians who thought India should first become modern and *then* adopt democracy.

A: True, we reversed the process. We became democratic first and now have to go through the electoral process to make our society, institutions, and practices modern.

H: Do you modern scholars think that that's been a good thing?

A: Well, Sir, the question of good and bad is a complex one. And it depends on personal preferences as well. The point is, like you said, we have to accept what has happened and make that our point of departure. The writing of history cannot escape our political history. The peculiarities of Indian democracy will no doubt have an impact on the writing of history in India. But let me get back to your work, Sir—it's not every day that I get a chance to speak to you like this.

H: Okay.

A: What would you regard as your enduring legacy? I am an admirer of your achievements. Everybody now acknowledges the groundbreaking nature of your research in Maratha and Mughal histories. Not only did you discover new documents and read Persian accounts alongside Maratha ones; you also pointed out errors in original documents, corrected them, located places on maps, and found correct dates for events. You were perhaps the first in India to demonstrate the close relationship between history and geography. I guess all this was your *Quellenkritik*—not quite a philological enterprise, but no less remarkable for that. You always said that the edifice of history should be erected on the bedrock of unassailable facts. You did not mind if the edifice—and your "philosophy of history"—was challenged, but research was about establishing facts, wasn't it? If you would concede me my point, Sir, that there would not be many takers today for your providentialist view of history, would you agree that your absolute commitment to facts is really your enduring legacy?

H: How could I be so sure? There are so many seminars and lectures in history that are organized in this very house these days. How many of them are about the period that I was concerned with? Very few. How many scholars today would care about learning Persian, scout around for new sources, interrogate them to establish basic facts? Partly, of course, sources are not so hard to come by these days; also, some of the basic work was done by our generation of scholars. But there is a bigger difference still. Your generation is not interested in source criticism. You pay more attention to narratives and points of view. You consider writing an alternative narrative "research"—well, research meant something else in my days. It meant getting to the basic facts of an event, separating facts from untruth. You know what I sometimes think these days? I lived too long. If I had departed the world in the 1930s, like Bhandarkar before me—but he was, of course, older—I wouldn't have lived beyond my own times.

A: But it's because you lived so long that we got so much more of you! It would have been such a loss if you had not been able to complete the *Fall*, for example. But, true, it is not your kind of history that won the day in the 1960s—our politics and politicians depend more on myths and legends, Sir, than the truth. Maybe that is the irony of history, of our history . . .

H: Ah, but see how you are speaking the language of literature! What's irony? It's a figure of speech. Didn't you say you people don't believe in literary qualities of history anymore? Anyway, I have been talking to you for a long time, much longer than the half hour I promised. I am afraid I have to go now. Susanta Ghosh and his people will arrive soon. They will not even notice that there is a plaque outside this house saying that this was my house, and that I lived here once.

A: Please don't feel sorry for yourself, Sir. Considering the fate of other Bengali intellectuals, you have been lucky. After all, academics still come to this house and discuss academic issues. Have you seen the house that the great linguist Sunitikumar Chattopadhyay lived in? Now it belongs to an American-owned Indian chain of fashion wear . . .

H: Yes, I know. Didn't Tagore say that the tide of time takes everything with it—life, youth, fame, everything? Who are we compared to him? But I suppose even he will be forgotten one day. Good-bye, then. Let me go and sit near where Kaliprasad Bose usually sits. He takes good care of books and readers. Besides, I overheard yesterday that Gautam Bhadra will bring in a new collection of historical documents he has discovered somewhere. I feel so curious to see what historians do with sources these days.

A: Good-bye, Sir.

Acknowledgments

I have heard it said as a complaint that scholars in the humanities do not collaborate with other scholars; they tend to write single-authored books. But single-authored books are also, deep down, collaborative efforts. This book would have been impossible to write without the innumerable acts of help, kindness, and collaboration that came my way. I cannot possibly thank all my benefactors by name; I seek the forgiveness of those whom I have missed here.

Several young scholars helped with research and computer problems at various stages of this project. They also acted as a preliminary sounding board for many of my ideas. I recall with affection and gratitude the assistance I have received in this regard from (in no particular order) Awadhendra (Dipu) Saran, Gerard Siarny, Rafeeq Hasan, Sunit Singh, Sharmistha Gooptu, Arvind Elangovan, Dwaipayan Sen, Siddharth Satpathy, Abhishek Ghosh, Nusrat Chowdhury, Arnab Dey, Rajarshi Ghosh, Lorena Mitchell, Esther Mansdorf, Ranu Roychoudhuri, and others.

Gautam Bhadra has been a partner in conversations related to this project and many others from their very inception. He shared his ideas, sources, time, and friendship in a spirit of generosity that is characteristically his own. Christopher A. Bayly and Anthony Grafton, readers of the manuscript for the University of Chicago Press, gave extremely valuable suggestions and criticism; Sanjay Seth did the same purely out of friendship. I have benefited immeasurably from their engagement with this book. Partha Chatterjee, a friend and a lifelong interlocutor, read several chapters with care and helped with both references and some sharp observations. James Chandler—the best teacher of poetry I have ever had—was equally helpful with instructive comments both on specific chapters and on the general framework of the book. The historian Daniel Woolf (Queen's University, Ontario, Canada) kindly took time out of his busy schedule to read the chapter on character and to direct me to some very useful literature. Thomas and Barbara Metcalf and Sheldon Pollock offered support and criticism from the very beginning of the project. Faisal Devji, Rosalind O'Hanlon, and Tapan Raychaudhuri at Oxford; Shruti Kapila, Christopher Bayly, Joya Chatterji, and David Washbrook at Cambridge; Ajay Skaria at Minneapolis; Sumit and Tanika Sarkar, Neeladri Bhattacharya and Chitra Joshi, Shahid Amin, Ashis Nandy, Kunal and Shubhra Chakrabarti, Sabyasachi Bhattacharya, Prathama Banerjee, Rajeev Bhargav, Dipu Saran, Adtiya Nigam, Rakesh Pandey, Ravikant, Ravi Sundaram, Nivedita Menon, Payal Chawla, Udaya Kumar, and Rashmi Bhatnagar in Delhi; Badri Narayan in Allahabad; Ahmed Kamal and Shahduzzaman from and in Dhaka; Susanta Ghosh, Biswajit Roy, Rosinka and Amit Chaudhuri, Raghab Bandyopadhyay, Semanti Ghosh, Rudrangshu Mukherjee, Tapati Guha-Thakurta, Sugata Marjit, Sukanta Chaudhuri, Anil Acharya, Anirban Chatterjee, and the late Arun and Manasi Dasgupta in Calcutta; Raja Dixit, Vijay Sathe, Suhash Palshikar, and Mahesh Kulkarni in Poona; Sekhar Bandyopadhyay in Wellington, New Zealand; Hans Medick and Doris Bachmann-Medick, Alf Lüdtke, Jürgen Kocka, Sebastian Conrad, Madeleine Herren, Ute Frevert, Margrit Pernau, Georg Iggers, Carola Dietze, Manuela Ciotti, Monika Baàr, Bo Strath, Ewa Domanska, and Henning Trüpper in different cities of Europe; and Rajyashree Pandey in London—these friends and scholars have all generously shared their time, research, and ideas with me. Many of the ideas were also developed in discussions with colleagues I had at the Wissenschaftskolleg in Berlin during my year (2008–9) there; it is a pleasure to recall, in particular, conversations with Sheila Fitzpatrick, Seyla Benhabib, Eva Illouz, Sina Rausenbach, Michel Chouli-Deer, Christophe König, Roger Chickering, Frank Rexroth, Héctor Pérez-Birgnoli, and Ibrahima Thioub in relation to this project. I have treasured these conversations and very much hope that they will continue beyond this book.

The late Barun De, Anthony Low, Asok Sen, Ranajit Guha, and the late Greg Dening have been my teachers of history in formal and informal ways. They all took a lively and affirmative interest in the project and encouraged me all along. It will be my lasting regret that Barun De and Greg Dening passed away before I could finish the manuscript.

Discussions with friends in North America—Homi K. Bhabha, Arjun Appadurai, Bill Brown, Lauren Berlant, Lisa Weeden, Claudio Lomnitz, Fredrik Jonsson, Bradin Cormack, Tom Gunning, Jennifer Pitts, Dilip Gaonkar, Uday Singh Mehta, Mrinalini Sinha, Anupama Rao, Geoff Eley, Ritu

Birla, William Mazzarella, Orit Bashkin, Kathleen Davis, Anand Pandian, Daud Ali, William Glover, Farina Mir, and Lee Schlesinger—have always sparked off new thoughts. The idea that the practice of research could itself be an object of research came from a conversation I had with Arjun Appadurai way back in the late 1990s. Kumkum Chatterjee, who, sadly, is no more, took a keen interest in this project. My close colleagues at the Chicago Center for Contemporary Theory—Leela Gandhi, Shannon Dawdy, Kaushik Sunder Rajan, William Sewell, Michael Dawson, Moishe Postone, Bill Brown, Anwen Tormay, William Mazzarella, Lisa Wedeen, and Lauren Berlant—have willingly subjected themselves, both individually and as a collective, to my ramblings on Jadunath Sarkar. Occasional conversations with Carlo Ginzburg, Luisa Passerini, C. M. Naim, Sumit Guha, Indrani Chatterjee, Gyan Prakash, and Sanjay Subrahmanyam have also been extremely helpful. I have learned a great deal from my dear friend and colleague Muzaffar Alam, a renowned specialist on Mughal history. Philip Engblom was generous to a fault in helping me read some documents in Marathi.

I recall with similar pleasure the many conversations with friends in Australia to whom this work—and my work generally—owes a deep debt: Robin Jeffrey, Debjani Ganguly, Iain McCalman, Bain Attwood, Donna Merwick, Devleena Ghosh, Kama Mclean, Jim Masselos, Heather Goodall, Miranda Johnson, Kate Fullager, Ann McGrath, Stuart Macintyre, Margaret Jolly, Geremie Barme, Tom Griffiths, Rosanne Kennedy, Tim Rowse, Stephen Muecke, Meaghan Morris, Christopher Healy, Assa Doron, Simon During, Kenneth George, Kirin Narayan, Kalpana Ram, Meera Ashar, Ian Hunter, Knox Peden, Gary Lanziti, and Marina Bollinger.

Draft chapters from this book were presented in the following forms: Nicholson Distinguished Faculty Lecture at the University of Chicago; annual lecture of the Indian and South Asian Studies Center at the University of California, Los Angeles; inaugural annual faculty lecture, Department of History, University of Göttingen; invited lectures at the Max Planck Institute for the History of Emotions, Berlin; annual faculty lecture, Faculty of History, University of Oxford; keynote lecture at "The Book and the Public Sphere" conference in Mälmo, Sweden; invited lecture, Davis Center, Princeton University; invited lecture, Asia and Europe Cluster of Excellence, University of Heidelberg; Distinguished Visitor's Lecture, Institute of Advanced Study, University of Minnesota; Sakharam Ganesh Deuskar Lectures, Centre for Studies in Social Sciences, Calcutta; B. N. Ganguly Memorial Lecture, Centre for the Study of Developing Societies, New Delhi; Radhakrishnan Memorial Lectures, Faculty of Oriental Studies and All Souls College, University of Oxford; and invited lecture at the Humanities Center, University of Michigan, Ann

Arbor. I sincerely thank the authorities of these institutions for their invitations and the audiences for their comments and criticisms.

My research in Calcutta and Delhi was made possible by a fellowship from the American Institute for Indian Studies. The University of Chicago has been my intellectual home for the past two decades. I am beholden to the very supportive deans and heads of departments with whom I have had the privilege to work while engaged in this project. I thank, in no particular order, Mark Hansen, Danielle Allen, Martha Roth, Mario Small, Gary Tubb, Prasenjit Duara, Bruce Cummings, and Ulrike Stark. Thanks are also due my supportive staff and colleagues in the Department of History and in the Department of South Asian Civilizations and Languages (especially Alicia Czaplewski). The Humanities Research Centre at Australian National University has hosted me every summer for the past twenty years—I thank their staff, fellows, visitors, graduate students, and the two successive directors, Iain McCalman and Debjani Ganguly, for their warm and unstinting support. I also thank the director, Luca Giuliani, the then secretary, Joachim Nettlebeck, and the staff of Wissenschaftskolleg, Berlin, for the wonderful home they provided for my various projects in 2008 and 2009. Thanks also to the authorities of—and my circle of friends and colleagues at—the University of Technology, Sydney, and in particular to Devleena Ghosh, for hosting me for a few days every year.

It is my pleasant duty to thank the archivists, the bibliographers, and the staffs of the following institutions for their collaboration and help in making this project possible: National Library, Calcutta, with very special thanks to Swapan Chakravorty, former director of the library; National Archives of India, New Delhi; India Office Library, London; Regenstein Library at the University of Chicago; Hitesranjan Sanyal Memorial Archive, Centre for Studies in Social Sciences, Calcutta, especially Abhijit Bhattacharya and his colleagues; Deccan College Library, Poona; and Nehru Memorial Museum and Library, New Delhi, especially Mahesh Rangarajan and his staff. I am also thankful to the authorities of the Centre for Studies in Social Sciences for permission to reproduce some photographs found in Jadunath Sarkar's residence in the early 1970s and now preserved in their archives. Fali Pastakiya's generosity toward some strangers from Calcutta made possible the "discovery" of Sardesai's house in autumn 2012, a story I tell in the book.

My editor at the University of Chicago Press, Alan Thomas, has guided me through the process of writing this book with an astute combination of patience, understanding, critical feedback, and the difficult but gentle art of effective nudging. I am deeply grateful to him and to his staff for their sustained interest in this project. Thanks are also due to my copyeditor, Lois Crum, for her many helpful suggestions.

And last but not least, a few pleasurable and deeply personal words of gratitude. I lost my friend Shiloo while I was on the last legs of this book. Rita, Debi, Tandra, Partha (Sengupta), Soumya, and Sabyasachi have been steadfast in their friendship. For their affection and humanity, my grateful thanks to Boria, Mamoni, Sharmistha, Shyam, and "Bnatul" in Calcutta; to Arko, Kaveri, Khurshid, and Peter, Stephen and Kate, Roger and Anh Thu, Sidhhartha and Chandana, Gautam and Ruplekha, and John Hanoush in Canberra; to Sanjay and Raju in London; and to Don and Barbara, Neeraj and Meenakshi, Muzaffar and Rizwana, Jim and Becky, Jai and Vandana, Julian and Jennifer, and Don and Lisa in Chicago. Rochona Majumdar, my partner in life and in academic work, has waited long and patiently to see her "Dipesh-da" finish this book. To her, I say this: Without your love and support, none of this would have been possible, so thank you profoundly from the bottom of my heart. This book is dedicated to her and to those I have had, or have come to regard, as my teachers of history.

Earlier versions of parts of chapters 1 and 3 were published in the *Oxford History of Historical Writing, 1900–1950*, vol. 4, ed. Stuart Macintyre, Juan Maiguashca, and Attila Pók (Oxford: Oxford University Press, 2011); in *Utopia/Dystopia*, ed. Michael G. Gordin, Helen Tilley, and Gyan Prakash (Princeton, NJ: Princeton University Press, 2010); and in *Economic and Political Weekly* 25 (2009). Chapter 8 was first published in Bengali in the Calcutta magazine *Charcha* (Autumn 2012). I am grateful to the publishers and editors of these volumes for allowing me to develop the ideas that became the chapters in this book first in their publications. Thanks also to the Centre for Studies in Social Sciences, Calcutta, and to Ranu Roychoudhuri and Sujit Patwardhan for permission to include some photographs from their collections.

Index